FORMAL ORGANIZATIONS

Chandler Publications in

ANTHROPOLOGY AND SOCIOLOGY

LEONARD BROOM, *Editor*

✦

PUBLIC LEADERSHIP
Wendell Bell, Richard J. Hill, Charles R. Wright

THE ARCHAEOLOGIST'S NOTE BOOK
Clement W. Meighan

AN INTRODUCTION TO INDUSTRIAL SOCIOLOGY
Charles B. Spaulding

FORMAL ORGANIZATIONS
Peter M. Blau and W. Richard Scott

SOCIAL DISORGANIZATION IN AMERICA
Reece McGee

EDUCATING THE EXPERT SOCIETY
Burton R. Clark

FORMAL ORGANIZATIONS:

A Comparative Approach

✦

BY *PETER M. BLAU*

UNIVERSITY OF CHICAGO

AND W. RICHARD SCOTT

STANFORD UNIVERSITY

CHANDLER PUBLISHING COMPANY

San Francisco

Copyright © 1962 by Chandler Publishing Company

Library of Congress Catalog Card No. 61-17328

PRINTED IN THE UNITED STATES OF AMERICA

Contents

PREFACE ix

CHAPTER ONE. INTRODUCTION 1
The Concept of Formal Organization 2
The Study of Formal Organizations 8
Methods in the Study of Organizations 15
The Comparative Approach 25

CHAPTER TWO. THE NATURE AND TYPES OF
FORMAL ORGANIZATIONS 27
Theoretical Concepts 27
Typologies of Formal Organizations 40
Types of Formal Organizations 45
Concluding Remarks 58

CHAPTER THREE. THE ORGANIZATION
AND ITS PUBLICS 59
Professional and Bureaucratic Orientation . . . 60
The Public 74
Conflicts with Clients 81
Concluding Remarks 85

CHAPTER FOUR. THE SOCIAL STRUCTURE
OF WORK GROUPS 87
Informal Organization 89
Effects of Group Structure 100
The Larger Organization and Work-Group Structure . . 108
Concluding Remarks 115

CHAPTER FIVE. PROCESSES OF COMMUNICATION . 116

Experiments on Communication and Performance . . . 116
Field Studies of Communication in Formal Organizations . 128
Variations in Communication Patterns 134
Concluding Remarks 139

CHAPTER SIX. THE ROLE OF THE SUPERVISOR . . 140

Styles of Supervision 141
Supervision and Performance 150
Hierarchical and Peer Relations 159
Concluding Remarks 163

CHAPTER SEVEN. MANAGERIAL CONTROL . . . 165

The Hierarchy 167
Impersonal Mechanisms of Control 176
Questioning Some Prevailing Assumptions 183
Concluding Remarks 192

CHAPTER EIGHT. THE SOCIAL CONTEXT
OF ORGANIZATIONAL LIFE 194

The Social Environment of Organizations 195
Organizational Analysis 206
Interorganizational Processes 214
Concluding Remarks 221

CHAPTER NINE. ORGANIZATIONAL DYNAMICS . . 222

Organizational Development 223
Emergent Patterns 234
Dilemmas of Formal Organization 242
Dialectical Processes of Change 250

APPENDIX. DESCRIPTION AND COMPARISON
OF THE TWO WELFARE AGENCIES 254

BIBLIOGRAPHY 258

INDEX OF NAMES 303

INDEX OF TOPICS 306

Tables

1. Location of Reference Groups and Graduate Work . . 67
2. Type of Orientation and Professional Characteristics . . 68
3. Type of Orientation and Loyalty to the Agency . . . 69
4. Type of Orientation and Criticism of the Agency . . 72
5. Type of Orientation and Criticism of
   Administrative Policies 73
6. Seniority, Informal Acceptance, and Orientation to Clients 97
7. Seniority, Popularity, and Reference Group . . . 99
8. Group Climate, Individual's Orientation, and Attitudes . 102
9. Group Climate, Acceptance, and Individual's Orientation 106
10. Group Cohesion, Popularity, and Reaction to Clients . 108
11. Reciprocity in Consultations, Work Pressure, and
    Per Cent Regularly Consulting Colleagues . . . 136
12. Reciprocity in Consultations, Self-Confidence, and
    Per Cent Regularly Consulted 137
13. Worker Visits to Recipients and Orientation of Supervisor 155
14. Supervisor's Self-Confidence, Supervisor's Approach,
    and Worker Loyalty 158

Preface

Modern man is man in organizations. If the most dramatic fact that sets our age apart from earlier ones is that we live today under the shadow of nuclear destruction, the most pervasive feature that distinguishes contemporary life is that it is dominated by large, complex, and formal organizations. Our ability to organize thousands and even millions of men in order to accomplish large-scale tasks—be they economic, political, or military—is one of our greatest strengths. The possibility that free men become mere cogs in the bureaucratic machineries we set up for this purpose is one of the greatest threats to our liberty.

This book presents a sociological analysis of some of the main facets of organizational life. We shall examine the nature and types of formal organizations, the connections between them and the larger social context of which they are a part, and various aspects of their internal structure, such as peer group and hierarchical relations in organizations, processes of communication, management and impersonal mechanisms of control. The investigation of the various topics will involve the discussion of many studies of organizations and numerous related studies from the literature. Our aim, however, has not been to cover the entire relevant literature. No single work could achieve such complete coverage, since there exist literally thousands of books and articles on organizations. (The extensive bibliography at the end of this book contains only about one-third of the sources we have collected, with the help of Patricia Denton, and our own compilation is undoubtedly far from exhaustive.) Our intent, rather, has been to select those empirical studies and general discussions that help to clarify a particular problem under review. Frequently we have drawn on our own research on organizations, not only because we are most familiar with this material, but also to provide some continuity in the empirical examples.

We are indebted to Ivan C. Belknap, Leonard Broom, and Otis Dudley Duncan for many helpful criticisms and suggestions. We gratefully acknowledge financial support from the Ford Foundation and the Social Science Research Committee of the University of Chicago (to Blau) and a fellowship from the Social Science Research Council (to Scott). The typing services of Nancy Levinson Scott and Jayne Salzman Heron are appreciated, as is Joan Stelling's assistance with the indexes. Finally, we owe thanks for support and encouragement to Zena Smith Blau and Joy Whitney Scott.

PETER M. BLAU
W. RICHARD SCOTT

FORMAL ORGANIZATIONS

CHAPTER ONE

Introduction

This book is about organizations—organizations of various kinds, with diverse aims, of varying size and complexity, and with different characteristics. What they all have in common is that a number of men have become organized into a social unit—an organization—that has been established for the explicit purpose of achieving certain goals. If the accomplishment of a task requires that more than a mere handful of men work together, they cannot simply proceed by having each do whatever he thinks needs to be done; rather, they must first get themselves organized. They establish a club or a firm, they organize a union or a political party, or they set up a police force or a hospital, and they formulate procedures that govern the relations among the members of the organization and the duties each is expected to perform. Once firmly established, an organization tends to assume an identity of its own which makes it independent of the people who have founded it or of those who constitute its membership. Thus organizations can persist for several generations, not without change but without losing their fundamental identity as distinct units, even though all members at some time come to differ from the original ones. The United States Army today is the same organization as the United States Army in the World War of 1914–1918, even though few if any of its 1918 personnel have remained in it and its structure has undergone basic alterations.

Even when men who are living together do not deliberately plan and institute a formal organization, however, a social organization develops among them; that is, their ways of acting, of thinking, and in particular of interacting with one another come to assume distinct regularities. Neighborhoods, families, work groups, and play groups reveal such an organization of social life, and so do total societies. Indeed, the entire subject matter of the social sciences can be considered to consist of explanations of various aspects of social organization. Whenever a social scientist discovers a new principle or social pattern in what had previously appeared to be chaos—and this kind of discovery is the object of all social theory and research—he thereby demonstrates something about the orderly structure or organization of social life. The study of social classes and stratification is concerned with one aspect of the organization of societies; the study of economics, with another—for even an unplanned economy is not an economy without organization. But there is obviously a difference between a planned economy and an economy whose organization emerges as the result of the interplay between diverse forces; and there is a parallel, more extreme, difference between the way a business firm is organized and the way a relatively free market becomes organized. The contrast in both cases is not one between organization and chaos but one between two distinct principles of organization, and this contrast is what differentiates the specific subject matter of this book—*formal* organizations—from the general subject matter of sociology and other social sciences—social organization.

The Concept of Formal Organization

Social Organization and Formal Organizations. Although a wide variety of organizations exists, when we speak of an organization it is generally quite clear what we mean and what we do not mean by this term. We may refer to the American Medical Association as an organization, or to a college fraternity; to the Bureau of Internal Revenue, or to a union; to General Motors, or to a church; to the Daughters of the American Revolution, or to an army. But we would not call a family an organization, nor would we so designate a friendship clique, or a community, or an economic market, or the political institutions of a society. What is the specific and differentiating criterion implicit in our intuitive distinction of organizations from other kinds of social groupings or institutions? It has something to do with how human conduct becomes socially organized, but it is not, as one might first suspect, whether or not social controls order and organize the conduct of individuals, since such social controls operate in both types of circumstances.

Before specifying what is meant by formal organization, let us clarify the general concept of social organization. "Social organization" refers to the ways in which human conduct becomes socially organized, that is, to the observed regularities in the behavior of people that are due to the social conditions in which they find themselves rather than to their physiological or psychological characteristics as individuals. The many social conditions that influence the conduct of people can be divided into two main types, which constitute the two basic aspects of social organizations: (1) the structure of social relations in a group or larger collectivity of people, and (2) the shared beliefs and orientations that unite the members of the collectivity and guide their conduct.

The conception of structure or system implies that the component units stand in some relation to one another and, as the popular expression "The whole is greater than the sum of its parts" suggests, that the relations between units add new elements to the situation.[1] This aphorism, like so many others, is a half-truth. The sum of fifteen apples, for example, is no more than fifteen times one apple. But a block of ice is more than the sum of the atoms of hydrogen and oxygen that compose it. In the case of the apples, there exist no linkages or relations between the units comprising the whole. In the case of the ice, however, specific connections have been formed between H and O atoms and among H_2O molecules that distinguish ice from hydrogen and oxygen, on the one hand, and from water, on the other. Similarly, a busload of passengers does not constitute a group, since no social relations unify individuals into a common structure.[2] But a busload of club members on a Sunday outing is a group, because a network of social relations links the members into a social structure, a structure which is an emergent characteristic of the collectivity that cannot be reduced to the attributes of its individual members. In short, a network of social relations transforms an aggregate of individuals into a group (or an aggregate of groups into a larger social structure), and the group is more than the sum of the individuals composing it since the structure of social relations is an emergent element that influences the conduct of individuals.

To indicate the nature of social relations, we can briefly dissect this concept. Social relations involve, first, patterns of social interaction: the frequency and duration of the contacts between people, the tendency to initiate these contacts, the direction of influence between persons, the degree of cooperation, and so forth. Second, social relations entail people's sentiments to one another, such as feelings of attraction, respect, and hostility. The differential distribution of social relations in a group, finally, defines its status structure. Each member's status in the group depends on his relations with the others—their sentiments toward and interaction with him. As a result, integrated members become differentiated from isolates, those who are widely respected from those who are not highly regarded, and leaders from followers. In addition to these relations between individuals within groups, relations also develop between groups, relations that are a source of still another aspect of social status, since the standing of the

---

[1] For a discussion of some of the issues raised by this assertion, see Ernest Nagel, "On the Statement 'The Whole is More Than the Sum of Its Parts'," Paul F. Lazarsfeld and Morris Rosenberg (eds.), *The Language of Social Research*, Glencoe, Ill.: Free Press, 1955, pp. 519–527.

[2] A purist may, concededly, point out that all individuals share the role of passenger and so are subject to certain generalized norms, courtesy for example.

group in the larger social system becomes part of the status of any of its members. An obvious example is the significance that membership in an ethnic minority, say, Puerto Rican, has for an individual's social status.

The networks of social relations between individuals and groups, and the status structure defined by them, constitute the core of the social organization of a collectivity, but not the whole of it. The other main dimension of social organization is a system of shared beliefs and orientations, which serve as standards for human conduct. In the course of social interaction common notions arise as to how people should act and interact and what objectives are worthy of attainment. First, common values crystallize, values that govern the goals for which men strive—their ideals and their ideas of what is desirable—such as our belief in democracy or the importance financial success assumes in our thinking. Second, social norms develop—that is, common expectations concerning how people ought to behave—and social sanctions are used to discourage violations of these norms. These socially sanctioned rules of conduct vary in significance from moral principles or mores, as Sumner calls them, to mere customs or folkways. If values define the ends of human conduct, norms distinguish behavior that is a legitimate means for achieving these ends from behavior that is illegitimate. Finally, aside from the norms to which everybody is expected to conform, differential role expectations also emerge, expectations that become associated with various social positions. Only women in our society are expected to wear skirts, for example. Or, the respected leader of a group is expected to make suggestions, and the other members will turn to him in times of difficulties, whereas group members who have not earned the respect of others are expected to refrain from making suggestions and generally to participate little in group discussions.

These two dimensions of social organization—the networks of social relations and the shared orientations—are often referred to as the social structure and the culture, respectively.[3] Every society has a complex social structure and a complex culture, and every community within a society can be characterized by these two dimensions of social organization, and so can every group within a community (except that the specific term "culture" is reserved for the largest social systems). The prevailing cultural standards and the structure of social relations

[3] See the recent discussion of these concepts by Kroeber and Parsons, who conclude by defining culture as "transmitted and created content and patterns of values, ideas, and other symbolic-meaningful systems" and social structure or system as "the specifically relational system of interaction among individuals and collectivities." A. L. Kroeber and Talcott Parsons, "The Concepts of Culture and of Social System," *American Sociological Review*, 23 (1958), p. 583.

serve to organize human conduct in the collectivity. As people conform more or less closely to the expectations of their fellows, and as the degree of their conformity in turn influences their relations with others and their social status, and as their status in further turn affects their inclinations to adhere to social norms and their chances to achieve valued objectives, their patterns of behavior become socially organized.

In contrast to the social organization that emerges whenever men are living together, there are organizations that have been deliberately established for a certain purpose.[4] If the accomplishment of an objective requires collective effort, men set up an organization designed to coordinate the activities of many persons and to furnish incentives for others to join them for this purpose. For example, business concerns are established in order to produce goods that can be sold for a profit, and workers organize unions in order to increase their bargaining power with employers. In these cases, the goals to be achieved, the rules the members of the organization are expected to follow, and the status structure that defines the relations between them (the organizational chart) have not spontaneously emerged in the course of social interaction but have been consciously designed a priori to anticipate and guide interaction and activities. Since the distinctive characteristic of these organizations is that they have been formally established for the explicit purpose of achieving certain goals, the term "formal organizations" is used to designate them. And this formal establishment for explicit purpose is the criterion that distinguishes our subject matter from the study of social organization in general.

Formal Organization and Informal Organization. The fact that an organization has been formally established, however, does not mean that all activities and interactions of its members conform strictly to the official blueprint. Regardless of the time and effort devoted by management to designing a rational organization chart and elaborate procedure manuals, this official plan can never completely determine the conduct and social relations of the organization's members. Stephen Vincent Benét illustrates this limitation when he contrasts the military blueprint with military action:

> If you take a flat map
> And move wooden blocks upon it strategically,
> The thing looks well, the blocks behave as they should.
> The science of war is moving live men like blocks.
> And getting the blocks into place at a fixed moment.
> But it takes time to mold your men into blocks

---

4 Sumner makes this distinction between, in his terms, "crescive" and "enacted" social institutions. William Graham Sumner, *Folkways*, Boston: Ginn, 1907, p. 54.

And flat maps turn into country where creeks and gullies
Hamper your wooden squares. They stick in the brush,
They are tired and rest, they straggle after ripe blackberries,
And you cannot lift them up in your hand and move them.[5]

In every formal organization there arise informal organizations. The constituent groups of the organization, like all groups, develop their own practices, values, norms, and social relations as their members live and work together. The roots of these informal systems are embedded in the formal organization itself and nurtured by the very formality of its arrangements. Official rules must be general to have sufficient scope to cover the multitude of situations that may arise. But the application of these general rules to particular cases often poses problems of judgment, and informal practices tend to emerge that provide solutions for these problems. Decisions not anticipated by official regulations must frequently be made, particularly in times of change, and here again unofficial practices are likely to furnish guides for decisions long before the formal rules have been adapted to the changing circumstances. Moreover, unofficial norms are apt to develop that regulate performance and productivity. Finally, complex networks of social relations and informal status structures emerge, within groups and between them, which are influenced by many factors besides the organizational chart, for example by the background characteristics of various persons, their abilities, their willingness to help others, and their conformity to group norms. But to say that these informal structures are not completely determined by the formal institution is not to say that they are entirely independent of it. For informal organizations develop in response to the opportunities created and the problems posed by their environment, and the formal organization constitutes the immediate environment of the groups within it.

When we speak of formal organizations in this book, we do not mean to imply that attention is confined to formally instituted patterns; quite the contrary. It is impossible to understand the nature of a formal organization without investigating the networks of informal relations and the unofficial norms as well as the formal hierarchy of authority and the official body of rules, since the formally instituted and the informally emerging patterns are inextricably intertwined. The distinction between the formal and the informal aspects of organizational life is only an analytical one and should not be reified; there is only one actual organization. Note also that one does not speak of the informal organization of a family or of a community. The term "informal organization" does not refer to all types of emergent patterns of social life but only to those that evolve within the framework of a formally established organization. Excluded from our purview are social institutions that have evolved without explicit design; included are the informally emerging as well as the formally instituted patterns within formally established organizations.

The decision of the members of a group to formalize their endeavors and relations by setting up a specific organization, say, a social and athletic club, is not fortuitous. If a group is small enough for all members to be in direct social contact, and if it has no objectives that require coordination of activities, there is little need for explicit procedures or a formal division of labor. But the larger the group and the more complex the task it seeks to accomplish, the greater are the pressures to become explicitly organized.[6] Once a group of boys who merely used to hang around a drugstore decide to participate in the local baseball league, they must organize a team. And the complex coordination of millions of soldiers with thousands of specialized duties in a modern army requires extensive formalized procedures and a clear-cut authority structure.

Since formal organizations are often very large and complex, some authors refer to them as "large-scale" or as "complex" organizations. But we have eschewed these terms as misleading in two respects. First, organizations vary in size and complexity, and using these variables as defining criteria would result in such odd expressions as "a small large-scale organization" or "a very complex complex organization." Second, although formal organizations often become very large and complex, their size and complexity do not rival those of the social organization of a modern society, which includes such organizations and their relations with one another in addition to other nonorganizational patterns. (Perhaps the complexity of formal organizations is so much emphasized because it is man-made whereas the complexity of societal organization has slowly emerged, just as the complexity of modern computers is more impressive than that of the human brain. Complexity by design may be more conspicuous than complexity by growth or evolution.)

The term "bureaucratic organization," which also is often used, calls attention to the fact that organizations generally possess some sort of administrative machinery. In an organization that has been formally established, a specialized administrative staff usually exists that is responsible for maintaining the organization as a going concern and for coordinating the activities of its members. Large and complex organizations require an especially elaborate administrative apparatus. In a large factory, for example, there is not only an industrial work

---

6 For a discussion of size and its varied effects on the characteristics of social organization, see Theodore Caplow, "Organizational Size," *Administrative Science Quarterly*, 1 (1957), pp. 484–505.

force directly engaged in production but also an administration composed of executive, supervisory, clerical, and other staff personnel. The case of a government agency is more complicated, because such an agency is part of the administrative arm of the nation. The entire personnel of, say, a law-enforcement agency is engaged in administration, but administration of different kinds; whereas operating officials administer the law and thereby help maintain social order in the society, their superiors and the auxiliary staff administer agency procedures and help maintain the organization itself.

One aspect of bureaucratization that has received much attention is the elaboration of detailed rules and regulations that the members of the organization are expected to faithfully follow. Rigid enforcement of the minutiae of extensive official procedures often impedes effective operations. Colloquially, the term "bureaucracy" connotes such rule-encumbered inefficiency. In sociology, however, the term is used neutrally to refer to the administrative aspects of organizations. If bureaucratization is defined as the amount of effort devoted to maintaining the organization rather than to directly achieving its objectives, all formal organizations have at least a minimum of bureaucracy —even if this bureaucracy involves no more than a secretary-treasurer who collects dues. But wide variations have been found in the degree of bureaucratization in organizations, as indicated by the amount of effort devoted to administrative problems, the proportion of administrative personnel, the hierarchical character of the organization, or the strict enforcement of administrative procedures and rigid compliance with them.

THE STUDY OF FORMAL ORGANIZATIONS

Outline of Subject Matter. This book is a survey of theory and research on formal organization. Our aim is to examine some of the principles that govern organizational life. To discover those theoretical principles that can explain the structure and dynamics of organizations, we shall examine studies of a large number of organizations. Wherever possible, we shall systematically compare various organizations or segments of organizations in order to increase the scope and, so we hope, the validity of the tentative generalizations derived from the analysis.

Theory is both the end product and the starting point of scientific research. On the one hand, the objective of all scientific endeavor is to develop a body of substantive theory, that is, a set of interrelated verifiable generalizations that account for and predict the empirical phenomena that can be observed. On the other hand, scientific research must be guided by a theoretical framework, that is, a system of interrelated concepts that suggest theoretically fruitful lines of empirical investigation. The field of formal organization is still at a very early stage of development. There exists as yet very little substantive theory in this field, not only far less than in the natural sciences but also less than in other fields in sociology. Most theoretical analysis is on the level of developing a conceptual framework, combined with some speculation about possible substantive propositions. It is, therefore, appropriate to precede the analysis of empirical studies, which occupies most of the book, with a chapter (Chapter II) that presents theoretical discussions of formal organizations.

Max Weber's theoretical analysis of formal organizations and their bureaucratic characteristics is critically examined in Chapter II, and so are two other theoretical conceptions of formal organizations. These discussions define the major dimensions that characterize organizations in general and that must be taken into consideration in the study of every kind of organization. But just as important as a knowledge of what all organizations have in common is an understanding of what distinguishes various types. Hence, we discuss in the second part of Chapter II, criteria for differentiating organizations into distinct types. A presentation of empirical studies follows, to illustrate the differences among four types.

Organizations do not exist in a vacuum but in communities and societies. It has often been pointed out that much research on organizations neglects to investigate the important relationships between them and their environment. To avoid this omission, we devote two chapters to this topic. Chapter III deals with the relations between the members of an organization and the public with whom they have direct contact, for example, their clients. We shall examine the significance of the orientations of members of the organization to the public and of the orientations of the public to the organization and its personnel, paying special attention to two kinds of implications of conflict between these two parties: implications for the informal organization of the members of the organization, on the one hand, and implications for that of the client group, on the other. Chapter VIII is concerned with the broader social context of organizational life. Cross-cultural comparisons and time trends are used to infer how the environment influences organizations and what organizational attributes tend to occur and to change together, and the dynamic interrelations between organizations are analyzed.

Chapters III and VIII, in which the external relations of organization are examined from two different perspectives, provide the framework that precedes and follows the discussion of the internal structure of organizations in Chapters IV to VII. In Chapter IV we discuss peer-group relations and the informal structure of work groups, with particular emphasis on two problems, namely, how the group structure influences operations, and how the group structure, in turn, is affected by the conditions in the formal organization and in the society at large. In Chapter V, experiments and field studies are drawn upon to investigate processes of communication and their implications for task performance. The analysis of the interdependence between patterns of communication and status structure in this chapter furnishes a bridge between the discussion of peer relations in Chapter IV and that of hierarchical relations in Chapters VI and VII. Chapter VI deals with supervision and the structure of hierarchical authority. Management is examined in Chapter VII, as are impersonal mechanisms of control and some problems posed by pseudo-democratic practices in hierarchical organizations.

Viewed in another way, Chapters III to VIII proceed from the analysis of simpler aspects of the organization of social life to that of more complex ones. Starting with research on sociopsychological orientations, we go on to study interpersonal relations and how they become structured in small peer groups; next we look at the implications of communication for differentiation in the social structure, and only then do we investigate the complex hierarchical structures and control mechanisms in formal organizations, to turn finally to the relations among different organizations and those between them and their social context.

Throughout the book, there are occasions for referring to processes of change in organizations. But only in the last chapter are the dynamic processes of organizational change made the focus of attention around which a summary of the main points covered is organized. We shall suggest that various conflicts in complex organizations, which rigid bureaucratization is designed to conceal and suppress, are an inevitable source of change, and that the resulting organizational developments can be conceptualized as dialectical processes.

Before starting this survey of organization theory and research, however, we must complete our introduction to the subject matter by presenting two methodological topics. We want to examine first a methodological dilemma posed by the study of organization, and then briefly review the research methods used in empirical investigation of organizations.

A Dilemma in the Study of Organization. The object of all science is to explain things. What do we mean by a scientific explanation? An observed fact is explained by reference to a general principle, that is, by showing that the occurrence of this fact under the given circumstances can be predicted from the principle. To first establish such an explanatory principle or theoretical generalization, many particular events must be observed and classified into general categories that make them comparable. To explain a principle requires a more general proposition from which this and other similarly specific principles can be inferred.

Not only testing but even originating an explanatory hypothesis requires information on a number of independent cases. The insight that produces the hypothesis may appear to rest on only a single instance, but this appearance is illusory. Assume that a worker has quit his job shortly after having been promoted. An intensive analysis of this one case might reveal that he had been liked and well integrated in his former work group but was an isolate in his present one, suggesting the conclusion that lack of social integration was responsible for his resignation. This change in social integration with peers, however, surely was not the only change that occurred in his life at this period. His duties had been altered, and so had his income; perhaps he had just turned fifty, and maybe his relatives had chosen this time for a visit. Hence, even the insight that lack of social integration might be the variable that accounts for the worker's resignation rests on an implicit comparison of this case with others, a comparison that indicates that reaching the age of fifty is not usually accompanied by quitting one's job, and neither is entertaining relatives, but that lack of social integration often is. If deriving hypotheses requires the implicit comparison of several cases, testing them requires the explicit and systematic comparison of many independent cases. To verify the explanatory hypothesis advanced it would be necessary to show that in a representative sample of workers those who lack social integration quit in larger numbers than those who are integrated in their work groups. Such use of samples to test hypotheses is the typical procedure in survey research.

But this procedure of the sample survey, by tearing each individual from his social context and treating him as an "independent" case, ignores the networks of relations between individuals and groups —the very core of the study of social organization. The community study of the anthropology type, which focuses upon the interdependence between parts in the social system, is in this respect better suited for the study of organization than is the survey. For if our object is to analyze the relations between the elements in a social structure, we must not atomize it into its component elements. The anthropological method, however, while retaining the structural characteristics of the subject under study, provides information on only a single case, and one case is not sufficient for arriving at valid explanatory generalizations.

A fundamental dilemma is posed for the study of organizations by the double requirement of examining the interdependence between elements in a social structure, on the one hand, and of observing many independent cases to substantiate generalizations, on the other. Various stages of industrial research illustrate how attempts to resolve this dilemma on one level reintroduce it on another. Early research conducted in factories was concerned with such problems as worker fatigue and morale. These surveys treated workers as independent cases, furnishing a basis for generalizations about individuals, but ignoring the social relations among workers. Under the influence of Mayo and his associates, the emphasis of industrial research shifted to the significance of the human relations on the job for work satisfaction and productivity. The method typically employed was the case study of a single work group, as exemplified by the well-known Hawthorne studies.[7] These case studies furnished important insights into the informal organization of work groups, but isolated cases are not an adequate basis for valid generalizations. In recognition of this problem, social scientists have turned more recently to the systematic comparison of a sample of work groups or all the groups in a large factory.[8] Treating groups rather than individuals as independent units of analysis permits making generalizations about the internal structure of work groups,[9] but it ignores the interrelations of these groups in the larger industrial organization. And if the investigator analyzes this interdependence among the various groups in the factory—that is, the structure of the formal organization—he again is left with only a single case. General propositions about formal organizations must be based on the investigation of a large number of them. And even when comparable empirical data on many organizations are available, conceptualizing the organizations as independent cases would involve ignoring their interdependence in the larger society, whereas focusing upon their interdependence would leave the investigator, once more, with only one case.

This dilemma cannot be definitively resolved. For regardless of which organizations are compared, they are inevitably part of a larger social organization that cannot be systematically examined. Even a

[7] F. J. Roethlisberger and William J. Dickson, *Management and the Worker*, Cambridge, Mass.: Harvard University Press, 1939, pp. 19–186; 379–548.

[8] For an example of this type of research, see Stanley E. Seashore, *Group Cohesiveness in the Industrial Work Group*, Ann Arbor: Institute for Social Research, University of Michigan, 1954.

[9] Although groups within an organization, or individuals within a group, are often treated as independent cases, they do not, strictly speaking, meet the statistical criterion of complete independence. The problem posed by the analysis of such data is quite similar to that of the economist working with time-series data or that of the geographer and ecologist working with data from contiguous areas.

comparative study of entire societies could advance generalizations only about their internal organization and not about the international relations that characterize the world-wide organization of societies, of which there is only one case at any one time. But while this dilemma cannot be resolved in principle, once it is recognized it poses little difficulty for specific empirical studies with limited objectives. A study of a sample of work groups in a firm makes it possible to generalize about group structure, although not about the structure of formal organization. To arrive at the latter type of generalizations requires systematic comparison of a fair number of different organizations— ideally, a representative sample of them. In short, the important practical implication of the dilemma is that the research design must be adapted to the level of organization to be explained.

It is in the light of these considerations that the study of formal organization assumes special significance at the present stage of sociological knowledge. If the early sociologists were primarily concerned with broad problems of social organization, and neglected questions of scientific evidence, later ones became preoccupied with refining methods for testing hypotheses, and were willing to sacrifice the sociological focus on organized social relations for neatness of research design. Most theories of the pioneer sociologists illustrate the first trend, and most attitude surveys and demographic analyses, the second. Recently, however, the gap has been narrowed between the methodologically naive students of social organization and the theoretically naive rigorous researchers. There has been a growing refusal to be impaled on the horns of this dilemma, and an increasing emphasis on obtaining systematic data about social organization instead of collecting rigorous data only about individuals and merely impressionistic information about the social relations and shared beliefs that link them into a common structure. The tremendous expansion of the field of small groups in the past two decades is a reflection of this concern. In the study of small groups it is easy to compare systematically a number of independent cases of social organization, often under experimentally controlled conditions, whereas it is not easy to do the same in, say, community studies. As a result, research on small groups has made important contributions to an understanding of various aspects of group structure, such as social cohesion. This kind of work has been an essential first step in the systematic study of social organization—a knowledge of simpler systems is needed before one can understand more complex ones—but only a first step. A host of problems of organizational life cannot be clarified on the basis of observations of small groups because they simply do not occur in these groups. Obvious examples are the influence of the institutional context on group structure and the interrelations between groups in a hierarchical system. Research on formal organizations, on the other hand, provides opportunities for investigating these kinds of problems.

We consider the study of formal organization to be capable of making the greatest contributions to the advancement of systematic sociology at this juncture. Organizations are, on the average, smaller and less complex than communities or entire societies, but even aside from these differences the study of the former is less complicated than that of the latter. In contrast to communities or societies, formal organizations are characterized by explicit goals, an elaborate system of explicit rules and regulations, and a formal status structure with clearly marked lines of communication and authority.[10] This is not to say that the formally instituted arrangements dominate all patterns of conduct in the organization; far from it. But they do undoubtedly exert considerable influence on these patterns and thus reduce the freedom of movement of the emergent social forces. Since the most serious problem in the investigation of social life is to establish causal relations by disentangling the interplay among a large number of social forces, the fact that some of these are relatively fixed in a formal organization and only others vary simplifies the analysis. The official institutions in the organization control some of the conditions of social life, just as the experimenter in the laboratory does. (An important difference, of course, is that the researcher in an organization can usually not decide what is to be controlled, whereas the experimenter can.) The advantage of this control is illustrated in a study of the effects of variations in supervision on the productivity of office workers.[11] Many factors besides supervisory practices affect the productivity of work groups. By selecting for study a large number of work groups, however, all recruited in the same way, engaged in similar tasks, using similar equipment, subject to the same rules, and working for the same rewards, the most important of these factors were probably held constant. Holding them constant made it possible to attribute the observed differences in productivity to contrasting patterns of supervision. By controlling in this fashion some of the conditions in the situation, the formal organization provides an anchoring point that facilitates deriving and testing generalizations about social organization. In sum, the comparative study of formal organizations offers great promise for advancing systematic knowledge about the organization of social life.

[10] March and Simon make a similar point when they emphasize the specificity of formal organizations in contrast to the diffuseness which marks many of the other social processes within a society. See James G. March and Herbert A. Simon, *Organizations,* New York: Wiley, 1958, pp. 2–3.

[11] Daniel Katz *et al., Productivity, Supervision and Morale in an Office Situation,* Ann Arbor: Institute for Social Research, University of Michigan, 1950, pp. 3–4.

In addition to its theoretical significance, the study of organizations has much practical significance today, particularly in a democratic society. While large bureaucracies have existed for thousands of years, it has been primarily in this century that they have expanded greatly and come to pervade all of social life. Since formalized organizations have become the dominant form of institution in modern societies, a thorough knowledge of them is essential for an understanding of contemporary social life. The centralization of power in the hands of management that organizational giants make possible, moreover, poses a challenge to democracies. An efficient administrative machinery vests tremendous power in the hands of the few—be they corporation managers, government officials, military officers, party bosses, or union leaders—and thereby undermines the sovereignty of the many to whom the few in a democracy are expected to be responsible. Acquiring knowledge about bureaucratic organizations is an important first step in meeting the threat they pose for democratic institutions.[12]

METHODS IN THE STUDY OF ORGANIZATIONS

Methods of Data Collection. The methods of social research can be classified in various ways. One classificatory scheme emphasizes the purpose for which the data are collected.[13] The types arrived at include (1) exploratory studies, in which familiarity is gained with some problem or new insights are achieved that can guide further research; (2) descriptive studies, which define and portray the characteristics of the object of research or determine the frequency of various occurrences and examine their associations with one another; and (3) hypothesis-testing studies, which focus on the collection of data that permit the confirmation of a given hypothesis, or set of hypotheses, and thereby help to determine the probable validity of the theory from which it is derived. Needless to say, many studies have a mixed purpose, as exemplified by a recent work in the area of formal organization—a case study of the International Typographical Union.[14] This

---

[12] Lipset suggests that while the great social theorists of the nineteenth century directed their attention to the study of the sources of conflict and consensus—these themes dominating the work of both Marx and Tocqueville—the major social scientists of the early twentieth century have been much more concerned with the problems posed for democracy by the growth of bureaucratic institutional arrangements, as evidenced particularly in the writings of Michels and Weber. See Seymour M. Lipset, *Political Man*, Garden City, N.Y.: Doubleday, 1960, pp. 28–30.

[13] Claire Selltiz *et al.*, *Research Methods in Social Relations* (2d ed.), New York: Holt, 1959, pp. 50–51.

[14] Seymour Lipset *et al.*, *Union Democracy*, Glencoe, Ill.: Free Press, 1956.

study is descriptive when the characteristics and history of the ITU are recounted; it is hypothesis-testing when specific propositions about the occupational community of printers and its relation to union politics are tested; and it becomes exploratory when an attempt is made to formulate propositions "aimed at identifying the factors which make for and sustain democracy in private organizations."[15]

Research methods may also be classified according to the techniques employed in the collection of data. In principle, there are three ways of obtaining information about people: by watching them, by asking them questions, and by examining materials that have been written by them or about them. The three categories of research techniques which correspond to these operations are: observation, interviewing, and the analysis of documents. One group of these techniques may be used to the exclusion of the others, or a study may combine all three approaches. Besides, each of these techniques may be employed more or less rigorously. The use of these three methods of data collection in organizational research will be briefly discussed.

Considering first observation, the operation of watching people may be unstructured in the sense that the observer attempts to keep as complete a record as possible of all the activities of the members of the group being studied. Such an unstructured technique was utilized by the observer placed in the now famous Hawthorne Bank Wiring Observation Room.[16] While unstructured observation is still often used, particularly in exploratory research, "the movement has been away from exhaustive recording of all the behavior which occurs toward the selection of particular aspects of behavior in order to answer specific questions."[17] The observer who utilizes systematic observation methods either classifies the behavior observed into a set of predetermined categories or assigns to it a numerical index. Two widely used techniques of systematic observation, both concerned with recording patterns of social interaction, are those developed by Bales[18] and by Chapple.[19] In addition to these direct methods of observation, there is the use of

---

15 *Ibid.*, p. 413.

16 Roethlisberger and Dickson, *op. cit.*, pp. 387–391.

17 Roger W. Heyns and Ronald Lippitt, "Systematic Observational Techniques," Gardner Lindzey (ed.), *Handbook of Social Psychology*, Cambridge, Mass.: Addison-Wesley, 1954, vol. I, p. 371. This essay contains probably the best survey of systematic observational techniques to be found in the literature.

18 Robert F. Bales, *Interaction Process Analysis*, Cambridge, Mass.: Addison-Wesley, 1950. This technique is perhaps too complex to be suitable for the analysis of many of the types of interaction occurring within formal organizations; however, the work of some investigators suggests that, with appropriate modifications, it can be adapted for organizational studies.

19 Eliot D. Chapple, "Measuring Human Relations," *Genetic Psychology Monographs*, 22 (1940), pp. 3–147.

various self-recording devices which may be characterized as indirect observation. Here participants are persuaded to record for the investigator their experiences or their reactions to experiences over a period of time. This operation, too, may be relatively unstructured, as when organization members are asked to keep diaries of their daily activities; or the investigator may enlist the aid of respondents in the collection of more systematic data, for example, a two-week record of all lunch partners. The study of formal organizations affords many opportunities for using direct and indirect observational techniques, which is an important advantage of this field over some others.

Like techniques of observation, interviewing methods may be direct or indirect, systematic or unstructured. The direct unstructured interview, exemplified by asking the manager of an enterprise a wide range of questions about the plant and its operations, is most useful during the early stages of the research, when information is desired on the range and variety of problems confronted by the organization and its members.[20] Once the specific questions and hypotheses that are to guide the research have been formulated, the investigator may choose to utilize the direct interview in a more systematic fashion, asking a list of identical or similar questions of a representative sample of organization members. A good example of this systematic use of the interview is a study in which a sample of 2,451 social scientists from 165 colleges and universities were questioned concerning their views on academic freedom.[21] Finally, the interviewing of organization members may be carried out indirectly by the use of self-administered questionnaires.[22] The advantages of this method are that it is cheap and saves time in comparison with direct interviewing, wherefore a much larger number of persons can be questioned at a given cost. The disadvantages include the relative rigidity of this instrument (all questions will not be understood by, nor be appropriate for, all respondents) and the bias in results introduced by selective returns (disproportionate numbers of uneducated persons, for example, fail to return questionnaires).

The analysis of the organization's documents may be unstructured, as when the analyst surveys the various manuals of operation, charts, rules, and other documents in order to understand its nature and func-

[20] For a study based almost entirely on such unstructured interviews with various representatives of management and the union, rank and file workers, and supervisors, see James C. Abegglen, *The Japanese Factory*, Glencoe, Ill.: Free Press, 1958.

[21] Paul F. Lazarsfeld and Wagner Thielens, Jr., *The Academic Mind*, Glencoe, Ill.: Free Press, 1958.

[22] See, for example, the study of the characteristics and attitudes of a sample of higher civil servants in Egypt conducted by Morroe Berger, *Bureaucracy and Society in Modern Egypt*, Princeton: Princeton University Press, 1957.

tion.[23] Some investigators have attempted a more systematic analysis of organizational documents by using methods of content analysis to establish the frequency with which given themes or topics occur.[24] Performance records, usually plentiful in formal organizations, are another kind of document which may be employed in social research. In the study previously cited, Katz and his associates were able to use company records as the basis for distinguishing between work groups with high and low productivity—a variable fundamental to the purpose of the research.[25] Performance records may also be used to derive indices not contemplated by those who collected them. For example, Blau used organization records to construct an index of competition for each official in two sections of an employment agency.[26] A particular advantage enjoyed by the student of formal organizations is precisely the existence of such documents and performance records; to overlook their significance as an inexpensive, valuable source of data on the policies of the organization and the conduct of its members is to fail to exploit the "natural resources" in this research field.

Types of Research Design. Empirical studies may also be classified on the basis of the research design employed. Three basic designs will be considered here: the sample survey, the controlled experiment, and the field study.[27] As has been pointed out above, sampling surveys are not well suited for studies of organizations; the selection of independent cases is achieved at the cost of tearing individuals from the social matrix in which they are embedded. But this defect is serious only in studies of organizational structure. The survey approach is eminently suited for the study of various other problems of organizational life. To take but a single example, it is appropriate and has been utilized for the study of the careers and attitudes of civil servants, business leaders, and other organization men.[28] In brief, the sample survey is an excellent research design for investigations concerned with the characteristics of the members of organizations but not for studies interested in the characteristics of organizational structure.

[23] Selznick has been particularly imaginative in the unstructured use of documents to gain insights into a new organization and the changes that occurred in it during the first years. Philip Selznick, *TVA and the Grass Roots*, Berkeley: University of California Press, 1949.

[24] For one such approach to organizational documents, see Roy G. Francis and Robert C. Stone, *Service and Procedure in a Bureaucracy*, Minneapolis: University of Minnesota Press, 1956, pp. 51–61.

[25] Katz *et al., op. cit.*

[26] Peter M. Blau, *The Dynamics of Bureaucracy*, Chicago: University of Chicago Press, 1955, pp. 50–55.

[27] For a similar classification of research methods and a full discussion of the several types, see Leon Festinger and Daniel Katz (eds.), *Research Methods in the Behavioral Sciences*, New York: Dryden, 1953, pp. 13–172.

[28] For one such study see W. Lloyd Warner and James C. Abegglen, *Big Business Leaders in America*, New York: Harper, 1955.

At the present stage of our knowledge, complex organizations can neither be placed nor created in the experimental laboratory.[29] Nevertheless, the controlled experiment has a vital contribution to make to the study of organizations, indirectly as well as directly. It provides the ideal model of a scientific research design, which both informs and reveals the limitations of other designs that are less rigorous. The essence of the experimental approach is the comparison of two situations that are identical in all respects except that some factor "A" is introduced in one situation but not in the other. Any differences that consequently develop between the two situations may be attributed to the presence (or absence) of factor "A" since it is the only condition that has been allowed to vary. When experimentation is not possible, in consequence of inability directly to control all factors in the situation, the investigator seeks to approximate the prototype of the controlled experiment by the use of indirect controls through statistical methods or comparative analysis. In the former case, controls are effected through statistical manipulation; in the latter, control is introduced by comparing cases having strategic similarities and differences. Such alternatives, however, are not fully effective since they cannot control all possible sources of variation.

In addition to providing a general model for all scientific research, the experimental method is also of more direct use in the study of social organization. Perhaps its greatest contribution is that it enables one to subject specific hypotheses derived from organizational research to rigorous experimental tests. For example, Blau's tentative conclusion that the prevalence of competition in a group lowers the quality of performance of its members, based on a case study of two sections in a formal organization, receives considerable support from Deutsch's study of the impact of cooperation and competition on task performance in experimental groups.[30] But utilization of the experimental approach by students of formal organization is not limited to such laboratory experiments. In the form of the "field experiment" and the

[29] Interesting attempts are being made, however, to simulate in the laboratory some of the properties of formal organizations, such as structural complexity, formalization, differentiation of units and statuses, integration through hierarchical authority arrangements, and the assignment of tasks where the achievement of one goal interferes with the achievement of others. See Anatol Rapoport, "A Logical Task as a Research Tool in Organization Theory," Mason Haire (ed.), *Modern Organization Theory*, New York: Wiley, 1959, pp. 91–114. The merits of such experimental approaches to the study of formal organizations are discussed in Morris Zelditch, Jr. and Terrence K. Hopkins, "Laboratory Experiments with Organizations," Amitai W. Etzioni (ed.), *Complex Organizations*, New York: Holt, Rinehart and Winston, 1961, pp. 464–478.

[30] Blau, *op cit.*, pp. 49–67; and Morton Deutsch, "An Experimental Study of the Effects of Cooperation and Competition upon Group Process," *Human Relations*, 2 (1949), pp. 199–231.

"natural experiment," this approach has been employed to study organizational patterns in their setting. In the field experiment the investigator actually manipulates some conditions in an existing organization for the purpose of determining causal relations.[31] For example, by actually controlling the amount of participation of various employee groups, Coch and French were able to test experimentally the hypothesis that the greater the participation on the part of these groups in discussing how to cope with changes in working conditions, the less would be their resistance to these changes and the smaller would be the loss in production.[32] In the natural experiment, the investigator does not himself manipulate certain factors within the research setting, but he "opportunistically capitalizes upon some on-going changes and studies their effects in an experimental design."[33] Thus, management may decide to introduce automation in some sections of its plant but not in others. If these sections are similar in other respects, an alert social researcher might grasp the opportunity to observe the impact of technological change on the social relations within the plant by contrasting developments in the automated and the nonautomated sections. In both of these types of situational experiments, unusual caution must be exercised in interpreting findings, since there is always the possibility that the observed changes may be the result of factors that remain undetected by the investigator.

The field study is the typical research design employed in the study of formal organizations. This approach is well adapted for providing an over-all picture of the organization and information about the interdependence of its constituent parts. In the early stages of its development this method was often employed in an impressionistic fashion without the use of rigorous research methods or the presentation of systematic evidence in support of the conclusions. In recent years, however, an increasing number of field studies have utilized carefully designed, systematic research procedures. The field study is particularly hospitable to the combined use of a variety of data-gathering methods, including direct observation, interviewing, and the analysis of documents and records. This advantage is crucial, for it means that the investigator can select from his research repertoire those methods that are the most appropriate for the study of a given problem. Should the field researcher desire data on patterns of social interaction, he can directly observe them; should he require information about the distribution of sentiments, he can inquire about them. A variety of approaches allows him to examine subtle differences which otherwise would escape atten-

[31] See John R. P. French, Jr., "Experiments in Field Settings," Festinger and Katz, *op. cit.,* pp. 98–101.

[32] Lester Coch and John R. P. French, Jr., "Overcoming Resistance to Change," *Human Relations,* 1 (1948), pp. 512–532.

[33] French, *op. cit.,* p. 99.

tion, like that between private feelings and public behavior. Interlocking methods also provide a check on bias by bringing into juxtaposition two or more sets of data on the same problem—say, the observation record of the members at each meeting, and the reports of these members of their attendance at each meeting. Besides, the reliability and validity of various techniques of data collection can be ascertained by comparison. Thus, it can be determined whether the inexpensive reports about meetings furnish data that correlate highly with the more accurate but more expensive data obtained through direct observation.

Although the field study does not approach the controlled experiment in rigor of design and hence in validity of conclusions, the use it permits of a combination of systematic research procedures concentrated on a single object of study can yield data of considerable scientific value. Moreover, its focus on social relations among individuals and groups in natural settings provides data of great importance for the study of organizations—data of a type not obtained by any other design.

Some Practical Problems in the Study of Organizations. We have emphasized that in the field approach to the study of formal organizations, a variety of research techniques may be utilized. We have briefly presented the basic techniques of data collection, and have cited sources where these methods are discussed more fully. We now turn to a general practical problem of field research in an organization, namely, that of the disturbance created by the observer. How can the investigator observe and inquire about social conduct without in the process completely altering that which he wishes to study? This problem is generic to the field study approach, but it is particularly acute in the study of hierarchical organizations.

A procedure frequently employed by the observer to allay suspicion and to minimize the disturbances his presence inevitably produces is to explain at the outset to the staff of the organization who he is and, in a general way, the purpose and methods of his research. This introduction may give him legitimacy in the eyes of the staff and enough prestige so that some doors that might have remained closed to him will be opened. The observer's explanation, however, will probably seem unsatisfactory to many organization members, because he must make his discussion sufficiently vague and general that his major hypotheses will not be revealed, inasmuch as their mere statement could bias the very behavior to be utilized as evidence for their confirmation or rejection. No matter how successful the general explanation and the further explications made to smaller groups and individuals, a certain amount of staff anxiety will probably always accompany the entrance of an observer into the organization. The sources of this anxiety will vary from situation to situation, but their general nature may be outlined. To begin with, the observer is an outsider and a stranger. He is a figure of some power—frequently of an unknown amount—and will typically have access to powerful people within the organization. Perhaps most importantly, the observer, if he so chooses, can be virtually omnipresent. Having no conflicting duties (as does a supervisor, for example), he can constantly observe the conduct of the group members under study. Merton has pointed out that few if any groups readily accept full and unrestricted observation of their behavior.[34] Finally, the fact that staff members are not certain as to just what the observer's purposes and interests are increases their discomfort. How is one to behave "properly" under observation when the observer's standards for proper behavior are unknown?

It is also likely that misconceptions of the observer's role develop among organization members despite the best efforts of the investigator. The observer may be identified by some as an efficiency engineer or a representative from headquarters sent down to check on the performance of the organization members. Often respondents look on the observer, quite wrongly, as an expert in their field who can help them in the solution of problems. Such misconceptions, whether flattering or disparaging, must be counteracted by the observer's statements and by his behavior; each encounter with organization personnel should be viewed as an opportunity to clarify his own role vis-à-vis the respondent. In short, he must be skilled in the art of "impression-management,"[35] for the observer is also the observed and his behavior is under constant scrutiny from all sides and in all situations.

There are a number of role attributes through which the observer can lessen the disturbance created by his presence and generally increase the reliability of his records, but while each of these solves some problem it tends to raise others. One of these attributes is impartiality: all members of the organization should have approximately equal access to the observer. The avoidance of bias in the selection of cases is a problem in all situations where data are collected; it is a particular problem in a field situation where the "cases" exercise considerable discretion over deciding whether and to what extent they will make themselves available to the observer. Impartiality of access is especially important when two or more different and possibly conflicting groups are being studied, such as various hierarchical levels in an organization.

---

[34] "Some measure of leeway in conforming to role-expectations is presupposed in all groups. To have to meet the strict requirements of a role at all times, without some degree of deviation, is to experience insufficient allowance for individual differences in capacity and training and for situational exigencies which make strict conformity extremely difficult," Robert K. Merton, *Social Theory and Social Structure* (2d ed.), Glencoe, Ill.: Free Press, 1957, p. 343.

[35] See Erving Goffman, *The Presentation of Self in Everyday Life*, Garden City, N.Y.: Doubleday, 1959, pp. 1–16.

To achieve impartial access the observer can utilize such tactics as often changing his position in the area under study and seeking out the more passive members of the staff. But impartiality will remain only an ideal: some respondents exercise more initiative in contacting the observer than others and are more eager to share with him information otherwise kept confidential, and he cannot afford not to avail himself of these opportunities. Moreover, contacts with certain respondents will prove to be more rewarding—socially as well as in terms of the information received—than contacts with others, and the human observer will inadvertently pay more attention to the former. It should be recognized that during the first few weeks of the study, and to a lesser degree even later, the observer will be an isolate and thus subject to feelings of anxiety and loneliness.[36] Outgoing respondents who are friendly and accepting in these circumstances quite naturally will receive more than their share of his attention.

A second and related attribute of the observer's role is neutrality: his expressions and reactions to all members of the organization's staff should remain neutral and nonjudgmental. Neutrality is essential if an observer is to avoid involvement in the organization with a consequent loss of objectivity and if he is not to inhibit the responses of his informants. But to maintain such neutrality is difficult. Respondents typically attempt to force the observer to express his opinion on various subjects, particularly as he always asks theirs, because his opinion helps them to identify him and to adapt their responses to the kind of relationship they want to maintain with him. In everyday life, such modification of responses by the interpersonal situation occurs continually; but it is precisely what the observer wants to minimize. Yet there is also danger that an impartial neutrality may make the observer seem so dull and colorless that respondents lose all interest in maintaining contact with him. The passively neutral observer may give the impression that he is really not interested in what the respondents have to say, and this impression may inhibit them in his presence. To use an exaggerated example, just think of the effect on the joking banter around a water cooler that an observer would have who never cracked a smile for fear of showing partiality by revealing whose jokes he found funny.

A further attribute of the observer's role is that he is usually not a technical expert in the subject-matter with which respondents deal. Their discovery of his ignorance serves to prove that he is a genuine outside observer and not a "spy" of management, thereby lessening the threat his presence poses. But his technical ignorance may also lower

---

[36] Not only is the observer an isolate but he is constantly confronted by an on-going network of interpersonal relations among the workers observed, which serves to emphasize, by contrast, his own relative isolation.

his prestige in their eyes and thus make some respondents less interested in devoting time to answering his questions.

Another problem confronting the observer in the field is that of maintaining a favorable balance of obligations in interaction with respondents. The observer often finds himself in a position of forever asking and accepting favors from the members of the organization—to let him observe them, to give him information, to explain some document—and his consequent feeling of obligation may impair his effectiveness. But it should be remembered that he has no reason for feeling uneasy about accepting favors from respondents. He offers the staff favors in return: opportunities for demonstrating superior skills before an appreciative audience, for explaining their work and expressing their opinions to an attentive listener, and for making contributions to a scientific study. These are experiences most people enjoy. In addition to these favors inherent in his role, the observer can, and should, take advantage of any occasion to do favors for respondents that do not jeopardize his research role. In our own studies, for example, a number of respondents inquired about the university with which we were affiliated, its course programs, and its degree requirements, and we made it a point to obtain such information for them. Thus the observer can produce a favorable balance of obligations which motivates the members of the organization to cooperate with the research. But it should be mentioned that there is the opposite danger of having respondents too eager to cooperate, since this situation may also bias their verbal statements as well as their overt behavior.

Several situational factors, fortunately, lessen the disturbance created by the presence of the observer. The main one is the network of relations among the members of the organization. Once respondents have become accustomed to the investigator and, particularly, have accepted him as a genuine outside observer, his presence changes little in their situation. Each respondent has his familiar duties and is surrounded by his colleagues and his superiors, all of whom have developed distinct expectations of him and specific relations with him. The constraints exerted upon the individual by the expectations of other members of the organization and his relations with them appear generally to be too great to let him permit the presence of the outsider to alter his conduct very much.[37] The influence of interpersonal relations is most pronounced in the very areas where the observer's presence would otherwise distort conduct most. Members of an organization typically seek to conceal conflicts from outsiders, but if the observer happens to be present when a conflict arises, the emotional involve-

[37] Note that the same safeguards do not operate in the interview situation. Here the person is temporarily separated from his social context and may distort his comments in any way he sees fit without fear of retaliation from his peer group.

ment of participants in the argument makes it difficult for them to dissimulate because he is there. Another aid to the observer in collecting reliable data is what may be termed the bias-correcting action of respondents. Most organization members will be anxious to make sure that the observer obtains what they consider to be a "true" picture of their activities and opinions. Thus, if one member in the presence of his fellows makes a statement with which they do not agree, they will often challenge it. Since the observer cannot easily challenge the statements of his respondents, these workers perform a valuable service for him by uncovering misleading statements or areas of disagreement between organization members.

In short, the observer would do well to keep constantly in mind that he is playing a social role in a social situation and to adapt his role to his research objectives. This recommendation does not imply, however, that he should be manipulative, but rather the contrary; attempts to simulate and dissimulate are too easily detected in a group situation to be useful strategies for the observer.

THE COMPARATIVE APPROACH

The objective of this book is theoretical: to suggest tentative generalizations that help to explain the structure and dynamics of organizations. The emphasis in this book, however, is on the analysis of research findings. Since valid generalizations must be both derived from and tested in empirical research, we shall be largely concerned with empirical studies rather than with general discussions of administrative principles or criticisms of the bureaucratic tendencies in American life. The major empirical sources to be used are: (1) reports of research on various organizations; (2) experiments and other studies from the literature having bearing upon some organizational problem; and (3) our own investigations, especially our research on two welfare agencies.

The approach of this book, finally, is comparative. By "comparative" we mean that the importance of comparing different organizations for generalizing about them informs our thinking throughout the analysis. We cannot claim more than that, inasmuch as most research on this subject that has been reported in the literature consists of case studies. Indeed, in view of this situation, our attempt to be comparative may seem hazardous if not foolhardy. Nevertheless, we believe that the fruits to be attained by even partial success justify the risks involved. How do we propose to proceed with this comparative study, and from where shall the data come? First, it will be possible to attempt to make comparisons between several of the case studies of formal organizations in the literature. Second, we shall draw on those studies that make internal comparisons, for example, of one department with another. Third, we can make use of the few studies that have attempted to make systematic comparisons of several organizations, such as Udy's analysis of the organization of work in primitive societies.[38] Finally, we shall draw extensively on our own separate studies of two welfare agencies, which are described in the appendix. Since we shall have many occasions to refer to these two studies in the following chapters, it should be noted that the fact that these organizations are public welfare departments is incidental to our purpose here; we are interested not in public assistance but in formal organization.[39] The intent of our extensive use of these two studies is to provide some continuity in the illustrative materials throughout the book.

[38] Stanley H. Udy, *The Organization of Work,* New Haven: Human Relations Area Files, 1959.
[39] For a general characterization of social welfare agencies in this country—both with regard to program content and structural characteristics—see Harold L. Wilensky and Charles N. Lebeaux, *Industrial Society and Social Welfare,* New York: Russell Sage Foundation, 1958.

CHAPTER TWO

The Nature and Types of
Formal Organizations

To clarify the nature and characteristics of formal organizations, we shall first deal with the major conceptions advanced by organization theorists and then discuss the various forms that such organizations may assume. We begin by presenting Weber's classical theories of authority and of bureaucratic organization. Following a critical analysis of Weber's conception, we shall briefly deal with two other general theoretical treatments of formal organizations. With regard to types of organizations, our main purpose is to suggest some of the dimensions along which classification may occur and to illustrate the utility of one approach for the development of a classificatory scheme.

THEORETICAL CONCEPTS

The Concept of Authority. Max Weber's perceptive and incisive theoretical analysis of the principles of bureaucracy is undoubtedly the most important general statement on formal organization. Since its publication in *Wirtschaft und Gesellschaft* about 40 years ago, it has had a profound influence on almost all subsequent thinking and research in the field. Weber analyzes formal organizations as part of his theory of authority structures, or systems of legitimate social control; we shall follow his procedure and begin with a discussion of the concept of authority.

Authority must be distinguished from other forms of social influence—from power, on the one hand, and from persuasion and other kinds of personal influence, on the other. Weber defines power as "the probability that one actor within a social relationship will be in a position to carry out his own will despite resistance."[1] Power, as used by Weber, is a very general and comprehensive concept. It includes control through the use or the threat of physical coercion (as exercised by the stick-up man or by the rapist) and it includes the control of one who can manipulate conditions in such a way that others are forced to

[1] Max Weber, *The Theory of Social and Economic Organization,* A. M. Henderson and Talcott Parsons (trans.) and Talcott Parsons (ed.), Glencoe, Ill.: Free Press and Falcon's Wing Press, 1947, p. 152.

act in his interests rather than their own (as exemplified by a monopoly or by the one-company town).

The stick-up man and the monopolist exercise power, but they do not exercise authority, since the essence of the latter is that directives issued by the one in control are *voluntarily* obeyed. Weber defines authority as "the probability that certain specific commands (or all commands) from a given source will be obeyed by a given group of persons."[2] The group willingly obeys because its members consider it legitimate for this source to control them. The source of authority may be a person or it may be an impersonal institution, such as a system of laws. The fact that one individual voluntarily permits another to influence his behavior, however, is not necessarily indicative of an authority relation. There are also other types of personal influence, such as persuasion. In persuasion, one person lets the arguments of another person influence his decisions or actions. Persuasion is distinguished from authority inasmuch as the latter involves an a priori suspension of the first person's judgment, obviating the need for persuasion. In an authority relation the subordinate "holds in abeyance his own critical faculties for choosing between alternatives and uses the formal criterion of the receipt of a command or signal as his basis for choice."[3]

Two criteria of authority, then, are voluntary compliance with legitimate commands and suspension of judgment in advance of command. In concrete situations of social control, however, it is often difficult to determine whether these two criteria are actually met. Take the extreme case of the slave driver whose coercive power rested on his whip. He did not use his whip continually, since the very knowledge of the possibility of its use sufficed to make the slaves obey his orders. While few would classify this case as one of voluntary compliance, it differs only in degree from the case of the employer whose economic dominance over his employees motivates them to carry out official directives; yet, the latter relationship is usually considered to be one of authority. Again, when a person has often persuaded another in the past, his opinion may well carry so much weight that the second person lends a willing ear to his arguments and requires hardly any persuasion to be influenced. Does the first person have authority over the other, or not?

A major reason why there are so many borderline cases is that other forms of social control often develop into authority. For this change to occur, however, another social condition must be met, and this condition provides a final and basic distinguishing criterion for authority. The condition is that a value orientation must arise that

---

[2] *Ibid.*, p. 324.

[3] Herbert A. Simon, *Administrative Behavior* (2d ed.), New York: Macmillan, 1957, pp. 126–127.

defines the exercise of social control as legitimate, and this orientation can arise only in a group context. A single individual forced to comply with the commands of another may seek to adapt to this situation by rationalizing that he really wants to be guided by the other's directives. That this attitude is a mere rationalization would be indicated by the fact that once the coercive power were withdrawn he would not continue to comply. If, however, an entire group finds itself in the same situation, and if its members share the beliefs that it is good and right and, indeed, in their best interest to obey, the rationalizations of individuals become transformed into a common value orientation. For group agreement and approval of what is right constitute a social value that validates the beliefs of individuals and thereby makes them "really" right. Given the development of social norms that certain orders of superiors ought to be obeyed, the members of the group will enforce compliance with these orders as part of their enforcement of conformity to group norms. The group's demand that orders of the superior be obeyed makes such obedience partly independent of his coercive power or persuasive influence over individual subordinates and thus transforms these other kinds of social control into authority.

A fundamental characteristic of authority, therefore, is that the willingness of subordinates to suspend their own judgment in advance and follow the directives of the superior results largely from social constraints exerted by the collectivity of subordinates and not primarily from the influences the superior himself can bring to bear upon them.[4] Such social constraints are not characteristic of coercive powers, persuasion, or other types of personal influence. If a boy is in love with a girl, for example, he will be eager to do what she wants in order to make his company more attractive to her. Similarly, if a person depends on a colleague for advice, he will feel obligated to accede to this colleague's wishes. In both of these cases, one person's dependence on another for certain rewards motivates him to comply with the other's requests in exchange for obtaining these rewards. But it would not be correct to classify such patterns of personal influence, which are rooted in exchange processes, as authority, even though compliance is voluntary, because there is no social collectivity whose norms require compliance with the directives of the superordinate person in the relation.

Authority relations can develop only in a group or larger collectivity, and not in isolated pairs, because only group values can legitimate the exercise of social control and only group norms can serve as an independent basis for enforcing the pattern of compliance. Once an authority structure has become institutionalized, however, it can find

---

[4] The compliance of subordinates in authority relations is voluntary but not independent of social constraints. It is as voluntary as is our custom of wearing shoes on the street.

expression in apparently isolated pair relationships. Thus, a father exercises authority over his son, even though there is only one child in the family. The father's influence does not entirely depend on his superior power, or his success in persuasion, or his willingness to exchange favors for obedience, because culturally defined role expectations obligate the son to obey his father; and members of the community, such as teachers and neighbors, help to enforce these obligations. To be sure, other forms of influence often exist side by side with authority and extend the influence of superiors. Pure authority relationships are analytical abstractions that are found rarely, if at all, in concrete situations, but this rarity makes the analytical distinction between them and other forms of influence no less important.

Weber's Types of Authority. We have seen that authority exists only when a common value orientation in a collectivity legitimates the exercise of control as appropriate and proper. The types of legitimating beliefs that support the exercise of control vary, and Weber uses these differences as the basis for distinguishing three types of authority.[5]

The first type is authority legitimated by the sanctity of tradition. In "traditional" authority, the present social order is viewed as sacred, eternal, and inviolable. The ruling person or group, usually defined by heredity, is thought to have been ordained by supernatural powers to rule over the rest. The subjects are bound to their ruler by traditional feelings of personal loyalty and other cultural beliefs about the social order that reinforce his position, such as the concept of the divine right of kings. Absolute monarchies exemplify traditional authority, as does the patriarchal family or a shop under a paternalistic boss. The ruler's power is great under this system. Although it is limited by the traditions that legitimate it, this restriction is not severe, since a certain amount of arbitrariness on the part of the ruler is often part of the tradition and since a precedent in the past usually can be found to justify his new commands. The need to turn to past traditions for legitimation of present actions, however, sets this type of authority apart from others. In general, traditional authority tends to perpetuate the existing social order and is ill suited for adaptation to social change; indeed, change undermines its very foundation.

The values that legitimate a "charismatic" authority, Weber's second type, define a leader and his mission as being inspired by divine or supernatural powers. The leader, in effect, heads a new social movement, and his followers or disciples are converts to a new cause. There

---

[5] Weber, *op. cit.*, pp. 324–386. Note the following comment by Bendix: "In Weber's view beliefs in the legitimacy of a system of domination are not merely philosophical matters. They can contribute to the stability of an authority relationship, and they indicate very real differences between systems of domination." Reinhard Bendix, *Max Weber*, Garden City, N.Y.: Doubleday, 1960, p. 297.

is a sense of being "called" to spread the new gospel, a sense of rejecting the past and heralding the future as symbolized in Christ's words, "It is written . . . , but I say unto you . . ." Devotion to the leader and a conviction that his actions embody the newly adopted ideals are the source of the group's willing obedience to his commands. Charismatic leaders may appear in almost any arena of social life, as prophets in religion, demagogues in politics, and heroes in battle. Charismatic authority generally functions as a revolutionary force, rejecting the traditional values and rebelling against the established order.

Initially, charismatic movements tend to be anarchistic and eschew even internal organization. Revolutionary ideals and the urgency of the mission make the charismatic leader and his followers contemptuous of anything associated with routines or "business as usual." No confining organization or rigid rules must be allowed to fetter the leader's inspiration, and the devotion to the sacred mission must not be profaned by mundane economic considerations. But it seems axiomatic that the demands of reality—for some routine, some organization, some stable means of economic support—cannot be ignored indefinitely. If it is to persist, the movement must become organized. Accordingly, the members' interest in perpetuating the movement constrains them to overcome their distaste for formal routines and to develop a formal organization. The necessity for organization becomes particularly apparent with the impending death of the charismatic leader. This event confronts the movement with the dangers of collapsing due to lack of inspired guidance or of being torn asunder by struggles over succession unless a regular procedure has been developed for transferring the leader's mantle to a legitimate heir. Charismatic movements are inherently unstable, since they are linked to the life of one man; to endure, they must take on some of the characteristics of that mundane world which initially they arose to combat and change. This process of "the routinization of charisma," as Weber called it, transforms charismatic authority into a different type; it may crystallize into a traditional system or, more often, become bureaucratized into the legal authority of a formal organization.[6]

Weber's third type, "legal" authority, is legitimated by a belief in the supremacy of the law. This type assumes the existence of a formally established body of social norms designed to organize conduct for the rational pursuit of specified goals. In such a system obedience is owed not to a person—whether a traditional chief or a charismatic leader— but to a set of impersonal principles. These principles include the re-

---

[6] Dostoyevsky's "Grand Inquisitor" graphically deals with the conflict between charisma and organization in the form of a fictional discussion between Christ and a Cardinal of the Church. Fyodor Dostoyevsky, *The Brothers Karamazov*, New York: Random House, 1937, pp. 292–314.

quirement to follow directives originating from an office superior to one's own, regardless of who occupies the higher office. All formal organizations—the government, a factory, the army, a welfare agency— are examples of legal authority structures. The epigram for this type might well be: "a government of laws, not of men." Although superior officials command the obedience of their subordinates, they in turn are subject to the authority of the same body of impersonal regulations, and their authority is accordingly limited.

Each of the three types of authority creates an appropriate staff of assistants. Thus, under the traditional form the feudal lord has his vassals and the king his court and retainers; the charismatic prophet has his disciples; and under the legal form, a staff of administrative officials becomes established and rationally organized. The distinctive characteristic of the latter type is that this bureaucratically organized administrative staff is capable of tremendous expansion and often becomes the dominant feature of legal authority systems.

Weber's Theory of Bureaucracy. Almost all modern administrative organizations (as well as some ancient ones) are bureaucratically organized. Weber enumerates the distinctive characteristics of this type of organization in the following way:[7]

(1) Organization tasks are distributed among the various positions as official duties. Implied is a clear-cut division of labor among positions which makes possible a high degree of specialization. Specialization, in turn, promotes expertness among the staff, both directly and by enabling the organization to hire employees on the basis of their technical qualifications.

(2) The positions or offices are organized into a hierarchical authority structure. In the usual case this hierarchy takes on the shape of a pyramid wherein each official is responsible for his subordinates' decisions and actions as well as his own to the superior above him in the pyramid and wherein each official has authority over the officials under him. The scope of authority of superiors over subordinates is clearly circumscribed.

(3) A formally established system of rules and regulations governs official decisions and actions. In principle, the operations in such administrative organizations involve the application of these general regulations to particular cases. The regulations insure the uniformity of operations and, together with the authority structure, make possible the coordination of the various activities. They also provide for continuity in operations regardless of changes of personnel, thus promoting a stability lacking, as we have seen, in charismatic movements.

---

[7] Weber's discussion of these characteristics may be found in H. H. Gerth and C. Wright Mills (trans. and eds.), *From Max Weber: Essays in Sociology*, New York: Oxford University Press, 1946, pp. 196–204; and in Weber, *op. cit.*, pp. 329–336.

(4) Officials are expected to assume an impersonal orientation in their contacts with clients and with other officials. Clients are to be treated as cases, the officials being expected to disregard all personal considerations and to maintain complete emotional detachment, and subordinates are to be treated in a similar impersonal fashion. The social distance between hierarchical levels and that between officials and their clients is intended to foster such formality. Impersonal detachment is designed to prevent the personal feelings of officials from distorting their rational judgment in carrying out their duties.

(5) Employment by the organization constitutes a career for officials. Typically an official is a full-time employee and looks forward to a lifelong career in the agency. Employment is based on the technical qualifications of the candidate rather than on political, family, or other connections. Usually such qualifications are tested by examination or by certificates that demonstrate the candidate's educational attainment —college degrees for example. Such educational qualifications create a certain amount of class homogeneity among officials, since relatively few persons of working-class origins have college degrees, although their number is increasing. Officials are appointed to positions, not elected, and thus are dependent on superiors in the organization rather than on a body of constituents. After a trial period officials gain tenure of position and are protected against arbitrary dismissal. Remuneration is in the form of a salary, and pensions are provided after retirement. Career advancements are "according to seniority or to achievement, or both."[8]

In Weber's view, these organizing principles maximize rational decision-making and administrative efficiency. Bureaucracy, according to him, is the most efficient form of administrative organization, because experts with much experience are best qualified to make technically correct decisions, and because disciplined performance governed by abstract rules and coordinated by the authority hierarchy fosters a rational and consistent pursuit of organizational objectives.

Refinements of Weber's Conceptions. Weber analyzes bureaucratic organizations not empirically but as an ideal type. He does not characterize the "average" administrative organization; rather, he seeks to bring together those characteristics that are distinctive of this type. Just as we can imagine physicians constructing a model of the perfectly healthy man, so Weber attempts to characterize a perfectly bureaucratized organization. A question which remains to be answered is, what is the criterion of perfection employed by Weber?

Weber's construct of ideal type is an admixture of a conceptual scheme and a set of hypotheses. As a conceptual scheme it defines the

8 *Ibid.,* p. 334.

phenomenon to be studied. His conception calls attention to what he considers the key elements of bureaucratic organization—those essential for understanding such organizations. Weber provides a definition of the concept of bureaucracy by pointing to these characteristics. He says in effect: bureaucracies are those organizations that exhibit the following combination of characteristics. Such conceptual schemes provide important frameworks for analysis and research, although they themselves are not subject to empirical testing. They are neither correct nor incorrect, only more or less useful in guiding scientific investigations.

But in addition to its conceptual elements, the ideal type contains a series of hypotheses. Weber suggests that many of the characteristics attributed to bureaucracies are interrelated in particular ways; for example, specialization is said to promote expertness, the authority structure and the existence of formal rules are assumed to make vital contributions to the coordination of activities, and detachment is held to increase rationality. Further, Weber states that these characteristics, and, specifically, their combination function to maximize administrative efficiency. A careful reading of Weber indicates that he tends to view elements as "bureaucratic" to the extent that they contribute to administrative efficiency. This contribution to efficiency appears to be the criterion of "perfect" embodied in his ideal type. However, whether or not each of these elements, or their combination, enhances administrative efficiency is not a matter for definition; these are questions of fact—hypotheses subject to empirical testing.

To exploit Weber's insightful theoretical analysis, it is necessary, in our opinion, to discard his misleading concept of the ideal type and to distinguish explicitly between the conceptual scheme and the hypotheses. The latter can then be tested and refined rather than left as mere impressionistic assertions. We can ask, for example: does tenure promote efficiency? under what conditions does it have this effect, and under what conditions does it not? Only in this way can we hope to progress beyond Weber's insights to the building of systematic theory.

Weber has often been criticized for presenting an idealized conception of bureaucracy. His statements appear to entail an implicit functional scheme; again and again he addresses himself to the problem of how a given element contributes to the strength and effective functioning of the organization. What is missing is a similar systematic attempt to isolate the *dysfunctions* of the various elements discussed[9] and to examine the conflicts that arise between the elements comprising the system. Thus, even if it is true that the hierarchy of authority promotes discipline and makes possible the coordination of activities, does it not

---

[9] Merton has called for this balanced approach in his paradigm for functional analysis. Robert K. Merton, *Social Theory and Social Structure* (2d ed.), Glencoe, Ill.: Free Press, pp. 50–54.

also discourage subordinates from accepting responsibility? Or, granted that promotion should be based on objective criteria rather than on personal considerations or family connections, which of the two major criteria is to be selected—seniority or merit? When questions such as these are raised, it is seen that Weber's one-sided concern with the functions of bureaucratic institutions blinds him to some of the most fundamental problems in the study of formal organizations.[10]

Another criticism that has been advanced against Weber's analysis is that he is preoccupied with the formally instituted aspects of bureaucracies and ignores the informal relations and unofficial patterns which develop in formal organizations. Selznick has emphasized that the formal structure is only one aspect of the actual social structure and that organizational members interact as whole persons and not merely in terms of the formal roles they occupy.[11] Many empirical studies demonstrate that friendship patterns, unofficial exchange systems, and "natural" leaders arise to modify the formal arrangements.[12] Weber's conceptual scheme, by concentrating on the officially instituted aspects of bureaucracies, neglects the ways in which these are modified by informal patterns and thus excludes from analysis the most dynamic aspects of formal organizations.

Finally, Parsons and Gouldner have called attention to an implicit contradiction in Weber's conception of bureaucracy; in Gouldner's words, "On the one side, it was administration based on expertise; while on the other, it was administration based on discipline."[13] By emphasizing both expert judgment resting on technical knowledge and disciplined compliance with directives of superiors as the basis for bureaucratic decisions, Weber implies that there is no conflict between these two principles; that is, he implicitly assumes that in every disagreement between superior and subordinate, the superior's judgment is also the better judgment in terms of technical expertise. This is not a realistic assumption. Executives in complex organizations are not merely occasionally but typically less qualified to make expert technical judgments than their professional subordinates, since they cannot possibly be the

[10] Defenders of Weber will argue that he did note certain conflicts or dilemmas inherent in bureaucratic structures. The point here is, however, that he did not subject these dysfunctions to the same kind of systematic analysis that he furnished for the functions of various characteristics for bureaucratic efficiency.

[11] Philip Selznick, "Foundations of the Theory of Organization," *American Sociological Review*, 13 (1948), pp. 25–35.

[12] See, for example, Charles H. Page, "Bureaucracy's Other Face," *Social Forces*, 25 (1946), pp. 88–94, and Ralph H. Turner, "The Navy Disbursing Officer as a Bureaucrat," *American Sociological Review*, 12 (1947), pp. 342–348.

[13] Alvin W. Gouldner, *Patterns of Industrial Bureaucracy*, Glencoe, Ill.: Free Press, 1954, p. 22. See also Talcott Parsons' "Introduction," in Weber, *op. cit.*, pp. 58–60, footnote 4.

leading expert in each of the specialties under their jurisdiction. Often, indeed, they are experts not in any of these specialties but in administration. Administrative considerations, moreover, tend to conflict with technical professional considerations. Hence, the judgment of superiors, who are concerned with administrative problems, will recurrently differ from the judgment of their professional subordinates, who are concerned with technical problems. Generally, one of the central issues in contemporary professional organizations, which will occupy us repeatedly in later chapters, is the conflict between disciplined compliance with administrative procedures and adherence to professional standards in the performance of duties.

Weber's pioneering analysis of bureaucracy has stimulated much further analysis and research on formal organizations, and these studies make it possible critically to review and to refine some of his theoretical concepts. Our criticisms of parts of his discussion on the basis of more recent work in sociology are not intended to disparage the outstanding contribution Weber has made to this field.

Other Conceptions of Formal Organizations. Weber is not the only social scientist who has attempted to develop a theoretical framework for the analysis of formal organizations. The approach of two other students of social organization will be briefly considered here, although our list could easily be extended.

Herbert Simon conceives of administrative organizations primarily as decision-making structures.[14] He has characterized his own focus in the following passage:

What is a scientifically relevant description of an organization? It is a description that, so far as possible, designates for each person in the organization what decisions that person makes, and the influence to which he is subject in making each of these decisions.[15]

Effective administration, according to Simon, requires rational decision-making; decisions are rational when they select the best alternative for reaching a goal. But administrative decisions are highly complex, and rationality is limited for various reasons: all the consequences that follow from a given course of action cannot be anticipated; the consequences of action lie in the future and thus are difficult to evaluate realistically; and rationality requires a choice among all possible alternatives, but many of these will never even come to mind and so will not be considered. In short, individuals are not capable of making complex decisions rationally. The function of the organization is to limit the scope of the decisions that each member must make; only in

14 See Simon, *op. cit.*, pp. 1–11, 45–78, *et passim.*
15 *Ibid.*, p. 37.

this way can rationality be approached.[16] How does the organization accomplish this feat? First, it defines the responsibilities of each official, thus supplying him with goals to guide his decisions. Second, it sets up the mechanisms, such as formal rules, information channels, and training programs that help to narrow the range of alternatives the official must consider before making his decisions.

This conclusion may be somewhat amplified. Decisions, says Simon, are based on two types of premises. There are factual premises, which are subject to empirical testing in order to ascertain their truth or falsity, and value premises, which are not subject to such tests since they are concerned not with what "is" but with what "ought" to be, what is good or preferable. The former have to do with the choice of means, the latter with the choice of ends. Rational behavior may be viewed as consisting of means-ends chains. Given certain ends, appropriate means are selected for their attainment; but once reached, the ends often become the means for the attainment of further ends, and so forth. For example, a student studies in order to obtain a high mark in a course; he desires a high mark because this will help him attain a high over-all grade average; he desires a high grade average in order to be able to graduate from college; college graduation, in turn, is only a means to the end of getting a desirable job; and so on. The important point about organizational behavior is that the hierarchical structure permits all decisions, except those defining ultimate objectives, to rest on factual rather than on value premises, that is, to be decisions about means rather than ends. Once the objectives of the organization are formally established, the hierarchical organization of responsibilities serves as a framework for means-ends chains—specifying for each official the ends of his tasks and thus confining his duties to the selection of the best means for achieving these ends. To illustrate, the duty of the top manager may be described as finding effective ways for accomplishing the established objectives of the organization; the means he employs for this purpose are work assignments to his department heads. These assignments provide each department with its objectives, which the head seeks to attain by means of assigning responsibilities to the supervisors under him, and so on down the line. The ends of every member of the organization are defined by the directives of his superior, and his responsibility is primarily to decide on the best means for attaining these ends. In other words, each official in the hierarchy

---

[16] Rationality is always only approached, never achieved. The organization member must be willing to forgo a search for the best of all possible alternatives and be content with finding a satisfactory one; in Simon's language, administrators must "satisfice [sic] because they have not the wits to maximize." *Ibid.*, p. xxiv· see also James. G. March and Herbert A. Simon, *Organizations*, New York: Wiley, 1958, pp. 140–141, 169.

has his value premises supplied by his superior; besides, his search for alternative means is narrowed by procedural regulations. The combination of these two limits, according to Simon, permits rational decision-making in an organization.

Simon's suggestive conception of administration as a decision-making structure deals largely with the effects of the formal blueprint on decision-making and does not include a systematic analysis of those interpersonal processes that are not part of the formal structure. Our discussion, in contrast, will be particularly concerned with the significance of these informal interpersonal influences for decision-making. Another limitation of Simon's analysis is that he directs all his efforts to explaining how the various conditions in the organization—the hierarchy, the communication system, training programs—influence rational decision-making and omits consideration of their influence on one another. Such a specific focus on choice behavior as the sole dependent variable makes it impossible systematically to analyze social structure, since it reduces all problems of social structure to sociopsychological problems; that is, all questions of "what produces these characteristics of the organization?" are turned into a concern with "what produces this behavior of the members in the organization?"

Talcott Parsons provides yet another conception of formal organization in the recent application of his general theoretical framework for the study of social systems to such organizations.[17] According to Parsons' schema, all social systems must solve four basic problems: (1) adaptation: the accommodation of the system to the reality demands of the environment coupled with the active transformation of the external situation; (2) goal achievement: the defining of objectives and the mobilization of resources to attain them; (3) integration: establishing and organizing a set of relations among the member units of the system that serve to coordinate and unify them into a single entity; and (4) latency: the maintenance over time of the system's motivational and cultural patterns.[18] This scheme has sufficient generality to be applicable to all social systems. For example, if our focus is the society, then the economy may be said to function as the subsystem meeting the problems of adaptation faced by the society. Formal organizations, although they serve different specific functions, are part of the goal attainment subsystem of the larger society. Parsons thus views formal organizations as a major mechanism in modern societies for mobilizing power in the interest of achieving collective objectives.

But each formal organization may also be viewed as a social system in its own right that must possess its own set of subsystems concerned

17 Talcott Parsons, *Structure and Process in Modern Societies,* Glencoe, Ill.: Free Press, 1960, pp. 16–96.
18 See Talcott Parsons *et al., Working Papers in the Theory of Action,* Glencoe, Ill.: Free Press, 1953, pp. 183–186.

with the solution of the four basic problems. Accordingly, each organization must have structures that enable it to adapt to its environment and mobilize the resources required for its continued functioning. Mechanisms are also required to enable the organization to implement its goals, including structures devoted to specification of objectives, to allocation of resources within the organization, to "production," and to distribution. To solve its integrative problems the organization must find ways to command the loyalties of its members, to motivate their effort, and to coordinate the operations of its various segments. Finally, institutions must be developed to cope with the latency problem, that is, to promote consensus on the values that define and legitimate the organization's goals. All organizations are faced with these problems; however, the particular structures devised to meet them will vary with the type of organization under consideration.

Three major hierarchical levels in formal organizations are distinguished by Parsons. There is first the technical level, where the actual "product" of the organization is manufactured or dispensed; this level is exemplified by workers on assembly lines, doctors in hospitals, and teachers in universities. Above the technical employees is the managerial level, whose primary concern is to mediate between the various parts of the organization and to coordinate their efforts. Finally, the institutional level of the organization connects it with the wider social system; for instance, the function of a board of directors is to oversee the operations of the organization in the light of its position in the larger society. It appears that the first level is chiefly concerned with problems of adaptation and goal attainment, the second with integrative problems, and the third with latency problems.

Parsons suggests that there are clear-cut breaks in the hierarchy of authority and responsibility between these three levels. Only within a level can the superior supervise the work of subordinates and assume responsibility for it, since the differences in function between the levels are too great to make supervision of the lower by the higher possible. Senior professionals, for example, direct the work of junior professionals, but top management does not direct their work in the same sense, since managers do not have the technical qualifications to do so. Indeed, it is not correct even to say that the executive delegates responsibility to professionals. The latter assume full responsibility for technical decisions, and the executive must rely on their expert judgments in discharging his managerial responsibility, which is the area of his special competence. Similarly, the board of directors does not supervise managerial decisions but seeks only to adjust the organization to external conditions by defining general objectives and policies. In matters of internal policy and organizational management, it must permit the independent judgment of executives free scope.

Parsons' analysis of formal organizations is of special interest because it involves the application of the general theory of social systems he has developed to the investigation of this particular institution. A criticism that has been leveled against Parsons' work is that his extremely abstract conceptions yield a theoretical scheme devoid of a system of propositions from which specific hypotheses can be derived; in short, that he has only developed a theoretical framework and noι a substantive theory. Cognizant of this criticism, Parsons has recently suggested some theoretical propositions implied by his scheme.[19] But these propositions are again on such a high level of abstraction that it is by no means clear whether empirically testable hypotheses can be derived from them, an essential requirement of scientific theory.

TYPOLOGIES OF FORMAL ORGANIZATIONS

Various Classifications. Since formal organizations are complex social objects having diverse characteristics, any one of which may be seized upon as a basis for grouping them in one manner or another, many different classification schemes have been proposed. Some students have emphasized the distinction between private and public ownership as a basic one; some have classified organizations by size; others have concentrated attention on the specific purposes served. Another system of types focuses on the criterion of membership; thus, we may distinguish organizations manned largely by volunteers (the Red Cross), by employees (industrial firms), or by conscripts (citizen armies). Organizations have also been assigned to broad institutional areas on the basis of the function they perform for the larger society; such attempts may provide types like economic, political, religious, and educational organizations.

In contrast to these classifications which stress fairly obvious differences between organizations, there are others that use more analytical criteria of distinction.[20] Thus, Parsons differentiates four types on the basis of which one of the four fundamental problems confronting a society an organization helps to solve. Since this category system is derived from a theoretical scheme, it cuts across traditionally defined institutional areas.[21] Another analytical criterion ·of distinction is whether the "materials" worked on by the technical personnel of the organization are physical objects or people. The crucial difference be-

[19] Talcott Parsons, "Pattern Variables Revisited," *American Sociological Review*, 25 (1960), pp. 481–482.

[20] For examples, see Robin M. Williams, Jr., *American Society* (2d ed.), New York: Knopf, 1960, pp. 488–489.

[21] Banks and credit agencies, for instance, are assigned to the political sphere rather than to the economic. Parsons, *Structure and Process in Modern Societies*, op. cit., pp. 44–47.

tween the two resulting types—production and service organizations—is that only the latter are confronted with problems of establishing social relations with the "objects" of their endeavors and of having to motivate them in various ways. The success of a teacher depends on doing this; that of an engineer does not.[22] It should be noted that the term "service organizations" is misleading for the general type, since not all organizations dealing with people provide a service for these same people; it is hardly correct to say that the function of a prison is to furnish services to prisoners.

Hughes provides yet another analytical classification by attempting to describe several basic models of organization found in modern society, which yields five types: (1) the voluntary association of equals, where members freely join for a specific purpose; examples include sects, clubs, and professional associations; (2) the military model, which emphasizes a fixed hierarchy of authority and status; (3) the philanthropic model, consisting of a governing lay board, an itinerant professional staff, and the clients served, as illustrated by hospitals and universities; (4) the corporation model with its stockholders, board of directors, managers, and staff; and (5) the family business in which a group of people related by kin and marriage carry on some enterprise for profit.[23]

A typology, strictly speaking, is a multidimensional classification. If organizations were, for example, divided into large public, small public, large private, and small private ones, this would be a simple typology based on the dimensions of size and ownership. A more complex typology is illustrated by Thompson and Tuden's analysis of the decision-making strategies in organizations.[24] They suggest that the type of decision made depends on two factors: (1) whether there is agreement on objectives; and (2) whether cause-effect relations are known, that is, whether there is agreement on how to bring about given objectives. The combinations of these two factors produce four types of decision-making strategies and four types of organizations considered appropriate for them. First, if there is agreement on both the

[22] See *ibid.*, pp. 20–21. Parsons mentions, as a third type, organizations that deal with cultural objects; for example, research firms which add to knowledge. For an analysis of the ways in which people are similar to as well as different from physical objects as material to be worked with by organizations, see Erving Goffman, "Characteristics of Total Institutions," Walter Reed Army Institute of Research, *Symposium on Preventive and Social Psychiatry*, Washington, D.C.: U.S. Government Printing Office, 1957, pp. 66–69.

[23] Everett C. Hughes, "Memorandum on Going Concerns," unpublished paper read before the Society for Applied Anthropology, 1952.

[24] James D. Thompson and Arthur Tuden, "Strategies, Structures, and Processes of Organizational Decision," James D. Thompson *et al.* (eds.), *Comparative Studies in Administration*, Pittsburgh: University of Pittsburgh Press, 1959, pp. 195–216.

objectives and on how to attain them, what Thompson and Tuden call "computational" strategies are possible; that is, decisions can be based on rational calculations. This is the situation for which the rational bureaucracy described by Weber is ideally suited. Second, if there is agreement on objectives but cause-effect relations are not fully known so that insight is needed to decide on the best course of action, a "judgmental" strategy will be used. In this case, a collegium or self-governing body of peers is preferable as an organizational form to bureaucracy. A board of directors illustrates this type, and so does a colleague group of professionals. Third, if there is agreement on how to achieve various objectives but dispute on which objectives have first priority, a "compromise" strategy is required to make collective decisions. The appropriate organization in this case is a representative body, such as the United States Congress. Finally, when there is disagreement on both the objectives and on how to achieve them, "inspirational" strategies are likely to be resorted to. These conditions are usually characterized by the absence of formal organization and by a state of anomie, and would seem to be conducive to the development of charismatic movements.

A Classification Based on Prime Beneficiary. Even though the foregoing review of classificatory schemes is only cursory, it suggests that there is no dearth of such schemes in the literature on organizations. In proposing yet another classification, we take upon ourselves the burden of demonstrating the usefulness of our scheme for increasing the understanding of formal organizations. We hope to do so by using it as a basis for discussing several of the recent empirical studies of formal organizations. First, however, we must present the typology.

Four basic categories of persons can be distinguished in relation to any given formal organization: (1) the members or rank-and-file participants; (2) the owners or managers of the organization; (3) the clients or, more generally, the "public-in-contact," which means the people who are technically "outside" the organization yet have regular, direct contact with it, under whatever label—patient, customer, law violator, prisoner, enemy soldier, student; and (4) the public-at-large, that is, the members of the society in which the organization operates.[25] We propose to classify organizations on the basis of *cui bono*—who benefits: Which of these four categories is the prime beneficiary of their operations? It must be emphasized that the prime beneficiary is not the only beneficiary, for each of the various groups who make contributions to an organization does so only in return for certain benefits received. Thus, the owners, the employees, and the customers of a

---

[25] The first three of our four types are similar to those used by Simon in his discussion of the economic firm. See Simon, *op. cit.*, pp. 16–17.

business concern must each receive some recompense for their various contributions; otherwise, they would not provide the investment capital, the labor power, or the purchase price for goods, all of which are necessary for the firm's continued operation. The public-at-large also benefits from the contribution that business concerns make to the "general welfare," specifically, to the production and distribution of desired goods, and this benefit is the reason why the society permits and encourages such firms to operate. But although all parties benefit, the benefits to one party furnish the reason for the organization's existing while the benefits to others are essentially a cost. In the example cited, the prime beneficiary is the owner of the firm. He established it for the purpose of realizing a profit, and he will close it should it operate for very long showing a loss. Indeed, the public expects the owner to operate his business for his own benefit and not as a welfare institution. Contrast this situation with that of organizations whose prime beneficiary is the public. The city is not expected to close its police department or the community hospital because it fails to show a profit, but to operate it in the interest of the public even at a financial loss.[26]

Four types of organizations result from the application of our *cui bono* criterion: (1) "mutual-benefit associations," where the prime beneficiary is the membership; (2) "business concerns," where the owners are prime beneficiary; (3) "service organizations," where the client group is the prime beneficiary; and (4) "commonweal organizations," where the prime beneficiary is the public-at-large. (This classification can be combined with others to yield more refined typologies.) The following discussion of empirical studies illustrating these four types of formal organizations will clarify the distinction and show that special problems are associated with each type. Thus, the crucial problem in mutual-benefit associations is that of maintaining internal democratic processes—providing for participation and control by the membership; the central problem for business concerns is that of maximizing operating efficiency in a competitive situation; the problems associated with the conflict between professional service to clients and administrative procedures are characteristic of service organizations; and the crucial problem posed by commonweal organizations is the development of democratic mechanisms whereby they can be externally controlled by the public.

[26] The reader will note that our typology is not as unequivocal on this point as it might be. In the case of a police department, is not the public also the owner, and is not therefore the owner, as in the case of the business concern, the prime beneficiary? Technically speaking, of course, the public is the owner and prime beneficiary. However, it appeared to us that there were such major differences separating the two types—public organizations and privately owned ones—that more would be lost than gained by combining them into a single type.

The significance of the *cui bono* criterion for defining the character of a formal organization is indicated by the fundamental changes that occur when there is a shift in prime beneficiary from one to another of the four categories. Often such changes are strongly disapproved; sometimes they are heralded as revolutionary improvements; in either case, they signify radical alterations in the basic nature of the organization. Thus, unions are mutual-benefit associations, which are expected to serve the interests of the rank and file. If union leaders usurp the role of prime beneficiary and run the union as if they owned it for their personal benefit, the organization is condemned for no longer serving the proper functions of a labor union. The same is true for a union whose membership has been displaced as prime beneficiary by its public-in-contact—the employers or their representatives—as exemplified by company unions or those whose leadership has "sold out" to management.

In the case of business concerns, the owners are expected to be prime beneficiaries. But public corporations transform owners into mere stockholders and vest controlling power in the hands of top-level employees, enabling them to govern the enterprise in their own interests.[27] Moreover, if unions become more powerful than individual employers, a situation illustrated by some segments of the garment industry, the possibility arises that instead of the owners the employees represented by the union become the prime beneficiaries. Government regulations, notably the extreme case of nationalization of industry, might succeed in making the public-at-large the prime beneficiary of a business concern. This change may, of course, be a good thing. Whether such shifts in prime beneficiary are evaluated as advantageous or disadvantageous depends on one's ideological position, but there is no doubt that they would constitute fundamental transformations of business concerns into distinctly different types of organizations.

In service organizations, if the members of the professional staff lose interest in serving clients and become primarily concerned with making their own work easier or furthering their own careers, service will suffer, since the energies and resources devoted to it will no longer be considered as contributing to the prime function of the organization but rather as a necessary cost for obtaining benefits for the staff or some segment of it.

Commonweal organizations, in sharp contrast, are not expected to be oriented to the interests of their "clients," that is, those persons with whom they are in direct contact. A police department, for example, that enters into collusion with racketeers fails to discharge its responsibility to the public-at-large and is no longer the protective

[27] See Adolf A. Berle and Gardner C. Means, *The Modern Corporation and Private Property*, New York: Macmillan, 1932.

organization it is assumed to be. Likewise, if policemen solicit bribes instead of enforcing the law, or if the police commissioner runs the department primarily to further his political ambitions, the public's position as prime beneficiary of the organization suffers.

Note also that the criticism that an organization is "overbureaucratized" means quite different things in the four types of organizations.[28] In the case of mutual-benefit associations, such as unions, overbureaucratization implies centralization of power in the hands of officials. Here it does not refer to inefficiency; indeed, bureaucratized unions are often ruthlessly efficient. But in the case of business concerns overbureaucratization implies an elaboration of rules and procedures that impairs operating efficiency, and here the term is not used in reference to the power of management officials to decide on policies, since such managerial direction is expected and legitimate. Finally, service and commonweal organizations are considered overbureaucratized if in consequence of preoccupation with procedures rigidities develop which impede professional service to clients or effective service of the public interest.

TYPES OF FORMAL ORGANIZATIONS

Mutual-Benefit Associations. Examples of organizations in which the membership is expected to be the prime beneficiary include political parties, unions, fraternal associations, clubs, veterans' organizations, professional associations, and religious sects. There are some borderline cases. Share corporations, insofar as they can be analytically distinguished from the business concerns they own, may be considered mutual-benefit associations of shareholders. The philanthropic organization is a mixed type—part mutual-benefit, part service—because it serves its members' interests in serving the interests of others. Only "causes" that interest the members obtain their help, but such organizational activities as parties and balls must make a contribution to some outside client group.

As was suggested, the crucial issue facing this type of organization is maintaining membership control, that is, internal democracy. This involves coping with two main problems: membership apathy and oligarchical control.

Most members of mutual-benefit associations are apathetic in the sense that they are willing to leave the running of their association to

---

[28] For a discussion of the conditions that lead to overbureaucratization and its opposite, see S. N. Eisenstadt, "Bureaucracy, Bureaucratization, and Debureaucratization," *Administrative Science Quarterly*, 4 (1959), pp. 302–320.

an active minority.[29] This situation conflicts with the idealized conception of these associations as collectivities whose members are highly interested and actively engaged in achieving some common objective. Apparently this image of the mutual-benefit association is faithful primarily at the time of its origin and during its early struggle for existence. Evidence of widespread vigor and enthusiasm is ample in the early days of such associations as religious sects (which benefit their members by showing them the correct way to salvation). However, the very enthusiasm that marks the activities of the devoted original members leads them to attempt to persuade others of the moral superiority of their beliefs, and such proselytizing brings in new members less strongly identified with the goals of the association. Whether this infusion or other factors lead to the cooling of initial ardors, it is well established that the majority of members of mutual-benefit associations are not sufficiently interested to devote much time or energy to conducting the business of the association and are content to leave the running of the organization to a corps of active members or to a hired staff.[30] Once the organization is under the control of a minority or of hired officials, a vicious cycle begins, for in such cases business meetings are usually uninteresting and concerned with unimportant matters; members who come to these meetings obtain meager rewards for their efforts, and this condition curtails participation still further.[31]

Given a generally low level of participation in mutual-benefit associations, it is important to know what factors are related to participation—that is, what characteristics differentiate between members who participate much and those who participate little. Many studies, beginning with Komarovsky's, have shown that persons of higher socioeconomic status tend to belong to more associations and to participate more actively in them than persons of lower status.[32] Other studies show that males tend to participate more than females, those in their middle years more than those either younger or older, and those belonging to minority groups more than those in the majority.[33] The

[29] Bernard Barber, "Participation and Mass Apathy in Associations," Alvin W. Gouldner (ed.), *Studies in Leadership,* New York: Harper, 1950, pp. 477–504.

[30] Barber suggests two reasons for membership apathy: (1) in our society, a strong cultural value defines these associations as being of less importance than family and job obligations; and (2) the existence of formal structures makes it possible for a minority to achieve the goals of the association with the majority of the members participating little or not at all. *Ibid.,* pp. 486–487.

[31] See Seymour M. Lipset *et al., Union Democracy,* Glencoe, Ill.: Free Press, 1956, pp. 261–262.

[32] Mirra Komarovsky, "The Voluntary Associations of Urban Dwellers," Logan Wilson and William Kolb (eds.), *Sociological Analysis,* New York: Harcourt, Brace, 1949, pp. 378–392.

[33] See Wendell Bell *et al., Public Leadership,* San Francisco: Chandler, 1961, pp. 21–23, 44–47, 64–66, 82–84, 111–113.

most extensive research in this area has been carried out on participation in trade unions.[34]

The measures of participation in unions utilized by different studies vary somewhat, but attendance at meetings and holding office are most frequently used. Several investigations have found that socioeconomic status exerts the same influence within the union as in the larger society: the higher the status of union members, the greater is their participation. Thus, there is usually more membership participation in craft locals, and within the same local the most active members come in disproportionate numbers from those who hold the better-paid and higher-status jobs. A somewhat contrary finding is that "union activists are disproportionately drawn from specific ethnic groups— Negroes, Mexicans, Jews, and Catholics."[35] Such underprivileged groups are, of course, the ones expected to be particularly responsive to the union's emphasis on collective effort for improvement. This expectation makes the finding that the best-paid workers are often the most active unionists particularly interesting.

Another factor that appears to exert considerable influence on participation in union activities is social contact among workers. Men who hold positions that permit them frequently to interact with fellow workers tend to be active in the union, whereas those who hold jobs that isloate them from others tend to be apathetic. In situations where an "occupational community" develops, which encourages widespread contacts between workers both on and off the job, union participation is also high.[36] The most militant unions seem to develop in industries whose workers form an "isolated mass," as Kerr and Siegel call it— that is, whose workers are segregated from the rest of the community but closely integrated with one another, as in mining and shipping.[37] Sayles and Strauss indicate that homogeneous work groups tend to participate more in union activities than heterogeneous ones, the former being groups whose members work closely together, are under the same supervisor, are engaged in the same type of work, have equal pay, belong to the same ethnic groups, or come from the same neighborhood.[38]

[34] In considerable measure the following discussion is based on a survey of this literature by Spinrad. This article provides documentation for all the statements made in our discussion of union participation for which no specific reference is provided. See William Spinrad, "Correlates of Trade Union Participation," *American Sociological Review*, 25 (1960), pp. 237–244.

[35] *Ibid.*, p. 241.

[36] Lipset *et al., op. cit.*, pp. 71–75; 88–89.

[37] Clark Kerr and Abraham Siegel, "The Interindustry Propensity to Strike," Arthur Kornhauser *et al.* (eds.), *Industrial Conflict*, New York: McGraw-Hill, 1954, pp. 189–212.

[38] Leonard R. Sayles and George Strauss, *The Local Union*, New York: Harper, 1953, p. 198.

Surprisingly enough, studies find that workers who report high job satisfaction are more likely than dissatisfied workers to be active union members.[39] Contrary to the common stereotype, therefore, the strongest supporters of labor unions are not disgruntled workers incapable of earning an average wage but the most satisfied and highest paid ones. Workers who do not aspire to supervisory positions, and those who are highly identified with the working class are also more apt than others to participate in union activities. Putting these findings together, it becomes apparent that participation in labor unions is promoted not so much by feelings of resentment against management or more privileged groups as by a positive identification with one's work, the work group, and the working class in general.

Studies of participation and apathy deal with one aspect of the problem of internal democracy in formal associations; another facet of at least equal importance is the problem of oligarchy. A fundamental dilemma confronting mutual-benefit associations is that democratic controls are often sacrificed in the interests of promoting the effective accomplishment of objectives. To win a strike, for example, democratic procedures through which union members control their leaders may be set aside. Generally, an overriding concern with "results" easily leads to disenchantment with the often slow and tortuous democratic process—a process which sacrifices efficiency in the interests of preserving freedom of dissent—and to the development of bureaucratic mechanisms which do not depend for success on widespread membership interest or participation.[40] It was Michels who called attention to a general tendency of associations to move toward increasing centralization of control and hierarchical organization as a consequence of these processes as well as the desire of the leaders to retain and extend their power.[41] But Gouldner has pointed out that Michels' gloomy proposition of an "iron law of oligarchy" may be in part counteracted by the "iron law of democracy," which holds that no superordinate group can for very long flout the will of those it would control.[42]

What are the structural conditions that help to sustain democratic control in large-scale organizations? The writings and research of Lipset have focused on this problem.[43] Basic to the maintenance of

[39] See, for example, Joel Seidman *et al., The Worker Views His Union,* Chicago: University of Chicago Press, 1958, p. 178.

[40] For a general discussion of the issue of efficiency vs. dissent in formal organizations, see Peter M. Blau, *Bureaucracy in Modern Society,* New York: Random House, 1956, pp. 105–110.

[41] Robert Michels, *Political Parties,* Eden Paul and Cedar Paul (trans.), Glencoe, Ill.: Free Press, 1949 (first published, 1915), pp. 37–41.

[42] Alvin W. Gouldner, "Metaphysical Pathos and the Theory of Bureaucracy," *American Political Science Review,* 49 (1955), p. 506.

[43] Seymour M. Lipset, *Political Man,* Garden City, N.Y.: Doubleday, 1960, pp. 357–399; and Lipset *et al., op. cit.,* pp. 3–16; 393–418.

democractic control appears to be the existence of a two-party system, resting on two strong factions that have become institutionalized and legitimated. Simply holding periodic plebiscites without the existence of a two-party or multiparty system does not produce democratic control, as the elections held in one-party nations and those held in "one-party" unions demonstrate. The chances of the existence of two or more parties or permanent factions appear to be enhanced by such conditions as the autonomy of local groups within the larger organization, the absence of severe threats to the organization's survival from its environment, a high level of skill and education among the membership, the absence of a large disparity of income and status between leaders and members, the presence of many and varied links between members, the existence of opportunities for members to acquire political skills, and the presence of channels of communication between members independent of those maintained by the officials in control. But the case study on which these conclusions are largely based does not permit a reader to tell which of these conditions are most important or what the chances are for other mutual-benefit associations to develop arrangements that sustain effective democratic control.

Business Concerns. The prime beneficiaries of business concerns are expected to be their owners. Obvious examples of this type are industrial firms, mail-order houses, wholesale and retail stores, banks, insurance companies, and similar organizations privately owned and operated for a profit. The dominant problem of business concerns is that of operating efficiency—the achievement of maximum gain at minimum cost in order to further survival and growth in competition with other organizations. To be sure, efficiency is important for other types of formal organizations as well, but only in business concerns is its significance not limited by that of other factors. All formal organizations are goal-oriented, that is, established to accomplish certain objectives; hence, efficiency in the sense of effective accomplishment of objectives without undue cost is a crucial problem for all of them. Barnard uses the term efficiency differently to refer to the work satisfaction and loyalty of the organization's personnel that promote its strength beyond that needed for immediate goal attainment.[44] Efficiency in this second meaning of the term is also important for other types of formal organizations as well as business concerns. In the other three types, however, considerations of administrative efficiency in both senses of the term are expected to be subordinated to some more fundamental considerations. Thus, in mutual-benefit associations, such as unions, concern with efficiency is expected not to interfere with the membership's ability democratically to decide on the specific objec-

[44] Chester I. Barnard, *The Functions of the Executive*, Cambridge, Mass.: Harvard University Press, 1938, pp. 56–61, 92–94.

tives in the organization. In service organizations, considerations of administrative efficiency must ideally not jeopardize the quality of professional service. And in respect to commonweal organizations, such as armies, maximizing of their efficiency and strength is assumed to take second place to assuring that they do not dominate the government they were created to serve but remain under its control. In business concerns, on the other hand, considerations of operating efficiency are expected to reign supreme within the limits *externally* imposed on them. Since productivity, work satisfaction, and other factors pertaining to efficiency will be discussed at length later, we shall illustrate problems of business concerns only briefly at this point with two studies of white-collar offices.

The first study, conducted by Katz and his colleagues, focused on groups of clerical workers and their supervisors in the home office of a large insurance company.[45] In a comparison of supervisors of work groups with consistently high and with consistently low productivity, it was discovered that supervisors of highly productive groups were most likely to report that they spent 50 per cent or more of their time on supervision rather than in doing the same kind of work as their subordinates. This difference seems to indicate the significance of the administrative function for productive efficiency. There was also a tendency for supervisors of the highly productive groups to describe as most important the "human relations" part of their jobs, while low-production supervisors stressed more often the production and technical aspects of their jobs. These findings suggest that, paradoxically, the more important productivity is for the supervisor the less productive is his unit. It should be noted, however, that this attitude of the supervisor might be a result of the group's low productivity as well as a determinant of it. (Cross-sectional data like these do not enable us to tell which of two related factors influences the other.) It is quite plausible that supervisors whose subordinates produce well are less concerned about productivity and accordingly less apt to mention it as the most important part of their job. The more interesting possibility, of course, is that the supervisor's anxious concern with production impedes work satisfaction and congenial informal relations—perhaps by inducing him to supervise more closely—thereby lessening productivity.

In another study of a business concern, Argyris found that superior officials in a bank were obliged to spend so much time with customers that they had little time left for supervision of subordinates.[46]

45 Daniel Katz *et al.*, *Productivity, Supervision and Morale in an Office Situation*, Ann Arbor: Institute for Social Research, University of Michigan, 1950.
46 Chris Argyris, *Organization of a Bank*, New Haven: Labor and Management Center, Yale University, 1954.

This situation appeared to have some positive consequences since one of the main sources of work satisfaction reported by junior employees was that "nobody breathes down your neck all the time." However, the fact that some of these junior employees, for example the tellers, also spent most of their time interacting with customers meant that they had little opportunity to interact with one another; this focus resulted in a weak informal structure and a low degree of group solidarity. Argyris also found that the hiring procedure of the bank led to the selection of a particular type of employee—persons who possessed a strong desire for economic security and job stability, a desire to be left alone, and a dislike of aggressiveness in themselves or in others. While this type of employee was well suited for performing the routine work of the bank, promotion created problems because the very qualities that were desirable in subordinates tended to make "passive and weak" leaders, impairing the efficiency of the organization.

Service Organizations. A service organization has been defined as one whose prime beneficiary is the part of the public in direct contact with the organization, with whom and on whom its members work—in short, an organization whose basic function is to serve clients. Included in this category are social-work agencies, hospitals, schools, legal aid societies, and mental health clinics. The crucial problems of these organizations center around providing professional services. The welfare of their clients is presumed to be the chief concern of service organizations.

In the typical case, however, the client does not know what will best serve his own interest. For example, the patient is not qualified to judge whether or not it would be best for his health to undergo an operation. Hence, the client is vulnerable, subject to exploitation, and dependent on the integrity of the professional to whom he has come for help. The customer in a store, on the other hand, presumably can look after his own interests.[47] Consequently, while the businessman's decisions are expected to be governed by his self-interest—as epitomized in the phrase *"caveat emptor"*—the professional's decisions are expected to be governed not by his own self-interest but by his judgment of what will serve the client's interest best. The professions are institutionalized to assure, in the ideal case, that the practitioner's self-interest suffers if he seeks to promote it at the expense of optimum service to clients.[48]

Professional service also requires, however, that the practitioner

---

[47] See the discussion of this point with particular reference to the medical profession in Talcott Parsons, *The Social System*, Glencoe, Ill.: Free Press, 1951, pp. 433–445, 463–465, 471–473.

[48] Talcott Parsons, *Essays in Sociological Theory* (2d. ed.), Glencoe, Ill.: Free Press, 1954, pp. 34–49.

maintain independence of judgment and not permit the clients' *wishes,* as distinguished from their *interests,* to influence his decisions. There are two reasons for this distinction: First, professional services are specific; the client may wish to borrow money from his lawyer, but the latter is not obligated to lend it to him; he is obligated only to serve the client's legal interests to the best of his abilities. Second, since clients are not qualified to evaluate the services they need, the professional who lets his clients decide what services he is to furnish does not provide optimum service to them.

A fundamental difference between the benefits obtained by clients of a service organization and those secured by the members of mutual-benefit associations (or by the owners of a business concern; or by the general public in the case of a commonweal organization) is the assumption that the client beneficiaries are not qualified to determine what is in their own best interest but that the member beneficiaries are so qualified. Since the members of mutual-benefit associations are the only judges of which of the many objectives the association might pursue are in their greatest interest, the problem of internal democratic control is basic. Since one group in service organizations must decide what is in the best interest of another, the basic problems here are to assure that the former serve the interest of the latter but that they do *not* let the latter determine how they are to be served.

The professionals or semiprofessionals in a service organization must steer between two dangers. On the one hand, they must not lose sight of the welfare of their clients, either through concern with their own status and career or through preoccupation with administrative problems. The latter may become manifest in rigid adherence to and enforcement of procedures or in permitting budgetary considerations to dominate all decisions (for example, considering it more important to protect the taxpayer than to serve clients adequately in a public agency). On the other hand, the professionals must not become "captives" of their clientele and surrender to them the power to determine the nature of the service furnished. To err in the first direction is to become despotic or overly rigid; to err in the second is to become subservient.[49] Both types of error are illustrated in a study of the relations between Israeli officials and new immigrants to that country.[50] Some officials became despotic and attempted to use their bureaucratic position to force clients to assume certain political and ideological roles contrary to their own predilections. By contrast, other officials

[49] See Morris Janowitz *et al., Public Administration and the Public,* Ann Arbor: Institute of Public Administration, University of Michigan, 1958, p. 6.

[50] Elihu Katz and S. N. Eisenstadt, "Some Sociological Observations on the Response of Israeli Organizations to New Immigrants," *Administrative Science Quarterly,* 5 (1960), pp. 113–133.

sent to work as instructors in immigrant villages became subservient to the village communities and turned into their representatives for presenting the demands to the authorities, losing sight of their specific responsibility to serve the welfare of these immigrants by teaching them new skills. An illustration of an entire service organization that became subservient to its clients is provided by Clark in his study of the adult-education programs in Los Angeles.[51] Here the marginality of the entire program and the policy that only classes with a certain minimal attendance would be maintained gave the students control over the character and content of the curriculum and even the selection of instructors; clients assumed "a position of dominance over professionals in influence on program content."[52] To convert a university into a business concern that "gives the customers what they want" does not serve the best educational interests of students; rather, students are best served when professional educators determine what and how they are to be taught.

Failure to serve the welfare of clients is probably a more prevalent problem in service organizations than becoming subservient to them, and the former issue will occupy us again later, particularly in the next chapter. Now we turn to another problem, which has received considerable attention from students of mental hospitals, namely, the sensitive nature of the professional-client relationship. Stanton and Schwartz found that when a patient in a private mental hospital was the subject of covert but basic staff disagreement he tended to become pathologically agitated; furthermore, once the disagreement was brought into the open and resolved, the patient's excitement terminated, often abruptly.[53] Apparently such conflicts subtly influence the interaction between staff and patient, and the disagreements among staff members are inadvertently communicated to the patient, causing his emotional disturbance. Caudill's study of another small hospital tends to confirm this conclusion.[54] In this case, changes in the hospital's treatment program upset hospital routines and confused staff roles; disagreements remained covert and led to less frequent encounters among the various staff groups—senior psychiatrists, residents, and nurses. Shortly thereafter, a period of rather intense collective disturbance occurred among the patients. Early attempts of each of the staff groups to deal with patient problems proved unsuccessful, partly because the endeavors of different groups were in conflict, and

[51] Burton R. Clark, *Adult Education in Transition,* Berkeley: University of California Press, 1958.

[52] *Ibid.,* p. 86.

[53] Alfred H. Stanton and Morris S. Schwartz, *The Mental Hospital,* New York: Basic Books, 1954, pp. 342–365.

[54] William A. Caudill, *The Psychiatric Hospital as a Small Society,* Cambridge, Mass.: Harvard University Press, 1958, pp. 87–127.

it was not until disagreements were brought into the open and discussed that the situation was restored to normal. Both studies suggest
that conflict within an organization must become overt before it can
be resolved. In many ways this situation seems analogous to individual disturbances—the mental conflict of a person must also become
conscious before he can resolve it. Another study, however, did not
find disagreements among the staff to be associated with disturbance.[55]
Wallace and Rashkis administered a paper-and-pencil test to staff
members in a mental hospital over a seven-week period to obtain measures of degree of consensus on every patient; at the same time systematic observational data were collected on amount of patient disturbance. No significant relations were found between these two sets
of data, although an increase in over-all consensus and a decrease in
patient disturbance were noted over the period of study.[56]

Commonweal Organizations. It is not always meaningful to speak of
the clients of an organization, since this term refers to both the segment of the public in direct contact with the organization and the
segment that benefits from its services. In service organizations, the
two are identical; hence, only when referring to these is it appropriate
to speak of clients. But who would be the clients of, say, an army?
Surely not the enemy it fights; neither would it be the citizens who
benefit from its operations, since they are not in direct contact. An
army has no clients in the above sense.

The distinctive characteristic of commonweal organizations is that
the public-at-large is their prime beneficiary, often, although not necessarily, to the exclusion of the very people who are the object of the
organization's endeavor. Examples of this type are the State Department, the Bureau of Internal Revenue, military services, police and
fire departments, and also the research function as distinguished
from the teaching function in universities. Most of these organizations either perform protective services for the community or
serve as its administrative arm. As was pointed out earlier, the
public could be considered the owners as well as the prime beneficiaries, and this type could then have been subsumed under our second category: organizations serving the interests of their owners.

[55] Anthony F. C. Wallace and Harold A. Rashkis, "The Relation
of Staff Consensus to Patient Disturbance on Mental Hospital Wards,"
American Sociological Review, 24 (1959), pp. 829–835.

[56] Two possible interpretations of these conflicting findings are:
First, the relationship between consensus and disturbance may be
spurious; there is more consensus about those patients who have been
in the hospital for some time, and patients also tend to become less
disturbed the longer they have been in the ward. Second, the important
factor in promoting disturbance is not the total number of disagreements concerning a patient but rather disagreements on particularly
salient issues or between particularly significant staff members.

However, it seems preferable to separate these types since great differences in the nature and function of an organization depend on whether the community at large or a select number of owners are the prime beneficiaries.

The issue posed by commonweal organizations is that of external democratic control—the public must possess the means of controlling the ends served by these organizations. While external democratic control is essential, the internal structure of these organizations is expected to be bureaucratic, governed by the criterion of efficiency, and not democratic. The challenge facing these organizations, then, is the maintenance of efficient bureaucratic mechanisms that effectively implement the objectives of the community, which are ideally decided upon, at least in our society, by democratic methods. (*Internal* democratic control by the membership might well be at the expense of efficiency and thus lessen the organization's ability to effect the democratic will of the community.)

Three problems of commonweal organizations will be briefly discussed: the problem of power, the problem of promoting extraordinary performances, and the problem of dealing with outcasts.

The problem of power is perhaps best exemplified by the military service. In the interests of national security, most countries maintain military organizations of considerable strength. The existence of such a force creates the danger that it can be used to dominate the society that produced it, thus destroying democratic control or other forms of civilian government. This situation is illustrated by the army coups which have occurred in South American countries and the Algerian adventures of the French generals in 1961. The problem of maintaining democratic control over the military is accentuated by the background and the political orientation of its senior officers, although recent evidence reported by Janowitz indicates that changes are occurring in the composition of the officer corps.[57] Thus, in the past the officers in most countries were recruited from the aristocratic groups: half a century ago 92 per cent of the military leaders of the United States originated in the upper-middle class or above it. By 1950, however, the proportion of leaders having their origin in these higher classes had decreased to about 50 per cent. Similar shifts occurred in other countries; in Germany, for example, 97 per cent of the military elite were recruited from the nobility in 1824, 67 per cent in 1911, and by 1944 only 18 per cent could claim such origins. As might be predicted from their background, military officials have been traditionally conservative in politics. This statement has been particularly

[57] See Morris Janowitz, *The Professional Soldier*, Glencoe, Ill.: Free Press, 1960, especially pp. 89–94; 236–241.

true in Europe; in the United States, military leaders more often have tended to be apolitical, but most of them also have had a conservative viewpoint, and still do. The persistence of their conservatism despite the broader base of recruitment appears to result from the socialization of recruits to army traditions. For example, graduates of military academies were found to be more conservative than nonacademy men. While there are several aspects to this military conservatism, perhaps the most important and disquieting is the belief held by a considerable number of the military elite that the formation of policy on national security should be removed from civilian control and placed in the hands of the military. Janowitz concludes: "The effectiveness of civilian political control over the military is dependent only to a small extent upon the political beliefs held by the military profession."[58]

A second problem confronting some commonweal organizations is that of promoting such extraordinary performance as bravery or creativity. Military organizations must find ways of eliciting bravery from their members under combat circumstances; police and fire work also frequently call for individual heroism. Of course, bravery by itself may be insufficient for guaranteeing military success. Weber has suggested that bureaucratic discipline is more important than individual heroism for the success of an army,[59] and Janowitz indicates that the military manager has come to replace the military hero.[60] Nevertheless, it would seem to remain true that military success depends on fielding soldiers who are brave, not cowardly. And if there is less need for great heroes in today's battles, even "routine" action in combat requires much courage. Another form of extraordinary behavior is required in research organizations, namely, scientific creativity. This elusive quality is considered by many to be inborn and thus, by definition, outside the sphere of organizational influence. Actually, however, as we will see later, organizations do influence research creativity. If extraordinary qualities are required of individuals to insure the successful operations of an organization, it is important to learn how an organization can select personnel that possess such qualities, can stimulate their further development among its staff, and can motivate and help its members to apply their relevant talents to the pursuit of organizational objectives.

A special problem is posed for organizations that are required to deal with society's outcasts, such as prisoners, against whom the public is being protected. What complicates the work of these institutions is

[58] *Ibid.,* p. 253.
[59] Weber cites Cromwell's victory over the Cavaliers as an illustration of his thesis that discipline is more significant than bravery. Gerth and Mills, *op. cit.,* pp. 256–257.
[60] Janowitz, *op. cit.,* p. 21.

that stamping men as outcasts not only removes them from society but also from society's control. Cloward has discussed in detail the dilemma faced by prison officials who must control inmates.[61] On the one hand, physical force is not very effective for routine control, and society has placed severe strictures on its employment in prisons. On the other hand, the attempt to offer the prisoner incentives by promising him rehabilitation and social reintegration is inhibited by society's refusal to accept prisoners after their release.

In this situation the guard finds himself in a difficult position. He is the one in continual interaction with prisoners, and he must find means to control them. It is not easy to treat a person with whom one has frequent contacts as an outcast. Moreover, the failure of the formal reward and sanctioning system forces the guard, according to Cloward, to rely on informal means of control. The guard can obligate prisoners to himself by providing them illegitimate access to desired goods and services. Such illegal alliances between guards and prisoners provide the structure by which the other prisoners are controlled—the prisoner confederates helping the guards to maintain control in the interest of retaining their own favored position.

One attempt to solve the problem of control, as well as that of rehabilitation, is to transform prisons from commonweal organizations (concerned with the protection of the public) into service organizations (oriented primarily to the needs and interests of the prisoner "clients"). An interesting problem this raises for the organization is discussed in Grusky's study of a small Midwestern prison camp.[62] He reports that the adoption of a therapeutic orientation toward prisoners resulted in enhancing their status, a circumstance likely to be disruptive for the organization, because it tended to be perceived by the guards, not without justification, as lowering their own status relative to that of the prisoners. Other consequences of the therapeutic approach were an increase in the interaction between the staff members and prisoners, a decentralization of authority (a change which may enhance the status of the middle-level staff), and a reduced dependence on bureaucratic procedures.

These studies suggest that the identity of the prime beneficiary of the organization's operations has far-reaching consequences for its structural characteristics, a conclusion which indicates the usefulness of the typology of formal organizations here proposed.

[61] Richard A. Cloward, "Social Control in the Prison," Richard A. Cloward *et al., Theoretical Studies in Social Organization of the Prison,* New York: Social Science Research Council, 1960 (Pamphlet No. 15), pp. 20–48.

[62] Oscar Grusky, "Role Conflict in Organization," *Administrative Science Quarterly,* 3 (1959), pp. 452–472.

Concluding Remarks

This chapter has presented an analysis of the nature of formal organizations and of the diverse forms such organizations exhibit. It began with a summary of Weber's theory of types of authority and of bureaucratic organization. We emphasized that his work provides both a conceptual scheme, defining the main characteristics of bureaucracies, and many hypotheses concerning the relations between characteristics and their significance for administrative efficiency. We proposed some modifications of Weber's conceptions, notably the inclusion of the informal as well as the formal, and the dysfunctional as well as the functional aspects of such organizations in the study design. We also called attention to the importance of the distinction between expertness and discipline as two different criteria for the rational organization of conduct. Next, we examined two other approaches to the analysis of formal organizations—those of Simon and Parsons. Finally, we attempted to differentiate between various types of formal organizations. After summarizing a number of other classifications of organizations, we suggested a typology based on the criterion *cui bono* —who benefits. Using this criterion, four types of organization were distinguished—mutual-benefit associations, business concerns, service organizations, and commonweal organizations. In the course of illustrating these four types and discussing certain problems associated with each, we had the opportunity briefly to survey some of the research on formal organizations.

All organizations, regardless of the group whose interest they are designed to serve, have regular contacts with persons who are not officially part of the organization. The characteristics of those publics have important implications for the organization's structure and functioning. This statement is particularly true for service organizations, where the orientation of officials to clients and that of clients to officials is of crucial significance for operations. In the following chapter we shall examine several aspects of the relations between organizations and their publics.

CHAPTER THREE

The Organization and Its Publics

Formal organizations are associated with diverse publics. There is the larger society which permits the organization to operate (if only by default, as in the case of criminal organizations). There is the population of the society in its capacity as a pool of potential members. There are the other organizations with whom the organization competes, cooperates, or enters into various exchange relationships. There are, finally, two special publics which should be distinguished: the public-in-contact, with whom or on whom the organization's members work, and the public served. Only in service organizations are the two identical, constituting the clientele—recipients of public welfare, students, or patients are both worked with and served by the organization.

What are the publics-in-contact in the other types of formal organizations? In business concerns, the main public-in-contact is, of course, the customer. While customers receive a service, they must look after their own interests; in this respect they differ decidedly from the clients of service organizations. In mutual-benefit associations the public-in-contact and acted on is those on whom depend the benefits sought by the membership. Thus, in the case of unions, the major public acted on is management, since negotiations with management are needed to improve the situation of the union members. In a like manner, the public-in-contact of the political lobby is the legislature, on whose action the lobby's success depends. In commonweal organizations the public-in-contact is frequently some source of danger to the community. In the interests of serving the larger public, these organizations must have direct contact with such threatening and disreputable elements as law violators, prisoners, and enemy soldiers.[1]

Many organizations have several publics-in-contact. For example, business concerns relate directly to customers, to suppliers of needed materials, to unions, to the government, and to other groups. The internal organization of such concerns frequently reflects these basic divisions; thus, an enterprise will have a sales department, a department concerned with purchasing, a labor-relations department, and a

---

[1] But the source of danger may also be impersonal; thus, other commonweal organizations are concerned with the control of fire or contagious disease.

legal branch to deal with government regulations. Some of the internal organizational conflicts which develop between departments result from their orientation toward different publics.

Which level in the organizational hierarchy deals with the major public-in-contact varies greatly. In unions, for example, it is the top level: leaders negotiate with management. But in prisons, it is the bottom level: guards have direct contact with inmates. Two main factors appear to determine the hierarchical level from which are selected the organization's representatives who work with a given public. The smaller the number of these representatives (compared to the entire organization), and the higher the status and power of the public with whom they deal, the higher will be their relative standing in the organization.

This chapter is broadly concerned with various aspects of the relations between organization members and their publics. In the first part we shall discuss the orientations of officials, concentrating on the contrast between professional and bureaucratic orientations. While these orientations have relevance for many aspects of organizational life, they are of particular importance in service organizations, where they vitally affect the worker-client relation. Following this discussion, we shall concentrate directly on the public itself and examine its orientation, its organization, and the repercussions of official-client relations on the social structures in formal organizations.

PROFESSIONAL AND BUREAUCRATIC ORIENTATION

Similarities and Contrasts. The professional form of occupational life and the bureaucratic form of organizational administration are two institutional patterns that are prevalent today and that in many ways typify modern societies. Professional principles share many elements with bureaucratic ones, but include some that are not common. Let us briefly survey the underlying characteristics of professionalism and compare them to those of bureaucratic organization, focusing on principles rather than on specific practices.

First, professional decisions and actions are governed by universalistic standards; that is, they are based on certain objective criteria which are independent of the particular case under consideration. These principles rest upon and are derived from a body of specialized knowledge, such as the science of medicine, and practice consists of applying these principles with appropriate skill to particular cases. The mastering of this body of knowledge and the acquiring of appropriate skills requires a period of specialized training. The character of bureaucratic administration does not differ greatly in this respect. Bureaucratic operations are also governed by abstract principles and consist of the application of these principles to particular cases. Although the period of training for professionals is generally longer than that required of bureaucrats and contains some unique features, to be discussed presently, bureaucrats too undergo a period of technical training and indoctrination to qualify for their positions.

A second characteristic of professionalism is the specificity of professional expertness. The trained professional is a specialized expert qualified to deal with problems in a strictly limited area; he makes no claim to generalized wisdom—he is neither sage nor wise man. The practitioner's authority over his clients rests on their confidence in his expertness in some specific area; he enjoys no authority outside that sphere. In the interests of good health, for instance, the physician can tell his patient what he should eat, but he cannot tell him with authority what friends to choose. Contrast the limited authority exercised by the professional over his clients with the diffuse authority exercised by the parent over his children. The principle of specificity applies with equal force to the bureaucrat; in his case, too, specialization is the key to expertness, and the essence of bureaucracy is circumscribed authority.

Third, the professional's relations with clients are characterized by affective neutrality. Professional codes of ethics condemn emotional involvement with the client. These norms protect the client from being emotionally exploited and the practitioner from being torn apart by sympathy for his troubled clients. In addition, detachment insulates the professional so that he may exercise reasoned judgment. The relations between bureaucrats and clients are also marked by such impersonal detachment, with similar ends being served.

Fourth, professional status is achieved by an individual's performance, not ascribed to him because of some qualities he cannot change, such as sex or birth order. The professional's success rests upon outstanding performance in accordance with the principles laid down by his colleague group. In a similar manner, the bureaucrat is appointed to a position because of his technical qualifications rather than because of who he is or what connections he has, and his career advancement is governed by objective and explicit official criteria.

A fifth element in professionalism, essential to protect the welfare of dependent and vulnerable clients, is that professional decisions must not be based on the practitioner's self-interest, whereas in business life self-interests are expected to govern decisions. This difference does not mean that professionals are less selfish than businessmen, or less interested in economic advancement. It means that while each party to a business transaction is assumed, by the other and by the community, to act strictly in terms of his own interests, it is not legitimate for a professional to let his decisions as to what services to render be influenced by self-interest. If he does, the condemnation and the sanctions of his colleagues and of the community will hurt his interests in the long run. Thus, the structure of a profession tends to make the practitioner's own interests dependent on his serving the interests of his clients to the best of his abilities. Businessmen, on the other hand, are not condemned for acting in terms of their own interests. Moral disapproval attaches to the surgeon who recommends an appendectomy when the patient does not need one, but not to the auto or appliance salesman who recommends the super-deluxe model although the customer does not need the extra trim.[2] Another aspect of this principle is that the nature of the services the professional renders to his clients is presumed to depend on their need and not their ability to pay; whereas the kinds of services rendered by a business to its customers depend, of course, on what they can afford to purchase.

In contrast to the first four principles, this fifth one is not characteristic of all formal organizations but only of certain types. Lack of self-interest is not expected to govern the operations of business concerns or of mutual-benefit associations, but it is expected of commonweal organizations and, particularly, of service organizations. As a matter of fact, the conditions for realizing this principle are probably more favorable for professionals working in service organizations than for professionals working outside this organizational context. The traditional practitioner in the free professions is not only a professional but also a businessman who makes a living by collecting fees from clients. His economic dependence on clients comes into conflict with the requirement to set self-interest aside in rendering service to them. For example, a physician's need to earn a livelihood puts pressure on him not to devote all his time to clients who are too poor to pay for his services. The salaried professional in the service organization is free of this pressure, and the organization supported by community or philanthropic funds is not dependent on fees from clients either. These conditions would seem to be more conducive to promoting disinterested service.

A final characteristic of the professions is their distinctive control structure, which is fundamentally different from the hierarchical control exercised in bureaucratic organizations. Professionals typically organize themselves into voluntary associations for the purpose of self-control. As Goode explains, "the larger society has obtained an *indirect* social control by yielding *direct* social control to the professional com-

2 Life insurance agents have sought to support their claim to professional status by emphasizing that the properly trained agent does not try to sell as much insurance as he possibly can but only the amount and kinds called for by the needs of the customer-client. For a discussion of the problems inherent in such an attempt to attain professional status in an occupation whose members are dependent on sales commissions, see Robert K. Bain, "The Process of Professionalization: Life Insurance Selling," unpublished Ph.D. dissertation, Department of Sociology, University of Chicago, 1959.

munity, which thus can make judgments according to its own norms."[3] Professional control appears to have two sources. First, as a result of the long period of training undergone by the practitioner, he is expected to have acquired a body of expert knowledge and to have internalized a code of ethics which governs his professional conduct. Second, this self control is supported by the external surveillance of his conduct by peers, who are in a position to see his work, who have the skills to judge his performance, and who, since they have a personal stake in the reputation of their profession, are motivated to exercise the necessary sanctions. Professionals in a given field constitute a colleague group of equals. Every member of the group, but nobody else, is assumed to be qualified to make professional judgments. To implement these values, professional organizations usually seek to have them enacted into laws establishing the exclusive jurisdiction of the organized colleague group in a given area of competence and granting it the right to license practitioners. The medical profession, for example, enjoys such a mandate in the area of healing; psychologists are now seeking legislation to obtain the right to license psychological counselors and testers, and even other practices in which their expertise is more questionable.

It is clear that this type of control structure differs greatly from that employed in bureaucratic organizations. The source of discipline within a bureaucracy is not the colleague group but the hierarchy of authority. Performance is controlled by directives received from one's superiors rather than by self-imposed standards and peer-group surveillance, as is the case among professionals. This difference in social control, which is related to that between expertness and discipline discussed in Chapter II, constitutes the basic distinguishing feature between professional and bureaucratic institutions, which have otherwise many similar characteristics. The significance of this difference is brought into sharp relief if one examines people who are subject to both forms of social control; that is, professionals in a bureaucracy.[4]

---

[3] William J. Goode, "Community within a Community: The Professions," *American Sociological Review*, 22 (1957), p. 198 (italics in original).

[4] The model of the professions presented in this section is heavily indebted to the writings of Parsons and Hughes. See Talcott Parsons, *Essays in Sociological Theory* (2d ed.), Glencoe, Ill.: Free Press, 1954, pp. 34–49; and *The Social System*, Glencoe, Ill.: Free Press, 1951, pp. 433–436, 454–465; and Everett C. Hughes, *Men and Their Work*, Glencoe, Ill.: Free Press, 1958, pp. 78–87, 116–130, 140–142. Despite differences in their terminology both Parsons and Hughes appear to agree on the basic elements of the model with one major exception: Hughes focuses on self-determination by the colleague group as a crucial characteristic of professions, whereas Parsons hardly deals with this topic. In this respect we have followed Hughes since this factor seems to us to be essential for understanding the differences and conflicts between professionalization and bureaucratization.

Cosmopolitans and Locals.[5] The professions in industrial societies, having long been typified by the independent practitioner, appear to be
undergoing a vast and far-reaching period of transition. During recent
years a large number of the members of the "old" professions, such as
physicians and lawyers, have become salaried employees of formal organizations; the "new" professional groups—social workers, librarians,
nurses, accountants—are almost exclusively employed by organizations
rather than engaged in private practice.[6] The salaried professionals are
increasing in numbers many times faster than are the independent professionals.[7] The advantages to be gained from the collaboration of
varied specialists in the same administrative structure and the increasing cost of professional equipment, much of which a single practitioner
no longer can afford, are two factors that have encouraged the development of this new pattern of professionals working in formal organizations.

The transition from private practice to salaried employment has
no doubt been facilitated by similarities in the principles that govern
professional and bureaucratic practice. But while some of the principles
are similar, others, as noted above, are divergent, and the latter have
tended to engender conflicts between the professionals and their administrative organization. Conflicts created by the merger of the two
institutional forms are resolved by the bureaucratized professionals in
different ways. Some retain their identification with their professional
group, are highly committed to their professional skills, and look for
social support to professional colleagues outside the organization as
well as within. Such involvement in the larger network of professional
relations that cuts across organizations may be said to indicate a "professional" orientation. Others have less commitment to their specialized
skills, come to identify with the particular organization by which they
are employed and its program and procedures, and are more concerned
with gaining the approval of administrative superiors inside the organization than that of professional colleagues outside. These may be
said to have a "bureaucratic" orientation.

The tendency of some professionals to place their loyalty to their
profession above their loyalty to their employer is a phenomenon that

[5] The terms "cosmopolitan" and "local" were first used by Merton
to describe two different types of community leaders. See Robert K.
Merton, *Social Theory and Social Structure* (2d ed.), Glencoe, Ill.: Free
Press, 1957, pp. 387–420.

[6] See Hughes, *op. cit.*, pp. 131–138.

[7] Corey reports that the number of salaried professionals has increased thirty times over during the period from 1870 to 1940, while
free professionals have grown at a much smaller rate during the same
period. See Lewis Corey, "The Middle Class," *Antioch Review* (1945),
pp. 1–20.

has received considerable attention, although only recently has there been any systematic attempt to marshall evidence on the conditions under which this occurs. Hughes has long since called attention to the "itinerant" professional, who, being "more fully committed and more alert to the new developments, will move from place to place seeking ever more interesting, prestigeful, and perhaps more profitable positions."[8] Reissman confirmed this observation in his study of forty middle-level bureaucrats, suggesting the label "functional bureaucrat" for the type of worker "who is oriented toward and seeks his recognition from a given professional group outside of rather than within the bureaucracy."[9] Two recent studies of professional groups examine the conflict between the professional and the organization. Caplow and McGee in their study of the process of recruitment in a sample of universities provide a specific example of this loyalty struggle:

Today, a scholar's orientation to his institution is apt to disorient him to his discipline and to affect his professional prestige unfavorably. Conversely, an orientation to his discipline will disorient him to his instituton, which he will regard as a temporary shelter where he can pursue his career as a member of the discipline.[10]

And in Wilensky's study of intellectuals in labor unions, the largest and most stable category was the "professional service" type, whose distinguishing characteristics included an orientation to a colleague group outside the union.[11] Unlike the other types described by Wilensky, these experts were less concerned about loyalty to the labor movement, many admitting that they would consider company employment. In general, they desired positions where their skills could be used to best advantage and were willing to consider any moves that would enhance this possibility.

The most systematic study of the conflict between professional and organizational commitment was carried out by Gouldner in a small private liberal-arts college.[12] Gouldner constructed Guttman-type scales to measure loyalty to the employing organization, commitment to specialized professional skills, and reference-group orientation. He found that high commitment to professional skills and an orientation to outside reference groups were associated with low loyalty to the college.

8 Hughes, *op. cit.,* p. 136.
9 Leonard Reissman, "A Study of Role Conceptions in Bureaucracy," *Social Forces,* 27 (1949), p. 308.
10 Theodore Caplow and Reece J. McGee, *The Academic Marketplace,* New York: Basic Books, 1958, p. 85.
11 Harold L. Wilensky, *Intellectuals in Labor Unions,* Glencoe, Ill.: Free Press, 1956, pp. 129–144.
12 Alvin W. Gouldner, "Cosmopolitans and Locals," *Administrative Science Quarterly,* 2 (1957–1958), pp. 281–306, 444 480.

Generalizing from his data, Gouldner concludes that although Weber implied that the more expert an organization's personnel, the more efficient and stable the organization, his findings suggest that "there seems to be some tension between an organization s bureaucratic needs for expertise and its social-system needs for loyalty. '[13] In short, several studies have concluded that professionals tend to assume a "cosmopolitan" orientation, manifesting itself in a lack of loyalty to particular organizations and a willingness to move from one employer to another, whereas only those less committed to professional skills are usually "locals" with strong feelings of loyalty to their organization.

Data gathered in our research on County Agency (the county welfare department which is described in the Appendix) allow us to further explore this problem and to test the hypothesis that there is an inverse relationship between professional commitment and organizational loyalty.[14] The index employed to measure a professional orientation among the social-work staff consists of two parts: (1) commitment to professional skills as indicated by some graduate training in social work, and (2) orientation to professional reference groups outside the agency. Considering the first criterion, it was felt that in an agency where the majority of workers lacked any graduate training in social work, the fact that a worker had started such training, regardless of how far he had as yet advanced, was indicative of superior commitment to professional skills. It should be emphasized that we are not concerned here with amount of education as such but that we use graduate courses in social work as an indicator of the worker's commitment to the profession and of his exposure to the professional subculture in social-work schools, where he comes into contact with norms and values that are independent of those promulgated by his employing agency.[15] With regard to reference-group orientation, workers who chose both professional people outside the agency and professional books and journals as two of the three sources from which they obtained most

13 *Ibid.*, p. 466.

14 For a fuller discussion of these data and findings, see W. Richard Scott, "A Case Study of Professional Workers in a Bureaucratic Setting," unpublished Ph.D. dissertation, Department of Sociology, University of Chicago, 1961. Only data from the County Agency study are utilized in this section because comparable data from the City Agency were not gathered. Specifically, we do not have any measures on orientation to the profession as opposed to the agency for City Agency workers. Throughout, we shall present data from both agency studies whenever they are available.

15 Some graduate training in social work was found to be positively associated with the following characteristics: being female, Negro, single, of high seniority, from middle- or upper-class origins, deciding early to enter the field, holding few jobs prior to entering the field, and, if married, having few children. Some of these characteristics are, of course, interrelated.

intellectual and professional stimulation were considered to be oriented to outside reference groups.[16]

We expected that workers with graduate training (hence, high professional commitment) would be more likely to choose reference groups external to the agency. Table 1 shows that there was some ten-

TABLE 1. LOCATION OF REFERENCE GROUPS AND GRADUATE WORK

Graduate Training in Social Work	Location of Reference Groups	
	Outside Agency	Inside Agency
Yes	56%	36%
No	44%	64%
N (= 100%)	25	61

dency for workers with graduate study to choose outside reference groups in disproportionate numbers, but the relationship observed is far from pronounced. Therefore, instead of dealing only with the two pure types—professional and bureaucratic—we shall add to them the two mixed types, giving us four types of orientation, each corresponding to one of the four cells of Table 1. These four types are: (1) Professionals—workers having graduate training and choosing outside reference groups. (2) Reference group only—workers oriented to outside reference groups but lacking graduate training. (3) Training only—workers having graduate training but not choosing outside reference groups. (4) Bureaucrats—workers without graduate training and not oriented to outside reference groups. By retaining these four groups for our analysis, we shall be able not only to compare the two extreme orientations but also to distinguish the significance of commitment to skills from that of choice of reference group.

How successful is this attempt to differentiate workers by their orientation? One method of validation is to determine how workers in these categories differ on certain activities and attitudes that should be associated with the underlying orientations. Thus, workers with a professional orientation might be expected to attend more social-work conferences and to be more active in local welfare activities than workers with a bureaucratic orientation. Professionally oriented workers might

[16] Inside agency sources of stimulation which completed the choice list furnished on this question were: colleagues in the agency; supervisor; division head; and the director of the agency. The stipulation that the professionals chosen be outside the agency under consideration carries with it no reflection on the quality of professionals within the agency. As our concern is with the possible conflicts between professional workers and bureaucratic structures, workers selecting reference groups outside these structures were thought to be exposing themselves to influences relatively "unstained" by bureaucratic "contamination."

be expected to express the belief that supervisors should have a graduate degree in social work rather than have only work experience in the field; they might also be expected to be more concerned than workers with a bureaucratic orientation about furthering the interests of clients. The data in Table 2 confirm these predictions and help to validate the measures of orientation.[17] Professionals were in all cases most likely to exhibit professional characteristics, bureaucrats, least likely, and mixed types tended to be intermediate.

TABLE 2. TYPE OF ORIENTATION AND
PROFESSIONAL CHARACTERISTICS

Professional Characteristics	Type of Orientation			
	Professional	Reference Group Only	Training Only	Bureaucratic
Attended two or more conferences in past year	93%	81%	78%	72%
Active in two or more local welfare groups	46%	18%	18%	11%
Think supervisors should have an M.S.W. degree	86%	50%	45%	34%
Think assistance to clients should be increased	77%	73%	55%	41%
N (= 100%)	13	10	20	37

To ascertain the degree of loyalty of workers to their employing agency, workers were asked whether or not they would be tempted to leave their present job if a "fairly large private family-service agency" were established in their community. Those workers who stated that they would consider leaving their present position at a similar or lower salary were considered to exhibit low loyalty to County Agency. A second measure of loyalty was also utilized. Workers were asked whether or not they expected to be working in the agency "five years from now" and, if not, what they expected to be doing. Those who expected to leave the agency during this period but to go on working in the field of social welfare were considered to exhibit low loyalty.

[17] The numbers on which the percentages are based in Tables 2 to 5 vary slightly from question to question since some workers did not answer all questions. The numbers reported at the bottom of the table indicate the number of workers answering the question on which there was the *lowest* response.

The data presented in Table 3 indicate that professionals were somewhat more apt to be willing to leave and to expect to leave County Agency than were bureaucrats. These findings confirm the hypothesis derived from other studies that a professional orientation is inversely related to organizational loyalty. Professionals tend to be cosmopolitans and not locals. The data further suggest that reference-group orientation is more significant for loyalty than is training.[18]

TABLE 3. TYPE OF ORIENTATION AND
LOYALTY TO THE AGENCY

Loyalty to County Agency	Type of Orientation			
	Professional	Reference Group Only	Training Only	Bureaucratic
Would leave present job for one in private agency	31%	27%	18%	8%
Expect to leave agency within five years	21%	27%	15%	6%
$N (= 100\%)$	13	11	20	36

A study of nurses in several out-patient departments in Boston hospitals conducted by Bennis and his associates reports results that qualify the generalization that a professional orientation is typically associated with a cosmopolitan one and clarify the relationship between orientation to the profession and organizational loyalty.[19] Contrary to expectation, Bennis and his colleagues did not find a professional orientation among nurses to be associated with being a cosmopolitan rather than a local. The more professionally oriented nurses did not differ from others in their loyalty to the hospital, and they were *more* apt than others, not less, to express loyalty to the local work group. One possible explanation of these unanticipated findings is that they are due to the narrow visibility of the nurse's professional competence —her performance is observable only to her colleagues in the immediate work group, not to those outside the organization. The nurse who is committed to her professional skills expresses a high loyalty to her

---

[18] The influence of reference groups alone is indicated by the difference between the first and third columns and that between the second and fourth; the influence of training alone is indicated by the difference between the first and second columns and that between the third and fourth. In this table, the former differences are, on the average, larger than the latter.

[19] W. G. Bennis *et al.*, "Reference Groups and Loyalties in the Out-Patient Department," *Administrative Science Quarterly*, 2 (1958), pp. 481–500.

work group since only this group can give her praise and recognition for work well done.

If this interpretation is correct it should apply to other groups where professional performance is hidden from the view of all but the local work unit—groups such as social workers. But we have already reported that a professional orientation was inversely related to loyalty to the organization among social workers in County Agency, which is unlike the finding Bennis obtained for nurses and like that obtained by Gouldner and others. Moreover, loyalty to the local work group in County Agency, as indicated by a caseworker's unwillingness to be transferred to another agency division,[20] was unrelated to professional orientation, again failing to replicate the positive relationship obtained among nurses; in fact, there was a slight negative relationship between professional commitment and loyalty to work group in County Agency.[21]

These differences in findings can be explained by suggesting that the crucial underlying factor is not so much the visibility of performance as the nature of the limits of professional opportunity. If there is little opportunity for advancement *within the profession,* regardless of the organization by which a professional is employed, a commitment to professional skills comes into conflict with aspirations for advancement. Such limits apply to nurses, whose major opportunities for advancement involve forsaking nursing practice and going into administration, or possibly into teaching.[22] The more committed a nurse is to her professional skills, therefore, the less attractive will she find the formal reward of a promotion that removes her from the work for which she was trained, and the more she will have to rely on the informal rewards of being highly esteemed for her skills as a nurse by colleagues working in close association with her. Hence, commitment to nursing skills promotes an attachment to the local colleague group, although not necessarily to the entire hospital, since this organization is composed primarily not of colleagues but rather of non-nursing groups, and since one hospital offers from this standpoint no particular advantage over another. (Moreover, whatever differences there may be between hospitals in the opportunity to advance to specialized nursing

20 That divisions were perceived as the significant work groups in this agency is indicated by the fact that when workers were asked sociometric questions concerning the members of their "units" (groups of workers sharing the same supervisor) they almost invariably ignored this subgroup and instead reported peer choices extending throughout their division. Each division was housed in a single large room, and the largest one contained only about 30 workers.

21 If respondents are divided on the basis of professional commitment (training), we find that 64 per cent of the (33) committed workers and 78 per cent of the (49) others felt loyal to their group.

22 See Bennis *et al., op. cit.,* pp. 497–498.

positions are not reflected in a sample of nurses drawn from a variety of hospitals, such as that of the Bennis study.)

If, on the other hand, there is ample opportunity for advancement in a profession but this opportunity is much more restricted in some organizations than in others of the same type, commitment to the profession comes into conflict with loyalty to the organization and encourages a cosmopolitan orientation. Limits of this type would seem to apply to the faculties of small colleges, such as the one studied by Gouldner. These faculty members knew that research opportunities and other professional advantages were superior in large universities, and thus those most interested in cultivating their professional skills were usually the ones most eager to leave the college and move to "greener pastures." The same considerations apply to the public welfare agency. Since the opportunity for doing professional casework was not as good there as in private agencies, professional commitment motivated workers to hope for positions in private agencies, thus making them less loyal to their present employer. Caplow's and McGee's scholars and Wilensky's intellectuals were in a similar situation, since they could strive for a better professional position in other universities or with other employers. We suggest, then, that a commitment to professional skills will be associated with low organizational loyalty only if professional opportunities are more limited in the organization under consideration than in others with which it competes for manpower. In other words, only if it is the structure of the organization rather than the structure of the profession that restricts opportunities for professional advancement do we expect professional commitment to be accompanied by a cosmopolitan orientation.

When a given organization curtails opportunities for professional development, the locals who express strong loyalty to the organization do so at the expense of a weakened affiliation with their profession. They may surrender their professional ambitions in favor of administrative aspirations, or simply restrict their level of aspiration and remain content to carry on their work in ways defined by the organization. Locals who choose the first of these alternatives and become successful administrators may, in turn, become "cosmopolitans" oriented to administrative positions in larger and better organizations; their skills have qualified them to compete in a new market. Those who choose the second alternative may devote their energies to the development of new skills outside their original profession: the research scientist may attempt to become a good teacher of undergraduates, and the social worker may obtain satisfaction from becoming an expert in public assistance.

Significance of Professional Reference Group. So far, our discussion of the professional reference group has centered on its influence on organizational loyalty. We now shall consider its significance for behavior toward clients. It has been suggested that professional reference groups function to provide standards of judgment and conduct, as well as social support for living up to these standards, for individuals working in varied organizational contexts. In social work, a primary concern of these standards is to maintain and improve the quality of service rendered to clients. This is also a concern of social-work agencies. In terms of general service principles, there is no conflict. But general principles must always be adapted, and often compromised, in applying them to specific cases. Hence, the basic question is, what are the criteria that govern these necessary compromises—professional standards or administrative considerations? In a complex public-welfare organization, administrative requirements cannot be ignored, especially since the agency is also subject to pressures from other publics, such as taxpayers, as represented by the legislature, who are interested in keeping expenditures at a minimum. For workers who are oriented to professional casework, administrative adjustments made in the agency's program and procedures as accommodations to local circumstances or pressure groups are seen as defections from professional standards.[23] For these reasons we hypothesized that a commitment to professional standards would make workers more critical of agency practice and less apt to conform to established administrative procedures.

These predictions were tested using data from County Agency. As Table 4 shows, professionally oriented workers were more critical of their agency than were workers not so oriented. They were more apt

TABLE 4. TYPE OF ORIENTATION AND
CRITICISM OF THE AGENCY

Criticism of Agency	Type of Orientation			
	Professional	Reference Group Only	Training Only	Bureaucratic
Agency is far from being professional	43%	9%	10%	5%
Discrepancy between social work theory and agency practice is large	31%	24%	18%	8%
N (= 100%)	13	11	21	38

[23] Various examples of conflict between the demands of the taxpaying public and those of professional social workers, and between the requirements of administration and professional standards, are cited in Harold L. Wilensky and Charles N. Lebeaux, *Industrial Society and Social Welfare,* New York: Russell Sage Foundation, 1958, pp. 179, 245–246.

"strongly" to agree with the statement that the agency has a "considerable distance to go before it can claim to be offering a fully adequate, professional welfare program," and they were more likely to believe that there was a "large" discrepancy between "professional standards and social-work theory on the one hand and the actual work performed by this agency on the other." A professional orientation was also associated with a tendency to criticize agency policies and procedures explicitly for interfering with service to clients. Table 5 shows that workers identified with the profession were more likely than bureaucratically oriented ones to feel that the laws under which the agency operated, its administrative procedures, and specifically the responsibility to check the qualifications of clients interfered with casework service.[24]

TABLE 5. TYPE OF ORIENTATION AND CRITICISM OF
ADMINISTRATIVE POLICIES

Criticism of Policies	Type of Orientation			
	Profes-sional	Reference Group Only	Training Only	Bureau-cratic
Laws limit casework	77%	82%	73%	32%
Procedures interfere with helping clients	50%	36%	36%	21%
Checking on clients interferes with case-work	29%	18%	14%	14%
N (= 100%)	13	11	22	36

One might assume that a professional orientation not only increases interest in doing casework, as these findings imply, but also improves the quality of service. But what is good performance in terms of professional criteria may be poor performance in terms of administrative standards, and when there is such a conflict professional identification may well lead to failure to live up to administrative standards. A measure of such failure to conform to official standards was obtained from the formal records of the agency by compiling the number of "de-

24 Interestingly enough, professionally oriented workers were less prone than bureaucrats to criticize the agency for changing procedures too often. Such criticism was most affected by professional training, that is, workers with some graduate work were less critical of changes in procedures than were untrained workers. This finding is similar to that of an earlier study which showed that the more competent officials were less resistant to change. (See Peter M. Blau, *The Dynamics of Bureaucracy*, Chicago: University of Chicago Press, 1955, pp. 197–198.) These results suggest that knowledge and skills, by lessening anxiety, reduce rigidity.

linquent" cases for each worker for one year. Every case accepted for service by the agency was officially classified, on the basis of how severe the problems were, as requiring visits at specified time intervals. A case not visited on schedule was considered delinquent. This administrative solution to the problems posed by large caseloads created rigid schedules, which recurrently faced workers with the dilemma of visiting one case because a visit was administratively required or visiting another case in urgent need of attention and thereby adding a delinquency to their record. Hence, the number of delinquent cases a worker had per month is used as an indicator of his willingness to rebel from the dictates of administrative procedures in the interests of client services.[25] Professionally oriented workers were, indeed, found to have disproportionately high numbers of delinquencies. As in most other comparisons, the crucial factor was professional reference group rather than graduate training. Of the 11 workers oriented to professional colleagues outside the agency, one-third had many delinquencies, in contrast to only 2 per cent of the 41 without such an outside reference group.[26] Apparently, an orientation to the profession as a reference group makes a worker somewhat independent of organizational pressures and thus more inclined to deviate from administrative procedures in the interest of professional service to clients.[27]

THE PUBLIC

The Orientation of the Public to Government Organizations. One serious shortcoming of most organizational research, including our own, is that there is no investigation of the publics related to the organization. Studies of organizations have not included within the scope of their analysis the publics directly in contact with the organization, let alone the larger public which is potentially in contact. The neglect of this aspect of organizational research means that a one-sided picture of the

[25] This index is not perfect since delinquencies could result from the actions of a poor worker who neither took care of emergency cases nor of his regular visits.

[26] These data were available for only 52 workers; in general, only full-time workers carrying regular public-assistance and child-welfare caseloads were included. "Many delinquencies" are operationally defined as 12 or more per month for Aid to Dependent Children caseloads and 2 or more per month for Old Age Assistance and child-welfare caseloads.

[27] Data from City Agency suggest that workers oriented to professional service (using a criterion different from that applied in County Agency) were also more independent from peer-group pressures than workers not so oriented. The former were more apt than those oriented to bureaucratic procedures to differ from the majority of their work group in their judgments of the supervisor. See Peter M. Blau, "Patterns of Deviation in Work Groups," *Sociometry*, 23 (1960), pp. 254–256.

official-client relation has been constructed: we are beginning to know something about the orientations of officials to clients, whereas we know little of the orientations of clients to officials and organizations.

Studies of public opinion toward government agencies, notably a recent one by Janowitz and his associates, make an important contribution to a fuller understanding of official-client relations, although such survey research is no substitute for specific organization studies that include data on the organization's clientele. In the Janowitz study a representative sample of 764 adults in the Detroit area were interviewed in 1954.[28] The respondents were questioned about a variety of federal, state, and local government agencies that have contacts with a wide public, such as the Bureau of Internal Revenue, the state and county police, and the public schools.

Information and opinions were sought from the sample of respondents concerning four basic problems. First, the study assessed the amount of the public's knowledge concerning government organizations. By any standard, this knowledge was very limited. For example, nearly half of the respondents did not know the amount of earnings at which income tax started, and only one out of ten knew approximately what portion of the national budget was spent on defense and foreign aid. The knowledge concerning specific agencies and their operations was even more limited, particularly among those who had not had any actual contact with the agency in question. Persons of low socioeconomic status, Negroes, and women tended to be even less well informed than others.

Second, the study was interested in the "worth" of government services to the people. The majority of respondents felt that the government was serving the public interest well. However, a sizable minority (41 per cent) thought that the government took more from the people in the form of taxes than it returned to them in services. There seemed to be considerable ambivalence toward government service, particularly among the underprivileged. They favored the extension of government services but were dissatisfied with the burdens that the government imposed on them. The proportion dissatisfied rose to 59 per cent among lower-class Negroes.

The third problem examined was that of morality in public administration. Only 13 per cent of the respondents thought that many government officials were corrupt, but two-thirds of the sample believed that political pull influenced the decisions of officials. In general, there

---

28 Morris Janowitz *et al., Public Administration and the Public,* Ann Arbor: Institute of Public Administration, University of Michigan, 1958, especially pp. 15–27, 29–71. For a study of public attitudes toward big business, see Burton R. Fisher and Stephen B. Withey, *Big Business as the People See It,* Ann Arbor: Institute for Social Research, University of Michigan, 1951.

was a lack of confidence in the government's ability to extend impartial treatment to its clients, and this feeling increased among those in the lower socio-economic groups.

The fourth major area explored was the prestige of public officials. Such prestige has traditionally been high in continental Europe but low in the United States. Using as a benchmark a study conducted by White in 1929,[29] Janowitz and his associates found that there had been a considerable increase in the status of public officials in the last generation—so much so that a slight majority of the persons questioned said that they would rather work for the government than for a private firm, pay held constant. Only a small number of the respondents questioned by White took this position. Attitudes had also changed toward officials in other respects. For example, whereas 60 per cent of White's respondents considered private employees to be more courteous than public ones in 1929, only 29 per cent of Janowitz's sample did in 1954. Janowitz, like White, found that those for whom public employment had the highest prestige value tended to come from the bottom of the social structure, possibly because the job security characteristic of civil service seems particularly attractive to this group whose jobs are typically so insecure. Interestingly enough, however, public employees and their relatives tended to accord lower prestige to public employment than did others.

The Janowitz study provides information on the general context of public opinion within which government organizations must function. But attitudes of the public towards various types of organizations differ, of course, providing a more specific context of public opinion for each type. To complement our research on the internal structure of two social welfare agencies, we shall briefly review a few studies dealing with public attitudes toward this type of organization and the prestige of its members.

The first study provides a picture of social agencies as viewed by a group of white residents living in two depressed areas of Chicago in 1952.[30] Since a large proportion of those interviewed had regular contacts with the organizations they were asked to discuss, this study deals essentially with the attitudes of clients toward welfare agencies. Borash and his colleagues report that almost all of their respondents had postponed making formal application for public welfare until they had exhausted all their own resources as well as the informal sources of

[29] Leonard D. White, *The Prestige Value of Public Employment*, Chicago: University of Chicago Press, 1929.

[30] Saul Borash *et al.*, "Conceptions of Social Agencies, Community Resources and the Problems of a Depressed Community," unpublished M.A. thesis, Department of Sociology, University of Chicago, 1952, pp. 113–168. A total of 159 respondents were interviewed, 95 interviews were conducted in the two areas and an additional 64 in the waiting rooms of the social agencies.

assistance in their neighborhood. Agency service was evaluated not in terms of official policies or other general criteria but in terms of the treatment the respondent had received in his contacts with the agency and from his particular caseworker. Generally, there was much dissatisfaction: 74 per cent of the respondents complained that they were treated as inferiors, 69 per cent said they were kept waiting too long on their visits to the agencies; 58 per cent felt that they received insufficient funds from these organizations; and 81 per cent expressed unfavorable attitudes toward the caseworker, the representative of the welfare agency. Such widespread dissatisfaction among clients, regardless of its source, cannot but hamper the operations of social agencies and cause difficulties for their personnel. Of course, we do not know how typical these opinions are of those held by welfare clients in general.

Turning briefly to the prestige of the caseworker, a national opinion survey reported that the social worker in public welfare was accorded less prestige than most other professional public employees, being given a status approximately equal to that of skilled blue-collar workers, reporters, and bookkeepers.[31] Studies reporting the self-evaluation of social workers show that they tend to rank themselves roughly in the same prestige grouping as does the general public.[32]

We can only speculate on the ways in which widespread client dissatisfaction and low prestige of officials affect the operation of welfare departments. But recruitment of new workers, turnover of personnel, and level of job satisfaction are probably only the most obvious of the areas adversely affected.

Client Characteristics and Department Organization. It is perhaps a truism to say that organizations will reflect the characteristics of the publics they serve. A technical high school differs in predictable ways from a college-preparatory school, and an upper-middle-class church is unlike the mission church of the same denomination in the slums. While such differences seem to be important and pervasive, there has been little attempt to relate client characteristics systematically to organizational structures. As a step in this direction, we have analyzed some aspects of two departments within County Agency from this point of view.

Although no data were collected on the client groups served by this agency, we do know something about their characteristics, particu-

31 National Opinion Research Center, "Jobs and Occupations," Reinhard Bendix and Seymour M. Lipset (eds.), *Class, Status and Power*, Glencoe, Ill.: Free Press, 1953, pp. 412–413.
32 See, for example, Norman Polansky *et al.*, "Social Workers in Society," *Social Work Journal*, 34 (1953), pp. 74–80; and R. Clyde White, "Prestige of Social Work and the Social Worker," *Social Work Journal*, 36 (1955), pp. 21–23, 33.

larly about the differences between the clients of the Public Assistance Division (PAD) and those of the Child Welfare Division (CWD). PAD clients came to the agency to apply for assistance under one of the categorical programs. They appeared to occupy a position clearly subordinate to the worker since they had come to request help and had to accept it on terms defined by the agency or do without. On the other hand, the clients served by CWD were, technically, dependent children. However, serving these children involved the workers in client relationships with adults who were not only requesting a service of the agency but also providing one; these were the foster-home parents and the adoptive parents who furnished homes for children. These parent surrogates were not in a subordinate position to the agency but rather enjoyed some measure of power because they could withdraw their contributions of service and thereby seriously impair the functioning of the placement program.

How did these differences in the power of the clientele affect the structure of the two departments? First, caseloads in CWD were less than half the size of caseloads in PAD; this arrangement would seem to indicate that administrators were concerned to provide more regular and adequate service to CWD clients.[33] A second differentiating characteristic was the assignment of work in the two divisions. In PAD, clients were assigned to workers entirely on a geographic basis, without regard to the peculiar problems of the case. By contrast, assignments in CWD were made on a case-by-case basis by the division head, a procedure that allowed cases with special problems to be given to the more competent and experienced workers. Further, the geographical method of assignment in PAD necessitated a periodic reshuffling of clients among the workers when the distribution of cases became inequitable, and also a transfer of the case whenever a client changed residence; neither of these disruptions of worker-client relations occurred in CWD. Thus, in PAD the professional principle of the importance of a stable and continuing relation between worker and client was sacrificed for the distinctly bureaucratic principle of the interchangeability of one worker for another.

These differences between divisions were formal and explicit in character. In addition, some informal differences developed. Data from the questionnaire revealed that although all divisions were officially considered to be equal in status and there were no differences in qualifications or salaries, CWD enjoyed much higher prestige than did PAD

---

[33] This extreme difference in amount of worker time allocated to a given case was probably also a function of the amount of responsibility assumed by workers in the two divisions. CWD was legally responsible for the welfare of the children assigned to it; PAD did not assume such legal responsibility.

among workers.[34] A final difference was the racial composition of workers in the two divisions. In the agency as a whole 57 per cent of the workers were white; but in CWD the proportion of white workers was 73 per cent, and in PAD it was only 41 per cent, although there were certainly no explicit policies to account for this unequal distribution.

Some differences between CWD and PAD were not related to differences in their clientele, but many of those noted may well have been. Although our conclusions must be highly tentative, being based on a comparison of only these two cases, it appears that the clients with the higher socio-economic status and greater power enjoyed more attention from workers and more stable relations with them, and that formally instituted procedures served to maintain these differential conditions. Moreover, the agency division serving the clients with superior status and power was more highly esteemed among workers, and it was largely staffed by workers with culturally preferred ethnic characteristics.

An Organized Public. In many organizations the public-in-contact is an aggregate of people unrelated to one another, who have only intermittent contact with the institution. But in other organizations this public is actually a part of the organization,[35] and under these conditions it develops its own social structure. Such publics-in-contact are found, for example, in prisons, mental hospitals, and schools. A distinctive social structure also characterizes some publics-in-contact that are not a part of the organization, such as enemy armies and firms supplying the needs or buying the products of an organization. The latter situations, however, lead to an analysis of the relations between organizations, and we shall put this discussion over to a later chapter. When the public-in-contact is a part of the organization, it often organizes itself in opposition to the organization. This situation is to be expected in commonweal organizations such as prisons, where this public is an enemy against whom the institution protects society. But it also occurs in service organizations, where the public is a clientele whose interests are served—for example, in schools and mental hospitals—since clients do not necessarily agree with what the professionals in the organization judge to be in their best interests. We shall discuss three illustrations of an organized public, based on research in prisons, in mental hospitals, and in high schools.

In the prison organization, the problems faced by guards often induce them to single out some prisoners to help control the rest, as was

[34] Of the workers, 34 per cent ranked CWD highest in prestige of the four agency divisions, while 3 per cent ranked PAD highest.

[35] See Erving Goffman, "Characteristics of Total Institutions," Walter Reed Army Institute of Research, *Symposium of Preventive and Social Psychiatry*, Washington, D.C.: U.S. Government Printing Office, 1957, pp. 43–48.

mentioned in Chapter II, and the guards, thereby, foster the development of an informal organization among inmates. Although this informal organization facilitates short-run control over prisoners, it undermines long-range control, as indicated in a study by Sykes and Messinger.[36] They suggest that the system of common values and norms that emerged among inmates, and the set of roles associated with it, helped the prisoners face the deprivations of prison life. For this social system enabled and, indeed, encouraged the prisoner "to reject his rejectors," and it provided him with social support from a community where he was not an outcast. To serve these functions, the informal organization exerted social pressures on the prisoner to refrain both from obeying the prison authorities and from taking advantage of fellow prisoners. The role of "right guy" most closely conformed with inmate norms and was accorded the highest status; roles that departed from the norms elicited disapproval, since they constituted a threat to the cohesiveness of the inmate group.[37] Such an inmate social system, whatever its function for prisoners or for the prison, clearly impedes efforts to control and rehabilitate criminals.

Caudill and his associates, in research of unusual design, were able to collect data on the informal organization of patients in a mental hospital.[38] Caudill entered the hospital in the guise of a patient, his real identity and purpose being known only to the top administrator; his data were collected by participant observation. The study suggests that the group structure that developed among the patients provided its members with the opportunity for "playing" a variety of social roles and supplied social support. The formal organization was unaware of this social structure among patients, and the group, being ignored, tended to turn inward and insulate itself further from the larger organization. Here, then, the client organization was not hostile to the host organization but the failure of hospital officials to recognize the client group structure and its needs led to friction between the two organizations.

A recent study of twelve high schools by Coleman reveals that the student prestige structure tends to conflict with the academic goals of the formal organization.[39] In most of the schools included in the study,

[36] Gresham M. Sykes and Sheldon L. Messinger, "The Inmate Social System," Richard A. Cloward *et al., Theoretical Studies in Social Organization of the Prison,* New York: Social Science Research Council, 1960 (Pamphlet No. 15), pp. 5–19.

[37] For a discussion of a number of social roles identified among prisoners, see Gresham M. Sykes, *The Society of Captives,* Princeton: Princeton University Press, 1958, pp. 85–107.

[38] William Caudill *et al.,* "Social Structure and Interaction Processes on a Psychiatric Ward," *American Journal of Orthopsychiatry,* 22 (1952), pp. 314–334.

[39] James S. Coleman, "The Adolescent Subculture and Academic Achievement," *American Journal of Sociology,* 65 (1960), pp. 337–347.

the peer group rewarded students for their achievements in athletics and in other extracurricular activities with high prestige, while achievement in academic areas earned a student far less prestige, if any. It was found that the less value students in a school placed on obtaining good grades, the lower was the intelligence (as measured by tests) of students making high grades. The implication is that if scholastic achievement does not earn a student prestige in his peer group then the most intelligent students do not seek to attain it, and the educational goals of the formal organization are consequently thwarted.

It would appear that a clear recognition on the part of organization officials of the existence and nature of the structures linking together the members of their publics-in-contact would allow them to operate more effectively. Service organizations, in particular, would profit by harnessing the forces for support and control operating in their client groups—forces that now are often at cross purposes with their own.

CONFLICTS WITH CLIENTS

Who Are the Aggressive Clients? Conflicts between members of the organization and its public occur not only in commonweal organizations, where they are expected, but also in other types, where they are not. Conflicts occur between service organizations and their clients, and between business organizations and their customers. In discussing some empirical studies of conflicts with clients we shall at the same time illustrate the difference between a sociopsychological approach to this phenomenon and a structural approach.

A study on aggressiveness among recipients of unemployment insurance conducted in the depth of the depression by Lasswell and Almond is an example of the sociopsychological approach.[40] Workers at the complaint desk were asked to distinguish between aggressive and nonaggressive clients, and a sample of 100 of each type was selected.[41] Background data on these 200 cases were then assembled from agency records in order to determine the characteristics associated with aggressiveness. Almond and Lasswell found that the aggressive clients had been in contact with the agency over a longer period of time than the others, and that more of them had been employed by the government. According to court records, more of the aggressive than of the nonaggressive clients had broken the law, and more had had contacts with

[40] Gabriel Almond and Harold D. Lasswell, "Aggressive Behavior by Clients Toward Public Relief Administrators," *American Political Science Review*, 28 (1934), pp. 643–655.

[41] Aggressiveness was quite loosely defined and appeared to include mere self-assertiveness on the part of clients.

penal institutions. In contrast to the nonagressive clients, aggressive clients tended to come from higher income and education groups, and more of them had been employed in occupations dealing with people rather than with things. More aggressive clients were of native birth, and more were raised in urban areas.

The findings were interpreted in the following manner: Familiarity with government agencies in general, and this one in particular, encourages assertive conduct that may lead to conflict. Experience in dealing with people also promotes assertive conduct in interaction with officials. Resentment against having been penalized by the government may be displaced in the form of aggression against the present organization and its representatives. Finally, deprivation is relative: a person of higher socio-economic status is probably more frustrated than one of lower status by being on assistance, and his middle-class standards may make him feel more guilty about it; such frustration and guilt lead to aggressive behavior.

The focus of this study is clearly on personality characteristics of individuals rather than on social structure. It explains the observed conflicts by reference to the internal and psychological processes that motivated them. Note that the approach is *socio*psychological, that is, that psychological differences are traced back to the past social experiences that produced them. For example, the authors do not assume that aggressiveness is an inherent trait that accounts for both the tendency to violate laws and the tendency to have conflicts with officials, but suggest that the social experience of having been arrested engenders negative attitudes toward government officials. The sociopsychological approach asks: what are the past experiences and the characteristics of participants that foster conflict? But one can also ask, and this is the structural approach: what are the conditions in the social situation that promote conflict? Both approaches deal with the influence of social conditions on patterns of conduct, but the former examines the influence of *past* social conditions on personality characteristics and hence on conduct, whereas the latter is concerned with the influence of *present* social conditions on conduct.

Let us consider an illustration of the structural approach.

What Social Conditions Make Waitresses Cry? Whyte in his study of social relations in restaurants observed that waitresses sometimes broke down and cried.[42] After careful observation of the situations in which such behavior occurred, he concluded that it was the result of cross-pressures on the waitress. The nature of these pressures can be clarified by analyzing the "flow of demand" in the organization, that is, by

[42] William F. Whyte, *Human Relations in the Restaurant Industry*, New York: McGraw-Hill, 1948, pp. 64–81.

studying who makes demands on whom.[43] Demands that flow contrary to status lines—from lower to higher status—create conflicts. Thus, male cooks and countermen did not expect to be ordered around by females, yet the waitresses often had occasion to tell them what food to prepare or serve. Whyte found that this discrepancy produced conflicts, which could be reduced if some sort of impersonal barrier was erected at the point of encounter. For example, a spindle on which waitresses placed their food orders reduced tensions and conflicts by changing the flow of demand, since it enabled the counterman to fill the orders at his discretion instead of at the command of the waitress and then tell her that the food was ready.

Orders from superiors made demands on the waitress, as did the "orders" of the customers, and even the requests for help from her co-workers. A waitress was often caught in the cross currents of these demands, as when an impatient customer insisted on services that upset her routine. The tensions produced by these conflicting pressures sometimes built up to a point where they exploded, that is, made the waitress break down and cry.

Whyte's analysis illustrates a structural as distinguished from a sociopsychological focus. He does not discuss the psychological traits of customers or waitresses. He deals neither with the typical personality of the waitress nor with the past experience and psychological characteristics that distinguish those that cry often from those that rarely do. He explains an observed pattern of conduct not in terms of personality traits, even socially acquired ones, but in terms of existing social conditions. The social element in the approach is not the significance of past social experiences for present personality characteristics but the significance of the present structure of social relations for patterns of conduct. The question that Whyte attempts to answer, then, is: how does the social structure give rise to conflict? However, one can also ask how conflict affects the work-group structure, and this question too exemplifies the structural approach.

How Do Conflicts with Clients Affect Work-Group Structure? A study conducted by Blau in a public employment agency is concerned with this problem.[44] Anyone seeking employment was entitled to avail himself of the services of this public agency, but recipients of unemployment-insurance benefits were obligated to do so. Conflicts with clients developed in two situations: when a client needed a job and the interviewer decided he was not qualified for any of those available, and

---

[43] This concept is derived from a combination of two earlier concepts: "flow of work" and "organization of action," as discussed *ibid.*, and in Conrad Arensberg, "Behavior and Organization," John H. Rohrer and Muzafer Sherif (eds.), *Social Psychology at the Crossroads*, New York: Harper, 1951, pp. 324–352.

[44] See Blau, *The Dynamics of Bureaucracy, op. cit.*, pp. 82–96.

when a client was referred to a job although he did not want it. The latter usually occurred in cases of temporary lay-offs where the client was not seeking employment but had come to the agency only because continued receipt of his unemployment benefits required it. These conflicts with clients aroused tensions for officials, directly and also indirectly, by creating guilt feelings, particularly if an interviewer found it necessary to use sanctions against uncooperative clients, because most of the interviewers were fundamentally oriented to providing service and helping clients, not to policing them. These tensions impeded operations in various ways; for example, officials might displace their aggression onto subsequent clients after an unpleasant episode.

Discussions among colleagues served to relieve the tensions engendered by conflicts with clients. Informal observation over a period of several months and interviews with the staff revealed that there were three topics of conversation prevalent among staff officials during working hours. The most frequent topic involved complaints about clients. An interviewer would, in effect, say to a colleague, "Look what this client did to me!" These discussions served as an escape valve for releasing aggressive feelings against clients in a harmless form. But this could not have been their sole function, for they often occurred after an official had penalized a client, perhaps by sending a notification that might disqualify him from further unemployment benefits. In these cases, the practice did not serve to relieve pent-up aggression, which had already been expressed directly by penalizing the client, but to obtain social support for one's decisions and thereby mitigate feelings of guilt. The sympathetic listener, who laughed at the client's stupidity or expressed indignation at his impertinence, implicitly justified the speaker's punitive or inconsiderate action by condemning the client's behavior, and this social approval relieved impending feelings of guilt.

A second type of discussion took the form of joking about clients. Ridicule is a form of aggression, but it also relieves guilt. The laughter elicited by a story about a client constituted social evidence that his behavior was ludicrous or incongruous, thus placing the blame for the client's troubles on his own shoulders and relieving the official from having failed to mitigate these difficulties; it conveyed the message, "Nobody could have helped such an impossible person!" This practice is analogous to that of teachers who tell one another jokes about the "ridiculous" answers students give on examinations, thereby eliciting laughter that absolves them from feeling guilty for not having taught their students better. Joking about clients not only relieved tensions created by the work situation but also strengthened group cohesiveness by uniting its members in laughing together. Simultaneously, however, the practice of ridiculing clients established and perpetuated anticlient norms in the work group by legitimating inconsiderate treatment of clients.

Finally, some interviewers did not joke or complain about clients but often told colleagues about outstanding clients they had encountered. This third topic of conversation was characteristic of the interviewers who were most considerate in their treatment of clients. Their sympathetic attitudes toward clients constituted overconformity with the service ideals in violation of group norms, according to which concern with helping clients must be tempered by willingness to "put them in their place" when necessary. By selecting for their conversations with colleagues accounts of exceptional clients who clearly deserved special consideration, interviewers with overly favorable attitudes toward clients sought to escape the onus of being defined as deviant by soliciting social approval of their treatment of clients. In these cases, the listeners were invited to agree, the extremely considerate treatment was surely justified. Thus, officials felt compelled to seek the social approval of colleagues for both inconsiderate and overly considerate treatment of clients, because the former violated their service philosophy and the latter their unofficial norms. These discussions about clients furnished social support and reduced tensions, thus contributing to effective operations in the employment agency. But they did so at a social cost: joking and complaining resulted in less considerate treatment of clients. The organization benefited from smoother operations at the cost of a modification of service principles. The work group made a net gain; the clients had to bear the brunt of the cost.

This study provides another illustration of the structural approach. The social situation is not taken as given, as in the sociopsychological approach, but as problematical. The investigator asked how observed patterns influence social structure and social processes, not how given social conditions influence personality structure and psychological processes.

CONCLUDING REMARKS

This chapter began with an examination of the orientations of members of organizations and continued with a discussion of the orientations of the public. We first analyzed the orientations of members to their organization and to its clients, with particular emphasis on two conflicting orientations: the professional and the bureaucratic. Next we considered the orientation of the public to government organizations in general and to public welfare agencies in particular. At this point our focus began to shift from orientations—a sociopsychological datum—to more structural considerations. We briefly examined the connections between the characteristics of clients and those of the departments that served them. Then we discussed the emergent organizations of publics that are a part of a formal organization. Finally, we contrasted the sociopsychological and the structural approach to the study of conflict between clients and officials, and with the latter approach we came to focus on the structure of social relations among the members of formal organizations. But we shall soon show that it is not enough merely to focus on the organized social relations in a group. To isolate the significance of group structure requires the use of systematic comparisons of a number of work groups, a method illustrated in the next chapter.

CHAPTER FOUR

The Social Structure of Work Groups

Looking back over the past several decades, one can note progressive changes in the focus of industrial research. Much of the empirical research on workers in industrial organizations has been motivated by an interest in practical problems of productivity. Earlier studies were chiefly concerned with physiological and economic factors relating to production. Researchers probed the nature of fatigue, experimented with pay incentive schemes, and examined the efficiency of worker efforts by means of meticulous time-and-motion studies. Taylor and his followers in "scientific management" attempted to dissect manual tasks in the hope of improving output by training workers to eliminate all body movements that were not essential, and they searched in vain for a set of "basic" activities to which all work behavior could be reduced.[1] As it became evident that scientific management's conception of workers as rational machines could not adequately account for their behavior, because it ignored the influence of sentiments and values, attention turned increasingly toward research on the underlying psychological processes that influence production. This psychological focus is best exemplified in studies of worker morale. But the morale of workers was found to depend at least as much upon the interrelations of the worker with his colleagues as upon his individual needs and dispositions. Hence, the recent trend has been away from an exclusive concern with the individual and toward an interest in the social factors in the work situation, beginning with the "human relations" approach in industry and expanding to include systematic research on the social structure of work groups.

These shifts in the focus of industrial research are rooted in changes in the organization of industry and in managerial ideology.[2] The development from small- to large-scale industrial enterprises has

[1] A critical discussion of the Taylor school appears in James G. March and Herbert A. Simon, *Organizations*, New York: Wiley, 1958, pp. 12–22.

[2] See Reinhard Bendix, "*Bureaucratization in Industry*," Arthur Kornhauser *et al.* (eds.), *Industrial Conflict*, New York: McGraw-Hill, 1954, pp. 164–175. For a more detailed discussion of changes in managerial ideology, with cross-cultural comparisons, see Reinhard Bendix, *Work and Authority in Industry*, New York: Wiley, 1956.

been accompanied by a corresponding shift in the ideological justification advanced for managerial authority. In the days of the small shop,
it could be argued with some plausibility that hard work and superior
ability led to success, and the ideological assumption that the entre-
preneur had demonstrated superior ability served to legitimate his
authority over employees. But as industrial concerns grew in size and
complexity, advancing within them rather than establishing a factory
of one's own became increasingly the major avenue of success. With
the development of the modern large-scale enterprise, moreover, the
abilities the worker has occasion to demonstrate have ceased to lead
to managerial success, since the latter depends on entirely different
skills—not technical ones but skills in coordination, that is, skills in
dealing with relations between people. The ideology consequently no
longer glorifies primarily the old Puritan values of hard work and
thrift, or even the later ones of entrepreneurial drive, but the new
ones of personality salesmanship—of the ability to handle human
relations effectively. The admonition "build a better mousetrap . . ."
has changed into advice on "how to win friends and [that is, in order
to] influence people." The idealized concept of the industrial organization as a "pyramid of opportunity" where advancement in a bureaucratic career is open to all who have the required social skills has replaced in large measure the earlier idealized concept of an industrial
environment where every technically able employee could open up
his own business some day. The problems of industry have come to
be viewed in terms of human relations rather than in individual terms
because "from the standpoint of the individual these techniques became a means of career advancement; from the standpoint of management they seemed to facilitate the coordination of a growing and increasingly specialized staff."[3] And this trend is reflected in parallel
changes in research focus.

While the human-relations approach to industrial research assumes a more sociological perspective than its predecessors, it still is
not adequate for the systematic study of social structure. It does avoid
the atomization of work groups into their individual members and
thus overcomes a limitation of most morale surveys. But the human-
relations approach does not avoid a second pitfall: it tends to atomize
the human relations in work groups by treating them as if they were
attributes of individual group members, and it consequently ignores
the organized network of social relations that characterizes group
structures. This distinction may be illustrated by considering the relations between workers on an assembly line. Assembly-line workers, like
others, establish friendly relations with co-workers nearby. But since
they are strung out along the line, each person's set of interpersonal

3 Bendix, "Bureaucratization in Industry," *op. cit.,* p. 174.

relations is different: a given worker will have contacts with workers on each side of him and with workers across the line, while his neighbor's contacts will include some of the same men, but not all, and will extend to others not included in the first worker's range of contacts.[4] On such an assembly line, therefore, we typically find human relations among workers but no work groups, since individuals are not involved in a *common* network of social relations set off from others by distinct boundaries. There are no definite subgroups within the larger collectivity with which workers can identify, and there are no subgroup norms defining common standards of conduct. In contrast to the assembly line, which inhibits the formation of work groups in the above sense, most industrial situations promote their formation. The study of the distinctive significance of group structure requires going beyond the human-relations approach to consider the networks of human relations and the common values which unite group members.

INFORMAL ORGANIZATION

A Pioneering Study. No single research has exerted more influence on the direction taken by students of industrial organization than the study carried out by Roethlisberger and Dickson in the Hawthorne plant of the Western Electric Company in Chicago.[5] A set of early experiments conducted in this plant had focused on the effects of varying degrees of illumination on worker productivity.[6] The first of these involved three different departments. When illumination was regularly increased, productivity increased in two of the three departments, but the increases were not parallel to the changes in illumination. A second study divided workers in one department into an experimental and a control group, with illumination being increased in the former and held constant in the latter; production increased in both of the two groups. A third study decreased illumination in the experimental group; again productivity of workers increased until the illumination had been reduced to a point where operators could no longer see their work. The conclusion seemed inescapable that the improved productivity noted was not due to increased illumination. The experimenters pointed out that many relevant conditions—including social ones—had not been controlled. Apparently what was involved in these strik-

4 See Charles R. Walker and Robert H. Guest, *The Man on the Assembly Line,* Cambridge, Mass.: Harvard University Press, 1952, pp. 67–68; and Abraham Zaleznik, *Worker Satisfaction and Development,* Boston: Graduate School of Business Administration, Harvard University, 1956.

5 F. J. Roethlisberger and William J. Dickson, *Management and the Worker,* Cambridge, Mass.: Harvard University Press, 1939.

6 *Ibid.,* pp. 14–17.

ing changes was that groups of workers routinely engaged in monotonous tasks were singled out for attention by management and by the researchers. This attention gave them a feeling of importance and made their jobs more interesting, and their consequent greater work satisfaction led them inadvertently to work faster.

Roethlisberger and Dickson, however, did not go so far in their interpretation at this point. They suggested only that the failure of the illumination experiments provided a stimulus for research in human relations and proceeded to set up the Relay Assembly Test Room.[7] Six girls were placed in a separate room (after their regular rate of production had been measured for two weeks prior to the transfer) where rest periods and other conditions, such as length of working day, could be varied. The experiment continued for more than a year. Regardless of the particular experimental variation in rest pauses introduced throughout the several phases of this experiment, the general course of the girls' productivity was upward. Several hypotheses were advanced to explain these surprising findings. For example, one possible explanation considered was that productivity increases were due to a reduction in fatigue produced by rest pauses. However, the productivity records for individual workers did not reveal the patterns that previous research had identified with fatigue, and hence this explanation was rejected. A second hypothesis was that the results obtained were due to changes made in the wage incentive factor.[8] To test this hypothesis, a second group of relay assembly workers were left in their regular work room but put on the same group incentive rate as that in the Test Room. Production increased in this group but far less than in the first group, a result the experimenters interpreted as indicating that although changes in earnings were important they did not account for all of the changes in productivity. Other explanations of the increase in productivity were similarly examined and dismissed. The conclusion finally arrived at was that increased productivity was a function of improved human relations. The entire social situation had been altered in ways that fostered friendly relations among workers. In addition, the supervision of workers had been taken over by the researchers who, in the interests of maintaining worker cooperation in the experiments, were very informal and nondirective in their approach.

Such findings as these led Mayo to reexamine some of his conclusions in an earlier study of a mule-spinning department in a textile

7 *Ibid.*, pp. 19–186.

8 From the third experimental period on, the test-room operators were formed into a separate group for the purpose of computing piece-work earnings. This change was important since each operator had more control over her earnings in a group of six than in the large department. See *ibid.*, pp. 34–36.

mill.[9] Mayo had been called to this mill in 1923 because of the extremely high turnover in the spinning department. He introduced rest periods, and when this change led to improved productivity and lower turnover, he concluded that the rest period relieved postural fatigue induced by work and interrupted the pessimistic revery of workers. Later, however, he decided that the results obtained could better be interpreted in social rather than physiological terms. The workers gained status as they discussed their problems with researchers and company officials. Besides, and this change is most important, the men had been transformed from "a horde of 'solitaries' into a social group" as they consulted together on the setting of rest periods and used this free time for socializing.[10]

As the Hawthorne studies continued, an increasing awareness of the significance of social relations for worker morale led the investigators to decide to observe the behavior of a group functioning under normal circumstances rather than attempt to manipulate work conditions experimentally. An observer was placed in a room with 14 workers selected from a larger department; since the workers were engaged in wiring banks of telephone equipment the study came to be known as the Bank Wiring Observation Room.[11] It soon became apparent that there were uniformities in the behavior of the group under observation that did not follow the formal organization's blueprint. Informal relations developed among the men and gave rise to organized patterns of conduct in the group—that is, there was an informal organization.

The observer painstakingly recorded the overt manifestations of the network of informal relations that developed among the workers. There were distinct patterns of interaction: some workers frequently helped out certain others; games were regularly played at lunchtime which included some workers but not others. Sentiments of liking and respect were expressed primarily toward some group members, while others were not respected and were disliked. These observable aspects of their informal relations divided the workers into two cliques and a few isolates who were not members of either clique. It was among members of the same clique that most friendship ties developed, most games were played, and even most lunchtime conversations took place. While there was some conflict between cliques, there were social bonds that united the entire group and made possible the enforcement of common norms.

[9] Elton Mayo, "Revery and Industrial Fatigue," *Personnel Journal*, 3 (1924), pp. 273–281.

[10] Elton Mayo, *The Social Problems of an Industrial Civilization*, Boston: Graduate School of Business Administration, Harvard University, 1945, pp. 66–67.

[11] Roethlisberger and Dickson, *op. cit.*, pp. 379–524.

What group norms were there to enforce? In the course of interaction a set of common rules of conduct emerged, which included the following prohibitions: Don't be a rate-buster by working too fast. Don't be a chiseler by working too slow. If you are a straw boss, act like a regular guy; don't try to get bossy. Don't be a squealer. Conformity to norms was rewarded by approval that bestowed a relatively high position in the informal status structure. Norm violations were punished by group members in a variety of ways. Minor violations might be met with "binging"—striking the offender on the upper arm —or with ridicule. Continued violation of important norms resulted in a loss of popularity, a reduction in social interaction, and ultimately in complete ostracism. One worker was isolated because he violated the most serious group norm: he "squealed" on his fellows to the foreman.

Group norms also defined "a fair day's work," and this productivity standard fell below the level that management deemed desirable. These norms are discusssed by the authors under the label "restriction of output"; but this emphasis seems one-sided, since the norms discouraged overly low as well as excessively high production.[12] It is true, however, that workers guided by their informal standard of a fair day's work made less money than they could have. The fastest workers simply stopped working earlier than others to conform to group norms. And workers would discourage a fellow worker from working faster than the unofficial norm even though his output would increase their pay under the group incentive system. Such behavior seems irrational. But what is irrational depends on one's objectives. The workers' conduct can be considered irrational only if maximizing immediate income is assumed to be their sole objective, and this was not the sole objective.

The common objectives of these workers are implicit in the functions of their output norms. First, these norms allowed workers to increase their control over the environment and lessen their dependence on management. The workers were afraid that increased productivity would result in a cut in their piece rates, and although Roethlisberger and Dickson insist that none of the workers "had ever experienced any of the things they claimed they were guarding against" because Western Electric did not engage in such practices,[13] the workers had no assurance of this safety. Piece rates had been cut in other

---

[12] Although Roethlisberger and Dickson use the phrase throughout their work, they suggest at one point that the term "restriction" is perhaps not a good one, and that the informal control of production might be more accurately described as "behavior which was not strictly in accordance with the logic of efficiency." *Ibid.,* p. 537.

[13] *Ibid.,* p. 532.

companies,[14] and management had signed no contract with workers guaranteeing wage rates, there being no union at this time in the company. The workers' endeavor to control output was hardly irrational in these circumstances; indeed, it would have been irrational for workers to put their faith in the good will of management. The rational course was for the workers to take collective action in order to maintain productivity below the level that might tempt management to cut rates.

Norms controlling worker output also served the function of increasing job security for workers. The central objective of the workers was not maximizing their current income but attempting to keep their jobs so that they would have *some* income. For this study was conducted during the depths of the great depression. Millions of persons in the country were unemployed, there had been many layoffs at Hawthorne, and, in fact, the Bank Wiring Room study itself had to be discontinued because so many workers were laid off.[15] Thus, quite independent of possible changes in piece rates, an increase in productivity would have forced management to lay off workers in a depression if it were to act rationally. It would seem that restricting productivity was the most rational course open to workers to prevent layoffs.

A third function of informal output controls was to strengthen group solidarity by preventing competitive conflicts among workers. In the depression, each worker had strong incentives to keep his job. Roethlisberger and Dickson state that all but one of the workers participating in the study were in "very poor financial condition and if they were unemployed could not escape public support for long."[16] These circumstances could easily have led to cut-throat competition among the workers, each attempting to demonstrate that he, rather than his fellows, should be retained on the job because of his superior performance. The consequent conflicts would have torn the group apart and made the work situation most unpleasant had not norms controlling output maintained group solidarity by discouraging such rivalry. Given the situation in which workers found themselves, therefore, it appears that norms regulating the output of each worker were highly functional in protecting the interests of the entire group—they were rational means for this end.

14 See S. B. Matthewson, *Restriction of Output among Unorganized Workers*, New York: Viking, 1931.

15 Roethlisberger and Dickson, *op. cit.*, p. 385. Landsberger in his generally very favorable appraisal of the Hawthorne studies states that one of the authors' most regrettable errors was their failure to "draw attention to the fact that the rapidly worsening depression in all probability had an important influence on the atmosphere in the Bank Wiring Observation Room." See Henry A. Landsberger, *Hawthorne Revisited*, Ithaca: Cornell University Press, 1958, p. 58.

16 Roethlisberger and Dickson, *op. cit.*, p. 531.

Informal Organization and Performance. Although the depression gave workers in the Bank Wiring Room a special incentive for controlling output, such adverse economic conditions are not necessary for the development of group norms regulating production. For example, Babchuk and Goode report a situation where a sales group developed a quota system that equalized sales volume for each member although management had established a commission arrangement encouraging competition among salesmen.[17] This unofficial system lessened competition among salesmen, improved their performance in nonsales areas, raised morale, and increased total group sales. A study by Roy of a group of workers in a machine shop also deals with regulation of output.[18] Roy's role as participant observer gave him access to practices that might well have been concealed from an outsider. Thus, he found that although workers deliberately restricted their rate of production, they often engaged in output races with one another. Such competitive games were concealed from management and did not affect the level of productivity since they were compensated for by goldbricking. Apparently, workers enjoy proving their skills through excellent performance and even relish competition among themselves; but they do so only when the stake in competition is limited and does not place in jeopardy the worker's earning power or his job. While quota restrictions give the workers collectively some self-determination over the conditions of their employment, they do so at the social cost of preventing the workers' pride in their skills and enjoyment of limited competition from making a contribution to operating efficiency. These conclusions imply that official procedures instituted by management to assure the employment security of workers might well improve operating efficiency; for they would obviate the need for informal regulation of output by workers and, thereby, free the inclinations of workers to strive to excel in their work.

The informal organization may contribute to as well as impede effective operations in the formal organization. It has already been mentioned that worker norms controlling production usually discourage too slow as well as too rapid work. Another important mechanism linking the formal and informal organization is the informal reward system. Among persons identified with their craft or profession, there is a tendency to look up to colleagues who are particularly expert in occupational skills. The respect and the popularity that such workers frequently enjoy are rewards for outstanding performance,

[17] Nicholas Babchuk and William J. Goode, "Work Incentives in a Self-determined Group," *American Sociological Review,* 16 (1951), pp. 679–687.

[18] Donald Roy, "Quota Restriction and Goldbricking in a Machine Shop," *American Journal of Sociology,* 57 (1952), pp. 427–442.

and the promise of informal status serves as an incentive to workers for becoming more skilled in their work. An association between competence and informal status has been observed in various kinds of work groups. For example, competence, as judged by the supervisor, was positively associated with being respected by colleagues in both the City and the County welfare agencies. The same positive relationship between competence and informal status among colleagues was found in an earlier study of a law-enforcement agency.[19] On the other hand, Homans concludes from a secondary analysis of the Bank Wiring Room data and other sources that high informal status goes with modal productivity, not with outstanding performance.[20] Other studies also have found that modal producers enjoy the highest informal status in work groups whose norms restrict productivity, because in these conditions the overproducers as well as the underproducers are penalized by loss of respect or even rejection.[21] It appears that the relationship between informal status and performance is contingent on work group norms: only if the expert exercise of skills is a dominant value in the group does high status tend to be associated with superior performance and to serve as an incentive promoting it; if the dominant norm standardizes productivity, high status is associated with modal performance.[22]

The cohesion of work groups often furthers operations. For example, cohesion has been shown to raise worker satisfaction and to lower turnover and absenteeism.[23] Cohesion also provides social support for workers; thus, it can neutralize the disturbing effects of conflicts with clients, as was noted in Chapter III. But the direct effects of cohesion on performance appear to be more variable. The findings of some studies suggest that cohesion promotes productivity. For instance, research on such varied groups as clerks, railroad employees, and factory workers found that workers in high-producing groups had greater pride in the accomplishment of their work groups (which may be considered an indication of cohesion) than did workers in low-

[19] Peter M. Blau, *The Dynamics of Bureaucracy*, Chicago: University of Chicago Press, 1955, pp. 114, 117–121.

[20] George C. Homans, *The Human Group*, New York: Harcourt, Brace, 1950, p. 141.

[21] See, for example, Abraham Zaleznik *et al.*, *The Motivation, Productivity, and Satisfaction of Workers*, Boston: Graduate School of Business Administration, Harvard University, 1958, pp. 231–232.

[22] And in groups organized in outright opposition to the formal organization, such as are found in prisons or concentration camps, high informal status probably accrues to those members who can most effectively resist organization pressures; that is, to the "low producers" from the standpoint of the formal organization.

[23] See, for example, Elton Mayo and George F. Lombard, *Teamwork and Labor Turnover in the Aircraft Industry of Southern California*, Boston: Harvard Business School (Business Research Studies, No. 32), 1944.

producing groups.[24] The researchers admit that the causal direction of the two variables measured is not clear, since a positive evaluation of the group's accomplishment may be either a cause or an effect of high productivity. However, they opt for the former because the workers had no objective information on their productivity as a group.

But other studies do not confirm this conclusion. For example, an experiment found that cohesion had no direct effect on productivity,[25] and so did a field study by Seashore of 228 work groups in a factory.[26] Both report, however, some indirect relationships between cohesiveness and productivity. Thus, Seashore did find, as he had predicted, that members of high-cohesion groups showed less variation in productivity than did members in low-cohesion groups, a datum which indicates that cohesion is associated with conformity to group standards. He also found that there was more variability in productivity *between groups* with high cohesion than between less cohesive ones. Finally, if the members of a highly cohesive group felt secure in their relations to the company, productivity tended to be high, but if they did not, it tended to be low. These findings suggest that cohesiveness increases the controlling power of the group over its members but that the direction in which this control is exercised—whether toward higher or lower productivity—is determined by other factors, such as the group's orientation to the organization.[27]

Informal Status. Informal status is not a unitary concept. Several dimensions of status have been identified, including power, prestige, and popularity. The various aspects of status are often but not always correlated.[28] One basic analytical distinction can be made at this point

[24] See Daniel Katz and Robert L. Kahn, "Some Recent Findings in Human Relations Research in Industry," Guy E. Swanson *et al.* (eds.), *Readings in Social Psychology*, New York: Holt, 1952, pp. 661–662.

[25] Stanley Schachter *et al.*, "An Experimental Study of Cohesiveness and Productivity," *Human Relations*, 4 (1951), pp. 229–238.

[26] Stanley E. Seashore, *Group Cohesiveness in the Industrial Work Group*, Ann Arbor: Institute for Social Research, University of Michigan, 1954, pp. 63–80.

[27] The work of Festinger and his colleagues tends to support these conclusions. In a study of housing groups, for example, they found that in the more cohesive groups there were fewer individuals who deviated from the group norm in their attitudes and behavior. Leon Festinger *et al.*, *Social Pressures in Informal Groups*, New York: Harper, 1950. The study by Schachter and his associates (*loc. cit.*, see footnote 25), however, does not completely confirm these conclusions: high cohesion in the experimental groups studied was not consistently associated with more successful control of member conduct.

[28] In fact, Lenski has suggested that one important dimension of status is precisely the amount of agreement between the various status positions held by an individual. Gerhard E. Lenski, "Status Crystallization: A Non-vertical Dimension of Social Status," *American Sociological Review*, 19 (1954), pp. 405–413. See also Leonard Broom, "Social Differentiation and Stratification," Robert K. Merton *et al.* (eds.), *Sociology Today*, New York: Basic Books, 1959, pp. 429–441.

between two dimensions of social status in work groups: informal rank and social integration. An individual's informal rank is defined by the respect he and his opinions command among his fellows, and their consequent tendency to defer to him in social interaction. Rank is a hierarchical concept and refers to the relative standing of the members of the group. Integration is defined by social acceptance in a group, which is reflected in the degree to which an individual is drawn into interaction by his fellows. Although the integration of various members in a group often differs, it does not necessarily differ since all the members of a group may be highly integrated, or none may be. Thus, while rank is by definition a scarce commodity, integration is not and may be enjoyed by all group members, as is the case in highly cohesive groups.

We have already noted that the relationship between informal status and performance depends on the values and norms that prevail in a work group, and in a later section we shall analyze in greater detail the connection between informal status and group pressure. But let us now examine the implications of informal status for a person's orientation to others in the work situation—to his clients and to his colleagues. Caseworkers from the City Agency (which is described in the Appendix) were classified as being either primarily concerned with checking client eligibility for assistance in accordance with agency procedures (procedure oriented) or as chiefly interested in providing casework service to clients (service oriented). This distinction is based on each worker's description of how he had spent a day in the field visiting clients.[29] Social integration among colleagues, whether it was measured by popularity (number of friendship choices received) or by informal acceptance (being called by one's first name by other workers), was found to influence worker orientation, but only among the newer workers (see Table 6). Among workers with less than

TABLE 6.   SENIORITY, INFORMAL ACCEPTANCE, AND ORIENTA-
TION TO CLIENTS

	Seniority			
Orientation to Clients	*More than 3 Years*		*Three Years or Less*	
	Informal Acceptance		*Informal Acceptance*	
	High	*Low*	*High*	*Low*
Service oriented	50%	50%	54%	22%
$N (= 100\%)$	10	8	24	18

[29] See Peter M. Blau, "Orientation towards Clients in a Public Welfare Agency," *Administrative Science Quarterly*, 5 (1960), pp. 341–361.

three years' experience, more than half of the highly integrated but less than a quarter of the unintegrated were oriented toward service rather than toward eligibility procedures, but among oldtimers (over three years' seniority), integration among peers did not affect orientation to clients. These findings can be interpreted by assuming that one factor that discourages casework service, although not the only one, is lack of familiarity with agency procedures, because it engenders anxieties that often find expression in rigid conformity with procedures. Several years of experience free workers from being preoccupied with procedures and thus make it easier for them to go beyond checking eligibility and provide some casework service. Half of the experienced workers did not provide much casework service, to be sure, but presumably the reason was that they were not interested in doing so rather than that anxious concern with procedures impeded their ability to do so. Social support from colleagues apparently relieves the anxieties typically associated with lack of experience, with the result that inexperienced workers who were integrated among peers were just as likely to furnish casework services as experienced workers. Only those workers whose anxieties were minimized neither by experience nor by social support were less inclined to provide such services.[30]

Now let us consider how informal status may affect relationships with colleagues. Caudill has shown that both formal and informal rank were related to participation in staff conferences in a private mental hospital.[31] With regard to formal position, senior doctors tended to participate most in the discussions concerning patients, residents were next highest in participation, and nurses and auxiliary workers, such as occupational therapists, participated least. Informal status rankings had an analogous effect on participation: the amount of participation of the various residents was directly associated with their competence as evaluated by their seniors and presumably with the respect they enjoyed among their colleagues.[32] Moreover, the outcome of a discussion varied according to the status of the individual raising the topic:

[30] Data from County Agency, using a different index of worker orientation to clients, essentially confirm these findings.

[31] William A. Caudill, *The Psychiatric Hospital as a Small Society*, Cambridge, Mass.: Harvard University Press, 1958, pp. 243–252, 295–296.

[32] Caudill's procedure was replicated in our study of County Agency. The weekly meetings of the division head and her supervisors were observed over a three-month period in two divisions. Caudill's findings on the relation between formal status and participation were supported; his findings on the relation between informal status (measured by the division heads' competence ratings of supervisors) and participation were supported in one division but not in the other. Besides, an earlier study by Blau found that the frequency of participation in staff conferences in a law-enforcement agency was directly associated with the social integration of the staff members. See Blau, *The Dynamics of Bureaucracy, op. cit.,* pp. 126–127.

on topics introduced by a senior doctor only 8 per cent of the discussions were inconclusive, whereas 14 per cent of the topics raised by residents and 21 per cent of the topics raised by nurses resulted in inconclusive discussions. Caudill notes that this situation evoked a sense of frustration among lower-status personnel.

How does a worker's standing among his colleagues influence his reference-group orientation? Data from City Agency again indicate that seniority in the agency was a crucial factor intervening between status and reference group. Workers were considered to define colleagues as their major reference group at work if they said that it was more important to them to be highly thought of by fellow workers than by their clients or by their supervisor. The pattern exhibited by the data in Table 7 was similar whether popularity, respect, or being

TABLE 7. SENIORITY, POPULARITY, AND REFERENCE GROUP

	Seniority			
Reference Group	*More than 1 Year*		*One Year or Less*	
	Popularity		*Popularity*	
	High	Low	High	Low
Colleagues	38%	15%	0%	41%
N (= 100%)	26	13	4	17

often consulted by colleagues was used to measure informal status.[33] Among newcomers (workers with less than one year of service) *low* status was associated with an orientation to peers, but among workers in the agency longer than one year *high* status was associated with a peer-group orientation.[34] It appears that newcomers who have already gained some popularity can turn their attention from their colleague group to concentrate on other problem areas associated with their jobs—their relations with clients and superiors. Newcomers who have not yet become popular continue to direct much of their energies toward achieving social status among peers. Older workers, on the other hand, have had time to adapt in some way to the social situation; if they have failed to win friends among peers they do not continue to look for social support to their colleagues but rather turn to clients or superiors. If old-timers have achieved popularity, however, the colleague group tends to

[33] Whereas respect is clearly a measure of informal rank, and informal acceptance is a measure of integration, popularity refers in part to both of these dimensions.

[34] Workers with one to three years' seniority were here classified together with those having over three years of experience because the response patterns of the two groups were similar.

be an important source of satisfactions for them and, hence, the reference group to which they often are oriented. In other words, it seems that unpopular workers lost interest in being highly thought of by colleagues over time (from 41 to 15 per cent), whereas popular workers became increasingly oriented to colleagues as their reference group with the passage of time (from zero to 38 per cent).[35]

Status relations are not confined to individual workers; groups also differ in status. The status of work groups is generally associated with their position in the organizational hierarchy. The standing of the groups to which a person belongs is one aspect of his own status, particularly in his outgroup relations, as is illustrated by the high informal ranks of the engineer who is part of management and of the secretary to the top executive. Changes in the wage structure may alter the relative standing of work groups; they therefore become a source of intergroup conflict. Whyte reports a controversy arising between work groups when the introduction of an incentive system in one department improved the take-home pay of a group of young machine operators. The older workers immediately demanded improvements in their incentive systems, transfers to better jobs, and other changes in an attempt to reinstate the former differential in their favor.[36] Both unions and management are continually faced with problems caused by changes that upset the established status order of work groups. Much of the resistance to change encountered in organizations is due to the disturbance which the proposed innovation would produce in the status structure.

EFFECTS OF GROUP STRUCTURE

Group Climate. The group climate or subculture is defined by the values and norms that prevail among group members. It is often asserted that the prevailing group climate influences individual conduct. But how do we know that the observed conduct is really the result of social pressures, since the individual may simply act in terms of his own attitudes and values? How can we distinguish between the influence of individual attitudes on behavior and the social constraints effected by group values and norms? To answer this question we must distinguish

35 Our interpretation receives additional support from the fact that the tendency of workers to direct friendship choices to other members of their own unit rather than to the outgroup reveals roughly the same pattern as that in Table 7. Since we lacked these reference-group data for workers in County Agency, it was not possible to replicate the analysis.

36 William F. Whyte *et al., Money and Motivation,* New York: Harper, 1955, pp. 67–70. The particular study reported is based on the research of Sayles.

two effects of group climate. First, the group climate can change the attitudes of individual members. We can observe this effect by noting the changes in attitude that occur in an individual after he joins a group, or we can infer such changes by comparing the attitudes of new-comers and of oldtimers as we did in the previous section. Second, and this effect is what concerns us now, the prevailing attitudes in the group can influence a group member's conduct *regardless* of his own attitudes. To isolate this type of structural effect, it is necessary to sep-arate the external influence of group pressure from the internal influ-ence of the individual's own orientation.[37] (The latter may have been brought by the individual to the group when he joined it, or it may be the result of earlier group pressure which he has internalized.)

The method used to separate structural effects from those of per-sonality attributes can be demonstrated with data from City Welfare Agency. Twelve work groups were divided according to their prevail-ing group climate: groups where the majority of members favored a raise in the assistance allowance without qualification were considered to exhibit a proclient climate; work groups in which the majority of the members were opposed to raising the allowance or who tempered their endorsement by various qualifications were considered to have an anticlient atmosphere. (The alternative of lowering the assistance al-lowance was not favored by any caseworker.) *Within* these groups in-dividuals were divided according to their attitudes toward raising as-sistance, using the same measure. In this manner it is possible to ascer-tain what effects of a proclient atmosphere on the individual's acting and thinking are independent of his own orientation, as the data pre-sented in Table 8 illustrate.[38]

The first row of percentages in Table 8 indicates the significance of proclient values for service to clients. Proclient individuals were somewhat more apt than anticlient individuals to extend casework services to clients rather than merely to check their eligibility for as-sistance (compare individuals with different attitudes *within* groups). But regardless of the individual's orientation, he was more apt to ren-der services to clients if he was in a group where proclient values pre-vailed than if he was in an anticlient group climate (note the difference between the first and third column, and that between the second and fourth column). The combined effect of group and individual values

[37] See Peter M. Blau, "Structural Effects," *American Sociological Review*, 25 (1960), pp. 178–193.

[38] It should be noted that this procedure does not control for the effects on the criterion variables of characteristics of individuals other than the specific counterpart of the structural variable. Neither does it control for the effects of other aspects of the group climate. Finally, Jack Sawyer has called our attention to the fact that failure to control the individual counterpart of the structural variable more effectively than by dichotomozing it may produce spurious structural effects.

TABLE 8. GROUP CLIMATE, INDIVIDUAL'S
ORIENTATION, AND ATTITUDES

Attitudes toward Clients	Group Climate			
	Proclient		Anticlient	
	Individual's Orientation		Individual's Orientation	
	Proclient	Anticlient	Proclient	Anticlient
Service orientation	60%	44%	44%	27%
Willing to delegate responsibility	55%	78%	33%	50%
Worry little about cases	25%	56%	11%	32%
$N (= 100\%)$	20	9	9	22

on service orientation was considerable: 60 per cent of the proclient in-dividuals in proclient groups were service oriented, in contrast to only 27 per cent of the anticlient individuals in anticlient groups.

These data suggest that a worker's orientation influences not only his own performance but also his reaction to the performance of other workers in his group. If a proclient orientation prevails in a group, then the individual who merely checks client eligibility without pro-viding casework services experiences disapproval, whereas the indi-vidual who provides services to clients earns the approval of his col-leagues. The desire for social approval thus constrains workers in pro-client groups to provide casework services to clients regardless of their own orientations to clients. In groups where the prevailing social climate is anticlient, social pressure works in the opposite direction, and the individual is socially rewarded for carefully checking eligibil-ity but not for furnishing casework services. It is in this way that social processes—the distribution and direction of sanctions in interaction— exert an influence on a worker's approach that is independent of his own orientation to clients.

In respect to service orientation, the effect of a proclient group climate was in the same direction as that of proclient individual atti-tudes, and the two reinforced one another. But this reinforcement does not necessarily occur. The structural effect of the common value orien-tation in a group may be the reverse of the influence of the individual's internalized value orientation. This situation is presented by the data in the two lower rows of Table 8. The measure of willingness to dele-gate responsibility to clients is whether or not workers said that cloth-ing should be made a regular part of the client's budget. At the time of the study, recipients of public assistance at City Agency received a regular allowance for food and rent but not for clothing, which was supplied as needed at the discretion of the caseworker and his supervisor. In many other welfare organizations, including County Agency, a clothing allowance is included in the regular assistance budget, and City Agency workers were asked whether they would favor a change from their system to this system. Such a change would have saved them some tedious paper work, but it would also have deprived them of the power to furnish extra benefits to their clients at their own discretion, or to withhold them. A preference for the existing procedure implies that a worker is not willing to give up some of his own power of discretion in order to increase that of his clients. As Table 8 indicates, proclient individuals were less willing to delegate this responsibility to clients than were anticlient individuals. But the prevailing orientation in a group had the opposite effect: proclient group values increased the willingness of workers to delegate responsibility, both among proclient and among anticlient individuals. The last row in Table 8 reveals the same pattern. Workers were asked whether or not they tended to worry about their cases after working hours. Proclient individuals reported that they more often worried than did anticlient individuals; but membership in proclient groups operated to reduce worrying among both types of individuals.

Why is the influence of group values here the inverse of that of individual orientations? The following interpretation might be suggested: Proclient attitudes increase an individual's concern with his client's welfare, as indicated by the proclient worker's greater tendency to worry about cases. These same attitudes make him less willing to delegate clothing responsibility to clients, because he receives gratification from doing favors for clients, and because he can use his power to give clients more money than they otherwise could get by interpreting clothing needs liberally.[39] Furthermore, the extra burden of paper work is less objectionable for proclient individuals (who obtain satisfactions from helping clients that make the extra work involved worthwhile) than for anticlient workers (who do not experience such compensating rewards).

We may turn now to the structural effects. The prevalence of proclient values in a group probably gives rise to norms protecting the interests of clients. These norms tend to favor delegating responsibility to clients, partly to guard their interests against the actions of any workers

[39] This interpretation implies that workers with proclient attitudes actually issued more clothing than others. This information is available only for a subsample of 17 workers. There is a difference in the expected direction, but it is too slight to be significant for so few cases; seven of the nine proclient workers and four of the eight others issued clothing frequently.

with anticlient attitudes, and partly to demonstrate confidence in and respect for clients. Norms that discourage too much worrying about clients are also more apt to develop in proclient groups, not only because emotional involvement is not conducive to optimum service to clients, but also because these peer groups must protect themselves against the inclination of their proclient members to worry excessively. Worried colleagues can make life unpleasant for those around them as well as themselves through their preoccupation with the misfortunes of clients and their tension. These problems confronted by proclient groups often give rise to agreement that the long-run interests of clients are best served by delegating responsibilities to them rather than keeping them dependent and by lack of involvement rather than feelings of great concern. In anticlient groups, on the other hand, there is no basis for such norms to emerge.[40]

Resistance against Group Pressure. The relationship between informal status and conformity has been widely discussed. Thus, Homans concludes that there is a direct relationship between these factors, because popularity and prestige are rewards for conformity to group norms and, conversely, low status is the penalty paid for deviancy.[41] Here the question under consideration is how conformity influences informal status. But we may also ask the opposite question: how does informal status influence conformity or resistance to group pressure. Homans suggests that, as the phrase *noblesse oblige* implies, high status constrains a person to conform meticulously to social norms. But other investigators have found that informal status—specifically, high integration or full acceptance in a group—promotes, at least under certain conditions, resistance to group pressures for conformity.[42] The latter findings suggest that the person not yet fully integrated has stronger incentives to comply with group standards in order to prove himself worthy of acceptance than the one who has already won the confidence of his peers.

40 Data from County Agency permitted the replication of these tests. Service orientation could be replicated only roughly. County data revealed a structural effect in the same direction as that shown by City data but no individual effect was discernible. Data permitted the replication of the last two rows of Table 8 more precisely. City findings on willingness of workers to delegate responsibility to clients were exactly confirmed by County data. But County data did not confirm the findings on worrying, there being no difference between work groups in respect to worrying.

41 Homans, *op. cit.*, pp. 140–144.

42 See especially Harold H. Kelley and M. M. Shapiro, "An Experiment on Conformity to Group Norms Where Conformity is Detrimental to Group Achievement," *American Sociological Review,* 19 (1954), pp. 667–677; and J. E. Dittes and Harold H. Kelley, "Effects of Different Conditions of Acceptance upon Conformity to Group Norms," *Journal of Abnormal and Social Psychology,* 53 (1956), pp. 100–107.

Data from City Agency make it possible to test these alternative hypotheses—that informal acceptance among peers promotes conformity, or that it promotes resistance to group pressures.[43] For this purpose, both the twelve work groups and the 60 individuals in them were divided in terms of a given variable, just as was done in the previous section. Thus, groups in which the majority of workers reported that they often worried about cases were considered to have a "worrying" climate; the remainder of the groups were considered to have a "nonworrying" climate. Individuals within groups were then differentiated on the basis of this criterion into high worriers and low worriers. The measure of informal acceptance or integration used was whether or not an individual was called by his first name by some of the members of his work group. The data presented in Table 9 indicate that in groups where worrying prevailed, integrated workers worried slightly less than others, but in groups where few worried, integrated workers worried more than others.[44] Thus, in both kinds of groups, although their climates were the exact opposite of one another, integrated workers were more apt than others to deviate from the prevailing climate. In fact, it appears that integrated workers were not at all influenced by the group climate with regard to worrying: half of them worried in either situation—whether most of their co-workers did or most did not. In contrast, the group climate was clearly reflected in the orientations of the unintegrated workers, as indicated by the difference between 62 and zero per cent.[45] Essentially the same pattern of findings was observed if other measures of orientation were used, such as attitude toward raising the assistance allowance, and if popularity (received friendship choices) was substituted as the index of social integration.

The allegiance of workers to their supervisor revealed a similar pattern. Using as index of allegiance whether or not workers chose their own supervisor when asked which of the agency supervisors they would most like to work under, groups and workers were classified into loyal and nonloyal ones. In those groups where the majority of workers

43 See Peter M. Blau, "Patterns of Deviation in Work Groups," *Sociometry*, 23 (1960), pp. 245–261.

44 The form of Table 9 differs from that of Table 8 because now the individual's orientation (worrying) is assumed to be the dependent variable; this form simply makes it easier to read the table.

45 Data from County Agency did not permit an exact replication of this analysis of social acceptance and worrying, because the relatively low amount of worrying about cases reported made it difficult meaningfully to differentiate between work groups on this criterion. Work groups were divided using two or more workers who worried much to define a "worrying climate," and fewer than two to define a "nonworrying climate." When popularity was used as the index of social integration, the results presented in Table 9 were not replicated. However, when *perceived* integration ("Do you feel that you are a part of your division group?") was used as a measure, the results tended to confirm the findings in City Agency.

TABLE 9. GROUP CLIMATE, ACCEPTANCE, AND
INDIVIDUAL'S ORIENTATION

Individual's Orientation	Group Climate			
	Worrying *Informal Acceptance*		*Nonworrying* *Informal Acceptance*	
	High	*Low*	*High*	*Low*
Worry much about cases	50%	62%	50%	0%
$N (= 100\%)$	18	13	16	13

were loyal to their supervisors, highly accepted workers tended to be less loyal than unintegrated ones (73 per cent versus 100 per cent expressing loyalty). But in groups where few workers were loyal, the integrated workers tended to be slightly more loyal to their supervisor than the unintegrated (48 per cent versus 31 per cent expressing loyalty).[46] Thus, in both situations integrated workers deviated from the majority in disproportionate numbers. These findings as well as the previous ones tend to support the second hypothesis: social acceptance among peers seems not to promote conformity but to increase resistance against group pressure.[47]

Can these conclusions be reconciled with those of Homans? We believe that they can be inasmuch as Homans himself qualifies his thesis of *noblesse oblige* by introducing a factor which he terms "social security." He explains: "Up to a point, the surer a man is of his rank in a group, the less he has to worry about conforming to its norms."[48] We would add, "to *all* its norms," suggesting that it is necessary to discriminate between group norms on the basis of their importance. Norms that pertain to basic values of a group, such as output standards or the taboo on "squealing," are too significant to permit any member to violate them; hence, only outcasts are apt to do so. But some group norms are not this salient for the membership. The prevailing climates of opinion we have just analyzed are less important for group members and exert less severe restraints on them. So far as these group pressures,

---

[46] The numbers on which these four percentages are based are, in order, 11, 13, 23, 13. No data on the allegiance of workers to supervisors were collected in County Agency.

[47] Our data do not permit us to determine the direction of influence between these variables, but since it seems unlikely that deviation is rewarded by greater acceptance and popularity, the plausible assumption is that the direction of influence is the opposite.

[48] Homans, *op. cit.*, p. 144. For a more recent and fuller statement, see George C. Homans, *Social Behavior: Its Elementary Forms*, New York: Harcourt, Brace, 1961, pp. 339–358.

as distinct from the group's most salient values, are concerned, it appears that integrated members, who have already proved their acceptability, are permitted greater freedom to differ from the majority than unintegrated ones, who have yet to prove it.

Group Cohesion. Social cohesion refers to the strength of the network of social bonds that unite the members of a group. Its reference is thus clearly to group structure. While the feelings of integration or identification of individual members with the group are undoubtedly related to cohesion, they are not an appropriate measure of this structural property. A sociometric measure of group cohesion frequently utilized is the proportion of ingroup choices made by group members, but this index encompasses two distinct factors. A high proportion of ingroup choices means, first, that several, and perhaps most, group members are popular, that is, have established friendly ties with colleagues; and it shows, second, that all members find themselves in a group characterized by the prevalence of friendly bonds. While both of these factors clearly describe relations between people, only the second one is concerned with the structure of these relations in a group, and this attribute of group structure is the specific referent of the concept of social cohesion. Whether or not group cohesion in this narrow sense influences conduct independently of any influences the group member's personal social ties (his "human relations") exert can be answered by using the method of isolating structural effects.

The work groups in City Agency were divided on the basis of the proportion of friendship choices (best "friends" *in agency*) going to the ingroup, and individuals were divided by whether or not they received any choices from the ingroup, in order to examine the effects of group cohesion while holding constant the individual's ingroup popularity. To determine reactions to clients, the caseworkers were asked what behavior of their clients they found particularly trying. Some workers seemed to react largely in personal terms: they were upset when they felt insulted or exploited or when clients "made demands" on them. Others appeared to react in an impersonal manner: they objected to a client who engaged in behavior that they considered morally wrong or disadvantageous for the client himself or his family. Workers in this latter group might say, for example, that they found clients trying "when they do not take care of their children."

The data in Table 10 indicate that members of cohesive groups were less apt to react in personal terms to client behavior. Nearly two-thirds of them reported impersonal reactions, in contrast to only a quarter of the members of groups with low cohesion. Further, how popular an individual was in his work group had no effect on this aspect of his behavior. These results suggest that cohesive ties make the work group a source of strong social support for members. In the ab-

TABLE 10. GROUP COHESION, POPULARITY, AND
REACTION TO CLIENTS

Reaction to Clients	Group Cohesion			
	High		*Low*	
	Individual's Popularity		*Individual's Popularity*	
	High	*Low*	*High*	*Low*
Impersonal	62%	66%	30%	20%
N (= 100%)	17	12	14	17

sence of such peer-group support, the caseworker's relations with his clients tend to become an important source of ego support for him, and his resulting dependence on clients leads him to react to them in personal terms. Group cohesion furnishes social support that makes relations with clients less significant for the caseworker and helps him to remain more impersonal toward them, while having personal ties with colleagues apparently does not furnish the social support needed for such independence from clients.[49]

Two other factors associated with cohesion may be briefly mentioned. The productivity of cohesive groups, as measured by total field visits per month, was slightly higher than that of other work groups. And the members of cohesive work groups were more likely than others to have respect for their supervisor (the index being that workers named him as one of the best supervisors in the organization). Perhaps cohesion creates a favorable disposition among workers toward the in-group and this attitude extends even to the supervisor. But perhaps the causal relation is the reverse: the fact that a supervisor has superior qualities, as indicated by the respect he commands, may be a condition that favors the development of group cohesion.[50]

THE LARGER ORGANIZATION AND WORK-GROUP STRUCTURE

Conditions of Group Solidarity. At this point we turn from the consequences to the determinants of group structure. We shall examine first some aspects of group composition that have been found to influence

[49] No data on personal versus impersonal reactions to clients were available from the study of County Agency.

[50] Data on field visits from County Agency did not replicate the findings from City Agency on the relation between cohesiveness and productivity. Data on respect for the supervisor were not available from County Agency.

group solidarity and then analyze the influence of the formal organization on the structure of work groups.

Group solidarity is a broader concept than cohesion. It encompasses not only the uniting bonds of group membership but also the collective strength derived from this unity. Indicators of group strength are to be found in cooperative activities and collective actions of various kinds. Sayles has pointed out that the significance of informal social ties among work group members has been exaggerated by Mayo and his followers. At least of equal importance is the degree of solidarity manifested in collective action and the accomplishment of common economic goals.[51] In his study, Sayles used the work group's union activity as an indicator of solidarity. Let us examine some research that explores the determinants of work group cohesion and solidarity.

There are indications that cohesive bonds are more likely to develop in homogeneous than in heterogeneous groups, that is, in groups whose members share interests and have a common background. This statement may be misleading, however, since individuals bring to their work group many characteristics and clearly cannot be alike in all of them. Besides, some differences will be more significant than others, and the salience of particular characteristics will vary from group to group. Systematic data often do not support the homogeneity hypothesis. Thus, Seashore found that variability in age and in education among the members of work groups were not related to cohesion.[52] And our data from the welfare agencies revealed no relation between group cohesion and homogeneity in age, in sex, or in religion. If anything, the mixed religious units in City Agency were more cohesive than those in which all members (or all but one) were Protestant. In general, it appears that heterogeneity in respect to those factors that are not particularly relevant for the work situation does not impede cohesion. Some aspects of heterogeneity, however, were found to be inversely associated with group cohesion and solidarity. In both agencies, for example, racially homogeneous work groups were more cohesive than were racially mixed units. In City Agency, moreover, cooperation[53] was greater in units that contained few newcomers and oldtimers but mostly workers with from one to three years' seniority. Sayles, having

51 Leonard R. Sayles, *Behavior of Industrial Work Groups,* New York: Wiley, 1958, p. 113.

52 Seashore, *op. cit.,* p. 82.

53 Cooperation was measured in terms of the willingness of the members of a work group to assume duties for which colleagues who were absent in the field were responsible. Of all clients who came to the agency when their worker was in, a certain proportion was seen; of those who came when their own worker was not in, a certain proportion was seen by other workers; the difference between these two proportions in a work group furnishes the index of cooperation (small differences show much cooperation).

examined 300 work groups in 30 plants but presenting no quantitative data, reports that occupationally heterogeneous work groups, whose members had diverse economic (union) interests, were less prone than others to engage in concerted union action.[54]

Research has also indicated that prestigeful background characteristics of workers are often associated with cohesiveness and solidarity. Seashore found that factory workers in cohesive groups had higher average seniority and were more likely to perceive their own job as having high status than those in other groups.[55] Zaleznik and his colleagues also report that the more solidary subgroups in the factory they studied were composed of workers possessing more prestigeful characteristics, including higher age, seniority, and education, and American or northwest European origins.[56] However, Sayles concludes that the work groups which exhibited most union solidarity tended to be composed of workers of medium status. He explains: "The highest prestige groups in the plant are so favored in their various endowments that they are less likely to exhibit open pressure tactics; the least favored are incapacitated for such tactics. Thus overt concerted interest behavior tends to be more concentrated in the 'upper middle groups' . . ."[57] The solidarity of the middle-status industrial groups may be the result of the ambiguity of the position of the semiskilled worker. The skilled occupations are similar in different firms, and hence their wage rates are determined by the market. The same holds for the unskilled. The positions of semiskilled workers seem to be more closely identified with a specific firm; these workers are often trained on the job and acquire skills that are not readily transferable. The worth of semiskilled labor is consequently ambiguous, since it is not determined by the market; the ambiguity gives these workers more leeway to improve their economic position and thus greater incentives to engage in collective action for this purpose.

Finally, the position of the work group in the larger organization's division of labor influences its social solidarity. Sayles found that groups engaged in tasks considered essential for the operations of the entire plant were more likely to exhibit union solidarity. The importance of the function performed increases a group's power and the chances for successful union action, and in this way promotes higher solidarity. Sayles also notes that union solidarity was lower in groups that performed interdependent differentiated tasks, such as those on assembly lines.[58] Two factors appear to be relevant here. First, in these

[54] Sayles, *op. cit.,* pp. 59–61.
[55] Seashore, *op. cit.,* pp. 87, 91.
[56] Zaleznik *et al., op. cit.,* pp. 69, 144–158, 198–212. But in the welfare agencies, group cohesion was not associated with high seniority.
[57] Sayles, *op. cit.,* p. 55.
[58] *Ibid.,* pp. 61–64, 83–84, 92–93.

work groups, in contrast to other kinds, those who worked in close association with one another had different skills and consequently different economic (union) interests. In addition, these workers were more closely tied to their work, because of its interdependent nature, and could not move about in the shop to associate with workers of like interests as could, for example, maintenance workers. But union solidarity requires that workers with the same economic interests have opportunities for freely associating with one another.

The complex and often contradictory findings with regard to the conditions that produce group cohesiveness and social solidarity suggest that much research remains to be done in this area. The results will probably show that the conditions of group solidarity are much more complex than is implied in the simple hypothesis that solidarity depends directly on membership homogeneity, or on prestigeful characteristics, or even on the importance of the group's function for the larger organization.

Comparison of Two Formal Organizations. It has long been asserted that work groups should not be studied in isolation but in the context of the larger organization of which they are a part.[59] However, few studies have used a comparative approach to show how specific differences between formal organizations influence work group structure. The data provided by our studies of the two welfare agencies make such a comparison possible. A discussion of the main characteristics of these agencies appears in the Appendix. Here we shall only summarize some of the main differences between the two formal structures. City Agency was considerably larger than County Agency, the former employing over 1000 persons, the latter, less than 200. The management of County Agency tended to place more emphasis on social-work training than did that of City Agency. There was a manual of operating rules for each worker in County Agency but not in City Agency. City Agency had considerably more turnover than County, and thus County employees enjoyed higher average seniority. Finally, the office ecology was not the same. Although in both organizations members of several units occupied the same work room, members of the same unit had adjoining desks in City Agency but not in County, where members of all units were scattered throughout the room. We shall explore some of the implications of these differences for social relations within the two agencies.

First, there was a difference in orientation to clients. Although the modal orientations of the caseworkers in the two agencies were quite similar, the extremes were different. For example, the proportion who

---

[59] For one statement calling for such an approach, see William F. Whyte, "Small Groups and Large Organizations," John H. Rohrer and Muzafer Sherif (eds.), *Social Psychology at the Crossroads,* New York: Harper, 1951, pp. 299–312.

firmly favored raising the assistance allowance was about the same in City Agency (48 per cent) as in County Agency (56 per cent), but while fully 18 per cent of the City workers expressed the opposite opinion—that grants were sufficient and should not be raised—only 1 per cent of the County workers did. Similarly, whereas most employees in both agencies felt that clients were basically honest, 12 per cent of the City workers held that many clients were dishonest while only 1 per cent of those at County did. These findings suggest that one function of a professionally oriented management, such as that in County Agency, is to screen and eliminate those workers with the most negative attitudes toward clients. Another factor that may well have contributed to these differences, however, was the lower turnover rate at County Agency, which enabled County management and supervisors to know and train their workers better than was possible in City Agency. County management could also better afford to weed out poorly qualified workers (such as those hostile toward clients) than City management with its perennial staff shortage.

We expected that the fact that members of a unit sat together at adjacent desks in City Agency but not in County Agency would provide more opportunity for intra-unit social interaction and result in more cohesive units in the former agency. This prediction was not borne out. When cohesion was measured by the proportion of ingroup friendship choices in a unit, the medians for the two agencies were similar: .19 for the twelve groups studied in City Agency and .22 for the eleven in County Agency. Moreover, the mean proportion of ingroup choices was higher in County Agency (.29) than in City (.18), as was the standard deviation (.24 and .09 respectively). Inspection of the unit scores revealed that only one unit in City Agency had a score above .30 but four units in County Agency were well above this figure. Thus, while both agencies had several units with relatively low cohesion, County Agency but not City Agency had several units with very high cohesion. It appears that ecological factors exerted little influence on ingroup friendship choices; instead, the relatively low turnover rate of workers in County Agency may well have been the decisive factor that explains the differences between the agencies. High turnover in City Agency prevented any work group from developing really high cohesion whereas low turnover in County Agency allowed some work groups to do so despite the scattered seating arrangement, although most groups did not, perhaps in part because of the office ecology.

Another difference observed between the two agencies was in the patterns of consultation among workers. In County Agency, workers who said they worried about their cases were more involved in the consultation network. They were more often consulted and, particularly, they were more apt to consult others. Thus, 39 per cent of the 18 high worriers, 15 per cent of the 48 medium worriers, and none of the 20 nonworriers reported that they consulted colleagues often.[60] In City Agency, on the other hand, worriers did not participate more in consultation than others. This difference may well have been due to the existence of a procedure manual in County Agency and its absence in City Agency. Consultation among colleagues is of great importance not only for obtaining information but also for social support that facilitates decision-making, as we shall point out in Chapter V. Most caseworkers in both agencies regularly discussed problems with colleagues. The absence of a procedure manual accentuates the need for informal consultation, especially for inexperienced workers, who must often ask colleagues or the supervisor what the official procedures are, whereas inexperienced workers can look up this type of information themselves if a manual is available. In City Agency, therefore, some workers had good reason to ask disproportionately many questions, whether they were particularly anxious about their work or not. But since the procedure manual in County Agency obviated this objective need for advice of some workers, the subjective need for advice experienced by workers primarily governed their participation in consultation, and this subjective need was greatest for anxious worriers who wanted to make doubly sure of their decisions before taking action.

This interpretation implies that inexperienced workers consult more and experienced ones are more often consulted in the agency without a manual, but that there are no such differences in the agency with a manual. The findings confirm this inference. In City Agency 78 per cent of the 18 oldtimers but only 50 per cent of the 42 less experienced workers were regularly consulted by colleagues, whereas in County Agency experience did not affect being consulted: 44 per cent of the 48 oldtimers and 43 per cent of the 37 others were regularly consulted. Frequency of consulting reveals complementary patterns. The absence of a rule book apparently puts a premium on experience. It seems that written procedures can become a functional substitute for personal experience, and that this aspect of bureaucratization affects informal relations in a formal organization in subtle ways by altering the characteristics of individuals that govern their informal status in the peer group.

Whereas seniority affected consultation in City but not in County Agency, it was associated with popularity in County but not in City Agency. In County Agency, 62 per cent of the oldtimers and 38 per cent of the workers with less than three years' service were chosen as

---

[60] Formal observation records also substantiate this pattern: 55 per cent of 11 high worriers, 31 per cent of 29 medium worriers, and 27 per cent of 11 nonworriers were found to be high on initiated contacts per hour to fellow workers.

"friends" by several colleagues. In City Agency, exactly 50 per cent of each group were popular by this criterion. These differences may be due to differences in outside opportunities for employment and in relative turnover, and thus in the process of selection. In the metropolis in which City Agency was located there were many private social-work agencies with superior standards of professional casework. This condition did not hold for the community in which County Agency was located: there were few private agencies, and none whose professional standards were superior to those at County Agency. Besides, other employment opportunities appropriate for college graduates were probably greater in the larger city; for example, there were undoubtedly more opportunities for employment in a variety of white-collar jobs in the metropolis than in the smaller community in which County Agency was located. As a result, some of the best workers in City Agency left for other jobs. Workers who were ambitious, versatile, and oriented toward professional social work often sought other employment offering better pay and more professional opportunities. However, the best workers in County Agency tended to remain, since there were no important competitors for the abilities that they had to offer. The process of negative selection that occurred in City Agency probably made old-timers there somewhat less desirable companions, while in County Agency the better workers and those most committed to social work stayed on and enjoyed high popularity.[61]

In this section, we have focused on the *differences* in the work-group structures of the two agencies. It should be noted, however, that many patterns were the same in both agencies. For example, seniority was directly associated with being respected by colleagues and with being judged competent by the supervisor in both agencies; experience promotes proficiency whether there is a procedure manual or not. But when there is no manual, experience enhances a person's chances of being consulted quite independently of his proficiency. If respect is held constant, seniority and being often consulted were still directly related in City Agency (but not in County Agency). In both agencies, consultants were more popular than workers rarely consulted. And popular workers in both agencies were more self-confident than others (stating that they could do their work without aid from the supervisor).

The foregoing comparison of two formal organizations has provided insights that could not have been derived from the study of a single case. For instance, our conclusion that a written procedure manual influences social relations in certain ways depends on data from two contrasting organizations. Since these interpretations are based on only

---

61 This interpretation assumes that the best caseworkers are typically most popular among colleagues. The data confirm this assumption: there was a direct relationship between being considered one of the best caseworkers and popularity in both agencies.

two cases, however, we cannot even tentatively test our explanatory hypotheses about the influences of given aspects of the formal organization. Differences other than those noted may have been responsible for the observed differences in social relations and group structures. A comparison of many formal organizations, or at least segments of organizations, is required to determine which one of many possible institutional characteristics actually has brought about an observed result.

CONCLUDING REMARKS

This chapter has been devoted to an examination of the social structure of work groups. We have discussed various aspects of informal organization, including norms, cohesion, and informal status, and have analyzed some of the effects exerted by group structure. In the final part dealing with some of the determinants of group structure, we explored first the influence of background characteristics of group members and then those of the larger formal organization. Another major factor influencing the structure of work groups is supervision. It may be thought of as the connecting link between the formal organization and the work group. Supervision will be analyzed in Chapter VI, after we have discussed processes of communication in organizations.

CHAPTER FIVE

Processes of Communication

In preceding chapters we have spoken much of social interaction but little of communication, although when people interact they communicate meaningful information. The two terms refer to the same social processes but to different aspects of them. The concept of social interaction focuses principally upon the formal characteristics of social relation: such terms as frequency, initiative, superordination, and reciprocity indicate its dimensions. The concept of communication, on the other hand, directs attention to the meaningful content conveyed in the encounter, and its characteristics are described by such terms as flow of messages, obstacles, positive and negative reactions, and exchange.

In this chapter we shall draw on both experimental and field studies to analyze the significance of communication processes for group life and particularly for the performance of tasks. Interaction as well as communication aspects of these processes will inevitably be involved in the analysis. Our procedure will be to attempt to interpret contrasting findings; we shall examine some cases and formulate tentative generalizations, then search for negative cases and refine our interpretation accordingly. The major focus will be upon communication among colleagues. Starting with the analysis of communication processes among peers, we shall turn to the significance of status differences for these processes. In a sense, this chapter provides a transition between the discussion of peer relations in Chapter IV and the analysis of hierarchical relations in Chapter VI.

EXPERIMENTS ON COMMUNICATION AND PERFORMANCE

The Significance of Social Interaction. A number of experiments have compared the task performance of individuals and groups; most have found groups to be superior. An early experiment conducted by Allport on the speed with which subjects were able to produce free associations from a word stimulus contrasted subjects who worked alone with others who worked in a room where several were engaged in the same task.[1] Subjects were instructed not to compete. The performance in the social setting was found to be superior to that in isolation. Allport's analysis suggests that, instructions notwithstanding, the social situation led to rivalry. The competitive element introduced by seeing how fast others worked was the factor responsible for the superior performance of individuals in the social setting. Another experiment, reported by Taylor and Faust, compared the performance of single individuals, of pairs working together, and of groups of four working together on finding correct solutions to problems which consisted of a standardized version of the parlor game "twenty questions."[2] Pairs and groups of four were found to be superior to individuals working alone, whether number of questions used, amount of time needed for reaching a correct solution, or number of failures was the criterion of performance. No significant differences in performance were found between the two-man and the four-man groups. Although both experiments were concerned with the effect of social factors on performance, they differed in the operational definition of "social": Allport examined the performance of individuals *working separately in the presence of others,* while Taylor and Faust studied the performance of several persons *working together.*

A third experiment allows us to isolate the effects of working together from the influence of simply being in a social situation. Perlmutter and Montmollin conducted an experiment in which 20 groups of three individuals each were asked to recall correctly a list of nonsense syllables previously presented.[3] In the first part of the experiment, half the subjects worked individually, the answers of each being scored separately, while the other half collaborated on a composite group score; in the second part the situation was reversed so that those who had previously worked as individuals collaborated and those who had previously collaborated in groups worked individually. Even when subjects worked as individuals, however, they were in the presence of others engaged in the same task. Hence, this design eliminates the effect of the social situation, the focus of Allport's study, and isolates that of collaboration. The results show that the performance of groups was, on the average, superior to that of individuals. Besides, the individuals who began by working in a group performed better later, when working on their own, than did those who did not have previous group experience. It appears that collaboration with others

[1] Floyd H. Allport, "The Influence of the Group upon Association and Thought," *Journal of Experimental Psychology,* 3 (1920), pp. 159–182.

[2] Donald W. Taylor and William L. Faust, "Twenty Questions," *Journal of Experimental Psychology,* 44 (1952), pp. 360–368.

[3] Howard V. Perlmutter and Germaine de Montmollin, "Group Learning of Nonsense Syllables," *Journal of Abnormal and Social Psychology,* 42 (1952), pp. 762–769.

in problem-solving improves performance quite independently of any improvements resulting from the mere presence of others, and that the skills acquired in group learning even contribute to subsequent individual work.

What accounts for the superiority of group over individual performance? Is it mere chance? Chance, in the sense of probability, does exert some effect. In the experiment just reported, the chance that a given syllable will be recalled by one of the several persons in a group is greater than the probability that it will be recalled by any single one of them. Studies have found that statistical probability accounts for some of the superiority of groups, but not for all of it.[4] What, then, are the other factors that account for the group's superior performance? An early experiment by Shaw provides one important clue to the answer.[5]

Shaw presented complex puzzles (for example, transporting missionaries and cannibals across a river under specified conditions, or arranging words to complete a poem) to individuals and to groups of four working together. Groups were found to be superior to individuals in solving the puzzles. Shaw also placed an observer in the room where the groups were working and obtained systematic data on the interaction that occurred in the course of trying to solve the problems. Analysis of the interaction data showed that incorrect suggestions were often made and then rejected; occasionally the person who made the suggestion later saw his own error, but more often (in 160 of 217 cases) another person corrected him. This experience seems to indicate that social interaction provides an error-correcting mechanism. It is not easy for an individual to see his own mistakes, for he approaches a problem within a particular framework of perceptions and assumptions. The fact that various individuals bring different frameworks as well as different experiences and knowledge to the group multiplies the chances that an error made will be detected. The error-correcting property of social interaction is one reason why groups are superior to individuals in solving problems.

Not all studies, however, have found group performance to be superior to that of individuals. An examination of those tasks that groups do not perform as well as individuals will allow us to refine our analysis by specifying the conditions under which groups are generally superior. An experiment by Thorndike reports that groups were superior to individuals in *solving* crossword puzzles but that individ-

---

4 See, for example, Irving Lorge and Herbert Solomon, "Two Models of Group Behavior in the Solution of Eureka-type Problems," *Psychometrika*, 20 (1955), pp. 139–148.

5 Marjorie E. Shaw, "A Comparison of Individuals and Small Groups in the Rational Solution of Complex Problems," *American Journal of Psychology*, 44 (1932), pp. 491–504.

uals were superior to groups in *constructing* them.[6] Both these tasks are quite complex. What is the crucial difference between them? In solving puzzles, there is one correct answer and each step taken toward the solution is either correct or incorrect. This description applies not only to solving crossword puzzles but also to most of the other problems utilized in experiments on task performance. On the other hand, in constructing crossword puzzles there is no single correct solution. The problem is not solved by finding the one right word but rather by coordinating early with later steps. Any word will do as long as it fits together with previous selections and does not obstruct later steps. A guiding framework is important for achieving such coordination, and an implicit framework, which is not easily communicated to others, guides individuals in constructing puzzles. The different frames of reference that individuals bring to a group aid in the search for a correct solution among several alternatives but impede the coordination of different ideas into one consistent whole.[7] Thus, we can refine our generalization and derive a principle that can account for apparently contradictory findings: social communication in a group working on a common task provides a battleground of ideas, which stimulates thinking and, particularly, facilitates detecting false leads, but which simultaneously interferes with coordination. Whether the performance of groups is superior or inferior to that of individuals depends, therefore, on whether the essential task requirement is finding the best solution for a problem or achieving effective coordination.

Social interaction not only provides a correcting mechanism for sifting ideas but also contributes to problem-solving in groups by furnishing social support to individual members. Problem-solving engenders anxieties. An individual makes a tentative first step and begins to wonder whether or not it is correct. His uncertainty produces mental blocks which interfere with his further associations and ideas. In a group situation, however, good suggestions are likely to receive the approval of others. Approval may be explicit in the form of verbal comments or may be implicit in the behavior of others as they nod, smile, look expectantly, or just refrain from interrupting. Such social approval mitigates anxieties and frees the individual to continue his train of thought. There seems to be a contradiction between saying that interaction involves error correction and that it involves social support—the rejection and the approval of ideas—but it does both, only for differ-

---

[6] R. L. Thorndike, "On What Type of Task Will a Group Do Well?" *Journal of Abnormal and Social Psychology,* 33 (1938), pp. 409–413.

[7] See H. G. McCurdy and W. E. Lambert, "The Efficiency of Small Human Groups in the Solution of Problems Requiring Genuine Cooperation," *Journal of Personnel,* 20 (1952), pp. 478–494, for another study where the task is coordination and where individuals were found to be superior to groups.

ent suggestions and for different persons. Since interaction provides a battleground for ideas that serves to sift the suggestions made by the various members of the group, the ideas of some members are rejected, and these members do not experience the support that facilitates their thinking. But the ideas of others, or even ideas of the same members at other times, are approved, and this support helps them to develop their ideas further. Ideally, only wrong suggestions are rejected, and the thinking of those whose early suggestions promise to lead to the correct final solution is facilitated by social approval. But actually, other factors may influence this interaction, causing group members sometimes to reject correct solutions and to accept incorrect ones.

Still another aspect of social interaction that contributes to problem-solving is illustrated by a paradox implicit in the conclusions of Allport and those of the other experimenters discussed. The social situation was usually found to improve performance, but in Allport's experiment this improvement was due to the competition engendered by the presence of others, whereas in most experiments it was the result of cooperation among group members. Competition and cooperation seem to be opposites, but both, nevertheless, apparently improve performance in comparison to what it would be without either kind of social interaction, that is, over the performance of individuals working in isolation. To be sure, we can also ask whether competition or cooperation in a group makes a greater contribution to task performance. Experiments as well as field studies indicate that performance in competitive groups is inferior to that in cooperative groups.[8] In the light of Allport's findings, as well as others, this difference should probably be interpreted to indicate not that competition inherently impedes performance but that some of its by-products do, notably, a lack of social support and an inability to pursue common goals in predominantly competitive groups. (We have seen in Chapter IV how work groups tend to protect themselves against these consequences of competition that threaten their solidarity.) Some forms of competition occur in most groups, if not in all, and contribute to task performance.

In most groups, and particularly in those that appear to be basically cooperative, social interaction contains competitive as well as cooperative elements. Thus, in the experimental groups under consideration, instructions that members were to work together and pursue common objectives gave them an incentive to cooperate and support one another's efforts, since all benefited from the contribution each made to the correct solution of the problem. (In solidary work

---

[8] For example, see the experiment by Morton Deutsch, "An Experimental Study of the Effects of Cooperation and Competition upon Group Process," *Human Relations*, 2 (1949), pp. 199–231; and the field study by Peter M. Blau, *The Dynamics of Bureaucracy*, Chicago: University of Chicago Press, 1955, pp. 49–67.

groups, too, there is much cooperation in the form of consultation, enforcement of common norms, and the like.) Within this fundamentally cooperative framework, however, interaction will give rise to competitive processes since the members of a group typically seek to gain the respect of one another. Each member wants to be highly thought of by the rest—preferably more highly than others are. Such competition has positive consequences for performance. In groups working together on a task, competition for respect motivates members to make good suggestions and also to prove their superior abilities by criticizing the suggestions of others. This competition is the social mechanism that mobilizes the energies of group members and encourages them to devote effort to finding solutions. It is this social mechanism that induces them to bring their different frameworks to bear on problems, resulting in the correction of errors. Such competition does, of course, interfere with the furnishing of social support to group members. Ideally, the two processes must be kept in balance so that the competition is not allowed to tear the group apart and the supporting processes are not allowed to lull the group into a situation where the members turn from working on task problems to an exclusive concern with one another's feelings.[9]

Dysfunctions of Hierarchical Differentiation. The superiority of groups over individuals in certain kinds of task performance has been attributed primarily to three factors: (1) the sifting of suggestions in social interaction serves as an error-correction mechanism; (2) the social support furnished in interaction facilitates thinking; and (3) the competition among members for respect mobilizes their energies for contributing to the task. If our interpretation is correct, a comparison of groups that differ in these characteristics should reveal appropriate differences in performance. The best test of these explanatory hypotheses would be to introduce experimental differences in each of the three factors while controlling the remaining two and other relevant conditions. In the absence of such experimental evidence, we shall attempt to test our interpretations indirectly by examining social conditions that appear to inhibit these processes and noting the consequences for performance.

---

[9] Bales has discussed this dilemma posed by, in his terms, "task" and "socio-emotional" problems. He suggests that concentration on the group task gives rise to disturbances in the relations between members and that these socio-emotional problems must be solved if the group is to continue to work successfully on the task. Two mechanisms to cope with this dilemma are differentiation of time (at one period, task problems are worked on, and at another, socio-emotional problems) and differentiation of roles (some members focus on the task and others concentrate on resolving conflicts and tensions). See Robert F. Bales, "The Equilibrium Problem in Small Groups," Talcott Parsons *et al.,* *Working Papers in the Theory of Action,* Glencoe, Ill.: Free Press, 1953, pp. 111–161.

Hierarchical differentiation of status, particularly when formally established, appears to curtail these three group processes. First, explicit status distinctions tend to reduce social interaction and social support. A field study by Wessen of the personnel in a large general hospital found that social interaction typically followed status lines and was inhibited by status boundaries. Most social contacts of doctors were with other doctors, nurses primarily associated with other nurses, and the same was true for lower-status ward personnel.[10] An investigation by Kelley found that in experimentally created hierarchies feelings of friendliness across hierarchical boundaries declined when the upper-status individuals were insecure in their positions and the lower-status individuals had no chance of upward mobility.[11] Several studies report a tendency for lower-status group members to direct their friendship choices disproportionately to upper-status members.[12] Since upper-status members tend not to reciprocate but to direct their choices to others also high in status, lower-status members do not receive their share of the social support that is needed for stimulating thought and making suggestions.

Second, formally instituted status differences tend to undermine the process of competition for respect. In a *peer* group, a member's standing rests primarily on the respect of others, and this fact makes their respect and deference most important. But in the presence of formal distinctions of status, the respect of others is not the primary basis of a person's social standing, and competition for respect loses much, though not all, of its significance. Besides, status distinctions generally destroy the *laissez-faire* character of competition for respect. Members no longer seek to be respected by any and all, inasmuch as being respected by those of high status is of more significance than being respected by others of lower status. A field experiment conducted by Hurwitz and his colleagues provides some support for this interpretation.[13] Participation in discussions at a conference on mental hygiene was found to be affected by the influence and the professional prestige of various members. Records of frequency of communication between conference members reveal that those of high prestige participated most in discussions, and that both

10 Albert F. Wessen, "Hospital Ideology and Communication between Ward Personnel," E. Gartly Jaco (ed.), *Patients, Physicians and Illness*, Glencoe, Ill.: Free Press, 1958, pp. 453–458.

11 Harold H. Kelley, "Communication in Experimentally Created Hierarchies," *Human Relations*, 4 (1951), pp. 39–56.

12 See the studies by Jacob I. Hurwitz *et al.*, "Some Effects of Power on the Relations among Group Members," Dorwin Cartwright and Alvin Zander (eds.), *Group Dynamics*, Evanston, Ill.: Row, Peterson, 1953, pp. 483–492; and Muzafer Sherif, "A Preliminary Experimental Study of Inter-group Relations," John H. Rohrer and Muzafer Sherif (eds.), *Social Psychology at the Crossroads*, New York: Harper, 1951, pp. 406–410.

13 Hurwitz *et al.*, *op. cit.*, pp. 486–489.

low- and high-prestige persons directed most of their remarks to high-prestige persons. Liking choices were disproportionately often directed to high-status individuals, and there seemed to be more concern with receiving liking choices from high- than from low-status members. In short, participants appear to have competed primarily for being regarded and liked by the most prestigeful others. Seeking to win the approval of an elite has undoubtedly implications for conduct quite different from those of striving to earn the respect of most members of a group.

Third, status differences distort the error-correcting function of social interaction. It is not easy to oppose the judgment of a person with superior power or prestige, and most people will think twice before doing so. At the very least, they will want to be quite sure of their criticism before voicing it. In contrast, people do not usually hesitate to criticize the opinion of a person whom they do not respect. Indeed, lack of respect will incline them to find fault with proposals. Hence, there is a reluctance to criticize the suggestions offered by high-status members and a ready inclination to reject the suggestions and criticisms offered by low-status members. This interpretation gains support from an experiment in which Torrance observed the interaction during problem-solving sessions in three-man groups composed of Air Force personnel of different military ranks.[14] He found that the incorrect suggestions of high-status group members (crew captains) were disproportionately often accepted and the correct suggestions of low-status members (sergeant gunners) were disproportionately often rejected. The fact that status influences whose opinion carries most weight interferes with the detection of errors in group problem-solving.

There is, then, some indication that differentiation of hierarchical status in groups attenuates the very characteristics that have been hypothesized to be responsible for the superiority of groups over individuals in problem-solving. The interpretation implies, consequently, that the more pronounced the hierarchical differences in a group, the less effectively it will perform. There is some evidence in support of this inference. For example, in Torrance's experiment, permanent combat crews performed less well in solving problems than did temporary crews composed of similar personnel. Torrance accounts for this finding by explaining: "In the temporary crews, the effects of status differences seems [*sic*] to have been diminished and all members less frequently fail to influence when they have the cor-

14 E. Paul Torrance, "Some Consequences of Power Differences on Decision Making in Permanent and Temporary Three-Man Groups," A. Paul Hare, *et. al.*, (eds.), *Small Groups*, New York: Knopf, 1955, pp. 482–492.

rect answer."[15] The famous studies on the effects of social climates inspired by Lewin and conducted by White and Lippitt also tend to support our prediction.[16] White and Lippitt conclude that groups of boys under "democratic" leaders performed more "efficiently"—if this term is defined to include member satisfaction as well as achievement of work goals—than those under autocratic leaders. The efficiency was especially evident in the groups' ability to work and cope with problems in the absence of the adult leader. Finally, several studies have reported that workers under authoritarian supervision do not perform as well as those whose supervisors minimize status distinctions by delegating work, encouraging discretion, and similar practices.[17] These studies suggest that, as was expected, a diminution of status differentials improves performance.

Functions of Hierarchical Structure. Research evidence, however, does not entirely support our expectation regarding the adverse effects of hierarchy on performance. Some studies have found groups with a status hierarchy to perform better than those with less differentiation of social status. Let us examine these studies and their implications for our theory. An experiment by Maier and Solem contrasts groups of five or six persons with and without an appointed discussion leader.[18] The task was solving mathematical problems. Groups with a leader proved to be superior in performance to those without one. An analysis of the interaction during the problem-solving sessions provides a clue for understanding this apparently negative case. Majority opinions on how to attack a problem tended to develop in these groups, and the majority often exerted pressures to suppress minority opinions, including correct suggestions. Discussion leaders, who acted as chairmen, saw to it that all members had an opportunity to express their views. The fact that persons in the minority had more opportunity to contribute to the correct solution in groups with a discussion leader than in those without seems to have been responsible for the superior performance of the former.

In this experiment, the social differentiation of a group into a majority and a minority created obstacles to the free flow of commu-

15 *Ibid.,* p. 485.

16 Ralph White and Ronald Lippitt, "Leader Behavior and Member Reaction in Three 'Social Climates,'" Cartwright and Zander, *op. cit.,* pp. 585–611. See also the same authors' *Autocracy and Democracy,* New York: Harper, 1960.

17 See, for example, the study by Robert L. Kahn and Daniel Katz, "Leadership Practices in Relation to Productivity and Morale," Cartwright and Zander, *op. cit.,* pp. 612–628; and Michael Argyle *et al.,* "Supervisory Methods Related to Productivity, Absenteeism, and Labour Turnover," *Human Relations,* 11 (1958), pp. 23–40.

18 Norman R. F. Maier and Allen R. Solem, "The Contributions of a Discussion Leader to the Quality of Group Thinking," *Human Relations,* 5 (1952), pp. 277–288.

nication, just as hierarchical differentiation did in many other groups, and both forms of differentiation had adverse effects on problem-solving. The presence of a leader who removed obstacles to communication—those created by other aspects of group differentiation—improved the group's problem-solving abilities. This new information allows us to refine our theory by specifying why and under which conditions a status hierarchy interferes with performance. We have seen that the free flow of communication—in the form of criticisms, suggestions, manifestations of respect, and expressions of approval furnishing social support—furthers problem-solving. Hierarchical differentiation of status usually impedes the free flow of communication, and for this specific reason such differentiation tends to be detrimental for task performance. If leadership does not block but frees the flow of communication—as in the case of a discussion leader or procedural chairman in contrast to a dominant power—then leadership will further rather than hinder problem-solving.[19]

Another investigation permits further refinement of our interpretation. Heinicke and Bales studied developmental trends over four sessions of initially leaderless groups engaged in the discussion of a human-relations case.[20] The groups were instructed to arrive at a common solution. Status differences between members (measured by sociometric choices) crystallized in some groups but not in others, and the former were found to be more successful in reaching consensus on case problems. Why did the groups that established a status hierarchy perform the task more successfully? The reason may well be that the task was chiefly one of coordination. The criterion of success was not the quality of the recommendation made but whether the group could agree on a single recommendation. As we noted earlier when comparing the performance of individuals and groups, the free flow of suggestions and criticisms facilitates the sifting of ideas to find the single correct one, but this same process impedes coordination. Hierarchical differentiation of status, by curbing the free flow of ideas, facilitates the coordination of opinions to achieve consensus, just as the complete absence of communication (individual performance) facilitates coordination. In sum, groups are superior to individuals, and groups in which there is a free flow of communication are superior to groups in which differentiation impedes communication, in solving problems which call for a single correct or best answer; but indi-

[19] This restatement may well also account for the finding in the White and Lippitt study that groups with "democratic" leaders were more efficient than groups with *"laissez-faire"* leaders. See the descriptions of these leadership styles in White and Lippitt, "Leader Behavior and Member Reaction in Three 'Social Climates,'" *op. cit.,* p. 586.

[20] Christoph Heinicke and Robert F. Bales, "Developmental Trends in the Structure of Small Groups," *Sociometry,* 16 (1953), pp. 7–38.

viduals are superior to groups, and hierarchically differentiated groups are superior to undifferentiated groups, in performing tasks that primarily depend on efficient coordination.

A final group of studies reinforces the conclusion that hierarchical organization is important for coordination. These are experiments in which the communication network in a group is manipulated. Research by Leavitt, based on earlier work by Bavelas, imposed various communication networks on groups of five subjects.[21] A variety of networks was used, but we shall consider only the two extremes of centralization and decentralization. In the "wheel" or "X," a central person could communicate with all others, and they could communicate only with him. In the "circle" or "O," every person communicated with two neighbors. All subjects sat in separate cubicles and communicated in writing only. Each subject was given a sheet with five symbols on it and his task was to determine which one symbol was common to all the sheets. This is essentially a problem of coordination. Although there is a single correct solution, the difficulty is bringing the appropriate pieces of information together; once they are brought together, arriving at the answer is a trivial problem. The performance of wheel groups has been consistently found to be superior to that of circle groups. A centralized network of communication apparently contributes to effective coordination.

Later studies suggest that the crucial factor is not the formal network of communication but the group's ability to become hierarchically organized. The wheel imposes such hierarchical organization on a group, since the person in the central position naturally assumes the dominant role of coordinator. But if other types of groups are able to achieve status differentiation, then their performance becomes as good as that of the wheel groups. For example, Guetzkow and Simon, using the same equipment and task as Bavelas and Leavitt, compared the performance of groups when members were linked by the wheel, the circle, and an all-channel network (all members can communicate with all others).[22] Previous calculations had indicated that there were no significant differences between the three networks in terms of the time needed to accomplish the task *if* they were efficiently utilized;

[21] Harold J. Leavitt, "Some Effects of Certain Communication Patterns on Group Performance," *Journal of Abnormal and Social Psychology*, 46 (1951), pp. 38–50; see also, Alex Bavelas, "Communication Patterns in Task-Oriented Groups," *Journal of the Acoustical Society of America*, 22 (1950), pp. 725–730.

[22] Harold Guetzkow and Herbert A. Simon, "The Impact of Certain Communication Nets upon Organization and Performance in Task-Oriented Groups," *Management Science*, 1 (1955), pp. 233–250. See also Maul Mulder, "Communication Structure, Decision Structure and Group Performance," *Sociometry*, 23 (1960), pp. 1–14.

that is, any differences among the groups using the three networks was not due to the intrinsic limitations of a given network but rather to the use made of it. However, the difficulty of the organizational problem varied from network to network. The circle groups were expected to have the most difficult organizational problem, since they needed to establish relays for message passing as well as select one member to coordinate and distribute information. The wheel groups faced the least difficult organizational problems, since the network imposed a structure upon them. All-channel groups were considered intermediate, their problems being to eliminate excess channels and decide upon one person as coordinator. After a trial period, 56 groups were given 20 successive tasks with two-minute breaks between them during which members were allowed to discuss ways of improving their organization (also by an exchange of written messages). Using as a measure of efficiency the time needed to complete the task, wheel groups reached their maximum efficiency after only a few trials, all-channel groups were slower during early trials but most eventually performed as well as wheel groups, and circle groups generally did not reach optimum performance during the 20 trials. When and whether all-channel and circle groups achieved maximum efficiency depended on their success in developing a differentiated structure for communication.

In short, performance was negatively correlated with the difficulty of the organizational problems facing the groups. Among the groups of each type that did develop a hierarchical organization,[23] however, there were no significant differences in the efficiency with which they performed their tasks. A later publication analyzed the messages sent by group members during the periods between trials and found that whether or not the all-channel or circle groups developed a hierarchical organization was related to the number of specific proposals made and promulgated in planning such organizational arrangements.[24]

These experimental results strengthen our previous conclusions that hierarchical organization serves important functions for achiev-

[23] All 15 wheel groups, 17 out of 20 all-channel groups, and only 3 of 21 circle groups developed hierarchies during the 20 trials.

[24] Harold Guetzkow and William R. Dill, "Factors in the Organizational Development of Task-Oriented Groups," *Sociometry*, 20 (1957), pp. 175–204. Guetzkow and Dill also tested the hypothesis that circle groups would be more likely to achieve organization if they were permitted all-channel communication between trials. The results, however, were negative: the circle groups that were permitted intertrial all-channel communication were slightly more likely to become organized than regular circle groups but the average performance of the two types of groups was similar because the performance of the unorganized groups among those with all-channel networks between trials was particularly low.

ing coordination and that it does so specifically by restricting the free flow of communication. There is also some support for our hypothesis that the free flow of communication without hierarchical or other barriers is best suited for advancing new solutions to problems, including the ideas necessary to create a hierarchical organization where none exists. While hierarchically organized groups performed the coordination task better than groups not so organized, all-channel groups were more successful in developing an effective organization than were those groups where communication was restricted (circle groups).

FIELD STUDIES OF COMMUNICATION IN FORMAL ORGANIZATIONS

Consultation among Peers. In turning from a discussion of controlled experiments to field studies concerned with communication, we are leaving behind the precision and safety of the laboratory. However, only by entering the field can we ascertain whether conclusions arrived at in the laboratory also hold for natural groups. One question is how accurately the experiment simulates the conditions it is supposed to represent, say, how well laboratory groups whose members are told they have similar interests reflect the salient aspects of solidarity in actual work groups. An even more fundamental problem is posed by the fact that experiments are designed to determine how a given factor in pure form and in the absence of variations in other conditions influences a second factor. Outside the laboratory, however, factors do not occur in pure form (there is no absolute vacuum, and neither is there completely unrestricted communication). Whether a condition occurs, or what effect it has if it does occur, is not independent of but contingent on other existing conditions. Field studies are needed to ascertain which social conditions typically occur together and which combinations of factors may be relevant for producing a given effect. Experiments are required to confirm the hypotheses derived from such field studies that a certain factor or set of factors actually has a certain effect. And field studies, in turn, must validate generalizations derived from experiments by showing that they apply outside the laboratory. The best approach, then, is to alternate between both methods; but in most areas of social research, experimentation is rarely used and, indeed, may not be feasible. Communication is one of the few subjects that have been investigated experimentally as well as in field studies and surveys, and this double-pronged approach lends it special significance.

As our first field study on communication, we undertake to analyze the interaction processes among colleagues in a federal law-enforcement agency.[25] The main duty of the agents was to investigate business establishments in order to determine their compliance with two federal laws. The work was complex and involved a high degree of discretion. Agents not only had to know—or at least to know about—the many general regulations that governed their work, including legislative acts and amendments, administrative interpretations, and court decisions, but they also had to be able to gather and sift information from many sources on the firms investigated. The duty to detect possibly concealed violations as well as the complexity of the task required that agents be able to exercise discretion; uniform law enforcement, however, required that decisions conform strictly to legal principles. The control system in the organization was designed to meet this double requirement.

The operations of the agents were controlled through an evaluation of results achieved rather than by means of detailed operating rules. The agents enjoyed considerable freedom in deciding how to proceed—for example, nobody checked on how they spent their time either in or out of the office—but their results (decisions) had to conform strictly to the law. They knew that their work required rigid conformity to the law of the land since making exceptions, even for the sake of adhering to the intent of the law, could open a Pandora's box of legal loopholes. The importance of attaining correct results in strict conformity with the legal standards was emphasized by having cases reviewed by both the supervisors and a special review unit, and statistical records of performance also focused attention on results; for example, records were kept on the proportion of cases in which violations had been discovered. Errors of decision detected by either review and the quantitative performance record were given great weight in the periodic rating of agents by their supervisors.

Indications were that evaluation on the basis of results achieved rather than methods employed fostered disciplined responsibility among agents. Emphasis in an organization on conformity with operating procedures discourages the exercise of initiative and the willingness to assume responsibility. The federal-agency system, in contrast, permitted individual agents considerable freedom in their work but exerted constraints to make their final decisions conform to general legal principles. Not the road taken but the destination reached was the test of performance. This reward system promoted responsibility among agents in both senses of the term: it encouraged them to assume responsibility for their decisions and to exercise discretion, and it also

25 See Blau, *op. cit.*, pp. 99–115.

held them accountable for making responsible decisions in conformity with all the relevant official standards.[26]

Because agents were free to arrive at their own decisions, their work satisfaction was high. The discretion they exercised made their jobs challenging and interesting. But such responsibility engendered anxieties over decision-making which interfered with the capacity to make correct decisions. If agents encountered problems in their work, they were expected to confer with their supervisors, who might in turn send them to a staff attorney for further advice. However, this official procedure did not and could not lessen the anxiety aroused by concern over the correctness of decisions. Since the supervisor's evaluation of their work was a major cause of this anxiety, agents could not relieve it by coming to him with their difficulties. In fact, agents were reluctant to go to a supervisor with their problems for fear that doing so would reveal their ignorance—or, at least, their inability to act independently—and thus have adverse effects on their ratings.

These obstacles to the use of official channels of communication led agents to satisfy their needs for advice and social support by consulting one another. While the practice of turning to colleagues for advice was officially prohibited, it was tolerated, inasmuch as such operating rules were generally not strictly enforced. Consultation among peers appears to have had important consequences for the organization. This cooperative practice transformed an aggregate of individuals who merely had the same supervisor into a cohesive group. Moreover, it improved decision-making, not only by supplying information and advice when needed but also by reducing anxiety over decisions generally. The mere knowledge that one could ask a colleague for help when in difficulty decreased the anxiety engendered by the need to make complex decisions. Besides, the experience of being regularly asked by others for advice increased an agent's confidence in his own decisions. Hence, the decision-making ability of both participants was likely to benefit from consultations. By reducing anxiety and strengthening self-confidence, the pattern of unofficial consultation probably improved decisions even when no consultation took place. It should be noted that this conclusion is inferential. Although participation in consultation was associated with superior performance,[27] it is impossible to tell whether this association actually indicates that participation improved performance or merely that competent agents were more apt to be drawn into consultation. The latter was undoubtedly the case, but the question is whether the former was

---

[26] On the double meaning of "responsibility," see Marshall E. Dimock, *Administrative Vitality*, New York: Harper, 1959, pp. 218–219.
[27] See Blau, *op. cit.*, pp. 106–107.

also the case. To demonstrate that consultation affects decision-making would require an experimental or panel design.

Hierarchical status differences created obstacles to communication in this field situation, just as they did in laboratory experiments. Other field studies provide further support for the validity of this generalization. Argyris reports that supervisors in an industrial setting were very selective in the information they communicated to their superiors, tending to minimize problems, to emphasize successes, and to relay information detrimental to other supervisors whenever possible.[28] And research conducted by Blau in an employment agency indicates how operating directives became adjusted, redefined, and amplified as they passed from the upper levels of the hierarchy to the lower.[29] Finally, a study by Zaleznik replicates the finding from the law-enforcement agency in a machine shop.[30] These manual workers were also reluctant to approach their supervisor with their problems and instead turned to their peers. In particular, workers focused their requests for help on one individual who was high in seniority and who appeared to function as an informal leader.

The Dynamics of Communication Processes. A case study in which Shepard analyzes the patterns of consultation in a university research organization provides some interesting contrasts and parallels.[31] Most of the staff members of this engineering laboratory were recent university graduates who held temporary positions, which they looked upon primarily as a valuable opportunity to acquire good research experience—an advanced program of postgraduate training. Salaries were low compared with those engineers could command in industry. The staff was willing to sacrifice present income for experience and anticipated future earnings. Salaries were determined by the university, and superiors in the research organization had no control over them. Moreover, there was little chance for (and little interest in) promotion. Hence, employees were not dependent upon their superiors for receiving formal rewards—a situation quite different from that in most organizations.

We have seen that hierarchical dependence blocks the free flow of communications and, more specifically, disinclines staff members to

[28] Chris Argyris, *Executive Leadership*, New York: Harper, 1953, pp. 46–48.

[29] Blau, *op. cit.*, pp. 21–28.

[30] Abraham Zaleznik, *Worker Satisfaction and Development*, Boston: Graduate School of Business Administration, Harvard University, 1956, pp. 36–41.

[31] Herbert A. Shepard, "The Value System of a University Research Group," *American Sociological Review*, 19 (1954), pp. 456–462. For a study that compares communication patterns in the administrative and the scientific sections of a large federal research bureau, see Robert S. Weiss, *Processes of Organization*, Ann Arbor: Institute for Social Research, University of Michigan, 1956.

discuss their problems with a superior for fear of revealing their ignorance to him. Where creativity is valued there is also the danger that
free discussions will not occur even among peers, since each person
will be concerned with "getting credit" for his new ideas. Such communication barriers were not prevalent in this research organization:
engineers readily discussed their problems with one another regardless of official rank.[32] Although he had no quantitative data it was
Shepard's impression that this practice of freely talking problems over
with colleagues stimulated ideas and improved research productivity.
Indeed, these discussions seem to have served as a means for acquiring
status and as an informal reward system. In the absence of formal rewards the prestige gained by demonstrating technical knowledge and
solving complex problems provided an incentive for exerting effort.
Moreover, the exchange of technical ideas in these discussions was a
learning experience for all participants, which constituted another
informal reward.

Let us contrast communication patterns in the university research group with those found in the federal law-enforcement agency.
The free flow of consultations among colleagues probably improved
performance in both organizations. Communications across hierarchical lines were more restricted in the law-enforcement agency than in
the research organization—an expected consequence of the lesser hierarchical dependence in the latter. As we have seen, however, hierarchical dependence did not appear to impede consultation among colleagues in the federal agency. Perhaps advice would have been given
less freely if the agents in the federal agency had received formal
credit for having original ideas. But they obtained formal rewards
only for ideas that contributed to their own cases, not for all good
ideas, such as those that might help solve the problems in a colleague's
cases. In other words, federal agents were engaged in similar but not
common work, and ideas were given official recognition only in relation to particular case problems. Since these agents, just as Shepard's
engineers but for different reasons, could not gain formal rewards by
withholding ideas from colleagues, the informal rewards they could
gain from freely giving advice governed their conduct.

Shepard suggests that in the research organization, earning the
respect of colleagues served as a substitute for formal rewards. But
if the unofficial pattern of rewarding competence in problem-solving
with high respect has the same function for performance as the official
institution of rewarding such competence with good ratings and ad-

---

[32] There did appear to be some communication barriers between
engineers and technicians (less highly trained employees). Shepard
felt (*op. cit.,* p. 461) that these stemmed from the difficulties of recipro-
cation: technicians could learn much from engineers but not engineers
from technicians.

vancements, may the two not also have the same dysfunctions? If the informal status structure constitutes an effective incentive system, just as the formal status structure does, one would expect differences in informal status to impede communications, just as differences in formal status do. Fear of losing face is probably not much less inhibiting than fear of losing one's place. The study of the research organization provides no information on this matter, but the study of the federal agency does.[33] The most competent agents were most often consulted, but most agents discussed the majority of their problems not with these experts but with others of lesser competence. Agents explained this preference by saying that they were reluctant to go regularly to other agents with whom they were not particularly friendly. Instead, they tended to establish partnerships for the purpose of mutual consultation.

Why did agents settle for advice which they knew to be not the best available? A person receives advice in exchange for paying respect. By repeatedly approaching another for advice, the questioner is implicitly acknowledging the superior competence of the adviser. The consultant earns respect, in exchange for which he must devote time and energy to helping colleagues with their problems. However, this system undergoes modifications that can be looked upon as resulting from marginal-utility functions. The respect received for any single consultation declines as the number of consultations increases. A person seldom consulted will appreciate the respect for his judgment shown by a colleague who asks for his advice much more than the one often consulted. Correspondingly, the expenditure of time becomes increasingly difficult to bear as frequent consultations infringe more and more on the time a colleague needs for work on his own cases. Consequently, popular consultants find requests for advice less welcome than others, and may even become impatient and uncooperative when colleagues ask too frequently for their help. The cost of advice to the one who requests it changes in similar ways. Continually paying respect and giving deference to colleagues by asking for their help threatens the self-confidence of an agent and his standing among peers. If the cost of obtaining expert advice becomes too high for an agent, partly because he needs so much of it, he will seek to obtain advice of inferior quality at a cheaper price.

These processes promote the establishment of partnerships for mutual consultation, particularly among officials in frequent need of assistance. No deference is implied by asking the advice of a colleague who often asks one's own advice. In these partnerships, therefore, agents paid for advice not with deference, which they could ill afford, but with consulting time devoted to the partner's problems. This was

[33] See Blau, *op. cit.*, pp. 106–110.

a cheap price, since little demand was made on the consulting time of the less competent agent and he enjoyed being asked for advice. Inasmuch as the anxiety aroused by having to submit decisions to superiors for evaluation interfered with decision-making, agents could benefit from consulting a colleague whose competence was not superior to their own, for *his* decision-making ability on *their* cases was not impeded by such anxiety. Furthermore, the development of consulting partnerships enabled agents to make fewer demands on the time of the experts and thus to approach them more freely when faced with a particularly difficult problem.

Let us summarize the implications of this analysis. The formal status hierarchy in an organization creates obstacles to the free flow of communication. Specifically, dependence on superiors for formal rewards restricts consultation across hierarchical boundaries. Under special conditions, it may also discourage consultation among colleagues, but probably the more typical situation is that hierarchical obstacles to communication foster consultation among peers. The processes of consultation among peers give rise to an informal differentiation of status, because some members of the colleague group earn more respect as consultants than others. Such emerging distinctions of informal status also create obstacles to the free discussion of problems, just as formal status differences do. These obstacles may further redirect the flow of consultation, so that the highest frequency occurs between persons of equal informal as well as formal status. But even consultations among persons of equal competence probably improve the quality of performance, for anxiety interferes less with making decisions on a colleague's cases than with making decisions on one's own.

Variations in Communication Patterns

Reciprocity in Consultation. The foregoing discussion has shown that whether consultations are reciprocal or one-sided has important consequences for the participants and the group structure. Unilateral consultations, where a given worker usually asks another for help, create a differentiation of informal status. By recurrently requesting a colleague's advice, a person socially acknowledges that the other's standing as an expert is superior to his own. Moreover, receiving advice creates social obligations, which constrain a person to return the favor by deferring to his consultant's wishes and suggestions. Hence, power as well as prestige becomes differentiated as the result of one-sided consultations. In unilateral consultations advice is exchanged for informal standing, while in consulting partnerships there is a reciprocal exchange of advice. In the latter situation no differentiation of status occurs between participants, since advice received at one time is repaid not by deference but by giving advice at a later time. We may further explore these patterns by attempting to determine what the conditions are that lead to more or less reciprocity in a group's consultation network and by examining some implications of such reciprocity.

A measure of perceived reciprocity in consultation was obtained in City Agency by asking caseworkers which colleagues they consulted on work problems and which ones regularly consulted them. If several members of a work group named the same person on both questions, the group was assigned a high score on the reciprocity index; if not, it received a low score.[34] Our data suggest that work pressure promoted reciprocity in consultations. The indicator of work pressure used was the number of new cases assigned to a worker in a month, because new cases made urgent demands on a worker's time.[35] In work groups marked by high reciprocity, 13 out of 22 workers were working under high pressure (more than 15 new cases); in low-reciprocity groups only 4 out of 23 workers were under high pressure. This association suggests that workers under high pressure were more likely to develop reciprocal partnerships to meet their need for consultation, since such networks make it easier to obtain advice.

Once a reciprocal-consultation structure has developed in a group, it influences other aspects of the communication patterns. In high-reciprocity groups the amount of work pressure on individuals was directly associated with their tendency to consult colleagues,[36] but in low-reciprocity groups this association was inverse (see Table 11). Thus, in groups with reciprocal-consultation networks hardly any of the workers under little pressure (fewer than 11 new cases) regularly consulted colleagues, but the majority of those under much pressure did so. In contrast, in groups with little reciprocal consultation the

[34] The index of perceived reciprocity was computed by dividing the number of identical choices on both questions in a unit by the total number of choices made and received by workers in the unit. Units above the median were considered high in reciprocity. A measure of *actual* reciprocity in sociometric choices of consultants based on the choices of both partners was also computed. However, this index showed little relation to perceived reciprocity, and it was not associated with other factors in the same way as perceived reciprocity. Perhaps reciprocity is effective only if it is so perceived by the subjects; but it is also possible that the actual reciprocity index was unreliable, since there were very few actual reciprocated choices among workers.

[35] These data taken from the official records were available for only 45 of the 60 workers.

[36] Frequency of consulting others was determined by sociometric methods. Workers were asked which colleagues frequently came to them for advice. If a worker was named on this question by one or more respondents he was considered to consult others regularly.

TABLE 11. RECIPROCITY IN CONSULTATIONS, WORK PRESSURE, AND PER CENT REGULARLY CONSULTING COLLEAGUES

Number of New Cases (Work Pressure)	Reciprocity in Group	
	High	Low
10 or fewer (low)	17% (6)*	60% (5)
11 to 15 (medium)	100% (3)	57% (14)
16 and more (high)	54% (13)	0% (4)

* Numbers in parentheses are those on which corresponding percentages are based.

majority of the workers with few new cases asked for advice frequently, but none of those with many (more than 15) did so. This association suggests that the presence of reciprocal-consultation channels reduced the effort and social cost required for obtaining advice. In the absence of reciprocal partnerships, the greater the pressure of his work the less inclined a worker was to expend the extra effort necessary to get advice. In work groups where reciprocal networks had been established, on the other hand, consultants were readily available and the tendency to ask for advice was primarily governed by the need for it, which was greater if a worker had many new cases with new problems than if he had few. In short, reciprocal-consultation networks made advice readily available to workers when they needed it most and not merely when relatively low work pressure permitted them to devote special energy to obtaining it.

The extent of reciprocal consultation in a group not only influenced the conditions under which a worker asked for advice but also influenced whose advice was most often sought. In low-reciprocity groups, highly competent workers were more often consulted than others and were less likely to ask colleagues for advice.[37] But in high-reciprocity groups, there was no relationship between competence and either being consulted or consulting. This pattern is exactly what one would predict: workers in low-reciprocity groups typically go to experts for advice, since they have not established consultation partnerships, while workers in high-reciprocity groups do not concentrate their requests for advice on experts but usually consult in partnerships.

Reciprocity was also found to reverse the relationship between self-confidence and being consulted, as Table 12 shows.[38] In low-reciprocity groups, self-confident workers were more likely than others

[37] Both of these variables were measured by sociometric choices: workers named by others as consultants and workers named by others as asking questions.

[38] The index of self-confidence was whether or not a worker stated he could do his job without help from the supervisor.

Table 12. Reciprocity in Consultations, Self-Confidence, and Per Cent Regularly Consulted

Worker Self-Confident	Reciprocity in Group	
	High	Low
Yes	41% (17)	73% (15)
No	77% (13)	47% (15)

to be regularly consulted by colleagues, just as highly competent workers were. This association again is not unexpected. The more competent caseworkers tended to be more self-confident, and a self-assured bearing as well as technical skills increased the chances that a caseworker would impress others as an expert and, consequently, become a popular consultant. Besides, being regularly consulted by colleagues probably also raises a worker's self-confidence. What is unexpected, however, is that this same association was not present in high-reciprocity groups. On the contrary, there self-confidence was inversely associated with being much consulted by colleagues. We have suggested in the preceding section that the ego-threat posed by frequently asking colleagues for help is what motivates workers to establish consultation partnerships, and this interpretation can also account for the finding here. Workers whose self-confidence had been undermined had most incentive to develop reciprocal consulting arrangements, and they probably found other modest workers more attractive partners than self-assured workers who would be threatening to them. Hence, self-confidence decreased the likelihood of being regularly consulted in groups where reciprocal partnerships prevailed, although it increased this likelihood in groups where most consultations were unilateral. Moreover, being regularly consulted in a reciprocal partnership, as distinguished from being often asked for advice in a nonreciprocal situation, is not particularly apt to promote self-confidence.[39]

Homophily and Heterophily in Consultation. An earlier chapter stressed the importance, for operations, of the orientations of members of the organization to their work. Now we shall briefly consider the significance of these orientations for the effectiveness of consultations among colleagues. The term "homophily" has been used to refer to friendships between persons having similar values or other characteristics.[40] We shall use the concepts of homophily and heterophily to refer to the similarity or difference in value orientations between associates.

[39] How typical these patterns are is, however, questionable, since data from County Agency did not replicate them.

[40] See Paul F. Lazarsfeld and Robert K. Merton, "Friendship as Social Process," Morroe Berger *et al.* (eds.), *Freedom and Control in Modern Society*, New York: Van Nostrand, 1954, p. 23.

The question we want to raise is: which benefits performance most, consulting colleagues who have values similar to one's own, or consulting those with different values? Pelz's study of a government medical-research organization attempts to answer this question.[41] The researchers were classified as being either "scientific" or "institutional" in their orientation. In general, these two orientations bear a close resemblance to Gouldner's "cosmopolitan" and "local" orientations, respectively.[42] Pelz averaged the orientations of the five colleagues named by each scientist as the ones with whom he often discussed his work, and also computed the mean frequency of contacts each scientist reported with those colleagues. It was found that heterophily of orientations among consultants improved scientific performance. Specifically, if the average orientation of a researcher's five colleagues was similar to his own, then frequency of consultation with them was not related to his performance, but if their orientations were different from his, then frequent contacts with them improved his performance. The results were reversed, however, if only the orientation of the one closest colleague was considered. If the closest colleague's orientation was different from that of the respondent, frequency of contact was inversely associated with performance—discussions seemed to be a waste of time. But if the two individuals shared the same orientation, then frequency of contacts was directly associated with research performance.

Pelz interprets these findings as indicating that research performance depends upon the challenging stimulation as well as the support the social environment affords. Discussions with one's closest colleague should furnish social support to facilitate thinking and reduce anxieties. They appear to do this if the colleague's orientation is similar to one's own. If his orientation is different, he is likely to play the role of critic, making discussions with him disturbing so that frequent contacts with him will impede performance. Discussions with other less closely related colleagues, on the other hand, should supply challenges and serve to correct errors resulting from the one-sided viewpoint produced by a person's own orientation. A person's social contacts with colleagues whose orientation is the same as his own will fail to accomplish this, whereas frequent discussions with heterophilous associates in the organization will furnish such stimulation and thus improve research performance. Other data presented support this interpretation. For example, if the field of specialization of a scientist's closest colleague and that of his superior were different from one another, his performance tended to be better than if they were similar

[41] Donald C. Pelz, "Some Social Factors Related to Performance in a Research Organization," *Administrative Science Quarterly*, 1 (1956), pp. 310–325.

[42] See above, at pp. 64 and 66, especially footnotes 6 and 12, Chapter III.

to one another (whether both were similar to or different from his own specialty). Thus, optimum performance resulted if one of the two people with whom a person consulted most often was similar and the other was dissimilar in orientation to him. One provides social support; the other provides challenges and an opportunity for correction of errors.

Suggestive as these conclusions are, they remain only plausible hypotheses at this point. They rest on the assumption that performance is affected by homophily or heterophily, but the direction of influence may be the reverse. For instance, the most competent scientists, those who perform best, may be less reluctant to consult colleagues whose orientations differ from theirs than are researchers who are less competent and consequently less secure. Although the combination of findings reported increases the plausibility of Pelz's interpretations, his survey data cannot demonstrate the validity of his causal inference.

Concluding Remarks

The central topic of this chapter was the significance of the free flow of communication among colleagues. By providing social support, challenging stimulation, error correction, and a *laissez-faire* competition for respect among participants, the free flow of communication contributes to finding solutions to problems, to making decisions, and to creative thinking. But the battleground of ideas generated by such a free flow makes coordination more difficult. Hierarchical differentiation of status tends to block the free flow of communication in a group and thus to impede problem-solving, although some types of leadership have the opposite consequences, such as that of the discussion chairman who prevents suppression of minority opinions.

A hierarchical organization, in part precisely because it restricts the free flow of communication, improves coordination; indeed, it seems to be essential for effective coordination of group effort. This is the dilemma posed by hierarchical differentiation: while it is necessary for coordination, it blocks the communication processes that are vital for stimulating initiative and facilitating decision-making. Moreover, even if there were no formal hierarchy in the organization, communication among peers would be likely to give rise to informal differentiation of status, which also creates obstacles to communication. These considerations illustrate the dynamics of organizational life. Hierarchical structures channel communication processes; communication processes give rise to structural differentiation, and the emergent social structures, in turn, redirect the communication processes. The existence of dilemmas that cannot be definitively and finally resolved is inherent in such dynamic processes.

CHAPTER SIX

The Role of the Supervisor

The authority of superiors in a formal organization is legitimated by legal contract rather than by traditional values or by an ideological identification with a charismatic leader. Employees assume the contractual obligation to follow managerial directives. Commons, in his famous discussion of the wage bargain, states that what the worker sells "when he sells his labor is his *willingness* to use his faculties according to a purpose that has been pointed out to him. He sells his promise to obey commands."[1] The directives controlling a subordinate include the various administrative regulations, the professional or technical principles guiding his activities, and, particularly, they include the orders he receives from his superiors.

The formal authority that has its source in this legal contract, however, is extremely limited. First, as Commons points out,[2] the labor contract is not really an enduring commitment of the employee, since he is free to leave his job if he can find a better one, and neither is it such a commitment on the part of the employer unless tenure provisions or union agreements specifically prohibit dismissals at his free discretion. Second, by its very legal nature, the contract obligates employees to perform only a set of duties in accordance with minimum standards and does not assure their striving to achieve optimum performance. The legal authority of management to assign tasks to employees is rarely questioned—there is willing compliance—but this legal authority does not and cannot command the employee's willingness to devote his ingenuity and energy to performing his tasks to the best of his ability. Important as formal authority is for meeting the minimum requirements of operations in a complex organization, it is not sufficient for attaining efficiency. It promotes compliance with directives and discipline, but does not encourage employees to exert effort, to accept responsibilities, or to exercise initiative.

The narrow scope of formal authority induces management, in the interest of effective operations as well as in its self-interest, to seek to widen the sphere of its influence over employees beyond the con-

---

[1] John R. Commons, *Legal Foundations of Capitalism,* New York: Macmillan, 1924, p. 284 (italics in original).
[2] *Ibid.*, pp. 284–286.

trolling power that rests on the legal contract or on formal sanctions. For this reason many books on management place heavy emphasis on administrative leadership rather than sheer legal authority.[3] They stress the importance of such executive functions as defining the goals and responsibilities of the members of the organization, inspiring them to identify with the objectives of the enterprise and to pursue them to the best of their abilities, motivating them to collaborate for this purpose, and resolving conflicts that may arise in the organization. Executive leadership evidently involves exerting influences that go far beyond the confines of the legal contract and thus cannot be legitimated by it. But, as a recent analysis by Bendix shows, managerial ideologies develop in modern societies that serve to justify the power of management in terms of basic cultural values.[4] These value orientations legitimate administrative leadership and, thereby, transform it into managerial authority.

The problem of finding ways to extend the scope of formal authority is not one that confronts higher management only: it also is a challenge that faces first-line supervisors. For the supervisor cannot effectively discharge his responsibilities without exerting more influence on his subordinates than his formal authority alone permits. The "style of leadership" of a supervisor is of great importance, since it governs the amount of influence he has over subordinates in addition to the power that derives directly from his formal status in the organizational hierarchy. Indeed, these variations in effective authority are what make the empirical study of supervision an interesting and fruitful task for the sociologist. If there were no such variations resulting from differences in leadership styles and if official authority alone determined supervisory practices, everything about them could be learned simply by reading the official procedure manuals and job descriptions.

STYLES OF SUPERVISION

Formal Authority and Leadership. A problem facing all supervisors is to find ways of extending the scope of their influence over subordinates beyond the narrow limits of formal authority. One possible strategy is that of domination. A supervisor may extend his controlling power over subordinates beyond the willing compliance his legal status com-

3 For a classic and a more recent work stressing managerial leadership see Chester I. Barnard, *The Functions of the Executive,* Cambridge, Mass.: Harvard University Press, 1938; and Philip Selznick, *Leadership in Administration,* Evanston, Ill.: Row, Peterson, 1957.

4 Reinhard Bendix, *Work and Authority in Industry,* New York: Wiley, 1956.

mands by resorting to formal sanctions, or to threats of using these sanctions. Quite a different strategy is that of leadership, in which a superior furnishes services that obligate subordinates to him. A supervisor has many opportunities for assisting subordinates. He is responsible for training and advising them, and they will appreciate it if he exerts special effort in doing so and is easily accessible when they need help. He can facilitate their work, for example, by getting tools in short supply or quickly locating a repairman when a machine breaks down. He may back his own work group in interdepartmental conflicts and represent them and their cause to the administration, and he may perform special favors, such as adjusting the vacation schedule to fit the personal preferences of workers. Rendering these kinds of services creates social obligations, and subordinates who are obligated to their supervisor for benefits received will feel they should reciprocate by complying with his requests and special demands. In this manner, the effective leader increases the sphere of his influence over subordinates.

The formal status and official powers of the supervisor help him to provide services to subordinates. To cite an obvious example, his formal status in the organization, which gives him greater access to management and other supervisors than his subordinates have, enables the supervisor to channel needed information, supplies, and services from other departments to his subordinates. But the supervisor who resorts to formal status prerogatives and sanctions in his relations with his subordinates will alienate them. He can use his formal powers to coerce them to do his bidding, to be sure, but this method of supervision is hardly designed to create social obligations and promote a willing compliance with his requests. Far from strengthening his authority, such authoritarian behavior undermines it. Indirectly, however, the supervisor can use the official powers granted him so as to broaden his influence over subordinates and promote willing compliance with his directives, for he can create social obligations by judiciously *refraining* from using all his power of control. For example, a supervisor who does not enforce an unpopular no-smoking rule obligates subordinates to him; but if this rule had not existed, or if he had not had the power to enforce it, he could not have established this social obligation. In short, one function of formal rules and status prerogatives in organizations, although clearly not the only one, is that they bestow powers upon the supervisor that enable him to obligate subordinates and win their good will simply by refraining from using these powers.

Merton points out that effective and stable authority requires that superiors be in a position to observe the actual performance of subordinates and become familiar with their prevailing norms.[5] But he adds that this visibility must not be unrestricted lest it create opposition which impedes effective operations, because subordinates demand some leeway to depart from the ideal requirements of their office. This proviso implies that any departure from official rules that becomes visible to the superior will be suppressed by him; however, it is not necessary for supervisors to act in this fashion. Our analysis suggests that it may not be visibility that must be limited but rather the superior's tendency strictly to enforce all official rules. The greater the field of vision of the superior—his knowledge of formal requirements, group norms, and actual practice—the greater will be his ability to judge which operating rules can be ignored without impairing efficiency and which unofficial practices are rooted in such basic work-group norms that he cannot afford not to tolerate them. Thus, the supervisor's greater range of vision enables him to decide rationally in terms of his responsibility which official rules he must enforce and which he can permit to be violated by subordinates in order to establish social obligations.

Influence over subordinates acquired by obligating them does not constitute an established authority over them, although it may lead to this. For authority requires legitimation. And while authority can be exercised in pair relations, it can originate only in a group because only a group can provide legitimation of the control exercised. What social process legitimates the control exercised by a supervisor? The supervisor's ability to help subordinates solve complex problems commands their respect; and his willingness to furnish help and do favors for them commands their allegiance. As the members of the work group share their respect for and loyalty to the supervisor, there develops a consensus among them that they should comply with his wishes and suggestions. Once established, these norms of allegiance and respect are enforced by the group because all might suffer if some members failed to repay their obligations to the supervisor. In this fashion, compliance within certain bounds becomes a group norm—internalized by group members and enforced by group sanctions. These values legitimate the extension of the supervisor's authority beyond the legally prescribed limits.[6]

Formal and informal authority can now be clearly distinguished. Authority has been earlier defined as the exercise of control that rests on the willing compliance of subordinates with the directives of their superior. To say that this compliance is voluntary, however, does not

---

[5] Robert K. Merton, *Social Theory and Social Structure* (2d ed.), Glencoe, Ill.: Free Press, 1957, pp. 339–350.

[6] A similar point is made by George C. Homans, in his *Social Behavior: Its Elementary Forms*, New York: Harcourt, Brace, 1961, pp. 294–295.

imply that it is independent of social constraints. On the contrary, the social value orientation that legitimates the exercise of authority constrains subordinates to obey the superior's orders. They voluntarily follow the mandates of their own values, which have become internalized, and which are enforced through social sanctions. Formal authority is legitimated by values that have become institutionalized in legal contracts and cultural ideologies, and the social constraints that demand compliance pervade the entire society. Informal authority, on the other hand, is legitimated by the common values that emerge in a group, particularly by the loyalty the superior commands among group members, and group norms and sanctions enforce compliance.

This theoretical analysis implies that superiors who command the loyalty of their subordinates are more likely than others to establish effective informal authority over them and thus to influence them. A number of empirical findings support this conclusion. For example, an experiment conducted by French and Snyder, which used groups composed of one supervisor and three members engaged in a group judgment test, indicates that the more accepted the leader was by the rest of the group, the more he attempted to influence them and the more successful his attempts to influence were.[7] In addition, group respect for the ability (intelligence) of the leader was associated with successful influence attempts. Similar results were obtained in a field experiment conducted by Lippitt and his colleagues.[8] Boys in a camp setting to whom other boys attributed much power made more influence attempts and in addition were more successful in these attempts. Further, the boys with high power were liked better than other group members and were more frequently identified with.

The implication of these findings is that superiors who command the loyalty of a group—who are liked, accepted, respected—have more control than others over group members partly because they have greater confidence in their authority to issue directives—influence attempts were more frequent as well as more successful. Since the ultimate criterion of effective supervisory authority is the performance of subordinates, our interpretation also implies that superiors who command loyalty will have more productive groups than those who do not. This interpretation was found to apply in the French and Snyder experiment: on a task involving card sorting, the acceptance of the leader was positively correlated with the productivity of the group ($r =$

[7] John R. P. French, Jr., and Richard Snyder, "Leadership and Interpersonal Power," Dorwin Cartwright (ed.), *Studies in Social Power,* Ann Arbor: Institute for Social Research, University of Michigan, 1959, pp. 118–149.

[8] Ronald Lippitt *et al.,* "The Dynamics of Power," *Human Relations,* 5 (1952), pp. 37–64.

+.42).[9] In City Agency, work groups whose supervisor commanded the loyalty of his subordinates performed better in various respects than work groups with a supervisor who failed to inspire loyalty. For example, groups with high loyalty to the supervisor were more productive than those with low loyalty, as indicated by both the number of field visits per month and the proportion of time spent in the field.

Measuring Differences in Supervision. Various research techniques can be used to study differences in supervisor practices in a formal organization. Three methods of major interest are: (1) the direct observation of the supervisor's interaction with his subordinates; (2) interviews with supervisors; and (3) interviews with those in contact with the supervisor—his subordinates, his superiors, or his co-workers. We shall consider each of these methods briefly.

Several studies have employed direct and indirect observation of supervisors as they go about their daily work. Barnard, for example, relies for most of his empirical material on his recollections of processes of management and supervision as a participant.[10] Lasswell, on the other hand, has utilized a method whereby supervisors record their own interaction in a systematic fashion—the contacts they have with others, their length, and their significance—as they carry out their responsibilities.[11] Barnard's method of participant observation is suitable for exploratory purposes—gaining new insights and suggesting hypotheses—but not for testing hypotheses, since it does not yield systematic data. Lasswell's approach may provide systematic data but has the shortcoming that it requires participants continually to change the focus of their attention from being a supervisor to becoming an observer and back again. The frame of reference needed for successful performance of one role would appear to conflict with effectively carrying out the other. As a result, the quantitative data may be of questionable reliability and validity. This specific problem can be overcome by introducing an outside investigator to observe the process of supervision in organizations, as Whyte did in his study of restaurants.[12]

Only quite recently have students of industry and administration begun to systematize the observation of supervision by adapting the quantitative methods of observing interaction in peer groups that have been developed in experimental laboratories to the study of supervisory processes in field situations. Thus, Lawrence has modified the Bales category system of interaction-process analysis for use in the

9 French and Snyder, *op. cit.*, p. 146.
10 Barnard, *op. cit.*
11 Harold D. Lasswell, "Self-Observation," Robert K. Merton *et al.* (eds.), *Reader in Bureaucracy*, Glencoe, Ill.: Free Press, 1952, pp. 425–430.
12 William Foote Whyte, *Human Relations in the Restaurant Industry*, New York: McGraw-Hill, 1948, pp. 359–368.

investigation of interaction between supervisors and subordinates.[13] Carter and his colleagues use a large number of categories divided into seven principal dimensions for the study of leadership in face-to-face groups.[14] And Wirdenius has developed and tested in field settings a method of classifying supervisory behavior.[15] Chapple's method for measuring interaction has received fairly widespread use in field situations because of its simplicity.[16] His system provides data on the frequency of interactions between various participants and the direction of interaction (who initiates each contact); the data yielded by the resulting who-to-whom matrix can be used to analyze, among other things, the role of the supervisor in his own work group and his relations to his peers and superiors. Such a quantitative record of the patterns of interaction that occurred in the office was kept for 12 of the 23 work groups in the two welfare agencies.[17] In addition, unit meetings and conferences between supervisors and workers were observed in 13 of the work groups, and quantitative measures on these sessions are available for 5 of these groups. In general, these data were used to validate other measures of supervision which are available for all (or nearly all) supervisors.

Data on supervision can also be obtained through interviews with supervisors; their attitudes, orientations, and descriptions of their role performance may be elicited in this manner. Interviews, like observation, may provide more or less systematic data. The studies conducted by the Survey Research Center provide a good illustration of an attempt to collect systematic data on supervisory practices by means of interviews with supervisors.[18] An important limitation of this method, particularly if it is used as the exclusive source of information on supervision, is that it provides a one-sided view of a social relationship,

[13] Paul Lawrence, *The Changing of Organizational Behavior Patterns*, Boston: Graduate School of Business Administration, Harvard University, 1958, pp. 130–141. Caudill has also utilized the Bales categories in the study of interaction in a field setting. See William Caudill, *The Psychiatric Hospital as a Small Society*, Cambridge, Mass.: Harvard University Press, 1958, pp. 231–265.

[14] Launor Carter *et al.*, "The Relation of Categorizations and Ratings in the Observation of Group Behavior," *Human Relations*, 4 (1951), pp. 239–254; and Carter *et al.*, "A Note on a New Technique of Interaction Recording," *Journal of Abnormal and Social Psychology*, 46 (1951), pp. 258–260.

[15] Hans Wirdenius, *Supervisors at Work*, Stockholm: The Swedish Council for Personnel Administration, 1958, pp. 86–111.

[16] Eliot D. Chapple, "Measuring Human Relations," *Genetic Psychology Monographs*, 22 (1940), pp. 3–147.

[17] The formal observation period was approximately 25 net hours in each agency.

[18] Robert L. Kahn and Daniel Katz, "Leadership Practices in Relation to Productivity and Morale," Dorwin Cartwright and Alvin Zander (eds.), *Group Dynamics*, Evanston, Ill.: Row, Peterson, 1953, pp. 612–628.

presenting only the perspective of the superordinate participant. Besides, the supervisor's perceptions of his activities and relations with others is subject to distortion by his attitudes and orientations. As a matter of fact, the artificial interview situation may not even result in accurate information about the supervisor's orientation, since he may continue, so to speak, a controversy he has had with colleagues in the past as he responds to a salient question. When asked whether supervisors should be businesslike or informal in their relations with workers, for example, some of those we interviewed began by saying, "Of course, it is important to be businesslike . . ." Only after they had considerably elaborated this point and their attitudes had been further probed did it become apparent that this introductory statement was a kind of strategic ploy utilized to ward off criticism that had presumably been previously directed at them for favoring a very informal approach. They were, in effect, saying, "I do too recognize that being businesslike sometimes is important." In a short-answer interview, the actual preference for an informal approach underlying such statements might remain undiscovered.

An extension of the principle underlying Moreno's sociometric method[19] is to ascertain a supervisor's approach and practices by asking his subordinates about them.[20] This method was used in our studies of the two welfare agencies. To illustrate this procedure: subordinates are asked whether they consider their supervisor to be easy or strict, and supervisors are then classified on the basis of whether the majority of their subordinates select the one or the other response. Of course, it is not known whether or not all supervisors classified as strict by this criterion would be found to be more strict on the basis of some objective measure than those categorized as easy. But this method does furnish a measure of social reality—it does tell us which supervisors are socially defined as being strict by their subordinates. (Instead of using the majority opinion, the median can be used if necessary to obtain a better distribution of supervisors.)

More complex methods of assessing the role of supervisors than those discussed have been utilized. For example, Foa has developed a measure of the supervisor's role which combines the responses of both the superior and his subordinates.[21] One of the measures developed in our research, an index of hierarchical independence to be described

19 Jacob L. Moreno, *Who Shall Survive?* Washington, D.C.: Nervous and Mental Disease Publishing Co., 1934.

20 This approach is utilized in A. L. Comrey *et al.*, *Factors Influencing Organizational Effectiveness*, Los Angeles: University of Southern California, Final Technical Report, The Office of Naval Research, 1954, pp. 12–41.

21 Uriel G. Foa, "The Foreman-Worker Interaction: A Research Design," *Sociometry*, 18 (1955), pp. 226–244.

later, also combines data from two sources to characterize supervisors.

Contrasting Styles of Supervision. The study carried out in City Agency included the analysis of several aspects of supervision, systematic data being collected on all twelve supervisors in two general-assistance field sections. A considerable number, though not all, of these supervisory characteristics were also examined in the study of eleven supervisors in County Agency; again only supervisors in the field sections were included. The concern of our analysis is with the interrelations between the various supervisory characteristics and with the effects of differences between supervisors on the groups of subordinates.

Data from City Agency suggest that a number of supervisory characteristics were so closely interrelated that they seem to define an overall syndrome of supervisor authoritarianism: supervisors who displayed these characteristics were labeled "authoritarian"; those who lacked them, "nonauthoritarian." An authoritarian approach, which is not to be confused with the exercise of effective authority, involves a somewhat rigid and domineering pattern of close supervision. The distinction was based on the responses of subordinates when asked to characterize their own supervisor.[22] Seven items were found to be closely related; together they constitute the operational definition of authoritarianism.[23] The authoritarian supervisor was considered to be strict rather than easy by most of his subordinates; he was felt to supervise closely rather than to let subordinates work pretty much on their own; the majority of workers did not describe his approach to them as friendly or in favorable terms; his instructions were felt to be sometimes unclear; he was said to stick closely to procedures rather than be willing to make reasonable exceptions to rules; his subordinates did not consider his approach to clients to indicate an orientation to casework; and, finally, some of his subordinates explicitly stated that he was authoritarian in his approach.

Validation of this syndrome of authoritarianism was attempted in several ways. Four of the above items were included in the County Agency study, and the same close interrelations between them were found there. Moreover, a number of observational measures were re-

[22] Responses on a large variety of supervisory practices were elicited in the interview, some in open-ended questions, others in paired comparisons (the workers being asked to choose the one of two descriptive statements that best characterized their supervisor), and still others in a list of statements the workers were asked to check if applicable.

[23] All items were dichotomized and relationships between any two were established in two-by-two contingency tables. Two items were considered to be related if ten or more of the twelve supervisors fell into a diagonal. Each of the seven items included in the syndrome was related to at least four others. No supervisor classified as authoritarian had more than two (out of a possible seven) nonauthoritarian characteristics, and vice versa.

lated as expected to this index of authoritarianism. An authoritarian supervisor was more likely than another to take the initiative in interaction with his subordinates, as revealed by the proportion of his contacts with workers originated by him rather than by them. This tendency probably indicates that authoritarian supervisors were more apt to check on workers instead of waiting for their subordinates to come to them with their problems. A quantitative record showed that caseworkers under authoritarian supervisors were more prone than other workers to report to the supervisor immediately after returning to the office from the room where they interviewed clients. Apparently these workers found it necessary to check with their supervisor before taking action and did not feel as free as workers under less authoritarian supervisors to act on their own initiative. There was a further indication of the unwillingness of subordinates under authoritarian supervisors to assume responsibility; observation of worker-supervisor conferences revealed that workers under authoritarian supervisors disproportionately often consulted the supervisor even when they already had the answer to their problem. Finally, a record of the discussions at workgroup meetings indicated that authoritarian supervisors were more likely than others to issue orders to their subordinates: a larger proportion of their statements in group meetings were directives. Their style of supervision was to tell workers what to do rather than to use the meetings for explaining issues and letting the group explore them or for discussions of problems raised by subordinates.

Two other important role attributes of supervisors are their social distances from subordinates and superiors, respectively. A supervisor's approach to his subordinates was defined as "detached" if a majority of them said that he "always remains calm and never really loses his temper" rather than that "he can get quite excited." Detachment seems to have been a salient and clearly visible role characteristic of supervisors in City Agency, as shown by the very high consensus among subordinates: seven supervisors were looked upon by subordinates as detached and five as excitable; only five of sixty caseworkers endorsed statements that disagreed with those of the majority in their unit.[24]

The concept of hierarchical independence refers to the fact that a supervisor maintains in his work a minimum degree of independence from his superior, the section chief. In order to determine the supervisor's independence, five of the characteristics of his role performance as defined by his subordinates were compared with the same five characteristics of his section chief as defined by the chief's subordinates (the

[24] There was a slight inverse relationship between detachment and authoritarianism, but it did not meet the criterion established for inclusion in the authoritarian syndrome (see footnote 23). In County Agency, few respondents said their supervisor was excitable (14 per cent), and consensus on this item was not as high as in City Agency.

supervisors directly under him). The five characteristics involved were: sticking closely to procedures rather than making reasonable exceptions; supervising closely rather than letting subordinates work on their own; a formal as opposed to an informal approach to subordinates; extensive knowledge of procedures as opposed to a lesser concern with knowing rules; and being strict as opposed to being lenient. Since the two section chiefs differed greatly with regard to these characteristics, the index of hierarchical independence reveals nothing about the style of leadership of different supervisors but measures specifically the amount of difference between a supervisor's approach and that of his superior.[25]

We shall examine the significance of different supervisory role characteristics by relating them to several effect criteria, using the findings from studies of various organizations reported in the literature as well as those from our welfare-agency research. The main effect criteria to be considered are: the loyalty the supervisor commands among his subordinates; the productivity in his unit; other aspects of the performance of his subordinates and their approach to their work, such as whether they are oriented toward service or toward procedure; the work satisfaction of his subordinates; and the group solidarity that prevails in his unit.

SUPERVISION AND PERFORMANCE

Effects of Authoritarian Practices. Recent studies carried out in organizational settings indicate that authoritarian styles of supervision lessen worker satisfaction and productivity. Studies in an insurance company and a tractor-manufacturing firm conducted by the Survey Research Center, for example, found that closeness of supervision was inversely related to productivity.[26] Group productivity was negatively affected not only if workers were closely supervised by their foremen, but also if foremen were closely supervised by their superiors; apparently pressures were transmitted from level to level. In the tractor company, closeness of supervision was also inversely related to the amount of job satisfaction reported by workers. An experimental study conducted within a telephone company by Westerlund reports that workers allowed to work under informal supervision in small groups showed an increase in productivity over those operating under more rigid, departmental supervision.[27]

25 The criterion of independence is that the supervisor's role differed from that of his section chief on two or more of the five items. The data necessary to construct this index were not collected in County Agency.

26 Kahn and Katz, *op. cit.*, pp. 617–620.

27 Gunnar Westerlund, *Group Leadership,* Stockholm: Nordisk Rotogravyr, 1952.

Comrey and his associates conducted twenty-nine questionnaire studies of different types of organizations. Summary results are based on the eleven studies that showed the highest proportion of significant findings.[28] The results pertaining to authoritarianism were that the most effective supervisors differed from others, according to the reports of subordinates, in the following respects: they communicated more information to their subordinates, were considered to be helpful, were not arbitrary in their decisions and judgments, and had a sympathetic approach to workers. Finally, a study by Argyle and colleagues of ninety roughly comparable work groups concludes on the basis of the empirical evidence that the combination of general, democratic, and nonpunitive qualities in supervision was most conducive to high productivity in a work group.[29] However, as a result of his own studies, and after a survey of the literature, Argyle cautions that the differences in productivity in work groups resulting from contrasting methods of supervision were typically small, usually not larger than 15 per cent of the total output.

In the two welfare agencies, authoritarian supervision appeared to decrease work satisfaction, as indicated by worker expectations to leave the agency. Thus, in City Agency 65 per cent of 29 workers under authoritarian supervisors, as compared with 48 per cent of 31 workers under nonauthoritarian supervisors, expected to leave the agency in less than ten years. In County Agency, differences were smaller but in the same direction: 31 per cent of the 52 workers under authoritarian supervisors and 23 per cent of the 27 workers under nonauthoritarian supervisors expected to leave the agency in less than five years.[30]

Worker orientation to clients was also affected by authoritarian supervision. Authoritarian supervisors, who were invariably the procedure-oriented ones,[31] seem to have encouraged a concern among their subordinates with checking the eligibility of clients at the expense of rendering casework services. In City Agency, only 24 per cent of the 29 workers under authoritarian supervisors, in contrast to 61 per cent of

28 Comrey *et al., op. cit.,* p. 55.
29 Michael Argyle *et al.,* "Supervisory Methods Related to Productivity, Absenteeism, and Labour Turnover," *Human Relations,* 11 (1958), pp. 23–40.
30 The proportion of all workers expecting to leave differed in the two agencies undoubtedly in part because the wording of the question was different (ten years as opposed to five). However, these proportions probably also reflect differences in the availability of outside employment opportunities in the two communities (see above, p. 114), as well as actual differences in worker satisfaction, which appeared to be higher in County Agency.
31 Differentiation between supervisors on the seven-item index of authoritarianism was found to be perfectly correlated with their differentiation on one of the seven items: all authoritarian supervisors, and none of the others, were thought by most of their subordinates to "stick closely to procedures."

the 31 caseworkers under the nonauthoritarian supervisors, were oriented to casework service.[32] This particular information was not gathered for County workers, but a different indicator of orientation to clients was available for both agencies. Visits with nonrecipients (collaterals) are usually conducted for the purpose of verifying information obtained from the client or for checking up on him in other ways.[33] In both agencies, workers under authoritarian supervisors made more visits to collaterals per month than did workers under nonauthoritarian supervisors. In other words, authoritarian methods of supervision tended to foster a narrow concern with enforcing eligibility procedures and to discourage a willingness to assume a broader responsibility for service. This conclusion is further supported by the finding that authoritarianism curtailed the desire of subordinates to assume more responsibility than they presently had. In City Agency, 52 per cent of the workers under authoritarian supervisors but 75 per cent of those under nonauthoritarian ones indicated an interest in extending the scope of their responsibilities. In County Agency, the corresponding proportions of workers who wanted increased responsibility were 36 and 45 per cent, respectively.[34]

Contrary to expectations, work-group productivity as measured by

[32] This type of relation raises an important methodological question. The finding that a supervisory characteristic *as defined by responses of subordinates* is related to the orientation of these subordinates may not indicate, as here assumed, that supervisory practices influence the orientation of workers but rather that these orientations find expression in the worker's perception of his supervisor. The specific relation examined, for example, may not be due to the influence of authoritarian supervision on the worker's orientation to clients but to the fact that workers who themselves are more rigid in their approach are more likely than other workers to describe their supervisor as procedure-oriented and as having other authoritarian characteristics. But when we statistically control the way in which a given worker describes his supervisor, we still find that the worker is less apt to be casework-oriented if he works under a supervisor whom other workers define as authoritarian than if he works under a nonauthoritarian supervisor. This finding indicates that the actual role of the supervisor, and not the worker's subjective perception of this role, is responsible for the relationship observed. Only relations for which this has been found true are reported.

[33] This statement does not apply for workers with Old Age Assistance caseloads in County Agency. Hence, OAA workers were excluded from this analysis.

[34] Differences in operating procedures in the two agencies made it necessary to ask different questions to ascertain the worker's interest in assuming more responsibility. In City Agency, workers had to submit the first assistance budget they worked out for a new client to the supervisor for his signature. Here the question asked was, "If they would permit you to sign your own first budgets, would you want to?" In the County Agency, so-called "independent" workers were permitted to make more decisions on their own than others, and the question asked was, "Would you like to be an independent worker?"

the numbers of visits to recipients per month, was not related to authoritarianism. Only small differences were found in the two agencies, and they were in opposite directions. This finding conflicts with the findings of other studies. Perhaps in a service organization, in contrast to factories and private offices, employees do not react to authoritarian supervision by reducing the effort they devote to their work. Neither was authoritarianism negatively related to commanding the loyalty of subordinates (as indicated by their preference for their present supervisor), another relationship which we had expected to observe. While this conclusion is based on data from City Agency alone,[35] data from both agencies are available on whether subordinates considered their supervisors helpful. In neither agency was there any association between the supervisor's authoritarianism and the tendency of his subordinates to describe him as helpful. In short, although authoritarian practices had an adverse effect on the orientations of subordinates to their job, their work, and their clients, these practices did not alienate subordinates as much as had been expected.

Effects of Detachment and Independence. The human-relations approach has correctly emphasized the importance of social relations for operations. We have, for example, just examined the dysfunctions of authoritarian supervisory practices for the tendency of subordinates to render service, assume responsibilities, and experience work satisfaction. But this approach has tended to ignore other important requirements of effective supervision. Maintaining "good" human relations is not the only prerequisite for being an effective manager of men. Indeed, there is a danger that relations between supervisors and subordinates will be "too good," since the supervisor may become personally involved in the network of relations among subordinates to the extent of being confined by them. Thus, the first manager in the gypsum firm studied by Gouldner had many informal contacts with workers and was on very good terms with them, but his consequent indulgent methods constituted ineffective management.[36] He seems to have succumbed to the temptation of letting a concern for maintaining good human relations interfere with his managerial responsibility for the operating efficiency in the plant. Effective leadership requires not only refraining from closely checking on subordinates but it also requires making challenging demands to stimulate their interest and, indeed, their ability to perform well.

These considerations imply that some social distance and independence from subordinates promotes effective leadership. This is the

[35] The data on loyalty to the supervisor were not collected in County Agency.

[36] See Alvin W. Gouldner, *Patterns of Industrial Bureaucacy*, Glencoe, Ill.: Free Press, 1954, pp. 45–56.

conclusion Fiedler draws from a series of studies.[37] Various types of leaders were given a test in which they selected words that characterized the co-workers they most and least preferred. Low scores on this test of Assumed Similarity between Opposites (resulting from large differences in the descriptions given) have been interpreted as a generalized index of social distance between the subject and the rest of the group, since they indicate the subject's tendency to discriminate between group members rather than to approve of all of them. Such different groups as basketball teams and surveying parties were more successful if their informal leader had a low Assumed Similarity score than if he had a high score. The same results were obtained for open-hearth shop foremen. Fiedler concludes that "leaders who perceive themselves to be more distant from their subordinates have more effective work units than those who perceive themselves to be closer to their men."[38]

Another indicator of a lack of involvement with subordinates is the supervisor's ability to maintain emotional detachment—to remain calm and rarely, if ever, lose his temper. Such detachment was perfectly associated with commanding loyalty in City Agency. All seven detached supervisors, but none of the five excitable ones, commanded the loyalty of most of their subordinates, that is, were preferred by them over any other supervisor, and were also most respected by them. The index of helpfulness, available for both agencies, confirms the conclusion that subordinates appreciated detachment in their supervisors. In County Agency, 85 per cent of the 55 workers under detached supervisors as opposed to 47 per cent of the 19 workers under excitable ones, considered their supervisor to be helpful. In the City, 56 per cent of 36 workers under detached supervisors and 17 per cent of 24 workers under excitable ones felt that their supervisor was helpful.

Detachment, unlike authoritarianism, was related to productivity

[37] Fred E. Fiedler, "A Note on Leadership Theory," *Sociometry*, 20 (1957), pp. 87–94.

[38] *Ibid.*, pp. 92–93. These are important insights but they are not as yet supported by other research. Comrey and his colleagues, for example, found no relationship between social distance and effectiveness of supervision (*op. cit.*, p. 40). Fiedler's proposition that the *superior's* perception of great social distance promotes *actual* performance is also somewhat at variance with, although not directly contradicted by, the finding of studies by the Survey Research Center that *subordinates* who perceive their superior as not distant have more favorable *attitudes* to the job than others (see Rensis Likert, "A Motivational Approach to a Modified Theory of Organization and Management," Mason Haire (ed.), *Modern Organization Theory*, New York: Wiley, 1959, p. 189). Finally, other studies by Fiedler himself dealing with bomber crews, tank crews, and farm-supply cooperatives suggest that optimum group performance results from certain combinations of sociometric closeness and psychological distance between leaders and "keymen" (group members whose behavior most directly influences team performance). See Fred E. Fiedler, *Leader Attitudes and Group Effectiveness*, Urbana: University of Illinois Press, 1958, pp. 27–45.

in both agencies (see Table 13). Two-thirds of the workers under detached supervisors, but only about one-third of the workers under excitable supervisors exerted much effort in making field visits to recipients. Worker satisfaction, however, was hardly associated with the supervisor's detachment in City Agency and not at all in County Agency.

TABLE 13. WORKER VISITS TO RECIPIENTS AND ORIENTATION
OF SUPERVISOR

Orientation of Supervisor	Workers with Many Recipient Visits		
	City Agency	County Agency	Total
Detached	69% (28)	66% (38)	67% (66)
Excitable	29% (17)	44% (16)	36% (33)

Supervisors, like foremen in industry, are men in the middle, subject to pressures from above as well as below, and their ability to exercise their leadership functions requires some independence from both kinds of pressure. Maintaining a degree of independence from superiors is no less important for effective supervision than remaining somewhat detached toward subordinates. Thus, Pelz's research indicates that a supervisor's ability to exercise influence independently of his superior conditions the reactions of his subordinates to him.[39] Subordinates were favorably disposed to their supervisor only if he engaged in "good" supervisory practices *and also* had enough autonomy from his superior to exercise effective power over the workers' environment. The absence of the latter neutralized the advantages of good supervisory practices.

To explore the significance of hierarchical independence, an index that measures the difference between the supervisor's approach and that of his superior was constructed in City Agency, as previously described. The effects of hierarchical independence differed decidedly from those of authoritarianism.[40] Independent supervisors had more loyal subordinates: four of the five independent supervisors commanded high loyalty in their work group, while only one of the seven others did.[41] It will be recalled that authoritarianism was not associated with loyalty. And whereas authoritarianism was inversely associated

[39] Donald C. Pelz, "Influence: A Key to Effective Leadership in the First-Line Supervisor," *Personnel*, 29 (1952), pp. 209–217.

[40] Despite the fact that there was a slight inverse relationship between the two variables: only one of the five independent supervisors was authoritarian, but five of the seven others were.

[41] Of the twelve supervisors in City Agency, five commanded a high degree of loyalty among their subordinates, two, a medium degree, and five, a low degree.

with work satisfaction and with a service orientation among subordinates, hierarchical independence was not associated with either. In contrast, a willingness to delegate more responsibility to clients was not affected by authoritarianism but was affected by independence. Among workers under independent supervisors, 63 per cent (of 24) favored delegating responsibility to clients by making the clothing allowance a part of the regular budget, whereas only 36 per cent of the (36) workers under more dependent supervisors favored this change in procedure. Perhaps the crucial factor here is the willingness to change existing procedures, which might be encouraged by supervisory practices that demonstrate some freedom from the constraints exerted by superiors in the organization.

Hierarchical independence was also found to promote group solidarity, whereas authoritarianism did not. Specifically, work groups under independent supervisors were more likely than other groups to be characterized by high perceived reciprocity in consultation (this measure was discussed in Chapter V). Thus, under independent supervisors, 32 per cent of 81 consulting relationships mentioned by workers were perceived as reciprocal, and under dependent supervisors only 20 per cent of 101 consulting relationships were so perceived.[42] Cohesive ties among workers, as measured by the proportion of ingroup choices, were also slightly more prevalent under independent supervisors.

These findings may be interpreted by suggesting that the value independent supervisors place on autonomy and self-direction motivates them to differ from their own superiors, on the one hand, and to refrain from interfering in the social interaction among subordinates, on the other. Moreover, supervisors who value independence might manifest this attitude not only in their relations to superiors but also in demands that their subordinates make decisions independently, thus constraining subordinates to obtain advice and social support from one another by establishing consultation partnerships and closer social bonds in general. Finally, work-group solidarity develops perhaps most readily in groups that are somewhat protected against adverse influences of the environment, and supervisors who feel free to differ from their superiors are more likely to furnish such protection than others. For example, conflicts between caseworkers and members of the audit department were frequent in City Agency; all independent supervisors, but only two of the six others, regularly backed their subordinates in

---

[42] The self-confidence of the supervisor was also found positively associated with the proportion of reciprocal consultations in his work group. Under the eight self-confident supervisors, 32 per cent of all (124) consultation ties were perceived as reciprocal; under the four supervisors lacking self-confidence only 10 per cent (of 58) were so perceived.

these conflicts. It appears, then, that the qualities associated with independence in a supervisor promote group solidarity, in part by facilitating the development of reciprocal bonds in work groups, and in part by creating a challenge that subordinates can best meet by establishing such social ties.[43]

Effects of Consistency. Turning now to another dimension of the supervisor's role, we will consider the effects of consistency in role performance on subordinates. Although there are many conflicting results reported in the literature dealing with the role of parent as it influences the development of the child, one of the most recurrent pleas is for consistency of parental behavior, some authors going so far as to insist that consistently "bad" practices are preferable to erratic behavior. We are not suggesting that the supervisor is a parent-figure for his workers but only that consistency in persons occupying authority positions may well be of generic significance. Lack of consistency in supervision and a lack of clarity in defining the duties of subordinates probably have adverse effects on leadership and on the performance of subordinates.

An experiment by Cohen deals with the effects on worker performance of an ambiguous definition of the task and inconsistent directives from a power figure.[44] Female employees of a public utility company were placed individually in a room with an experimental assistant who was identified as coming from the supervisory level directly above the subject. The power figure varied the consistency of his suggestions from subject to subject; also varied was the clarity of the task assigned. Ambiguous situations and inconsistent directives were found to raise the subject's anxiety, to create less favorable attitudes toward the power figure, and to lower productivity. The field studies of supervisory practices by Comrey and his colleagues also found a positive relationship between consistency and effectiveness of supervision.[45]

Consistency of supervisory performance should be reflected in the extent of agreement among workers when asked about the characteristics of the supervisor. If supervisory behavior varies from time to time and from worker to worker, we would expect workers to manifest little consensus when describing their supervisor; conversely, consistency should find expression in greater consensus. Following this reasoning, a measure of the consistency of role performance of each supervisor in City Agency was obtained by ascertaining the degree of consensus among his subordinates when asked about seven different aspects of his

---

[43] For an intensive study of variations in group structure resulting from differences in supervision based on data collected in City Agency, see Philip M. Marcus, "Expressive and Instrumental Groups," *American Journal of Sociology*, 66 (1960), pp. 54–59.

[44] Arthur R. Cohen, "Situational Structure, Self-Esteem, and Threat-Oriented Reactions to Power," Cartwright, *op. cit.*, pp. 35–52.

[45] Comrey *et al.*, *op. cit.*, p. 54.

behavior.[46] Role consistency, so measured, was found to be positively associated with worker loyalty to the supervisor. All but one of five consistent supervisors, and only one of the seven less consistent ones, commanded high loyalty in their work groups. The supervisor's role consistency also promoted group solidarity, there being a pronounced relationship between it and perceived reciprocity in consultation. Under the consistent supervisors, 34 per cent of the (88) consultation relationships were perceived as being reciprocal, but under the inconsistent supervisors only 17 per cent (of 94) were so perceived. These findings suggest that stability of supervisory practice promoted the loyalty of subordinates and the development of solidary relationships among them, although they might be interpreted alternatively as resulting from the influence of solidarity and loyalty on consensus about the supervisor.

Consistency of supervisory role performance also appears to account for another set of findings concerning the relationship between the supervisor's self-confidence and the allegiance of his subordinates in City Agency. Table 14 presents these data.[47] The more self-confident supervisors were somewhat more apt to command the loyalty of subordinates if they were strict, but the less self-confident supervisors were

TABLE 14. SUPERVISOR'S SELF-CONFIDENCE, SUPERVISOR'S APPROACH, AND WORKER LOYALTY

Worker Loyalty to Supervisor	Supervisor's Self-Confidence			
	High		Medium or Low	
	Supervisor's Approach		Supervisor's Approach	
	Strict	Easy	Strict	Easy
High	77%	53%	27%	87%
N (= 100%)	13	17	15	15

[46] The seven items on which worker opinion was solicited related to the supervisor's procedure orientation, knowledge of procedures, close supervision, social distance from subordinates, excitability, strictness, and self-confidence. Agreements (the more frequent response) among subordinates were summed for each item (counting one-half of the "don't know" responses) and then divided by seven times the number of subordinates to yield the index of consensus. This index was corrected for size of group, since consensus is more likely to occur by chance in smaller groups. No such measure was obtained in County Agency.

[47] Most supervisors in City Agency were considered self-confident by their subordinates. In order to have enough cases for the analysis in this table, supervisors were divided by the median. This division required that even supervisors who were considered to lack self-confidence by only one worker be classified in the "medium or low" category. (There were two such cases among the twelve supervisors.)

much more apt to command loyalty if they were easy. A possible inter-pretation of these findings is that the most natural and consistent ap-proach for a self-confident person is a firm one, whereas more lenient supervision is more natural for an individual lacking self-confidence. Some supervisors may feel constrained to use an approach to their subordinates that is not suited to their personalities—perhaps because of pressures from superiors, perhaps as a result of having acquired cer-tain conceptions as to the "proper" conduct for a supervisor, such as that a supervisor should be easy-going and foster "good human rela-tions" with subordinates, or, conversely, that he should be firm and should maintain social distance. It is probable that a person who self-consciously adopts a style of supervision that is at variance with his normal mode of conduct will feel uncomfortable and behave erratically on occasion, whereas one whose approach to subordinates does not con-flict with his personality and usual demeanor will be more at ease and consistent.[48] Supervisors whose approach is inconsistent with their dis-positions, whether they are strict or lenient, are apparently less likely to command the loyalty of subordinates than consistent supervisors. This conclusion may also account for the earlier-mentioned finding that supervisory detachment is associated with work-group loyalty. A detached supervisor is undoubtedly more consistent in his behavior toward subordinates than an excitable one, and this consistency may well be a main reason why he is more apt to win their loyalty.

HIERARCHICAL AND PEER RELATIONS

Testing a Hypothesis. Much of the work done in the field of formal organizations emphasizes two different facets of these social systems: the impersonality and emotional detachment of relations between in-dividuals and groups on different hierarchical levels, and the cohesive-ness and informality of relations among peers on the same organiza-tional level. This difference suggests a possible causal link between peer-group cohesion and hierarchical social distance. The following hypothesis may thus be offered: an official who enjoys social integra-tion among his peers will be more impersonal and detached in his rela-tions with subordinates than one who does not. For peer-group support allows the superior to be more detached by obviating the need for courting the support of his subordinates. To test this hypothesis, we used data from both welfare agencies. Specifically, we examined the association between the index of detachment to subordinates already

---

48 In this connection, note Likert's comment: "A subordinate tends also to expect his superior to behave in ways consistent with the per-sonality of the superior." Likert, *op. cit.*, p. 191.

described and three measures of social integration among peers: whether the supervisor felt integrated among the other supervisors in his department; the number of "friendship" choices he received from other supervisors in his department; and the total number of such choices he received from all supervisors in the agency.

The supervisor's social integration among other supervisors, regardless of which of the three measures was used, was not related to detachment toward subordinates in either agency. The hypothesis that peer-group integration makes supervisors more detached in their relations with caseworkers is clearly negated. Data from City Agency allowed us to determine whether or not peer-group integration among supervisors promoted independence from superiors. Again, the hypothesis was not supported by the data. Integrated supervisors were no more likely than others to exhibit hierarchical independence.

How can we account for this rejection of the hypothesis? With the benefit of hindsight, we realize now that an implicit assumption underlies our hypothesis, and this assumption proved to be incorrect. We had assumed that integrative peer relations and group solidarity tend to develop among supervisors, just as they often do among workers. But this tendency evidently was not present among the supervisors in the two organizations studied. Although supervisors had much more seniority on the average than workers, and seniority was related to integration among workers, supervisors tended to be much less integrated in networks of social relations with peers than did workers. Only three of the twelve supervisors in City Agency received two or more friendship choices from other supervisors, but exactly half of the 60 workers in this agency received two or more choices from colleagues; similarly, in County Agency, only one of the eleven supervisors received as many as two friendship choices, while more than half of the 87 workers did. In City Agency over one-third of the workers, but none of the supervisors, reported that they saw other members of the agency staff socially after working hours as often as once a month. Similar disparities were found for County Agency, where almost two-fifths of the workers but only one of the eleven supervisors reported that they saw other members of the agency socially as frequently as once a month. Social relations among supervisors in the same section were particularly weak, and this was especially pronounced for consultation. In City Agency, six of the ten supervisors interviewed said that they never consulted a colleague (supervisor) in their own section, whereas only 12 out of 60 workers said that they never consulted another worker in their own work group. Supervisors in County Agency were not asked about their consultation practices, but the observation record on the frequency of social interaction provides some clues about the extent of consultation among supervisors compared with that among caseworkers. On the average, caseworkers initiated 3.8 contacts with other workers in their own division per hour, whereas supervisors initiated only 0.9 hourly contacts with other supervisors. The difference in City Agency was even more pronounced, initiated ingroup contacts per hour being 4.8 for caseworkers and 0.3 for supervisors.[49]

In short, our findings indicate that supervisors in the two agencies tended to be somewhat isolated from supportive contacts with peers. Jaques, to name only one among several observers, has called attention to the isolated position of the top managers in large organizations;[50] but it is rather surprising to find comparable isolation for these first-line supervisors. The supervisors in a given section worked under the same superior, had weekly meetings as a group, and spent all day in close proximity in the office. Nevertheless, solidary bonds uniting them into a group hardly developed among them. Of special significance was the finding that they rarely consulted one another. Perhaps their conception of the supervisory role as being responsible for advising others discouraged them from seeking advice themselves. Perhaps, too, being a link in a hierarchical chain focused the supervisor's attention upon his superiors and subordinates rather than his peers. This suggestion receives some confirmation from the finding that none of the ten supervisors interviewed in City Agency felt that it was more important to be highly thought of by his peers than by his superior or his subordinates, whereas nearly one-third of the workers (19 of 60) considered the good opinion of their peers more important than those of either their supervisor or their clients.[51] Among these supervisors, then, there was no concern with winning the respect of their peers. And virtually no cooperative relations, such as consultation, developed among them. As a result, social relations among colleagues did not furnish sufficient social support for supervisors to have any bearing on their detachment from subordinates or their independence from superiors. This isolation was in contrast to the more significant peer relations that developed in work groups on the bottom level, which seemed to further detachment and independence from clients, as was discussed in Chapters III and IV.

[49] County Agency data are based on the observation of 54 workers and 7 superiors for 28 hours, and City Agency data are based on the observation of 22 workers and 4 supervisors for 24 hours.

[50] Elliott Jaques, *The Changing Culture of a Factory*, New York: Dryden, 1952, pp. 278–279.

[51] Although the difference between workers and supervisors is not as great, these findings are supported by roughly comparable data from County Agency. Workers and supervisors were asked from which of several sources they obtained the most intellectual and professional stimulation. Some workers (8 of 86) but none of the (11) supervisors chose their peer group on this criterion.

Loyalty of Subordinates and Loyalty to the Superior. What, then, is the source of social support that enables some supervisors to maintain detachment and independence? It may well be the loyalty of subordinates.[52] Detached supervisors had more loyal subordinates, as was previously shown. This relation is undoubtedly in part due to the adverse effects of excitability, and of the inconsistency it entails, on loyalty. But it may also result in part from the fact that commanding the allegiance and respect of subordinates is a source of strength for the supervisor that facilitates calm detachment. The supervisor's hierarchical independence, too, was found to be associated with high loyalty of his subordinates. The qualities of the supervisor that allow him to remain independent from his superior probably command the respect and loyalty of his subordinates, as we have suggested. But it may also be that the loyalty of subordinates helps the supervisor to attain and maintain his independence from his superior. This interpretation receives some support from the interview responses of ten City Agency supervisors.

Supervisors who commanded the loyalty of their subordinates were less likely than those who did not to express loyalty to their own superior (the section chief). None of the four supervisors whose subordinates did express high loyalty to them felt loyal to his own superior, while five of the six supervisors who did not command high loyalty from their subordinates expressed loyalty to their section chief. And although detachment from subordinates and hierarchical independence were not related to one another,[53] both were inversely related to the supervisor's loyalty to his superior.

The loyalty of subordinates thus appears to have been a source of social support for first-line supervisors. Social support from subordinates probably lessens the supervisor's need to seek the support and approval of his superior by becoming attached to him and emulating his style of supervision. Conversely, strong ties of loyalty to one's superior may reduce the need of the supervisor to win the respect and allegiance of his own subordinates.[54] This latter interpretation implies that loyalty to superiors in a hierarchical organization would be pronounced on alternate levels. If a manager does not command the loyalty of the section chiefs under him, it will be particularly important for them to obtain social support by commanding the loyalty of their subordinates, the first-line supervisors. And if a section chief is successful

[52] This discussion is based entirely on data from City Agency since no loyalty measures were available in the County study.

[53] Four out of five independent supervisors were detached toward their subordinates, but so were three out of seven dependent supervisors.

[54] Here again our survey data require us to present alternative interpretations of observed relations inasmuch as they do not allow us to determine the direction of influence between the variables.

in establishing supportive working relationships with the supervisors under him, the incentive of these supervisors to win the allegiance and respect of their subordinates will be reduced.[55] Hence, the orientations of alternate hierarchical levels would be similar, and those of adjacent levels, different. Although this conclusion is highly speculative, it parallels Caudill's observation that alternate levels in the hierarchy of the hospital he studied were more similar in orientation than adjacent ones.[56]

CONCLUDING REMARKS

Different styles of supervision apparently exert a variety of influences on workers. Emotional detachment, consistency, and hierarchical independence were found to be the supervisory characteristics most closely related to the ability to command the loyalty of subordinates. Authoritarian practices on the part of the supervisor, on the other hand, had no bearing on loyalty in the welfare agencies. Worker productivity was largely associated with factors that were related to loyalty, perhaps because supervisors who had won the loyal support of their subordinates were most successful in commanding willing compliance with their directives and in stimulating effort in their work group. Authoritarian practices by the supervisor adversely affected work satisfaction, the willingness to assume responsibility, and the tendency to extend casework service to clients. But in contrast to the findings obtained in other types of organizations, authoritarian supervision did not lower productivity in the two welfare agencies. The supervisory attributes that exerted most influence on group solidarity were hierarchical independence and consistency.

Contrary to expectations, the supervisor's relations with his peers did not affect his approach to subordinates, probably because only a low level of peer-group solidarity existed among supervisors. Workers seemed typically to derive their social support from cooperative relations with their peers, notably from consulting one another. Supervisors, on the other hand, obtained their social support not from working relations with other supervisors, but from loyal subordinates or from their relations with their superiors. The data suggest that a supervisor who expresses loyalty to his superior is less apt than another to command the loyalty of his own subordinates, to be detached in his relations with subordinates, and to exhibit hierarchical inde-

[55] But this statement would not hold true for caseworkers organized in work groups, since they have not two but three alternative sources of social support in the work situation—their peers, their superiors, and their clients.

[56] Caudill, *op. cit.*, pp. 155–157.

pendence. If this suggestion is generally true, it would imply that a manager's ability to command his subordinates' loyalty impedes their effectiveness as supervisors in their own right. This implication, in turn, suggests that effective management can be expected to occur only on alternate levels in the hierarchy.

CHAPTER SEVEN

Managerial Control

The discussions of management that appear in the literature differ considerably, because they tend to emphasize different facets of this complex topic. Let us briefly examine some of the implicit models of management underlying these discussions, without attempting to provide an exhaustive list or assuming that these conceptions are mutually exclusive.

One model views management as "executive leadership" and focuses on such functions as defining objectives, setting policies, and inspiring effort. The writings of Barnard exemplify this emphasis; for him the essence of executive responsibility is the ability "to bind the wills of men to the accomplishment of purposes beyond their immediate ends, beyond their times."[1] Selznick, too, views leadership as the key function of management and suggests that it is required for making critical as opposed to routine decisions—decisions that define the ends of the organization and constitute commitments that shape its essential character.[2] He considers administrative leaders responsible not only for making such "character-defining" decisions but also for seeing that the organization embodies and implements these purposes once they have been established, for defending the integrity of the institution against internal changes and external attacks, and for maintaining order and control over internal conflicts.

A second conception of management emphasizes the hierarchy of "bureaucratic authority" in the organization. The focus here is on impersonal discipline and rational expertness, and on control through directives originated at the apex of the authority pyramid and transmitted through channels down to its base. This, of course, is Weber's model of management. As has been suggested, there is a possible conflict between compliance with directives and the exercise of professional judgment, and the implications of this conflict have received increasing attention from recent students of administrative structures, such as Parsons and Gouldner.

[1] Chester I. Barnard, *The Functions of the Executive*, Cambridge, Mass.: Harvard University Press, 1938, p. 283.
[2] Philip Selznick, *Leadership in Administration*, Evanston, Ill.: Row, Peterson, 1957, pp. 30–37, 62–64.

A third model conceives of management as the "regulator of the incentive systems." The basic assumptions of this approach are that contributions are made to the organization for rewards received and that management induces contributions by regulating the structure of rewards. Attention was at first directed almost entirely to financial incentives; however, empirical studies as to their effects have been inconclusive. For example, a study by Dale of 305 individual wage-incentive arrangements in 29 different industries reports that wage incentives were found to improve productivity,[3] whereas a study by Behrend of 250 British firms found no evidence in support of the effectiveness of piece-work incentive payments.[4] And Roberts found that the compensation of the highest-paid official in a company was related to the company's size but not to its profit.[5] More recent conceptions of incentives have emphasized the significance of other rewards as well as monetary ones. Thus Whyte and his associates reject the simple model of economic man and stress that incentive systems must be broadly defined as including worker-company relations, intergroup work relations, interaction patterns, and symbols.[6] Likert has attempted to specify the interrelations between several factors that have been demonstrated to influence worker motivation.[7] In addition to distinguishing between monetary and nonmonetary rewards, some writers have distinguished between incentive systems that reward results and those that reward conformity with officially established procedures. Worthy has suggested that the former system "develops initiative and self-reliance and generates a far more powerful driving force than could ever be imposed from the top down."[8] Dimock also concludes that the rewarding of results promotes initiative as well as responsibility in performance.[9]

A fourth model conceptualizes management as "centralized plan-

[3] John D. Dale, *Wage Incentives and Productivity,* New York: George Elliott, 1958.

[4] Hilde Behrend, "Financial Incentives as the Expression of a System of Beliefs," *The British Journal of Sociology,* 10 (1959), pp. 137–147.

[5] David R. Roberts, "A General Theory of Executive Compensation Based on Statistically Tested Propositions," *Quarterly Journal of Economics,* 70 (1956), pp. 270–294. For further discussion of these findings, see Herbert A. Simon, "The Compensation of Executives," *Sociometry,* 20 (1957), pp. 32–35. And for an analysis of the general problem, see David R. Roberts, *Executive Compensation,* Glencoe, Ill.: Free Press, 1959.

[6] William F. Whyte *et al., Money and Motivation,* New York: Harper, 1955.

[7] Rensis Likert, "A Motivational Approach to a Modified Theory of Organization and Management," Mason Haire (ed.), *Modern Organization Theory,* New York: Wiley, 1959, pp. 184–217.

[8] James C. Worthy, "Organizational Structure and Employee Morale," *American Sociological Review,* 15 (1950), p. 178.

[9] Marshall E. Dimock, *Administrative Vitality,* New York: Harper, 1959, pp. 189–191.

ning"—the coordination of operations through advance planning of the work program. Some aspects of this focus are included in the foregoing models: the leader makes critical decisions relating to the over-all design of the enterprise, coordination of activities is a basic function of the bureaucratic hierarchy, and incentive systems are designed to coordinate efforts in the interest of effective achievement of organizational purposes. But the specific emphasis of the planning model is on creating conditions in the organization that influence its members rather than on influencing them directly. This distinction is illustrated by differences between job-lot and assembly-line production as discussed by Richardson and Walker.[10] In the former, which is the traditional organization of production, the coordination of specialized tasks of various sections depends on directives issued by management and transmitted through the hierarchy. But for the assembly line, the flow of production has been organized by management in advance to serve as the coordinating mechanism that obviates the need for much direct supervision.

This brief overview of various models underlying some of the treatments of management will serve as a background for our discussion of this topic. In this chapter we shall first consider the shape of the hierarchical pyramid and then examine social relations among managers. In the second part we shall analyze impersonal mechanisms of control and their significance for the management of formal organizations. Finally, we shall question some of the prevailing assumptions in the study of management.

THE HIERARCHY

The Shape of the Pyramid. While the significance of social relations for supervision has been particularly emphasized in more recent research, it was by no means entirely ignored by earlier students of administration. Graicunas, for example, called attention to some important implications for management of the fact that as the number of persons in a group increases the number of possible relations between group members increases at a much faster rate.[11] Thus, in a group of 2 persons there is only 1 social relation, while in a group of 6 there are 15 relations between members. Graicunas felt that inasmuch as the manager's responsibility requires an understanding of

---

[10] Frederick L. Richardson and Charles R. Walker, *Human Relations in an Expanding Company,* New Haven: Labor and Management Center, Yale University, 1948, pp. 54–85.

[11] The rate is $N(N-1)/2$, when N is the number of group members. V. A. Graicunas, "Relationship in Organization," Luther Gulick and L. Urwick (eds.), *Papers on the Science of Administration,* New York: Institute of Public Administration, 1937, pp. 183–187.

the social relations among subordinates as well as of his own with them, no manager should be in charge of more than a small number of subordinates. Many subsequent students of administration have agreed with this conclusion, and the ideal span of control for a manager has typically been set at about six subordinates.

However, this rational conception of the individual manager's functions ignores certain problems which the narrow span of control creates. One of these is that in large organizations a narrow span increases the number of hierarchical levels required, thus accentuating problems of communication.[12] Research by Worthy indicates further disadvantages connected with a narrow span of control.[13] In the organization he studied, the span of control had been extended in deliberate violation of the old principle, and managers had several times the number of subordinates that had earlier been considered ideal. In addition to reducing the number of hierarchical levels in the organization, this innovation meant that managers could not depend too closely on their own superiors, and independence from superiors, as we have seen, fosters effective management practices.[14] At the same time, managers had too many subordinates to exercise close supervision over them, and this condition too was functional for operations, because close supervision (as we have noted often) impedes performance. Further, the broad span of control prevented the manager from becoming too closely involved with his subordinates, and such supervisory detachment, it will be recalled, tends to promote the loyalty of subordinates.[15] In short, comparing the significance of acute and obtuse pyramids of control, it appears that the latter exert several constraints on managers that are functional for effective supervision. The increased span of control prevents managers from engaging in certain practices—close supervision, dependence on superiors, involvement with subordinates—which may be tempting because of their short-range advantages but which prove to be detrimental to managerial effectiveness in the long run.

To measure the shape of the hierarchical pyramid, a simple index of the average span of control can be derived by the formula $S = {}^L\sqrt{N}$,

[12] See Herbert A. Simon, *Administrative Behavior* (2d ed.), New York: Macmillan, 1957, pp. 26–28.

[13] Worthy, *op. cit.*, pp. 169–179.

[14] For another case where a broad span of control resulted in greater independence of middle managers, see Burton R. Clark, *Adult Education in Transition*, Berkeley: University of California Press, 1958, p. 72.

[15] An earlier study found that the smaller the work group, the less detached was the supervisor in evaluating his subordinates. Supervisors of small units tended to give higher and more uniform ratings to their subordinates than those of larger units. See Peter M. Blau, *The Dynamics of Bureaucracy*, Chicago: University of Chicago Press, 1955, p. 167.

where S is the span of control, L is the number of supervisory levels (the number of organizational levels above the operating level), and N is the total number of employees or members of the organization. Applying this formula to City Agency, which had 5 supervisory levels and about 1,000 employees, the span of control index is 4.0 (the fifth root of 1,000). County Agency had three supervisory levels and about 160 employees, yielding a span-of-control index of 5.4 (the cube root of 160). The index shows that the span of control for supervisors in County Agency was greater than that for City Agency supervisors. This difference is reflected on the lowest levels of the organizations in the size of the work groups, which contained five to six members in City Agency, but an average of seven caseworkers in County Agency.

Although this span-of-control measure is admittedly crude, it is useful as a reference against which variations between organizations as well as within organizations can be examined. For example, in the two welfare agencies the top managers had fewer subordinates than the number expected on the basis of the index, while the first-line supervisors had more than the expected number. This difference was probably due to the fact that top managers had many nonsupervisory responsibilities, such as representing the organization in its dealings with the environment, whereas first-line supervisors were chiefly engaged in overseeing the work of subordinates. In some organizations, however, the span of control of the higher officials is wider than that of the lower. In a plant studied by Dalton, for example, the number of superintendents under the assistant plant manager was greater than the number of subordinates under each of these superintendents.[16] This disparity reflects a division of labor in top management, with the second in command assuming primary responsibility for the internal operations of the plant, thus permitting the senior executive to devote most of his time and energy to external problems. The obtuse shape of the pyramid in the upper region of the hierarchy may well have been an important reason why middle management in this plant had much independence and maneuverability.

The range of managerial authority differs not only in terms of span of control but also in a different dimension, namely, the official's time perspective. Higher managers are generally expected to take a more long-range view than lower ones, taking into account not only the immediate but also the long-run consequences of decisions. This difference in perspective is related to differences in the way time is structured for the various levels in the organization. In the welfare agencies, for instance, the time of the caseworkers was highly fragmented. Their work was continually being interrupted, partly because

---

[16] Melville Dalton, *Men Who Manage*, New York: Wiley, 1959, chart facing p. 10.

emergency requests from clients urgently required action, but also partly as the result of supervisory practice. Supervisors felt free to disrupt the work of their subordinates by calling them to a conference or by telling them to stop what they were doing in order to start something else. In contrast, higher managers did not feel free to disrupt the work of their subordinates; accordingly, their conferences were scheduled by advance appointments. Neither do supervisors of more professionalized employees feel free to interrupt the work of their subordinates.[17] These differences suggest that the higher the level of responsibility—managerial or professional—the more control an employee tends to have over his own time.

Jaques has attempted to systematize these notions about the relationship between the freedom to decide how to use one's own time and the level of responsibility.[18] He recommends as a quantitative measure of responsibility the amount of time that elapses between successive reviews of an employee's performance by his superior. The time span during which a member of an organization makes decisions at his own discretion without accounting to his superior becomes, then, the operational definition of his level of responsibility.[19] Thus, a production worker may have his work checked by his foreman hourly, whereas the president of the company reports to the board of directors only annually. Jaques claims that his time measure of responsibility predicts salaries, and thus implies that management takes this factor implicitly into account when distributing financial rewards. This indicator also calls attention to the fact that exercising much responsibility involves the capacity to stand up under the uncertainty of not knowing the outcome or wisdom of one's own decisions for a period of time.[20] If the anxiety resulting from this uncertainty is so great that it impedes performance, it shows that an official has been given too much responsibility. Conversely, if an official finds his work routine and becomes impatient with his lack of discretion, it would indicate that he is ready for more responsibility than he has.

The physical distance separating the members of an organization is also relevant in this context. The frequency with which a superior checks on the performance of his subordinates depends not only on the amount of responsibility he or top management has explicitly

17 See, for example, the discussion in Blau, *op. cit.*, p. 102. Supervisors of workers in a state employment agency felt free to interrupt the work of their subordinates, but supervisors of the more highly skilled federal investigators did not engage in such practices.

18 Elliott Jaques, *Measurement of Responsibility*, London: Tavistock Publications, 1956, especially pp. 32–42.

19 Alternatively, the longer the time during which the decisions of an official commit the resources of the organization, the higher his responsibility. See *ibid.*, pp. 23, 138.

20 *Ibid.*, pp. 91–93.

decided to delegate to them but also on the ecological conditions, so to speak, that determine the opportunity for checking. On the one hand, subordinates may perform their duties continuously under the eyes of the superior; on the other hand, their work may carry them far from supervisory surveillance. If physical separation limits supervisors to intermittent contacts with subordinates, the latter often come to exercise more discretion than the official definition of their responsibility would warrant. Hughes, for example, calls attention to the increased level of unofficial responsibility that accrues to hospital nurses because their functional superiors, the physicians, are present for only short periods during the day and consequently exercise merely episodic control.[21] Clark reports that the geographical dispersion of the various centers of adult education in a metropolitan area resulted in a greater degree of autonomy for the officials in each of these centers.[22] Physical distance, then, decreases the degree of managerial control over subordinate units and hence increases the latter's autonomy. For it reduces the opportunities for checking on the performance of subordinates, just as a wide span of control does, and it is the actual frequency of such supervisory reviews rather than the official definition of the level of responsibility that governs the amount of discretion subordinates can and, indeed, must exercise.

From the standpoint of the management of an organization whose units are located in remote areas and dispersed over an entire country, these implications of physical distance constitute a challenge to devise long-range control mechanisms that maintain centralized control over local units and even over isolated members. In a recent study, Kaufman reports how the United States Forest Service has coped with this problem.[23] In addition to its elaborate manuals and guides, the Forest Service utilizes special techniques for detecting and discouraging deviations from official procedures among its scattered posts in the field. Rangers are asked to submit many written reports and to keep an official diary showing to the nearest half-hour how each work day is spent. They submit many statistics to be processed by regional headquarters, and while this processing is a service performed by headquarters for them, it also serves as a control device on ranger operations. Field inspections are regularly conducted covering both over-all and specialized technical programs. The public has the right to appeal decisions by rangers to the regional office. There are frequent transfers of Forest Service personnel from one post to another, a practice that reduces loyalty to a specific community and increases

---

[21] Everett C. Hughes, *Men and Their Work*, Glencoe, Ill.: Free Press, 1958, p. 74.
[22] Clark, *op. cit.*, pp. 71–72.
[23] Herbert Kaufman, *The Forest Ranger*, Baltimore: John Hopkins Press, 1960.

dependence on the Service. These external controls over rangers are supplemented by internal constraints developed during the early years of training and fostered by personnel policies. Promotions are made only from within and are relatively slow, so that a man has acquired considerable experience and has become properly socialized before he is given much responsibility. Finally, the use of uniforms and badges and the relatively high status of the Service promote *esprit de corps* among the men and their identification with the organization. Although the Forest Service seems to have achieved centralized control over widely dispersed and isolated local units, the elaborate arrangements instituted for this purpose indicate that such control is not easily accomplished.

Staff and Line. The distinction between staff and line is one that has long informed the study of formal organizations. Line organization places emphasis on differences in rank, and its members have authority over production processes. Staff organization directs attention to specialization, and its members usually function in a research and advisory capacity.[24] In short, line officials possess formal authority, whereas staff members furnish specialized and technical advice to the appropriate line officials in the organizational hierarchy. On the basis of their job content and the functions they perform for unions, Wilensky has developed a typology of union staff experts which illustrates the variety of staff roles even in such relatively unspecialized organizations.[25] Types include the "Facts and Figures Man," who supplies leaders with technical, economic, and legal information, the "Contact Man," who furnishes intelligence on the political conditions and ideological tendencies in the society at large, and the "Internal Communications Specialist," who furnishes intelligence on the members of the organization and its operations that is needed for successful internal control.

At first glance it would appear that the division of labor between staff and line officials résolves two dilemmas of hierarchy discussed earlier: the blocking of communication due to hierarchical authority and the dilemma of disciplined compliance versus expert judgment. The staff, standing outside the hierarchical line, provides a mechanism for upward communication. Besides, staff personnel supply expert judgments which the line managers can transmit with confidence as authoritative directives, so that the decisions of the line can be governed by discipline, and those of the staff by expertness. These neat distinctions, however, are oversimplified and distort the actual situa-

---

24 See Wilbert E. Moore, *Industrial Relations and the Social Order*, New York: Macmillan, 1947, pp. 96–104.
25 Harold L. Wilensky, *Intellectuals in Labor Unions*, Glencoe, Ill.: Free Press, 1956, pp. 39–108.

tion. The staff expert can submit accurate operational reports to management, but if he presents adverse information concerning the actions of lower managers he will earn their antipathy and distrust, and these attitudes will prevent him from obtaining accurate information from them in the future. Alternatively, he can attempt to modify his report in order to maintain the good will of his informants, but in so doing he suppresses information that reflects adversely on lower managers, making his report hardly more accurate than their own communications.

The distinction between line authority and professional expertness is also less clear-cut in reality than the abstract concepts of line and staff make it appear. Increasingly, the line as well as the staff must make professional judgments. Thus, the engineer in charge of a production department in a factory is no less a technical expert than the accountant in charge of a staff department, and the latter is no less in a position of authority over a staff of subordinates than the former. As a matter of fact, in certain types of organizations, as Etzioni has noted, the roles of staff and line are reversed.[26] In the prototype of a formal organization, the line officers discharge the major functions of the organizations, and the professional staff, auxiliary functions. Accordingly, a factory may hire experts to do market research or public relations, but the main business of the organization —production—remains in the hands of line officials. Similarly, the line officers in an army are in charge of military action, and the staff merely furnishes assistance in making strategic and tactical decisions— intelligence about the enemy, supplies, and so forth. But in a university, the professional staff discharges the major institutional functions—teaching and research—while the "line" administrators look after the auxiliary functions, such as arranging schedules, housing students, and collecting fees. The same structure characterizes the hospital: the physicians who cure patients are on the professional staff and not line administrators.

Conflicts and Coalitions. Conflicts often develop between staff and line personnel. Dalton has discussed some of the sources of these recurring conflicts.[27] In part, conflicts between staff and line are due to differences in the background and career interests of the two types of personnel, but often they are not caused by a pursuit of self-interest or a clash of personal values but by the concern of officials with discharging their job responsibilities. For example, in City Agency, an accounting section was in charge of determining the exact amount of

[26] Amitai Etzioni, "Authority Structure and Organizational Effectiveness," *Administrative Science Quarterly*, 4 (1959), pp. 43–67.

[27] See Melville Dalton, "Conflicts between Staff and Line Managerial Officers," *American Sociological Review*, 15 (1950), pp. 342–351; and Dalton, *Men Who Manage, op. cit.*, pp. 73–108.

assistance due to a client. There were frequent conflicts between these staff auditors and the caseworkers, since the latter defined their responsibilities as providing service to clients (compared to auditors, even the procedure-oriented workers did so) whereas the auditors defined their responsibilities as protecting the taxpayers' funds and assuring that clients were not overpaid. Such conflicts are not motivated by self-interests; rather, they result from each party's devotion to its job and endeavors to discharge its responsibilities effectively.[28]

Dalton's early research emphasizes the conflicts between staff and line personnel, and his later work shows that conflicts also prevail among line officers (and presumably among staff officers).[29] In a study of four organizations—three factories and a department store—Dalton found that the most effective managers were goal-oriented rather than method-oriented.[30] The former were strong enough to fight for the effective accomplishment of their mission and for expanding the jurisdiction of their department. They were partly motivated by self-interest as they sought increased power and promotions, but theirs was not a self-interest that opposed organizational interests, since they strove to maximize departmental objectives. Seeking to expand the jurisdiction of one's department is a managerial responsibility, in government as well as in industry.[31] Since expansion tends to lead to border disputes, power struggles often developed between managers. In these battles the less aggressive managers lost out, and so did their departments.[32] Coalitions frequently developed in the course of such struggles, sometimes between managers on the same level, and sometimes between managers on different levels. Similar coalitions occur among army officers, as Janowitz has noted.[33]

Far from condemning these power struggles, Dalton looks on them as important mechanisms of organizational change. Formal organizations are frequently slow to adjust their official structure to changing conditions. Innovations that adapt operations to a new situation, and thus benefit the organization, are often made informally, sometimes

[28] Note that the same point was made in Chapter III from a somewhat different perspective and using different language. There we talked about internal conflicts being engendered by the fact that different departments in an organization are oriented to different publics. The auditors in the example above were apparently oriented primarily to serving the taxpaying public, while the caseworkers were concerned with providing service to their clients.

[29] Dalton, *Men Who Manage, op. cit.,* pp. 18–70.

[30] *Ibid.,* pp. 246–248. This distinction is somewhat similar to that between a professional and a bureaucratic orientation.

[31] On this point see Marshall E. Dimock, *The Executive in Action,* New York: Harper, 1945, pp. 53–68.

[32] Dalton, *Men Who Manage,* p. 34.

[33] Morris Janowitz, *The Professional Soldier,* Glencoe, Ill.: Free Press, 1960, pp. 293–294.

in violation of official procedures. Power struggles play a significant role in this process of adjustment to change in the organization, since they provide managers with incentives for making informal innovations which help them cope with operating problems and extend the scope of their influence.[34]

Dalton's image of organization managers, as the foregoing makes clear, contrasts sharply with Whyte's conception of the organization man.[35] Unlike Whyte, Dalton does not see the individual pressed by the organization into a mold, lacking initiative and avoiding conflicts. On the contrary, in Dalton's view the organization exerts pressure on managers to exercise initiative in the interest of discharging their responsibilities successfully and strengthening their position. Only those left behind in the struggle for positions of dominant influence become method-oriented organization men.

Crozier's study of plants in the French tobacco monopoly adds new insights to our discussion of power struggles between managers.[36] The plants studied were highly bureaucratized: almost every situation was governed by formal rules, jobs were allocated strictly along seniority lines, and candidates for positions were recruited from the outside through open competition. Interviewing in a number of different plants revealed that among the three categories of employees at the lower level of the firm the maintenance workers were very satisfied with their situation, production workers were less satisfied, and supervisors were quite dissatisfied. An identical pattern was found at the managerial levels of the organizations, where the technical engineers were both more satisfied and more aggressive than were the top managers, their superiors. There was considerable conflict between the engineers who were in charge of machine maintenance and other managers, and the former seemed to possess a good deal of informal power. In analyzing these patterns, Crozier suggests that bureaucratic formalization eliminates many areas of uncertainty. Power accrues to those who can control the remaining areas of uncertainty. In the bureaucratized tobacco plants, machine breakdown was the main area of uncertainty still remaining; hence, social processes expanded the unofficial power of maintenance workers and particularly of the engineers in charge of their activities. Their power position produced conflict

---

[34] Likert arrives at a similar conclusion. He considers conflicts between organization members essential and healthy as long as mechanisms are available to deal constructively with these conflicts, effective interaction is skillfully maintained by the personnel, and there exists a basic loyalty to the organization. See Rensis Likert, *op. cit.*, pp. 204–205.

[35] William H. Whyte, Jr., *The Organization Man*, New York: Simon and Schuster, 1956.

[36] Michael Crozier, *The French Bureaucratic System*, Stanford: Stanford University Press (forthcoming).

in the organization as others questioned the legitimacy of their controlling influence.

The major implication of Crozier's work seems to be that technical expertness is a source of power in formal organizations, just as Weber pointed out. But whereas Weber saw expertness as a basis of formal authority, Crozier views it as an alternative to it that becomes manifest in areas not yet fully bureaucratized. Moreover, the power that rests on expertness in areas of uncertainty is not stable, since "the expert's success is constantly self-diminishing."[37] As the knowledge of experts increases, it transforms areas of uncertainty into areas that can be routinely handled (for example, advances in medicine enable nurses to perform tasks that previously required the judgment of physicians). The expert's own success, therefore, reduces the base of his power or, at least, shifts its base to a new area of uncertainty.

IMPERSONAL MECHANISMS OF CONTROL

Assembly-Line Production. The concept of "impersonal authority" in formal organizations is usually interpreted to mean hierarchical relations free of personal involvement, in contrast, for example, to charismatic authority where personal ties bind the followers to their leader. Indeed, in our discussion of the supervisor's role we noted the significance of detachment for effective supervision. But impersonal authority may also mean management through nonhuman mechanisms of control. It is possible for management to design and install an impersonal control system in such a manner that it, rather than the hierarchy, exerts continuous constraints on the performance of subordinates. The assembly line exemplifies such a control mechanism.[38]

Once the production process on the assembly line has been designed, the conveyor exerts the major constraints on workers, indicating what job they are to do next, what materials and tools are to be used, and setting the pace at which the work must be done. The foreman in this situation is consequently relieved of many of his traditional responsibilities. In spite of this change, however, most foremen do not think that the assembly line has made their job easier, but stress that it creates new problems for them.[39] Faced with the moving conveyor and a certain output level to be maintained, worker turnover and absenteeism become crucial problems. The foreman must

---

[37] *Ibid.*

[38] See Charles R. Walker and Robert H. Guest, *The Man on the Assembly Line,* Cambridge, Mass.: Harvard University Press, 1952, pp. 9–14.

[39] See Charles R. Walker *et al., The Foreman on the Assembly Line,* Cambridge, Mass.: Harvard University Press, 1956, pp. 12–33.

quickly train new workers and must be able to obtain replacements speedily from his superior. While waiting for a replacement, he must redistribute the work load among the men present. Tools must be kept in good repair, supplies must be readily available if the work is to proceed on schedule, and the foreman must make the necessary arrangements, since the workers themselves are bound to their place on the line. Finally, although the conveyor assures that a certain amount of work will be done in a specified time, the supervisor must see to it that the work is of satisfactory quality. Note that all of these supervisory responsibilities except the last—maintaining performance quality—involve helping the workers rather than checking on them. The assembly line reduces the foreman's responsibilities for checking on workers and increases his responsibility for helping them.

Assembly-line production tends to reverse the flow of demand in the organization. Typically, demands flow downward in the hierarchy: orders are received from the level above and transmitted to the level below. And usually the foreman must direct operations by giving instructions and orders and by checking on work. An intensive downward flow of demands constitutes close supervision, a practice which tends to impede effective performance, as we have seen. Since the presence of a conveyor assures coordination and a certain level of productivity, it obviates the need for supervisory direction to achieve these ends. As a result, the major task of the foreman is transformed from directing and checking on subordinates to helping them and being their trouble-shooter. With the assembly line to organize the work process, the typical pattern of interaction is that the worker requests the foreman's help (whether he needs advice or merely supplies) rather than that the foreman makes demands on the worker—to do this job now or to work faster. Thus, the worker, not the foreman, initiates most of their interaction, reversing the flow of demand typical of close supervision in formal organizations. The same sort of reversal occurs on higher levels. The foreman, seeking services and materials, initiates most of the interaction with his superiors and staff officials. And in contrast to the frequent conflicts that occur between staff and line in other types of organizations, assembly-line foremen tend to look on the staff as being helpful.[40]

These and related changes cast the foreman on the assembly line in the role of adviser and assistant to his subordinates, and his new role affects his behavior even when he does make demands on workers. As noted, the foreman must still check on the quality of work performed, but his role as trouble-shooter is likely to induce him to seek improvements by offering advice to his workers rather than by issuing commands. For to issue curt orders would interfere with his

[40] *Ibid.*, pp. 34–36.

ability to maintain the role of trouble-shooter and helper, and hence impede his effectiveness as a foreman on the assembly line. In short, the assembly line, by removing some of the sources of conflict between foreman and worker, improves the relations between them.[41]

Performance Records. The evaluation of performance on the basis of statistical records also acts as an impersonal mechanism of control, as was observed in the study of a state employment agency.[42] The agency developed performance records as an indirect means of control—to provide the supervisor with information which would serve as a basis for the evaluation and guidance of workers. But once introduced, the records themselves became a direct mechanism of control. Since the records were public, they provided each employee with precise knowledge of how his performance compared with that of others and of his chances for getting a high performance rating. If his record was below average, this knowledge frequently motivated him to improve his performance. In this way public records which made comparative performance visible to officials controlled operations without any direct intervention on the part of the supervisor.[43] Such performance records can be used to control some qualitative as well as quantitative aspects of performance. Various types of errors and successes can be recorded in addition to the total number of cases processed. With some ingenuity, the quality of performance on quite complex tasks can be assessed by management. For example, to measure how carefully interviewers selected qualified applicants for jobs in the employment agency, the proportion of referrals who actually obtained the job to which they had been referred was computed. By including some statistical measures in the performance record and not others, and by placing more or less emphasis on any one measure, management could regulate the amount of effort interviewers would devote to various aspects of the work.

Observation in the employment agency revealed that these per-

41 Although worker-foreman relations were good on the assembly line studied, this fact should not be taken to mean that workers were satisfied with their jobs. Most reported less satisfaction with present jobs than with previous jobs (not on the assembly line); the quitting rate for assembly plants in the automobile industry was higher than for other manufacturing industries; and there was some evidence that work on the assembly line generated aggression against the company. *Ibid.*, pp. 63, 120–121, 135.

42 See Blau, *op. cit.*, pp. 33–48, and "Formal Organization," *American Journal of Sociology*, 63 (1957), pp. 62–63.

43 It should, however, be noted that sometimes effective operations were impeded because making a good record became an end in itself. This situation was observed in the two welfare agencies as well as in the employment agency. In County Agency, for example, caseworkers sometimes worked on "easy" cases rather than on those with more urgent problems in order to increase the number of closings or to reduce the number of pending cases on their monthly statistical record.

formance records also reversed the flow of demand in the organization. The records provided supervisors with information about the performance of their subordinates and at the same time exerted direct influence on performance. In these circumstances the supervisor no longer needed to check frequently on the work of subordinates, and his task of critically evaluating their performance became easier and less onerous. He did not have to court the danger of antagonizing some of his subordinates by telling them that their work was inade-quate, since he could, as one put it, "let the records speak for themselves." The information provided by performance records permitted the superior to supervise less closely and to let subordinates come to him with their problems. This reversed flow of demand was reflected in the finding that the more supervisors relied on statistical records, the less frequently did they initiate the social interactions between themselves and subordinates.

Even when the supervisor talked to an interviewer with a poor record about improving his performance, the existence of statistical records completely changed the nature of the conference. In the absence of performance records, the supervisor would have to start the conference by first telling the interviewer that his performance was inadequate. The existence of public records made this opening super-fluous and, consequently, transformed the supervisor's discussion from a criticism that was likely to be resented to an offer to help the subordinate improve his record. Still another function of statistical records was that they served as an instrument for evaluating the work of interviewers on the basis of accomplished results, and such an evaluation system minimized the significance of detailed operating procedures on how to accomplish results and thus enabled management to permit officials more discretion in their work. The freedom from close supervision and from rigid operating rules that performance records make possible tends to enhance work satisfaction.

We have briefly discussed some of the consequences of two mechanisms of impersonal control: the assembly line and statistical records of performance. Note that these two mechanisms differ greatly in form and were observed in two very different kinds of organizations. Yet since both served as mechanisms for exerting impersonal constraint, their consequences in the organizations were quite similar. Both were in part substitutes for control through personal supervision; both reversed the flow of demand in the organization; and both improved relations between supervisors and subordinates. However, there was an important difference. Statistical records involved the evaluation of performance on the basis of results achieved, whereas the assembly line did not, and only the statistical performance records increased the discretion of employees and hence their job satisfaction. The assembly line had just the opposite consequences. It reduced the discretion of operators to a minimum, and as a result job satisfaction was extremely low.

Automation. Increased mechanization and specialization, exemplified by assembly-line production, has had the effect of reducing the skill level of workers as well as their discretion.[44] Skilled craftsmen have been replaced by semiskilled machine operators. However, further mechanization of the factory, particularly automation, has been expected to raise the level of skill and responsibility of operators again, since it would require that the modal worker be an expert mechanic who can maintain the complex machines. Specifically, we expected automation to serve as an impersonal mechanism of control more akin to performance records than to the assembly line. The same functions as those served by the assembly line—effecting coordination and maintaining rate of production with no need for close supervision —were expected from automation, but without the same dysfunctions—lack of discretion and low job satisfaction—because the worker would be highly skilled and could be evaluated on the basis of results, for example, his record of machine maintenance.

Studies of automated factories do not bear out these expectations. On the basis of interviews conducted with a random sample of workers in an automated automobile factory, Faunce discovered that workers felt they were more closely supervised than they had been in regular assembly-line automobile plants.[45] Workers reported more contacts with foremen,[46] and they were less satisfied with their relations with foremen. In addition, the number of foremen per worker had been increased in consequence of the greater complexity of the machines, their greater interdependence, and especially the costly delays occasioned by their breakdown. Also contrary to expectations is the finding that automation restricted the social contacts between workers even more than had the assembly line. In contrast to the assembly line, there were distinct social groups, but even so there was less chance for social interaction among workers in the automated plant. Faunce suggests that reduced interaction was due to the closer attention required by the work, the greater distances between workers, and the greater noise of the machines.

[44] For an early study of the breakdown of the skill hierarchy and its consequences for worker discretion and satisfaction, see W. Lloyd Warner and J. O. Low, *The Social System of the Modern Factory,* New Haven: Yale University Press, 1947, pp. 66–89.

[45] William A. Faunce, "Automation in the Automobile Industry," *American Sociological Review,* 23 (1958), pp. 401–407.

[46] No information was presented on who initiated these contacts, so that we do not know how or whether the flow of demand was affected.

A study by Simpson of a mechanized spinning department in a textile mill provides an interesting contrast with the foregoing case of automation.[47] Simpson found no evidence of close supervision in the spinning department, noting that first-line foremen had relatively few work-related contacts with their subordinates but interacted primarily with other foremen on their own level. This observation parallels the conclusion we deduced from the study of assembly-line foremen—that mechanized techniques which pace the work make close supervision unnecessary—but it differs from the situation observed in the automated factory, where supervision was quite close. Simpson interprets these results by suggesting that some degree of mechanization, such as that characteristic of the spinning department and of the assembly line, reduces the need for close supervision because the production process exerts some of the constraints on worker behavior that otherwise would have to be exerted by foremen. However, further mechanization, as occurs in automation, again increases the need for supervision and hierarchical communication because in the interest of effective operations the recurrent and very costly breakdowns of the complex machinery must be minimized and quickly dealt with when they do occur. The implication is that the operators in an automated plant cannot assume responsibility for machine maintenance by making minor repairs themselves and calling in expert mechanics when necessary.

Walker's study of a semiautomatic steel mill furnishes some explanation for this interpretation as well as confirmation of many of Faunce's findings.[48] Since workers had been transferred from another steel mill, it was possible to compare their new social situation and experiences with their former ones in a mechanized but nonautomatic plant. Workers reported greater social isolation in the new mill than in the old, and most felt that they were physically more isolated in the new plant. At first their attitudes toward supervision improved, but soon they deteriorated sharply. After a period of adjustment, attitudes to supervisors again improved but remained negative. No information was obtained on the closeness of supervision. In general, attitudes were also negative toward management. Workers felt that no attempt was made to improve undesirable physical conditions, such as excess smoke, and that they were not getting a fair share of the profits realized by the improved technology; they also feared that automation might result in layoffs during a depression.[49] With regard to

[47] Richard L. Simpson, "Vertical and Horizontal Communication in Formal Organizations," *Administrative Science Quarterly*, 4 (1959), pp. 188–196.
[48] Charles R. Walker, *Toward the Automatic Factory*, New Haven: Yale University Press, 1957, pp. 47, 51, 93.
[49] *Ibid.*, pp. 81, 94–96, 184–185.

their work, the men said they experienced less physical fatigue but more mental strain owing to tensions created by watching fast-moving machines closely. Their reported work satisfaction was only fair, but it was probably higher than that connected with assembly-line work. Surprisingly, the average skill level of the workers had not increased. There were fewer high job classifications in the automated plant than in the old one, and there was less opportunity for advancement, which was a source of great dissatisfaction to the workers.[50] The low skill level of operators of automated machines—not superior to that of other factory workers—helps to explain why responsibility for machine maintenance could not be assumed by these workers themselves but only by foremen.

Finally, a case history of the introduction of electronic data-processing equipment into the accounting division of a large light and power company is of interest because it provides some information about the effects of automation on white-collar groups.[51] As in the factory studied by Walker, the introduction of automation into the white-collar office did not significantly increase the average job grade or skill level. While most routine and menial jobs were eliminated by the change-over, so were a number of high-level non-supervisory jobs. The lack of improvement in job grades was a source of dissatisfaction among both workers and first-line supervisors. The new equipment also reduced discretion, particularly in the middle levels of the organization, and allowed less autonomy in setting the work pace for both groups and individuals. The greater interdependence of operations created problems of coordination and led to greater centralization of decision-making in the upper levels of the organization.[52]

A conclusion that emerges from these studies on the social consequences of automation is that as long as automation is not accompanied by a higher level of skill on the part of the workers involved, it does not result in increased discretion for them; hence, job satisfaction is not notably improved by such automation and may in fact be reduced. Given a low level of skill of operators, moreover, the complexity of the machines and the interdependence of operations appear to require closer supervision and greater centralization of decision-making to minimize the costly delays occasioned by machine breakdowns or by imperfect coordination. It may be that further automation and, particularly, a reorganization of the work force to assure that

[50] *Ibid.*, pp. 29–39, 59–61, 97–99, 192–193.

[51] Floyd C. Mann and Lawrence K. Williams, "Observations on the Dynamics of a Change to Electronic Data-Processing Equipment," *Administrative Science Quarterly*, 5 (1960), pp. 217–256. See also Floyd C. Mann and L. Richard Hoffman, *Automation and the Worker*, New York: Holt, 1960.

[52] Mann and Williams, *op. cit.*, pp. 247–252.

the technical expertness of operators is commensurate with the complexity of the mechanical equipment they handle (whether this involves skills in machine maintenance or in computer programming), will change conditions to make them correspond more closely to our original expectations, that is, will raise discretion and work satisfaction.

QUESTIONING SOME PREVAILING ASSUMPTIONS

Hierarchical Authority and Coordination. It is widely assumed that the hierarchy of authority is essential for coordination in complex organizations. Those who take this view recognize that hierarchical authority interferes with communications: specifically, that it often prevents accurate information from reaching higher executives to the detriment of effective management. But given the assumption that a hierarchy is a functional prerequisite for coordination in a formal organization, its dysfunctions are looked upon as an inevitable cost—a cost that may be reduced but cannot be eliminated. Moreover, given this assumption, some questions are never raised—questions such as how much and what kinds of coordination are actually required by various types of organizations.

To answer these questions it is necessary to distinguish between two forms of departmental specialization, which may be called "parallel" and "interdependent." Even if various departments have different responsibilities, they are not necessarily interdependent. A department store exemplifies such parallel specialization, where the work at the perfume counter is different from but not dependent on that in the shoe department. In contrast, the operations of a sales department and those of the corresponding group of buyers in the department store are interdependent, and so are the operations in various divisions of an automobile factory. It is only such interdependent specialization that makes coordination a fundamental managerial problem. In many organizations, therefore, problems of coordination are of minor significance. (And let us note also that quite large organizations are sometimes hardly specialized at all. The operations of different departments often are essentially alike, as is illustrated by the responsibilities of the various district offices of the Bureau of Internal Revenue. There is no interdependence between the work of these offices, and hence no problem of coordination. Instead, the crucial problem is that of uniform administration of tax legislation. The enforcement of strict conformity to legal standards throughout the entire organization is clearly a managerial problem, but it is not a problem of coordination.)

Another question seldom asked is how much coordination, when it is essential, is actually accomplished by means of hierarchical communication, that is, through managerial directives transmitted down the hierarchy to operating levels. Note that this model of hierarchical coordination implies that the solution of every new problem that arises between departments is delayed until relevant information has been passed up the hierarchy and a decision has been made and sent down again. (This procedure corresponds to the stereotype of the buck-passing bureaucracy encumbered in red-tape.) We want to suggest that in the very organizations where interdependent specialization is most pronounced, and where, consequently, the problems of coordination are most acute, coordination is typically not achieved by this method, undoubtedly in large part because it is so inefficient. In the assembly-line plant, not hierarchical communication but the a priori design of the production process, as manifested in the arrangement of work stations on the conveyors, is the primary mechanism of coordination; and the same is the case in the automated factory. But even where mechanization is less advanced and does not furnish the instrument with which management attains coordination, the coordination is often achieved by more direct methods than hierarchical communication.

The classical model of hierarchical coordination implies that supervisors discharge their duties by serving as vertical channels of communication. This function, however, is not what Simpson found in the spinning department he studied.[53] Communication there was predominantly horizontal rather than vertical. As we have mentioned, most work-related contacts of first-line foremen were not with superiors or subordinates but with other foremen on their own level, and the purpose of many of these contacts among foremen was to coordinate the operations of their interdependent specialized sections. This method of coordination through direct contact between employees on the same level was also observed in the welfare agencies. When the work of two departments required some coordination, the supervisors or even the caseworkers involved would establish direct contact and would jointly solve the problem or develop a common plan of action. Thus, a public-assistance caseworker might consult directly with a medical social worker, or a field supervisor with a supervisor from the auditing department. These consultations were not merely an informal practice but part of the formally established procedure. Why, given these considerations, did we find that the supervisors in the two agencies had relatively few contacts with one another?[54] The reason probably is that all the supervisors interviewed in City Agency and most of those in County Agency (within each division) were in charge

53 Simpson, *loc. cit.*
54 See above, pp. 159–161.

of units engaged in the same operations in different parts of the community. Since the responsibilities of these units were not interdependent, there were relatively few problems of joint concern to any two of them. Problems of coordination occur primarily between specialized sections whose operations are interdependent, and they are often solved not by communicating information up the hierarchy to a common superior and waiting for his decision to be transmitted downward, but through direct contacts between the members of the sections affected.

Finally, an implicit assumption of bureaucratic theory which we have had repeated occasion to question is that hierarchical authority and discipline are compatible with decisions based on expert judgments made in accordance with professional standards. It seems, on the contrary, that there is a conflict between these two conditions. Rigid discipline stifles professional judgments. Conversely, hierarchical authority is weakened by increasing technological complexity in an organization with its resulting emphasis on technical expertness for all personnel, including those on the lowest operating levels. Janowitz reports that even in the army—the prototype hierarchical structure—the requirements of modern warfare and its complex technology have brought about a reduction in hierarchical domination of lower levels and an increase in delegation of responsibility to them.[55]

These observations are not to be taken as indicating that management is becoming obsolete, only that its form and functions are changing. It appears that management's primary significance is no longer as the apex of the authority pyramid; rather its central function is to design, in collaboration with a staff of experts, appropriate impersonal mechanisms of control. These mechanisms centralize control in the hands of management and become functional substitutes for directives from supervisors, since they directly influence performance and effect the necessary coordination of specialized activities. Impersonal mechanisms take many forms. They include the old-fashioned rules and regulations in administrative organizations as well as the more recent technological control of the labor force through advance planning and mechanization of the work process. Another form of impersonal control is the use of performance records which serve as the basis for an objective evaluation of the results accomplished by employees and at the same time exert direct pressure on them to improve their performance. Recruitment and training procedures which assure that personnel will be qualified to make expert judgments are still other mechanisms of control available to management, and so

[55] Morris Janowitz, "Changing Patterns of Organizational Authority," *Administrative Science Quarterly*, 3 (1959), pp. 473–493. See also Janowitz, *The Professional Soldier, op. cit.*, pp. 8–9, 38–42.

are promotion policies established to furnish inducements for exercising initiative, responsibility, and effort. These and other techniques allow management to control operations without relying primarily on communicating directives through the hierarchy to operating levels.

Impersonal mechanisms of control, therefore, lessen the need for close supervision, but whether this lessening leads to more responsibility and discretion for employees depends on the nature of the control they exert. Important as problems of coordination are, they are not the only ones that require limiting the discretion available to members of an organization. If employees lack the skills to assume responsibilities, or if they receive no incentive to exercise their skills in the pursuit of organizational objectives, management will also find it necessary to restrict the scope of their discretion. Mechanization of the work process, as illustrated by the assembly line or automation, solves the problem of coordination but does not solve these other problems and, consequently, is not associated with greater discretion for workers. On the other hand, discretion, and therefore work satisfaction, can be increased by personnel policies and reward systems that increase the skill of employees and motivate them to exercise these skills in the pursuit of organizational objectives. In such a situation, management, relieved of much routine supervision, would be free to concentrate its efforts on improving the organization and, specifically, the impersonal mechanisms of control.[56]

Pseudo Democracy. Democracy implies that a group of people rule themselves, either directly or through elected representatives. We have just contrasted management through planning the conditions in the organization that in turn influence the activities of its members with management through transmitting directives down a hierarchy of authority. We have suggested that the former has several advantages over the latter, including a lesser emphasis on hierarchical authority relations. However, neither of these two approaches to management can be considered democratic. Indeed, the loose talk about internal democracy in private firms, government agencies, and similar organizations is simply misleading, since management in these types of organizations is not and cannot be governed by the principle of following the will of the majority of its members but must be guided by the principle of maximizing the effective accomplishment of given objectives. Only the type of organization we have called "mutual-benefit association" is expected to adhere to democratic principles of organization.

It is often assumed that permitting workers in a factory or business

---

[56] This is also the conclusion of Ackoff's attempt to forecast the implications of automation for management. See Russell L. Ackoff, "Automatic Management," *Management Science*, 2 (1955), pp. 55–60.

concern to discuss some problem that has implications for their work situation involves democratic management. But this practice would constitute democracy only if the workers had the right to make the most basic decisions about operations, not if they merely were permitted to decide how to implement decisions previously made by management. For example, if management should decide to install new machines in a department but allow the workers to discuss the problems involved in adapting to them and even to suggest ways by which the period of adaptation can be eased, this practice does not entail, in any meaningful sense, a democratic decision process. Research shows that workers who were given such opportunities for discussion accepted innovations in work procedures much more readily than did workers in situations where no discussion was allowed.[57] These findings indicate that such discussions are an effective managerial technique, but they do not involve, as is sometimes implied, democratic decision-making by the workers.[58] For the latter would require that the workers have the power to reverse management and decide not to make the suggested change.

In general, it appears that the hierarchical structure of an organization tends to defeat attempts at democratization. This effect is illustrated by some occurrences in a federal law-enforcement agency studied by one of the authors. The bureau chief in Washington decided that changes needed to be made in the evaluation procedure and that they should be democratically arrived at by a committee representing the employees. He therefore instructed each of the nine regional directors to send a nonsupervisory employee to represent his region to a conference; three of the regions were also to send a supervisory representative. This committee of twelve discussed problems of evaluation and democratically decided on a new evaluation procedure by a majority vote. Officials from the national headquarters participated only in an advisory capacity in the conference. But, appearances to the contrary, the hierarchical authority structure contravened the purpose of the bureau chief to make the decisions in a democratic manner. For the regional directors, wishing to make a good impression on the national officers, wanted the "right" person to represent them at the meeting. Only one of the nine directors permitted the employee organization to select their own representative. The rest appointed the representative themselves and tried to appoint an outstanding agent. Hence, workers most critical of the present evaluation system were not represented, and

---

[57] Lester Coch and John R. P. French, Jr., "Overcoming Resistance to Change," *Human Relations*, 1 (1948), pp. 512–532.

[58] Coch and French make no claim that their experiment involved democratic decision-making, only "participation in planning the change"; but their results are sometimes interpreted in this misleading fashion.

most agents felt that the committee did not represent them. Further, selection was biased in favor of the higher positions. Several of the agent-representatives were ex-supervisors, and two of the three supervisors attending the conference were not first-level supervisors but held higher positions. It appears that attempts to develop democratic decision-making machinery in formal organizations with hierarchical structures are almost sure to be frustrated by built-in conflicts of interest between management and operating officials, which make representatives selected by workers unsatisfactory to management, and vice versa. The widespread acceptance of the values of democracy, however, constrains officials to attempt to utilize democratic forms in the management of their organizations. Unfortunately, the forms alone are insufficient, and the result is often a kind of pseudo democracy which easily degenerates into a device for the manipulation of employees.

In certain types of service organizations, such as casework agencies and mental hospitals, pseudo democracy often takes the form of a therapy-oriented or psychiatric approach to supervision. In this approach the subordinate is not blamed for imperfections in his performance or for failing to conform to directives; instead, his behavior is analyzed to detect what unconscious forces have led to his resistance.[59] This practice was observed to occur frequently in the weekly supervisor-worker conferences in the welfare agencies, where the worker would bring his difficult cases for discussion. The supervisor would aid him in solving the technical questions involved in determining client eligibility, would help him to understand the behavior of his client, and sometimes would indicate to the worker how his own feelings and needs were influencing his relation with the client. Accordingly, the workers often found themselves rather than the clients to be the subjects of these discussions—so much so that there were many references among workers to the supervisory practice of "caseworking the worker." There were, of course, sometimes legitimate grounds for subjecting the worker's feelings and behavior to critical analysis—to help him refrain from projecting his own needs and interests into his casework relations, to encourage a more professional and detached orientation to clients, and to protect the welfare of the clients.

However, the psychiatric approach to supervision in social work is subject to abuse. What is conceived to be a very democratic method

[59] Gouldner refers to a "utilitarian" view of deviance when nonconforming acts are assumed to result from carelessness or ignorance. Our concept is broader and includes, particularly, acts that are assumed to result from internal forces over which the individual has no control. Gouldner contrasts the utilitarian with the "voluntaristic" view of deviance, according to which the offending individual has deliberately disobeyed and hence is subject to punishment. See Alvin W. Gouldner, *Patterns of Industrial Bureaucracy*, Glencoe, Ill.: Free Press, 1954, pp. 232–233.

of supervision—not blaming subordinates but helping them understand their problems—turns easily into a manipulative controlling device. When there were differences of opinion between the supervisor and the caseworker on how to deal with certain problems of a client, the supervisor was tempted to analyze the worker's motives for disagreeing rather than to demonstrate why his judgment was better in terms of professional or other objective standards. Workers whose judgment frequently differed from that of their supervisor might be accused of being "unable to accept supervision." The practice of questioning the worker's unconscious motives tended to elevate the superordinate into an omniscient power. Workers found that they could not be right in any disagreement since their arguments were not accepted at face value but dismissed as being rationalizations to mask unconscious resistance.[60] Subordinates are defenseless against this criticism because the very act of questioning it "proves it right."

Psychiatric terminology was also utilized to hide the exercise of power over clients. Such generalized phrases as "working through problems," "cooperating with the agency," and "accepting reality factors" could disguise from the supervisor, the client, and sometimes from the worker himself actions involving coercion or manipulation of the client. And here again objections and protests of clients could be interpreted as "resistance," which served to devalue their remarks and to depersonalize the hostility they expressed,[61] as the following incident in a worker-supervisor conference at County Agency illustrates. The worker had just returned from a field visit to tell a client that inasmuch as she had been neglecting her child the agency would institute wardship proceedings. The worker reported to the supervisor that the client had become quite abusive and had threatened to take the child and move to another city outside the county; the client further insisted that she had been willing to give up the child a year ago but that the agency had moved too slowly. The supervisor rejected the client's protests as reported by the worker in the following terms: "We know what this is, don't we? She is projecting blame onto others. We recognize this for what it is—a big defense. We anticipated some kind of reaction, didn't we? This is what to us? A threat! Is this going to take us off our course?"[62]

60 On similar tendencies to disregard the content of communications in a private mental hospital, see Alfred H. Stanton and Morris S. Schwartz, *The Mental Hospital,* New York: Basic Books, 1954, pp. 146–150, 200–206.

61 The interpretation of client hostility in nonpersonal terms is important for the worker as a means of protecting his own ego. It is also important for the organization, because it helps workers to enforce official policy even in the face of client hostility.

62 See W. Richard Scott, "A Case Study of Professionals in a Bureaucratic Setting," unpublished Ph.D. dissertation, Department of Sociology, University of Chicago, 1961, p. 199.

Since such psychiatric interpretations, often in terms of unconscious motives, leave the subject defenseless by devaluating the substantive content of his arguments, their legitimate use as a diagnostic or therapeutic tool requires a relationship in which the defenseless clients are protected—one where the decisions of the professional are exclusively oriented to serving the interests of the clients.[63] Such an orientation to clients prevails in social work as well as in other professional services, but other factors intrude in the operations of welfare agencies. For the responsibilities of these agencies include not only providing casework service but also some duties that involve a conflict of interests, such as determining eligibility for assistance, or deciding whether a mother's conduct justifies taking her child away from her against her will (an action that presumably serves the interests of the child but involves a conflict of interests with the mother). Psychiatric interpretations are a legitimate professional technique in the context of casework, but in a context where conflicts of interests occur they are simply manipulative devices to facilitate and conceal the exercise of power. They are particularly so in the supervisor-subordinate relationship, which is not a professional-client relationship, since conflicts of interest exist between the representative of managerial policies and the worker, and since conflicts of professional judgment are legitimate and are expected to be clarified rather than ignored by attributing the opinion of the subordinate to unconscious resistance.

A study by Lefton and his colleagues suggests that the pseudo democracy implicit in a psychotherapeutic approach to supervision may have boomerang effects.[64] Observation of staff conferences in a mental hospital revealed that nearly all decisions were made by the psychiatrists, the senior staff members, notwithstanding the conception of a "therapeutic community" where all members of the clinical team participate in decision-making. Interview responses also indicated the predominant influence position of psychiatrists. There were, however, interesting differences between wards in the staff reaction to this situation. In wards oriented toward organic treatment, the staff on lower levels did not expect or particularly want to participate in decision-making, but in wards with a strong psychotherapeutic orientation lower staff members did expect and want to exercise considerable influence on decisions. As a result, staff members in lower positions in the psychotherapeutically oriented wards found themselves frustrated and were less satisfied with the amount of influence they could exert than those in organically oriented wards, although the latter had no

[63] See Talcott Parsons, *The Social System*, Glencoe, Ill.: Free Press, 1951, pp. 463–465.

[64] Mark Lefton *et al.*, "Decision-Making in a Mental Hospital," *American Sociological Review*, 24 (1959), pp. 822–829.

more influence than the former. It appears, then, that the expectations engendered by a democratic ideology make low-influence positions unsatisfactory—more unsatisfactory than they are in the absence of a pseudo-democratic climate.

The managerial planning of impersonal mechanisms of control does not involve such pseudo-democratic promises or assumptions. Nevertheless, such mechanisms, particularly the evaluation of performance by results achieved, give the lower levels more responsibility and tend to identify their interests with the objectives of the organization. Consequently, the informal expectations and social pressures in work groups frequently further the interests of the organization rather than oppose them. For example, in the automatic steel mill studied by Walker, the introduction of a group incentive-pay plan had the result that workers put pressure on one another to maintain a high level of productivity.[65] They also demanded wider coverage of the incentive plan to include the maintenance workers, partly so that this group could participate in the higher earnings, but largely because they wanted the maintenance crews to have an incentive to make repairs quickly lest the production teams' earnings suffer from the more leisurely pace of the maintenance crews. Thus, in at least some respects, workers took over functions formerly exercised by management. The fact that work groups themselves exercise much controlling power in the interest of operating efficiency, however, is not an unmixed blessing for their individual members. The checks and balances resulting from some conflict of interest between informal work group, union, and management may give the individual a degree of freedom that he loses when a coalition develops between these three powers over him.

In the situation studied by Walker a group incentive plan led to increased output and mobilized the informal forces of the work group in the pursuit of objectives set by management. This result was precisely what the management in the Hawthorne plant studied by Roethlisberger and Dickson hoped for in their use of a group incentive system; however, as we have seen, the informal pressures of the workers in the Bank Wiring Observation Room did not increase production but limited it. What accounts for these different effects of similar incentive plans? We can, of course, only speculate, but the following differences may be in part responsible. First, the workers studied by Walker had no fear of immediate layoff since the country was not in the throes of a major depression when this study was conducted as it

[65] Walker, *op. cit.*, pp. 80–83, 169. See also Seymour Melman, *Decision Making and Productivity*, Oxford, England: Basil Blackwell, 1958, pp. 133–134; Melman concludes that the introduction of a gang system and group wage incentives into a British automobile-manufacturing firm reduced the need for supervision because work-group pressures assured a high level of productivity.

was at the time of the Hawthorne study. Second, group cohesion in the automated factory appears to have been weaker than in traditional work groups. Workers were scattered and communication between them was reduced. In such situations management and its reward system may be able to exert more influence on worker attitudes than is possible when workers are members of tightly knit groups. Third, and perhaps most important, the operations of workers in the automated plant were interdependent. Hence, there was no danger that they would compete with one another, and all had to attain high output together or none could. The men in the Bank Wiring Room, in contrast, were engaged in similar but not interdependent tasks. Competition for high productivity could have torn the group apart had not informal control measures to discourage it been instituted.

Finally, let us briefly examine another implication of pay-incentive systems. Piece-rate incentives are usually based on measuring working time and not idle time; however, if the task involves primarily mental and not physical labor, this distinction breaks down.[66] Unlike other workers, those employed in the automatic steel mill did not complain about the rates themselves, but they did complain about not getting paid for ideas they had and for judgments they made when they were apparently idle. A dysfunction of the pay incentives was that they tended to focus the worker's attention on his narrow task—to reward him for restricting his interest. But the interdependence of the work in the automated department made it important for the worker to scan the work of others and coordinate his task with theirs. Hence, the pay incentives discouraged the scope of attention most beneficial for automated production. This conflict suggests that the more professionalized tasks become—that is, the more they require expert judgment and breadth of perception—the less adequate will piece rates be as an incentive system. The evaluation of results of tasks that involve expertness requires more than measuring output rates, and the reward system appropriate for such tasks is one that does not focus on immediate earnings but on the employee's long-run career. This more complex reward structure would gear the evaluation system to a promotion system that provides opportunities for advancement to higher positions and thus assure that the worker's record of accomplishment would influence his chances for advancement.

Concluding Remarks

We discussed in this chapter some informal patterns that characterize the relations between managers, such as conflicts between staff

---

[66] See Walker, *op. cit.*, pp. 169–174.

and line, and power struggles that occur among managers and apparently serve important functions for organizational change. Our primary focus, however, was on organizational constraints. After examining the significance of the shape of the pyramid and of the structuring of time on different organizational levels, we contrasted impersonal mechanisms of control, such as mechanization and statistical records of performance, with management through hierarchical directives.

In the last part we questioned some prevailing assumptions in the field of formal organization. We asked whether the hierarchy of authority, as distinguished from managerial planning, is the most effective mechanism for coordinating the operations of specialized, interdependent segments of an organization or, for that matter, whether it actually is the method of coordination typically used. We questioned the assumption that the participation of workers in discussions of organizational problems involves democratic decision-making, and we critically examined other pseudo-democratic procedures in hierarchical organizations. We also raised the question of whether informal control of production through peer-group pressure, democratic as it appears, may not restrict individual freedom even more severely than do formal mechanisms of control. Finally, we queried whether the traditional pay-incentive systems are adequate to motivate and control workers in the increasingly complex and professionalized jobs of modern industry.

CHAPTER EIGHT

The Social Context
of Organizational Life

Organizations have their roots in larger social systems. In this chapter we shall examine formal organizations in relation to their social environment. This environment is complex, and while we cannot hope to deal with it in all its complexity, we can indicate a few of its components. In Chapter III, we analyzed one dimension of an organization's environment, namely, the publics associated with it—the public-in-contact, the public served, and the public-at-large. Now we are concerned with other dimensions of the social environment, such as the culture and the structure of the community in which an organization is located. One particularly interesting aspect of an organization's environment is other organizations, and the study of this aspect leads to a consideration of the web of interrelations between organizations.

The boundary between an organization and its social context is never entirely clear. Goffman has commented that organizations are surrounded by a "semi-permeable membrane," the degree of permeability varying with the type of organization.[1] The place of technology illustrates the ambiguity of this boundary. On the one hand, the stage of technological advancement in a society is part of the environment of organizations. On the other hand, however, it is a characteristic of the organizations themselves, because they are the bearers of the technology and also because organizations differ in technological complexity. Of course, this distinction does not refer to two different technologies but merely to two perspectives for looking at the same phenomenon. Since environmental conditions and organizational characteristics are so closely connected, the comparative study of organizations in different environments also provides an opportunity for analyzing the association between various organizational characteristics. For example, the study of organizations in different societies or cultures is most likely to reveal pronounced differences in technology and thus furnish the data most suitable for the investigation of the associa-

---

[1] Erving Goffman, "Characteristics of Total Institutions," Walter Reed Army Institute of Research, *Symposium on Preventive and Social Psychiatry*, Washington, D.C.: U.S. Government Printing Office, 1957, pp. 82–83.

tion between technological complexity and bureaucratic hierarchy in organizations.

The social environment influences organizations—their internal structure and their relations with one another—but there are also feedback processes through which organizations influence their environment. The social processes that characterize the relations between organizations, and that are affected by their internal structure, help shape the larger social system in which the organizations exist. We shall seek to analyze some of these dynamic processes.

THE SOCIAL ENVIRONMENT OF ORGANIZATIONS

The Web of Organizations. Merton has noted that any single status involves the individual in not one but a whole set of role relations and expectations.[2] Inherent in such a "role-set" is the possibility of conflicting expectations. For example, physicians in a hospital may expect the hospital administrator to purchase the latest diagnostic and therapeutic equipment whereas the hospital board expects him to hold down the cost of medical facilities. There are several mechanisms that help to articulate such conflicting demands: (1) differences in the importance and power of the various members of an individual's role-set help to determine whose expectations will govern his actions; (2) the fact that a person usually does not have contacts with all members of his role-set at once enables him to live up to the expectations of some at one time and to the conflicting expectations of others at a different time; (3) when the others realize that they are making conflicting demands on a person, they will themselves often attempt to resolve their differences; and (4) several individuals occupying the same social status can combine for mutual support, forming associations and developing codes to mitigate the conflicting expectations.

By extension, one can speak of organization-sets or webs of organizations, thus referring to the various other organizations to which any one organization is related. Like the persons who form an individual's role-set, these organizations often make conflicting demands on a particular organization. For example, a business concern may find that it is linked with a large number of organizations and groups—competing firms, suppliers, customers, the board of directors representing the stockholders, government agencies, unions, professional associations, and possibly consumer organizations. Each of these will have expectations of the firm's activities, some of which will not be compatible. The mechanisms that, according to Merton, provide a means of articulat-

[2] Robert K. Merton, "The Role-Set," *British Journal of Sociology*, 8 (1957), pp. 106–120.

ing the demands of an individual's role-set also appear to operate in the organizational sphere. First, power is certainly important in determining to whose demands the organization will yield. A union must have strength if management is to comply with its demands notwithstanding the contrary pressures of stockholders; and the public must become effectively organized to exert influence on a firm, in the manner, for example, of the recent sit-in demonstrations by Negroes in the South. Second, mechanisms that insulate organizations from observation offer some protection against conflicting demands. Thus, customers ordinarily are not informed about the contracts a firm has with its suppliers; meetings of the board are not open to the public; and the board has no knowledge of the informal compromises that have been reached between management and the unions. Third, business firms often go to great lengths to inform some segment of their set about the pressures and demands made by other segments. For instance, a concern will spend many thousands of dollars to inform the public through advertising that it cannot reduce or must raise prices because of union demands for higher wages or because of the high taxes imposed by the government.[3] Finally, organizations, like individuals, combine together in mutual-benefit associations for the protection of their common interests. For example, industrial concerns have joined forces in the National Association of Manufacturers to fight the demands of other organizations, hospitals have united in the American Hospital Association, and unions have gained strength from the A.F.L.-C.I.O.

What are some of the processes that govern relations among organizations? Thompson and McEwen have distinguished four types—competition between organizations for the output of third parties and three kinds of cooperation.[4] Cooperative relations involve one of the following processes: (1) bargaining, in which agreements are negotiated between two or more organizations for the exchange of goods and services; (2) cooptation, in which new elements are absorbed into the leadership of an organization as a means of averting outside threats;

---

[3] In this connection, it is interesting to speculate what will be the long-range consequences of sociological studies of the forces that impinge on formal organizations. As these studies are expanded in scope, and to the extent to which their results become widely disseminated, organizations may gain increased insight into the types of pressures operating on them and on the organizations with which they deal, and they may adjust their policies accordingly. We agree with Gouldner that not enough attention has been devoted to studying the consequences of applied social science. See Alvin W. Gouldner, "Organizational Analysis," Robert K. Merton *et al.* (eds.), *Sociology Today*, New York: Basic Books, 1959, pp. 407–408.

[4] James D. Thompson and William J. McEwen, "Organization Goals and Environment," *American Sociological Review*, 23 (1958), pp. 23–31.

and (3) coalition formation, in which organizations become formally committed to joint decisions. An organization's goals are defined and redefined in these relations with other organizations. Each of the above strategies is intended to obtain support from some other organization, but in each case support must be paid for in surrendered sovereignty. Competition among organizations entails the least reduction in the autonomy of the organizations involved, bargaining permits organizations to maintain more independence than does cooptation, and coalitions require the greatest reduction in autonomy.

Competition between firms does not involve direct interaction. As Simmel states: "Here the struggle consists only in the fact that each competitor by himself aims at the goal, without using his strength on the adversary."[5] But the other social processes that occur between organizations do entail some contact, the actual interaction between organizations being carried out by designated members as their representatives. Goldner has called attention to the importance of certain "boundary roles," which are often utilized by one organization to carry on interaction with others, and which serve the function of maintaining the boundary of the parent organization against pressures exerted on it by other organizations.[6] He examines the labor-relations representatives of a firm as an example of persons having such a boundary role. These men were hired as staff experts in order to deal with the union. However, as a result of their role activities, they soon were seen by line management as representing the union viewpoint. The unions also regarded them with suspicion and thus they became marginal men, working for the firm and with the union but not accepted by either. But Goldner reports that their marginal position was an asset to the labor-relations men in performing their duties. Strangely enough, a certain amount of marginality appears to be functional for discharging the responsibilities of boundary roles. This becomes apparent if we consider the kinds of strategies required for an organization to enter into or to alter relations with other organizations.

To establish a new or different relationship, one party must make overtures to another, but doing so is risky since the rejection of the overture may well harm the first party's interest. Thompson and McEwen suggest that these principles hold for relations between organizations as well as individuals, and they use the case of a boss with amor-

---

[5] Georg Simmel, *Conflict,* Kurt H. Wolff (trans.), Glencoe, Ill.: Free Press, 1955, p. 58.

[6] Fred H. Goldner, "Organizations and Their Environment: Roles at their Boundary," paper read at the meetings of the American Sociological Association, New York, 1960. The concept of "boundary role" was first suggested in Talcott Parsons and Robert F. Bales, *Family, Socialization and Interaction Process,* Glencoe, Ill.: Free Press, 1955, p. 13.

ous designs on his secretary to illustrate the strategy required in such a situation.[7] To have his advances rejected would be at best embarrassing for the boss and might be disastrous for his career. But he can avoid this risk by making his initial overtures ambiguous and waiting until these elicit signs from the secretary that his advances are not unwelcome before he makes his intentions explicit. Similarly, a firm known to have unsuccessfully sought a merger with another firm may suffer a loss of credit as its solvency becomes suspect. To prevent such damaging repercussions, a firm can send out "feelers" that are sufficiently ambiguous to provide an "out" if the overture is rejected and yet explicit enough to elicit expressions of interest and tenative commitments from others, and it can wait for some reaction before making its own position clear. This strategy is most readily employed in behalf of organizations by persons occupying boundary roles. Thus, the marginality of the labor-relations representative, known to be more sympathetic to the union than other executives, allows him to carry "trial balloons" concerning management's intentions to the union to elicit the reactions of union leaders without firmly committing management, since the latter can easily claim that the labor-relations man's own views have led him to misrepresent its official position. A similar function appears to be performed by those individuals whom Dalton calls "two-way funnels."[8] These are persons known to gossip, to whom various parties deliberately leak pseudo secrets for the purpose of having them spread around. Depending on the reaction that follows, the originating party can then deny the "rumor," since the source is known to be unreliable, or it can make a firm commitment.

Organizations are not only related but actually interpenetrate one another through overlapping memberships. Union members, for example, are necessarily also members of an employing organization and may, besides, belong to other associations. Another illustration of interpenetration is found in the report of the National Resources Committee that in 1935, 225 of the 250 boards of the largest nonfinancial and financial corporations in this country had one or more directors in common with at least one other corporation board on the list.[9]

A study by Coleman indicates that the density of organizations in a community and the extent of participation in them has paradoxical implications for community conflict.[10] On the one hand, pervasive membership in organizations draws more people into the conflict and

[7] Thompson and McEwen, *op. cit.*, pp. 29–30.
[8] Melville Dalton, *Men Who Manage*, New York: Wiley, 1959, pp. 232–235.
[9] National Resources Committee, *The Structure of the American Economy*, Washington, D.C.: United States Government Printing Office, 1939, pp. 153–170.
[10] James S. Coleman, *Community Conflict*, Glencoe, Ill.: Free Press, 1957, pp. 21–23.

thus increases its scope. On the other hand, organization membership tends to increase identification with the community and to keep controversies between factions within bounds by reducing the tendency that they will degenerate into "a fight to the finish." If there are many organizations and associations in a community and participation in them is high, it follows that a good proportion of the population belongs to several organizations. Such interlocking organizational memberships have the result that in case of controversy some individuals will belong to organizations that pull them in opposite directions. For example, their union may take one position, but most members of their church, another. The cross pressures introduced by many linkages of this type mitigate the intensity of community conflict in several ways. People who are under cross pressure from associates with divergent opinions tend to lose interest in the controversy and assume less firm and partisan positions, as studies of voting have shown.[11] Besides, their boundary role makes these persons continual arbitrators, who justify the position of either side to its opponents, and who can serve to bring about compromise. Finally, the role conflict experienced by these people under cross pressure dissipates, as it were, part of the conflict between factions, and so does the conflict that occurs within organizations. In the absence of overlapping memberships, on the other hand, conflicts tend to split a community into two hostile camps with little communication between them.

Influences of the Community. The relations between communities and their component organizations have long been a central concern of human ecologists and rural and urban sociologists. A recent survey of this literature by Form and Miller indicates that economic organizations exert a major influence on community structure, affecting such diverse aspects as the location of the community, its size and growth pattern, the functions it performs for the larger society, its occupational composition, its total land-use pattern, its power and class structure, and its general character (physical appearance and "goodness" as measured by Thorndike's index).[12]

Influence also flows in the opposite direction. The community's location affects which industries are established and which ones thrive, and the community's size influences the type and the degree of specialization of the firms located there.[13] In addition, community norms are often the basis on which management hires and promotes employees,

11 See, for example, Bernard Berelson *et al.*, *Voting*, Chicago: University of Chicago Press, 1954, pp. 97–99, 127–132.

12 William H. Form and Delbert C. Miller, *Industry, Labor, and Community*, New York: Harper, 1960, pp. 20–54. See also E. L. Thorndike, *Your City*, New York: Harcourt, Brace, 1939.

13 See Otis Dudley Duncan *et al.*, *Metropolis and Region*, Baltimore: John Hopkins Press, 1960, pp. 23–81.

as illustrated by the treatment of racial and ethnic groups in organizations[14] and, specifically, by differences in personnel practices in the South and the North, even when branches of the same firm are compared. Another example of community influence is provided by a study comparing the performance of social workers of a state welfare department in offices of varying sizes.[15] It was found that workers in small offices were more likely to have a service orientation and to perform better as caseworkers than those in large offices. However, further analysis indicated that the crucial factor was probably not size of office but size of community. The small offices were all located in small communities, where workers were more likely than those in anonymous cities to be concerned with the welfare of their clients, who were not complete strangers but neighbors; their greater interest in helping clients improved casework service.

A study by Kerr and Siegel suggests a relation between community structure and strike propensity among industrial workers.[16] Propensity to strike was measured by man-days lost due to strikes and lockouts, comparable data being available on about 15 industries in eleven different countries. The highest propensity to strike in most countries was in the mining, maritime, and longshore industries; the lowest, in agriculture, trade, and the railroad industry. The explanatory hypothesis offered for the strike patterns discovered is that men whose work isolates them from the regular social life of the rest of the community tend to form an isolated mass with strong union solidarity, whereas workers who are integrated into the larger community do not. Workers in the isolated mass were also more likely to be active participants in their unions, and factionalism was high in their unions. Other studies on union participation and solidarity tend to confirm this conclusion. As was noted in Chapter II, increased social contact on and off the job and high homogeneity among workers have been found to promote participation in the union by Sayles and Strauss, Lipset and his colleagues, and others.[17] And a study by Dean indicates an association between the extent of off-job contacts with fellow workers and attendance at union meetings.[18] Research also supports Kerr and Siegel's suggestion that social and physical isolation from other occupations strength-

---

[14] See, for instance, Orvis Collins, "Ethnic Behavior in Industry," *American Journal of Sociology,* 51 (1946), pp. 293–298.

[15] Edwin J. Thomas, "Role Conceptions and Organizational Size," *American Sociological Review,* 24 (1959), pp. 30–37.

[16] Clark Kerr and Abraham Siegel, "The Interindustry Propensity to Strike—An International Comparison," Arthur Kornhauser *et al.* (eds.), *Industrial Conflict,* New York: McGraw-Hill, 1954, pp. 189–212.

[17] Leonard R. Sayles and George Strauss, *The Local Union,* New York: Harper, 1953, pp. 148–149, 197–202; and Seymour M. Lipset *et al., Union Democracy,* Glencoe, Ill.: Free Press, 1956, pp. 106–140.

[18] Lois R. Dean, "Social Integration, Attitudes, and Union Activity," *Industrial and Labor Relations Review,* 8 (1954), p. 51.

ens union solidarity. Union activists are reported to be less apt than other workers to have close friends in occupations different from their own[19] and to be more class-conscious, perceiving industrial disputes from the vantage point of the working class.[20] The isolation of a large portion of printers from family and community due to night work, particularly in their youth, is apparently an important reason for the development of the extensive "occupational community" among printers, which in turn has led to very high union solidarity.[21] Seidman and colleagues and Lipset and colleagues also find that men in isolated geographic communities populated largely by workers of one industry tend to have strong pro-union attitudes, to participate actively in union affairs and in politics, and to vote "left."[22]

Finally, a case study of a strike in a New England community provides additional confirmation of the Kerr and Siegel hypothesis.[23] Warner and Low attribute a strike in a large shoe manufacturing company to the breakdown in the skill hierarchy resulting from mass-production methods, which alienated workers from their jobs and undermined their status and their integration with the rest of the community. As a result, shoe operatives were more apt than other workers to confine their social contacts to members of the working class. The removal of managerial control from a local Yankee City owner to outsiders led to further deterioration in management-worker relations. A loss of craft skills and alienation from a powerful distant management caused workers to feel like an isolated mass and to associate primarily with others of their own social class, thus encouraging their participation in the union and in the strike.

A study by Clark of a municipal junior college indicates the impact of the community as a source of clientele of an organization.[24] The unrestricted admission policy of the college recruited a student body over which it had no control and which molded the fundamental character of the institution. Although most entering students were of low aptitude, they expected to transfer from the junior college to a

[19] Cited in William Spinrad, "Correlates of Trade Union Participation," *American Sociological Review*, 25 (1960), p. 243.

[20] Daisy L. Tagliacozzo and Joel Seidman, "A Typology of Rank and File Union Members," *American Journal of Sociology*, 61 (1956), p. 552.

[21] Lipset *et al., op. cit.,* pp. 135–139.

[22] Joel Seidman *et al., The Worker Views His Union,* Chicago: University of Chicago Press, 1958, pp. 18–25; and Seymour M. Lipset *et al.,* "The Psychology of Voting," Gardner Lindzey (ed.), *Handbook of Social Psychology,* Cambridge, Mass.: Addison-Wesley, 1954, vol. II, pp. 1131, 1140.

[23] W. Lloyd Warner and J. O. Low, *The Social System of the Modern Factory,* New Haven: Yale University Press, 1947, pp. 159–180.

[24] Burton R. Clark, *The Open Door College,* New York: McGraw-Hill, 1960, pp. 41–102, 112–134.

regular four-year college. This situation required the junior college to adapt its curriculum and to set up various mechanisms whereby students could be confronted with the disparity between the demands of college education and their own abilities in order to interest them in alternative goals. The majority of instructors were recruited from public high schools, a policy which proved functional given the type of clientele served. Instructors with experience in high-school teaching proved to be better suited for their duties than those with a background in college teaching, because the latter had much less understanding of and sympathy for the students attending this college and for the program it offered.

Cross-Cultural Comparisons. Several recent studies of formal organizations in non-Western societies furnish an opportunity to examine the implications of varying cultural environments for organizations. Berger, for example, studied the careers and orientations of a sample of higher Egyptian government officials.[25] Among them, he found no relationship between a bureaucratic orientation (emphasis on rationality and universalism, hierarchy, and discretion) and a professional orientation (emphasis on skill, self-protection, and service). This finding agrees with our conception that professionalism and bureaucracy entail some conflicting as well as some common elements, and it is supported by other research, although Berger himself considers it atypical and assumes that these two orientations are positively related in the West.[26] A bureaucratic orientation was more prevalent among older government officials, those of superior rank, and those that had experienced upward mobility. In contrast to the trend in the United States, but similar to that in France, the prestige of civil-service employment in Egypt has declined in recent years. Familial and personal loyalties often came into conflict with formal and impersonal standards of decision-making. Outside commitments and interests generally seemed to impinge more on bureaucratic performance among these Middle Eastern officials than they probably do among Western officials.[27]

A study of factories in Japan conducted by Abegglen provides further information on non-Western organizations.[28] Abegglen's data were obtained from qualitative interviews and observations in 53 factories of varying size. All of these organizations were found to be governed by traditional values, in sharp contrast to the pervasive impersonality in Western organizations. Employment in a company was

[25] Morroe Berger, *Bureaucracy and Society in Modern Egypt*, Princeton: Princeton University Press, 1957, pp. 49–56.

[26] Morroe Berger, "Bureaucracy East and West," *Administrative Science Quarterly*, 1 (1957), p. 528.

[27] Berger, *Bureaucracy and Society in Modern Egypt*, op. cit., pp. 66, 111–112, 149.

[28] James G. Abegglen, *The Japanese Factory*, Glencoe, Ill.: Free Press, 1958, especially pp. 11–54.

looked upon as a personal commitment both by workers and management; hence, workers rarely were laid off or left their jobs. One result of such an employment policy was that most firms usually had a surplus of labor. This situation impeded adjustment to economic change and discouraged the introduction of technological innovations, since the cost of new machines could not be compensated for by reducing the cost of labor. Recruitment to various levels in these firms was largely based on formal education, and education depended to a considerable extent on family background and income, so that a person's status in the factory tended to be governed by his family's status in the community. Compensation was based on such features as age, education, and number in the family rather than being closely geared to performance, the worker being rewarded for his status and his loyalty to the firm and not his specific contributions to the production process. There was little demarcation between the worker's private life and his business life: "Management is involved in such diverse matters as the personal finances of the worker, the education of his children, religious activities, and the training of the worker's wife."[29] In general it appears that industrialization in Japan was accompanied by much less change in its traditional social organization and social relations than was the case in Western countries.

The lack of impersonality in Japan's formal organizations is also reflected in the use of a special female attendant in Japanese mental hospitals.[30] A woman called a *tsukisoi,* who may or may not have had special training, acted as a "motherly" servant for psychiatric patients. She was assigned to one patient, with whom she stayed day and night, serving as housekeeper and companion. Since she was not employed by the hospital but engaged in private practice, her allegiance was to the patient rather than to the hospital. Caudill feels that this type of role is consistent with Japanese values, which emphasize the interdependence between people as opposed to the Western emphasis on individuality. The use of the *tsukisoi,* and generally the very high ratio of staff to patients (there were 81 staff members and 50 patients in the private psychiatric hospital that Caudill studied intensively), made unnecessary many of the physical restraints used in American psychiatric hospitals. Although Caudill stresses that the therapeutic implications of the existence of such a supportive figure must be examined in the light of the particular needs of the Japanese personality, he notes that this institution entails the danger of mutual overinvolvement of the *tsukisoi* with her patient.

The comparison of industrial concerns in two Western countries

[29] *Ibid.,* p. 129.
[30] William Caudill, "Around the Clock Patient Care in Japanese Psychiatric Hospitals," *American Sociological Review,* 26 (1961), pp. 204–214.

reveals some interesting differences in administrative structure, even if the contrasts are not quite as striking as those between Eastern and Western organizations. A study by Harbison and his colleagues compares the characteristics of management in two steel companies of similar size, one in the United States and one in Germany.[31] Top management in the German firm had much more formal education than its counterpart in the American firm, and the same difference was found between managers on the next hierarchical levels. However, the American firm compensated for this discrepancy by employing a large staff of senior technicians—430 as compared to 43 in the German firm. Moreover, the American firm employed proportionately more foremen than did the German firm, and the American foremen were better educated than the German ones. The authors attribute these differences in part to the "much greater use of automatic machinery"[32] in the American plant, which requires more foremen (Faunce's study cited in Chapter VII also found that automation led to an increase in foremen), and which requires a large staff of technically trained experts, whose skills make it less important for management to have advanced training. But the fact that the American company was much younger than the German one may have contributed to the larger number of "self-made" uneducated managers in the former. The educational differences on lower levels, finally, are probably the result of the superior educational opportunities in the United States.

A study by Fallers of the governmental and administrative organization of the Soga, a Bantu-speaking people of East Africa, allows us to examine bureaucracy in a nonliterate society.[33] Unlike most tribes, the Bantu had a central government before the Europeans came. Fallers suggests that the ambiguity of the Soga descent system created a structural need for an administrative corps recruited on a nonkinship and nonhereditary basis. Hence, in addition to the hereditary ruler and the princes who were the ruler's classificatory siblings, there was an administrative staff composed of commoners raised to their position by the chief on the basis of their abilities and services to him and directly dependent upon him for their position. Although this staff was bound to the ruler by traditional authority, it was a hierarchical and nonkinship structure based on achieved status and as such was more receptive to bureaucratization when a Western nation took over the country than were the less centralized, more traditional political systems of other tribes. Moreover, the conflict between lineage and state inherent

[31] Frederick H. Harbison *et al.*, "Steel Management on Two Continents," *Management Science*, 2 (1955), pp. 31–39.

[32] *Ibid.*, p. 37.

[33] Lloyd A. Fallers, *Bantu Bureaucracy*, Cambridge, England: East African Institute of Social Research, by W. Heffer, n.d., especially pp. 126–135, 151–152, 241–243.

in the dual political structure facilitated bureaucratization by the British, since the ruler, insecure in his position and facing the threat of revolt by the princes, welcomed the British as allies. Among the Southern Bantu, where the lineage-state problem was of less importance, Westernization did not proceed as readily. Once the Soga rulers were committed to the new order—being dependent on the British as allies and sending their sons typically to schools in England—the British could introduce further bureaucratization, replacing the tribute system by salaries and the personal-appointment system by civil-service procedures. Attempts to introduce bureaucratic practices at the lower levels (for example, among the village headmen) were less successful, since these chiefs depended less for their authority on an administrative hierarchy and more on local personal ties with their villagers.

Fallers' study is concerned with the factors that have fostered bureaucratization in a particular society. Udy's cross-cultural comparison seeks to infer more generally the stages involved in the evolution of organizational complexity.[34] He investigates the characteristics of 25 bureaucratic production organizations located in 19 nonindustrial societies, his source materials being drawn from the Human Relations Area Files. "Production organizations" are defined in his study as social groups engaged in the combination or transformation of raw materials into material goods, and they meet his criterion of a "bureaucratic organization" if they possess three or more levels of authority. Udy reports that a consistent pattern of relations was found among four characteristics usually ascribed to bureaucratic organizations. These characteristics were: (1) dependence upon superiors for rewards, that is, rewards for participation allocated by a higher authority to lower positions; (2) specialization, operationally defined as three or more different operations carried on concurrently; (3) rewards for performance, that is, quantity of reward proportional to the work or effort contributed; and (4) contractual agreements—rather than, for example, kinship obligations—as a basis for participation. These characteristics were found to form a Guttman scale. Thus, all five bureaucratic organizations that had contractual agreements also had the other three characteristics: rewards based on performance, specialization, and allocation of rewards by superiors. All organizations that had three bureaucratic characteristics had the first three but not contractual agreements; all organizations with two characteristics had the first and second; and if a bureaucratic organization had only one of these characteristics, it was the first—allocation of rewards by superi-

[34] Stanley H. Udy, Jr., " 'Bureaucratic' Elements in Organizations," *American Sociological Review*, 23 (1958), pp. 415–418.

ors. Among the 25 cases, there was only one exception to this pattern.[35]

This pattern of findings permits us to make inferences concerning the evolution of organizational complexity in hierarchical production organizations. It appears that unless there is a system of allocating rewards which insures that the lower levels will be dependent on the higher ones, specialization is not likely to develop. Specialization, in turn, seems to be required before tendencies emerge in organizations to make rewards proportional to contributions. Finally, contractual agreements regarding the conditions of participation and of making contributions typically replace traditional reasons for participation only after complexity in the other areas has developed. Of course, the small number of cases makes these inferences hypothetical; even so, the consistency of the findings is remarkable and indicates that the relationships between various bureaucratic characteristics are by no means random.[36]

ORGANIZATIONAL ANALYSIS

Bureaucracy Reconsidered. In the preceding section we examined a few of the studies dealing with organizations in widely differing societies. These studies call attention to basic differences between organizations. Since the social context in which an organization operates often finds expression in its characteristics, the pronounced differences observed in cross-cultural comparisons provide an opportunity for testing hypotheses about the interrelations between organizational characteristics which have been suggested by investigations confined to organizations in one society. It will be recalled that Weber's conception of bureaucracy implies that certain characteristics will be found together in formal organizations. We did not accept Weber's formulation of an ideal type model but looked upon these implied interrelations between organizational characteristics as a set of hypotheses to be tested in empirical research. This testing requires the systematic comparison of different formal organizations. Recent research that compares formal organiza-

---

[35] Fishing practices among the Samoans had specialization but not allocation of rewards by superiors. *Ibid.*, p. 417.

[36] A recent issue of the *Administrative Science Quarterly* (vol. 5, June, 1960) is devoted to comparative public administration and contains several articles describing the characteristics of both Western and non-Western bureaucracies. For additional recent studies of non-Western bureaucracies, see: Ralph Braibanti, "The Civil Service of Pakistan," *South Atlantic Quarterly*, 58 (1959), pp. 258–304; William C. Beyer, "The Civil Service of the Ancient World," *Public Administration Review*, 19 (1959), pp. 243–249; Robert V. Presthus, "Social Bases of Bureaucratic Organization," *Social Forces*, 38 (1959), pp. 103–109; and Selo Soemardjan, "Bureaucratic Organization in a Time of Revolution," *Administrative Science Quarterly*, 2 (1957), pp. 182–199.

tions in order to establish the empirical relations between their various characteristics also helps us to answer a question that has been repeatedly raised in this book and in the literature in general; namely, whether hierarchical bureaucratic authority and professional expertness tend to go together, as Weber assumes, or whether they are alternative methods of administration and thus independent or perhaps even inversely related.[37]

A study by Stinchcombe compares the organization of construction and mass-production industries in the United States.[38] He reports that while construction industries are rationalized, just as are mass-production industries, they contain only a small bureaucratic apparatus through which the work process is hierarchically planned and governed, a situation which contrasts sharply with the organization of mass-production industries. Specifically, the proportion of clerical personnel in construction is far less than in other manufacturing industries; the proportion of authority positions occupied by professional administrators (administrators whose status derives from special education) is also much lower in construction; fewer specific directives flow from the superior (contractor) to the subordinate (the subcontractor);[39] and there is no career commitment to an organization, only to an occupation. This low degree of bureaucratization and rudimentary development of an administrative staff are probably due to the great seasonal variations of the operations in the construction industry. Evidence for this interpretation is furnished by comparisons within the construction industry: the higher the variation in seasonal employment in a given branch of the construction industry, the lower is the proportion of administrative staff (clerks) in the labor force of that branch. The formation of an administrative hierarchy and bureaucratic machinery requires continuity of personnel, but maintaining such a permanent staff is inefficient when an organization is faced by high seasonal fluctuations in volume and product mix. Stinchcombe argues that the greater degree of professionalization of its labor force

[37] Reference has already been made to the work of Parsons and Gouldner in this connection. For other criticisms of Weber's concept, see Helen Constas, "Max Weber's Two Conceptions of Bureaucracy," *American Journal of Sociology*, 63 (1958), pp. 400–409; Roy G. Francis and Robert C. Stone, *Service and Procedure in Bureaucracy*, Minneapolis: University of Minnesota Press, 1956, pp. 153–159; and Eugene Litwak, "Models of Bureaucracy That Permit Conflict," *American Journal of Sociology*, 67 (1961), pp. 177–184.

[38] Arthur L. Stinchcombe, "Bureaucratic and Craft Administration of Production," *Administrative Science Quarterly*, 4 (1959), pp. 168–187.

[39] In construction, only the broad goals (the products and prices) are specified; in industrial organizations there is also specification of responsibilities and procedures (by whom and how the work is to be done).

enables the construction industry to function with a minimum of bureaucratization. The workers employed are for the most part skilled craftsmen, who can perform their tasks without much direction and control from superiors, because their work is guided by standards of craftsmanship which are akin to professional standards. In short, a professionalized labor force constitutes an alternative to the bureaucratic organization of work.

Stinchcombe concludes that his data suggest a refinement of Weber's classic conception of bureaucracy, which involves distinguishing rational from specifically bureaucratic administration. Rational administration entails primarily (1) a work force with specialized competence; (2) pecuniary compensation in return for contributions made, and(3) a contract that defines the goals or the broad responsibilities of the participants. Bureaucratic administration involves, in addition, (1) a hierarchy of authority through which the higher levels supervise the lower ones; (2) an administrative staff maintaining the lines of communication; and (3) continuity of operations and employment. Bureaucratic administration is one form of rational administration, but not the only one. The existence of a professionalized labor force—a group of skilled craftsmen enjoying continuity of occupational status in a labor market rather than in an organization—provides an alternative to bureaucratic organization as a means of rational administration.

Udy's study of 150 formally established production organizations in 150 different nonindustrial societies arrives independently at the same conclusion as Stinchcombe's comparison of two American industries.[40] Udy examines the relations between seven characteristics of these organizations by means of a correlation matrix. Three of the characteristics are designated as "bureaucratic": (1) hierarchical authority, referring to the existence of three or more levels of authority; (2) a specialized administrative staff whose members are not engaged directly in physical work; and (3) a set of rewards differentiated according to office. It is evident that the first two of these characteristics refer to the same concepts as Stinchcombe's, although the operational measures are, of course, not identical. The four characteristics labeled by Udy as "rational" are also similar to Stinchcombe's: (1) specialization, meaning that the organization is exclusively devoted to the production of goods; (2) rewards for performance related to contributions; (3) contractual agreements to define the terms of participation; and (4) dependence on superiors for rewards. While the fourth characteristic is not included in Stinchcombe's list describing rational administra-

[40] Stanley H. Udy, Jr., " 'Bureaucracy' and 'Rationality' in Weber's Organization Theory," *American Sociological Review*, 24 (1959), pp. 791–795.

tion, it is clearly a characteristic of the organizations he examined. Udy's analysis shows that the three bureaucratic characteristics were directly related to one another,[41] and five of the six direct relations between the four rational characteristics were also significant.[42] Moreover, none of the twelve correlations between one bureaucratic and one rational characteristic were significantly positive, and three of them (all involving the factor "specialized administrative staff") were significantly negative. In sum, the extent of bureaucratization and the degree of rationality in these organizations were largely independent (and, if anything, inversely related). Thus, two entirely different sets of data yield essentially the same results.

What then may we conclude about the relation between professionalization and bureaucratization? Professional work, as we have previously noted, is increasingly being carried out in large, complex organizations which are bureaucratically organized. This trend would seem to contradict Stinchcombe's conclusion that professionalization and bureaucratization are alternative methods of rational administration. The contradiction can be resolved by suggesting that not all aspects of bureaucratization are incompatible with the exercise of professional judgment, although one is, namely, hierarchical supervision and discipline. The other factors included in Stinchcombe's conception of bureaucracy—centralized management, an administrative staff, and continuity of employment—are probably not found in the construction industry because of the particular circumstances there; specifically, because they are incompatible with seasonal fluctuations in operations. But managerial planning and coordination, the administrative staff they necessitate, and continuity of employment are not inherently incompatible with decision-making on the basis of professional expertness; only disciplined compliance with orders of hierarchical superiors entails a fundamental conflict with professionalism. In the absence of direct hierarchical supervision, genuine professional work can be and, indeed, frequently is carried out in otherwise bureaucratized organizations. To say this, however, is not to deny that conflicts between professional and administrative considerations often arise in these organizations.

Technological Complexity. Durkheim's classic analysis of the division of labor in societies holds that increases in social density promote specialization, which, in turn, changes the basis of social solidarity from common values—"mechanical solidarity"—to interdependence with a greater tolerance for differing value orientations—"organic solidar-

---

[41] The *Q* values using Yule's coefficient of association were +.79, +.79, and +.70. *Ibid.*, p. 794.

[42] *Q* values were +.66, +1.00, +.75, +.72, and +.61. The relationship between specialization and dependence was positive but not significant (+.35). *Loc. cit.*

ity."[43] Some implications of Durkheim's analysis may be explored by considering the relation between hierarchical differentiation and specialization in primitive production organizations.

Udy's research on production organizations in nonindustrial societies reveals, as we just mentioned, that a minimum of specialization —the mere fact that an organization is exclusively devoted to production—was not associated with the existence of a bureaucratic hierarchy of, at least, three levels. But further specialization—the carrying out of three or more different operations concurrently—was positively related to such hierarchical differentiation in an organization.[44] Does this difference mean, as Udy implies, that specialization, by creating a need for coordination, leads to the development of a bureaucratic hierarchy? We submit that the direction of influence between the two variables may be the opposite and that some evidence from Udy's own research supports this alternative interpretation. He found bureaucratic hierarchies more prevalent in organizations where membership was based on kinship or political-status obligations than in those where it was based on voluntary agreement or contract.[45] This observation suggests that hierarchical differentiation in a simple production organization tends to be rooted in the status structure of the community rather than to emerge in response to the need for coordination in the organization and that, consequently, the correlation between hierarchical differentiation and specialization implies that the differentiation promotes specialization, not the reverse. This interpretation is also supported by Udy's finding, cited in the discussion of the evolution of organizational complexity, that specialization tends to emerge in organizations only when hierarchical dependence, and thus surely hierarchical differentiation itself, have already developed. A further inference one might draw is that power differences and the opportunity of some members to exploit others encourage the development of specialization in production, since such specialization often means that some participants have more desirable duties than others. A bit of evidence in support of this speculation is provided by Udy's finding that the existence of a multilevel hierarchy is associated with the fact that one or more superiors in the organization (members above the bottom level) do not work.[46]

43 Emile Durkheim, *The Division of Labor in Society*, George Simpson (trans.), Glencoe, Ill.: Free Press, 1947, pp. 70–132, 256–282 (first published 1893).

44 Stanley H. Udy, Jr., "The Structure of Authority in Non-Industrial Production Organizations," *American Journal of Sociology*, 64 (1959), pp. 582–584; and *The Organization of Work*, New Haven: Human Relations Area Files, 1959, p. 38.

45 Stanley H. Udy, Jr., "Technology, Society and Production Organization," paper read at the meetings of the American Sociological Association, New York, 1960.

46 Udy, *The Organization of Work, op. cit.,* p. 39.

These conclusions, although highly tentative, suggest some specification of intervening variables in Durkheim's theory. Perhaps increases in social density foster specialization because and if they lead to a greater differentiation of power in the community, which is reflected in the organization of production inasmuch as it enables some members to assign the most burdensome tasks to others.

We turn now from a consideration of rudimentary technological systems to an examination of organizations exhibiting advanced technology. There can be little doubt that increased mechanization in production organizations has resulted in higher productivity. Using installed electrical horsepower per production worker as an index of the degree of mechanization, and output per man-hour as an index of productivity, Melman shows that in the United States between 1899 and 1950 productivity increases paralleled increases in mechanization.[47] A comparison between countries at different levels of mechanization also reveals some relation between installed horsepower and productivity per worker.[48] But data from 15 British and American industries show no consistent relation between the measures of mechanization and productivity. Melman suggests that this finding does not negate the finding of a relation between mechanization and productivity but merely indicates the importance of other factors, such as type of organization, for industrial productivity.

Changes in mechanization, in turn, appear to be related to labor costs, specifically, to the cost of labor relative to that of machine production. For example, Melman shows that between 1938 and 1950 the cost of manual handling of materials in British firms increased more rapidly than the cost of handling them by machine (fork-lift and elevating-platform trucks). As labor costs increased, the volume of work at which machine operation became less expensive than manual operation declined. As a result, it became economical even for the firms with a relatively small volume of work to mechanize.[49] Melman notes after visiting some 20 plants of the British motor-vehicle industry: "At every hand we found evidence of the mechanization of work that had previously been done by manual methods."[50] Labor and machine costs in the United States showed the same trends between 1940 and 1950; both increased but labor costs increased at a much faster rate. Increases in relative labor costs (measured by the ratio of man-hour costs to kilowatt-hour costs) paralleled increases in mechanization

[47] Seymour Melman, *Dynamic Factors in Industrial Productivity*, Oxford, England: Basil Blackwell, 1956, pp. 113–115.

[48] *Ibid.*, p. 114. However, Figure 9 on this page is somewhat misleading as it combines data from different countries with data from the same country at different periods.

[49] *Ibid.*, pp. 35–43, 97–99, 110–112.

[50] *Ibid.*, p. 24.

(measured by horsepower installed per production worker) in the United States during the period 1899–1950. In short, rising costs of labor provide strong economic incentives for manufacturing firms to mechanize.

The higher the relative cost of labor, therefore, the greater is the productivity per man-hour.[51] For high labor costs promote mechanization, and mechanization improves productivity. This conclusion of Melman is supported by Abegglen's observation that the low labor costs in Japan divest the management of Japanese factories of incentives for seeking to increase productivity by introducing technological innovations.[52] Here we have an interesting paradox: if high labor costs encourage mechanization and enhance productivity, as they seem to do, high wages and, particularly, strong unions that can effect recurrent raises in wages and fringe benefits, although typically opposed by management, serve important latent functions for technological progress and hence for long-run productive efficiency.[53]

Shortages of materials may have the same latent function for improving production methods as high labor costs. This effect is illustrated by changes that occurred in a large manufacturing company studied by Richardson and Walker.[54] During World War II the plant was converted from job-lot to assembly-line production, a change which involved not so much the introduction of new machinery as innovations in the organization of the production process. A major factor in the decision to reorganize was the shortage of materials resulting from the war, which made job-lot production unsatisfactory, because it required that a large supply of parts and materials be kept on hand in store rooms, which workers could draw on when needed. Since the new assembly-line production method not only mitigated the specific problem of wartime shortages but also seemed to improve productivity, the shortages that stimulated the innovation may be considered to have had the latent function of promoting efficiency.

This century has witnessed considerable growth in the administrative apparatus of production organizations, both in absolute terms

[51] For various countries and time periods combined, Melman found a correlation between labor cost and productivity of +.88; *ibid.*, p. 125. (The data on the United States and Great Britain are presented on pp. 117–118.)

[52] Abegglen, *op. cit.*, pp. 110–120.

[53] In a later case study of an automobile manufacturing company, Melman shows how high labor costs constrained management to increase mechanization. Seymour Melman, *Decision-Making and Productivity*, Oxford, England: Basil Blackwell, 1958, pp. 105–106, 141–143, 153.

[54] Frederick L. Richardson, Jr., and Charles R. Walker, *Human Relations in an Expanding Company*, New Haven: Labor and Management Center, Yale University, 1948, pp. 54–74.

and in terms relative to the size of the production force.[55] Melman shows that increases in the ratio of the number of administrative personnel to the number of production workers paralleled increases in productivity per worker in both the United Kingdom and the United States over the period 1900 to 1950.[56] But notwithstanding this association, Melman argues that growth in the administrative apparatus did not contribute to productivity; on the contrary, it impeded it. He supports his thesis with three arguments.

First, he reports that the two trends are not closely parallel. Specifically, the comparison of twenty-one manufacturing industries in the United States reveals little relation between the increase in the number of administrative personnel and the increase in productivity during the first few decades of this century. But these are very rough and indirect measures, and the trends are undoubtedly affected by other factors. Note that Melman found that comparisons by industry revealed no correlation between mechanization and productivity, as we have seen, just as he found they showed no correlation between administrative apparatus and productivity. In the first case, however, he disregards the negative finding, explaining that it is due to the interference of other factors, and concludes that mechanization and productivity are related; whereas in the second case he accepts the negative finding and concludes that administration and productivity are unrelated. But he cannot have it both ways. Differences in type of organization between industries are just as likely to be responsible for the absence of a correlation between administrative expansion and increased productivity as for the absence of a correlation between mechanization and productivity. If firms within an industry were compared, one might well find an association between administrative services and productivity, just as one does for the trend in all manufacturing industries, because an administrative staff makes possible a more complex organization of work processes.

Second, Melman reports that large differences in productivity between the United States and the Soviet Union are not accompanied by similar differences in proportion of administrative personnel. This difference, however, merely shows that conditions other than administration influence productivity, a fact that is hardly open to question.

Finally, Melman cites evidence that output (specifically, value added to the product through manufacturing) per production worker has increased more rapidly between 1907 and 1948 than has output

[55] See Seymour Melman, "The Rise of Administrative Overhead in the Manufacturing Industries of the United States, 1899–1947," *Oxford Economic Papers,* 3 (1951), pp. 64–66.

[56] See Melman, *Dynamic Factors in Industrial Productivity, op. cit.,* pp. 132–140.

per employee (including administrative as well as production personnel). This finding, however, apparently reflects primarily the disproportionate increase of administrative personnel in recent years and does not do justice to the indirect contribution administration makes. The question remains: how much of the increased efficiency of today's production worker has been made possible by the more extensive administrative apparatus? This question is not easily answered, because the contribution made to production by administration is necessarily indirect.

The data Melman cites do not, in our opinion, warrant the conclusion he draws. Pending empirical research explicitly designed to deal with this problem, it remains a moot question whether or under which conditions an enlarged administrative machinery contributes to productive efficiency.[57]

INTERORGANIZATIONAL PROCESSES

Ecological Processs and Organizations. What are some of the social processes that characterize the relations between organizations? Ecologists have distinguished between two basic types of relations: symbiosis and commensalism. The former term denotes relations of mutual dependence and advantage between unlike structures; the latter refers to competition between like structures for the scarce resources needed for survival and growth.[58] In this section we present an analysis of competitive and exchange processes that occur between organizations, of the ways in which these processes change like structures into unlike ones and vice versa, and of the resulting dynamics in the larger social system. In a sense, this is an analysis of the ecology of organizational life.

Urban growth is frequently conceptualized as being governed by processes of competition for optimum location.[59] Since all organizations are dependent to some extent on their social environment, there is competition among them for the most desirable locations. Thus, a business firm is interested in a location close to a large labor market, to its suppliers, and to its customers, but it will find itself competing with other firms for these advantages. Ready access to exchange partners makes a central location in the city particularly

[57] For another discussion of the relation between technology and administration see James D. Thompson and Frederick L. Bates, "Technology, Organization, and Administration," *Administrative Science Quarterly,* 2 (1957), pp. 325–343.

[58] Amos H. Hawley, *Human Ecology,* New York: Ronald, 1950, pp. 36–39.

[59] See Robert E. Park *et al., The City,* Chicago: University of Chicago Press, 1925.

desirable for many types of firms. The outcome of competition for a central location depends on two factors: (1) the significance that being easily accessible to a wide public has for the firm, which is greater for a retail store than for a manufacturing concern, since only the former depends on being personally contacted by many customers; and (2) the firm's capacity to purchase real estate in high demand which commands a high price. These competitive processes lead to the dominance of certain types of organizations in various areas of the city. For example, large stores and offices typically dominate the downtown business district of the city, while manufacturing firms cluster around its outer boundaries.[60] The dominant firms exercise control over the area, not by ordering or forbidding but by determining the conditions under which other types of firms can survive and thrive.[61] The lesser firms must settle for second-best locations unless they can establish a symbiotic relation with the dominant ones. For example, there are luncheonettes on Wall Street but no factories; powerful financial firms welcome the presence of the former because it is to their advantage to have restaurants easily accessible to their large office staffs, while no advantage would accrue to them from the proximity of factories.

The conclusion of human as well as plant ecology is that competition leads to the dominance of one type, and once dominance has been established competition between types subsides. Classical economics, in contrast, assumes that competition helps to maintain and simultaneously is perpetuated by an equilibrium between many competitors in the market. What accounts for these opposite conclusions? The crucial difference between the two underlying conceptions of competition is that ecology takes as its unit of analysis the species, in our case a *type* of organization; whereas in classical economics the competing unit is not the species but the individual, that is, a specific firm. Although there are several important differences between the species and the individual, the distinction that is most relevant for an examination of the consequences of competition is the *potential expandability* of each unit. An example from plant ecology illustrates this point. The very nature of a tree sets inherent limits on its growth, but there are no such *internally* determined limits to the expansion

---

60 It is recognized that this generalization is broad and imprecise. There are many types of stores, offices, and manufacturing establishments and their varying needs create different location pressures. See, for example, Edgar M. Hoover and Raymond Vernon, *Anatomy of a Metropolis*, Cambridge, Mass.: Harvard University Press, 1959, pp. 25–124.

61 See the discussion of dominance in Donald J. Bogue, *The Structure of the Metropolitan Community*, Ann Arbor: Horace H. Rackham School of Graduate Studies, University of Michigan, 1949, pp. 10–13.

of a species of trees. Thus, disregarding external limitations, a whole continent could conceivably be covered with oaks as the dominant species; but a single oak tree could not possibly grow so large as to dominate an entire continent. This example suggests the general hypothesis that in the absence of internal limits to the expansion of a competitor, competition is likely to result in the dominance of one or a few related units. Whether the outcome of competition between organizations approximate the dominance model of the ecologist or the equilibrium model of classical economics, therefore, is expected to depend on the degree of expandability of organizations.

How expandable are formal organizations? Their expandability is probably not unlimited because some restrictions are imposed on it by requirements of their internal structure.[62] But these limits to organizational expandability appear to be very broad ones, as is indicated by the tremendous variations in size of firms. According to the hypothesis, therefore, the result of competition among formal organizations should be closer to dominance than the model of classical economics implies. The individual firm can expand to such a degree that one or a small number of firms can dominate the system in its area of specialization, that is, a particular market. This, indeed, is the conclusion of several more recent studies by economists who have rejected Marshall's dichotomy between pure competition and pure monopoly. Both Chamberlin and Robinson suggest that the typical end product of competition is a state of monopolistic competition or oligopoly—the domination of the market by a few strong firms.[63] The hypothesis advanced also helps to explain the increase in oligopoly-dominated markets during the last century. In earlier years, the size of the individual or family fortune set practical limits on the expandability of firms. But the institution of the share corporation has removed these financial limits to expansion.[64] Other innovations, such as improved communication methods and better managerial tech-

[62] Boulding suggests that the principle of nonproportional change governs the growth of organisms and organizations. This principle holds that a uniform increase in the linear dimensions of a structure will increase its area as the square, and its volume as the cube. Although some compensation for these changes is possible, Boulding holds that "the size of the structure itself is limited by its ultimate inability to compensate for the non-proportional changes." See Kenneth E. Boulding, "Toward a General Theory of Growth," *Canadian Journal of Economics and Political Science,* 19 (1953), pp. 326–340.

[63] Edward Chamberlin, *The Theory of Monopolistic Competition,* Cambridge, Mass.: Harvard University Press, 1933; and Joan Robinson, *The Economics of Imperfect Competition,* London: Macmillan, 1933.

[64] "Just as the factory system brought large numbers of *workers* under unified direction and control, so the corporate system brought numerous bits of *wealth* together under a single management." Robin M. Williams, Jr., *American Society* (2d ed.), New York: Knopf, 1960, p. 182 (italics in original).

niques, have further facilitated organizational expansion, as Boulding notes.[65] As the limits to the expandability of economic organizations have widened, the chances that one or a few would dominate a given market have increased.

Competition and Exchange. Competition, of course, is not confined to economic markets.[66] Political parties compete for votes, fraternal and religious organizations for members, participants in a discussion for speaking time, and group members for popularity and respect. Social competition, whether between organizations or persons, always involves some kind of exchange relations with other organizations or persons. For example, a firm competes with other firms for the patronage of still other firms or individuals. Success in social competition, therefore, depends on the ability of the firm to establish symbiotic relations in which extensive advantageous exchanges take place. Social competition should be distinguished from other forms of competition that do not involve complementary symbiotic relations, exemplified by plants competing for sunlight. Exchange relations are required for competition if its immediate object is not a natural resource but some kind of output or product of another unit in the system.

In rudimentary competitive social structures, the distinction between competitive and exchange relations does not yet exist. For example, the federal agents discussed in Chapter V competed *with* one another for the respect *of* one another. An agent's exchange partners, whose output of respect was the object of the competition, were identical with his competitors for superior informal status. However, once differentiation in respect developed, and only then, exchange relations became differentiated from competitive ones. Those whose competent advice won them the respect of their colleagues continued to compete with one another for superior status—for power and informal leadership. This competition furnished the inducement for them freely to give advice in exchange for deference. On the other hand, those whose advice did not earn them the respect of their colleagues had no chance in this continuing competition for high status: since their advice was not in demand, they could not exchange it for deference. These agents, then, became the potential "customers" of those whose earlier success enabled them to continue to compete for superior status. The low-status agents' output of respect and deference (for which they received help and advice) determined the outcome of the high-status agents' competition for top status. In sum, the

[65] Kenneth E. Boulding, *The Organizational Revolution*, New York: Harper, 1953, pp. 25–32.

[66] "Even the most sacred institutions are subject to the necessity of competing, in some measure, to survive." Everett C. Hughes, "The Ecological Aspect of Institutions," *American Sociological Review*, 1 (1936), p. 188.

outcome of earlier competitive processes leads to a differentiation in the social structure which has the result that some remain competitors and others become exchange partners in subsequent stages of competition.

These processes in which competitive and exchange relations become differentiated are also characteristics of stratification systems of entire communities. The class structure of the Ifugao tribes in the Philippines illustrates this.[67] There are three broad social classes among the Ifugao, based primarily on wealth. Everybody competes for wealth, and the relative success of an individual governs his social status. The middle class is composed largely of property holders who work on the land. The lower-middle class is composed of people whose land holdings are barely sufficient to provide a living and who are threatened by bankruptcy, which would throw them into the property-less lower class. The upper-middle class, on the other hand, consists of families whose land provides a surplus income and who, therefore, have some chance of moving into the upper class. In effect, the members of the lower-middle class compete for staying in the middle class, while those of the upper-middle class compete for entry into the upper class. And exchange relations develop between these two strata within the middle class which help both partners in their respective competitive struggles. Members of the upper-middle class often make loans at interest to those of the lower-middle class, and this exchange process aids both in achieving the object of their competition. For the loan enables the poorer family to retain its land and thus its middle-class position, and the interest increases the wealth of the richer family and thus its chances of moving into the upper class. Greater advantage seems to accrue to the lender than the borrower in this exchange; this difference is not atypical for symbiotic relations that involve partners of unequal status and power. The reader may have noticed that the relations and exchange processes existing among the Ifugao are not unique but can be observed in some other societies as well. The point of major interest is that here again the outcome of earlier competition has differentiated between exchange relations and those that continue to be competitive.

Dominance involves an extreme form of this general tendency. If a few organizations become dominant in a market, symbiosis comes to replace competition as the central principle that governs relations between units in this larger system. This change is well illustrated by our earlier example taken from urban ecology concerning the dominance of the financial organizations in Wall Street. The entry of

---

[67] Irving Goldman, "The Ifugao of the Philippine Islands," Margaret Mead (ed.), *Cooperation and Competition among Primitive Peoples,* New York: McGraw-Hill, 1937, pp. 153–179.

other types of organizations into this area is no longer governed by competitive processes but by a need for their services. Lunch counters are found in this area not because they were able successfully to compete with the financial companies but because of their symbiotic relation with this dominant type of organization in the area. The same principle applies to economic markets. In an industry dominated by a few major companies, such as the automobile industry, the success of the smaller firms depends not on successfully competing with these giants but on establishing symbiotic relations with them, for example, as suppliers of various kinds of parts. It follows that the keystone to understanding these new markets is no longer an analysis of competitive processes but an analysis of the interdependence and power relations between the units in the system. This conclusion is similar to one Veblen reached long since,[68] and it is the focus of Galbraith's theory of countervailing powers.

Galbraith's main thesis is that the primary regulating mechanism of the modern market is no longer competition but rather the structure of power relations between exchange partners. In his own words:

The long trend toward concentration of industrial enterprise in the hands of a relatively few firms has brought into existence not only strong sellers . . . but also strong buyers . . . The fact that a seller enjoys a measure of monopoly power, and is reaping a measure of monopoly return as a result, means that there is an inducement to those firms from whom he buys or those to whom he sells to develop the power with which they can defend themselves against exploitation . . . Competition which, at least since the time of Adam Smith, has been viewed as the autonomous regulator of economic activity and as the only available regulatory mechanism apart from the state, has, in fact, been superseded . . . In the typical modern market of few sellers, the active restraint is not provided by competitors but from the other side of the market by strong buyers.[69]

The processes described by Galbraith are well illustrated in a government survey of United States business.[70] This report shows how the dominant market position of wholesalers was undermined at the end of the last century by the increasing power of manufacturing concerns employing mass-production methods. At the same time retailers, with the establishment of mail-order houses and chain stores, also became more powerful. The wholesalers, squeezed from both sides,

---

[68] Thorstein Veblen, *The Theory of Business Enterprise*, New York: Scribner, 1904.

[69] John Kenneth Galbraith, *American Capitalism*, Cambridge, Mass.: Houghton, Mifflin, 1952, pp. 118–119.

[70] Temporary National Economic Committee, *Investigation of Concentration of Economic Power: The Problems of Small Business*, Washington, D.C.: U.S. Government Printing Office, 1941 (Monograph No. 17).

consequently found themselves seriously threatened. In order to increase their power and meet these threats, they established trade associations and lobbied successfully for legislation that penalized chain
stores. These actions of wholesalers elicited counter-actions by retailers
and manufacturers. The former established trade associations of their
own and developed larger outlets, such as supermarkets, to escape the
tax on chain stores. Manufacturers also united by forming trade
associations and organized sales departments to bypass wholesalers.
Simultaneously, manufacturers and retailers were engaged in their
own power struggle, the former relying on product differentiation,
branding, and advertising to force retailers to carry their products,
the latter reacting by using their own brand names or even manufacturing their own brands to become more independent of manufacturers. In sum, as a few large organizations became dominant in
each market, the focus of their endeavors shifted from competing with
others in the same market to struggling over the conditions and terms
of exchange between buyers and sellers, a struggle that induced former
competitors to become allies and organize mutual-benefit associations.

Looking at these processes of development from another perspective, one can see that the outcome of competition at one stage changes
the object of the competition at the next. In the earlier stages, all units
compete against all others. Differential success in this competition
for relative standing has the result that the least successful are no
longer able to compete with the most successful, and this change leads
to the establishment of symbiotic relations that aid both parties in
their continued competition. But now the two groups have different
objects in their competition: the more successful units compete with
one another for dominance, while the less successful units compete with
one another for survival, as illustrated by the Ifugao middle class as
well as in economic markets. Relations between units have also
changed, since some former competitors have now become partners
in exchange relations. Differential success in further competitive
processes enables a few large organizations (or other units) to dominate
a given market. At this advanced stage when dominance has been
achieved, a new object of competition emerges, namely, the ability to
exercise controlling power in exchange relations. The consequent
power struggle between buyers and sellers puts the members of each
group under pressure to unite by establishing agreements and trade
associations. In this manner former competitors have once again been
transformed into partners. But the reverse change has also occurred
since organizations that were formerly partners in exchange relations—
the buyers and sellers—have become competitors for dominant power
over a set of interrelated markets. This latter competition for power in
exchange relations that link markets has, according to Galbraith, re-

placed the earlier competition for profit or dominance in one market as the main regulatory system of the American economy.[71]

The processes in which competitive relations become exchange relations and exchange relations turn into competitive ones furnish a graphic illustration of the dynamics that characterize the social context of organizational life.

CONCLUDING REMARKS

In preceding chapters of this work we have been concerned largely with the internal structure of formal organizations. We have analyzed the structure of colleague relations and of hierarchical ones, and we have discussed the relations between members of an organization and its public. But in this chapter our focus has shifted to the social context within which organizations function. We have briefly examined organizations in differing communities and cultures in order to note some of the interrelations between organizations and their environments. However, the social context is not merely an aspect of the external environment but actually penetrates organizational life. For example, the character of the labor force or the degree of technological complexity can be treated either as an attribute of the environment or as a characteristic of the organization itself. We examined some comparative studies to infer the nature of the interdependence between various basic characteristics of organizations. Finally, we turned to the relations between organizations and analyzed the processes that govern these relations and the dynamic changes in the larger social system resulting from these processes.

The internal dynamics of organizational life has been implicit in much of our earlier discussion. In our final chapter we shall make it our explicit focus as we summarize some of the main points of the previous analysis.

71 It is, of course, possible that the outcome of the competition between countervailing powers is that one supertrust comes to dominate the entire economy. In this case, the only remaining object of competition would be world domination.

CHAPTER NINE

Organizational Dynamics

This concluding chapter focuses attention on the internal dynamics of organizational life. We shall summarize the main points of our foregoing analysis with particular emphasis on the processes of change in formal organizations, processes that have sometimes been left implicit in the earlier discussion. To do justice to problems of organizational change, however, we shall not confine the analysis to material already presented in previous chapters but shall draw upon additional relevant sources whenever appropriate.

The concept of dilemma greatly contributes to an understanding of internally generated processes of change in a social organization. If we conceive of social systems as meeting basic needs and requisites, the implicit assumption is that adjustment prevails and change does not occur unless new *external* conditions require adjustments. But if we conceive of social systems as being confronted by dilemmas, that is, by choices between alternatives in which any choice must sacrifice some valued objective in the interest of another, the implicit assumption is that problems are endemic and, therefore, serve as a continual *internal* source of change in the system. The concept of dilemma by no means implies that improvements are not possible, but it does imply that final solutions and perfect adjustments are impossible. Dilemmas confront not only formal organizations, as we shall see in this chapter, but also the *study* of formal organization, as was mentioned in the first chapter.

A fundamental methodological dilemma in the study of social organization is posed by the necessity to investigate the interdependence between units in a larger social system, on the one hand, and the requirement to treat subunits of the totality under investigation as independent cases in order to derive generalizations about them, on the other. The investigator must choose between alternative approaches and invariably sacrifice one of these requirements. Research that is being conducted in one formal organization, for example, may either treat the various sections in the organization as independent units for analysis or focus upon their interdependence in the larger organization. The first alternative furnishes independent cases that permit deriving generalizations about work-group organization, but it ignores the principles that govern the ways in which work groups are organized into a larger formal structure. The second approach deals with these interrelations between sections that characterize the formal organization, but it thereby sacrifices the independent cases required for generalizing. The comparative study of many organizations would solve this specific problem—that is, make it possible to advance and test generalizations about formal organizations—but the generic dilemma would reappear as one raises the question of what principles govern the interrelations between these organizations in the larger society.

The comparative approach in the study of formal organizations offers probably the best heuristic solution for this methodological dilemma at this stage of knowledge in the social sciences. Ideally, this approach would involve a research design in which organizations in a sample are systematically compared. Since such studies are not as yet available, however, we have had to be content with approximating this ideal as best we could with less systematic comparisons. We have relied primarily on three methods: secondary analysis comparing case studies of various organizations; internal comparisons of different segments in one organization; and comparison of two organizations with many similarities—the two welfare agencies. We have tried to use the comparative approach in this book extensively, even though the cases we have examined were not always clearly comparable and many conditions had not been controlled. Hence, all of our conclusions are inferential and must be considered only suggestions, not confirmed propositions.

These problems are even more acute when we turn to the analysis of the processes of change in organizations. Systematic studies of organizational change are virtually nonexistent; therefore, the conclusions we reach about the dynamics of organizational life are mere hypotheses awaiting validation in future systematic research.

Organizational Development

Development of Organizational Complexity. Perhaps the minimum definition of formal organization is that collective effort is explicitly organized for specific ends. We have distinguished such formally established organizations from crescive organizations which emerge in the course of social interaction without explicit intent or deliberate design. Formal organizations vary in size and complexity from a modern army at one extreme to the collectively organized recurrent fishing expeditions found in nonliterate tribes at the other. Since the latter involve formally established procedures to accomplish an explicit objective, albeit rudimentary ones, they are included in our concept of formal organization. To be sure, the larger and more complex formal organizations are of special interest to students of contemporary social organization, partly because they are so prevalent today, partly because special problems are often posed by the bureaucratic apparatus that tends to develop with increasing organizational size and complexity. The typical characteristics of such bureaucratic machinery, according to Weber, include the division of work into areas of specialized jurisdiction and competence; a hierarchical authority structure; general rules and regulations that govern operations; an emphasis on impersonal detachment designed to eliminate personal considerations from official decisions; and personnel policies based on objective criteria which encourage commitment to a full-time life-long career.

Formal organizations can be classified in many different ways. We have proposed a classification based on the criterion *cui bono*—who the prime beneficiary is in whose interest the organization is expected to operate. The resulting four types of formal organizations are: (1) mutual-benefit associations, such as unions, which are intended to promote the interest of rank and file members; (2) business concerns, such as factories, which are established to serve the interest of their owners; (3) service organizations, such as social-work agencies, which are expected to be governed by the welfare and interest of their clients; and (4) commonweal organizations, such as police departments, which function to further the welfare of the public-at-large. If another group usurps the role of the prime beneficiary in any of these types, the objectives of the organization are thwarted and its original function is distorted or changed.

The fact that an organization has been formally established does not mean that all the social processes within it follow predesigned patterns. Large and complex formal organizations do not spring into existence full-blown but develop out of simpler ones. We shall examine such developmental processes in this first part of the chapter. Moreover, the formally institutionalized mechanisms for coordinating collective efforts merely set the limits within which social processes become informally organized. The next part of the chapter is devoted to these informally emerging patterns in formal organizations and their significance for official operations.

Some inferences can be drawn concerning the early development of organizational complexity from Udy's study of production organizations in nonliterate societies.[1] His cross-cultural comparisons suggest

[1] See, in particular, Stanley H. Udy, Jr., "'Bureaucratic' Elements in Organizations," *American Sociological Review*, 23 (1958), pp. 415–418, and "Technology, Society, and Production Organization," paper read at the meetings of the American Sociological Association, New York, 1960.

that a hierarchy of authority, in which persons in the lower levels are dependent for their rewards on those in the higher levels, tends to develop early in simple production organizations. There is also some indication that such rudimentary bureaucratic hierarchies are rooted in the ascribed status system of the community, inasmuch as these hierarchies were more frequently found in organizations where membership was based on kinship or political status rather than on a voluntary contract. Specialization typically evolves only in organizations already characterized by hierarchical differentiation, and it, in turn, tends to precede the development of more complex institutional arrangements, such as gearing rewards to contributions, and introducing contractual agreements to replace community status as the basis for defining the terms of membership participation. It would appear, then, that an organizational hierarchy rooted in an ascribed status system furnishes the initial impetus for the development of organizational complexity, but further developments tend to make participation in the organization independent of the community's ascribed stratification system. As organizations become more complex and differentiated in internal structure they also seem to become more differentiated from the larger societal structure, forming relatively autonomous subsystems with their own principles of organization.

Bureaucratization. Structural growth by its very nature involves increasing complexity. Boulding derives this conclusion from his "principle of non-proportional change": since the rates of growth of the various parts of an organization are not proportional, growth always entails internal adjustment and change.[2] One of the most important changes that occurs as organizations become larger and more complex is the development of an administrative apparatus. Many observers have lamented the trend toward larger administrative overhead in organizations as indicative of overbureaucratization. Parkinson has satirized the presumably parasitic character of administrative personnel most wittily, suggesting that the less work there is in an organization, the greater are the increases in its administrative staff. He cites in support of his "law" the fact that while the number of officers and men in the Royal Navy decreased by 31 per cent between the years 1914 and 1928, the number of Admiralty officials increased by 78 per cent.[3] Haire also comments on "the remarkable resistance of the staff to negative growth," noting that in 19 cases of layoffs observed in four different firms only line workers were involved and that in a few

2 Kenneth E. Boulding, "Towards a General Theory of Growth," *Canadian Journal of Economics and Political Science*, 19 (1953), pp. 326–340.
3 C. Northcote Parkinson, *Parkinson's Law and Other Studies in Administration*, Boston: Houghton-Mifflin, 1957, pp. 7–8.

instances new staff personnel was hired during the layoff period.[4] Powerful administrators undoubtedly can and often do protect their positions against being affected by reductions in staff. Parkinson's illustration, however, is quite misleading, since it unquestionably reflects in part technological advances in warfare and the changes that occur in a military service as it adjusts to peacetime—conscripts are discharged and regulars are gradually promoted, since it is important to maintain a core of staff officers for future emergencies.

It is widely assumed that large organizations tend to be over-bureaucratized, that is, that an increase in organizational size is accompanied by a disproportionate increase in administrative overhead; but the evidence does not support this assumption. To be sure, the average size of manufacturing firms has increased during the first half of this century, and so has the proportion of personnel devoted to administration rather than production.[5] These trends, which reflect basic changes in the organization of industrial concerns, may be responsible for the prevailing impression that size is associated with overbureaucratization. The growth of government services during the last few decades may also have contributed to this notion. Except for small firms, however, increases in size are not associated with increases in the proportion of administrative personnel. Only during an organization's early stages of growth does the proportion of administrative officials increase;[6] further growth is not accompanied by increases in administrative overhead. To cite specific cases, a study of 211 manufacturing firms in Ohio conducted by Baker and Davis found no relation between size of organization and proportion of administrative officials.[7] Melman's data on American manufacturing concerns even reveal an inverse relation between size and proportion of administrative personnel.[8] Data on German industries analyzed by Bendix also show an inverse relation between size and proportion of administrative staff; in 1933, for instance, the proportion of administrators was lower in firms employing more than 1,000 employees than in those employing between 51 and 200 workers.[9]

[4] Mason Haire, "Biological Models and Empirical Histories of the Growth of Organizations," Mason Haire (ed.), *Modern Organization Theory*, New York: Wiley, 1959, pp. 292–293.

[5] Seymour Melman, "The Rise of Administrative Overhead in the Manufacturing Industries of the United States, 1899–1947," *Oxford Economic Papers*, 3 (1951), pp. 64–66, 89.

[6] Haire, *op. cit.*, pp. 288–292, 305.

[7] Alton W. Baker and Ralph C. Davis, *Ratios of Staff to Line Employees and Stages of Differentiation of Staff Functions*, Columbus: Bureau of Business Research, Ohio State University, 1954, pp. 14–15.

[8] Melman, *op. cit.*, pp. 89–90.

[9] Reinhard Bendix, *Work and Authority in Industry*, New York: Wiley, pp. 221–222. Bendix shows that the proportion of technicians does increase as a function of size of firm; but since administrative officers are the larger group, "the over-all tendency remains for bureaucratization to be highest in the smaller firms."

In industrial organizations, then, bureaucratization as indicated by proportion of administrative personnel is, contrary to prevailing impressions, not directly related to size, and may even be inversely related to it. Two studies of other types of organizations have also dealt with this problem. Terrien and Mills present the only systematic data confirming the popular conception: the size of school districts in California was directly related to the proportion of administrative personnel, although the relations observed were small.[10] Anderson and Warkov, on the other hand, examining 49 Veterans' Administration hospitals, found an inverse relation between the size of a hospital and the proportional size of its administrative staff.[11] Their analysis also suggests that complexity[12] as distinguished from size, although the two usually go together, is directly associated with the proportion of administrative personnel, and this distinction provides a possible reason for the discrepancy between the results of the school-district study and those of other research on this problem. Larger school districts were probably more complex than smaller ones—administering several schools in different locations rather than a single one—and this complexity, not size itself, may have been responsible for their larger administrative staffs. The conclusions that emerge from the research findings are that large organizations do not typically have disproportionately large administrative machineries; that, however, size tends to be directly related to complexity, and complexity to a large proportion of administrative personnel; and that the size of an organization, particularly if complexity is held constant, may actually be inversely related to the relative size of its administrative staff.

In mutual-benefit associations bureaucratization poses the special problem of oligarchy. The functions of this type of organization, where the members are expected to be the prime beneficiaries and to govern themselves, are placed in jeopardy by the development of a bureaucratic apparatus that centralizes power in the hands of administrative officials, as was shown in Michels' famous study of unions and social-democratic parties in Germany.[13] The egalitarian ideology and objectives of these organizations would lead one to expect them to be democratically governed by their membership. But the need for efficient administration to insure success in bargaining or in elections

---

[10] Frederic W. Terrien and Donald L. Mills, "The Effects of Changing Size upon the Internal Structure of Organizations," *American Sociological Review*, 20 (1955), pp. 11–13.

[11] Theodore R. Anderson and Seymour Warkov, "Organizational Size and Functional Complexity," *American Sociological Review*, 26 (1961), pp. 23–28.

[12] Tuberculosis hospitals were considered noncomplex, whereas general hospitals, which serve other kinds of patients as well as tubercular ones, were considered complex. See *ibid.*, pp. 25–27.

[13] Robert Michels, *Political Parties*, Eden Paul and Cedar Paul (trans.), Glencoe, Ill.: Free Press, 1949, (first published 1915).

encourages the development of a bureaucratic machinery with effective control of the organization centralized in the leadership. Moreover, as the experience gained by the leaders makes them virtually indispensable for the successful implementation of organizational objectives, their dominant position is further strengthened. The examination of such consequences led Michels to propose his "iron law of oligarchy," according to which even initially egalitarian organizations invariably develop hierarchical structures in the interest of effective accomplishment of objectives. There can be little doubt that Michels directs attention to widely prevailing tendencies in mutual-benefit associations. The same developments that he describes have characterized the history of many American unions. Contrary to his assumptions, however, these developments, though prevalent, are not inevitable, as the study of the International Typographical Union by Lipset and his colleagues demonstrates.[14] This union has successfully resisted domination by a self-perpetuating oligarchy, because it has maintained a two-party system which safeguards the democratic election of union leaders.

Bureaucratization entails the danger that the original objectives of the organization are lost sight of as the result of preoccupation with administrative problems. Thus, Michels observes that the radical programs of socialist unions and parties became increasingly modified and conservative once bureaucratic hierarchies had developed. For the leaders, interested in preserving and increasing the organization's strength, willingly abandoned radical objectives in favor of more moderate ones that did not threaten the organization's survival in a hostile society. Note the dilemma implied here: a party or a union must build a strong organization and assure its survival to achieve its objectives, yet preoccupation with such organizational problems leads to the surrender of these very objectives. Modifications of this kind in the organization and its program occur not only in mutual-benefit associations but also in other types of formal organizations.

Selznick's analysis of the process of cooptation illustrates how a different mechanism brought about similar changes in a government agency, namely the Tennessee Valley Authority.[15] The reform program of the TVA encountered strong opposition from powerful entrenched forces in the area, and the TVA's grass-roots policy required that it achieve success by coming to terms with these opposition forces rather than impose its will upon them by relying on the power of the federal government. As a means for adjusting to its hostile environment, the TVA coopted some representatives of the opposition into its manage-

[14] Seymour M. Lipset *et al., Union Democracy,* Glencoe, Ill.: Free Press, 1956, pp. 201–269.
[15] Philip Selznick, *TVA and the Grass Roots,* Berkeley: University of California Press, 1949.

ment. However, since these new elements helped now to shape the policies of the organization in accordance with their own interests, the earlier objectives of the TVA were modified and transformed. For example, an initial policy of the TVA was to purchase large land strips around the reservoirs created by its dam-building operations in order to enable the public to benefit from the increased value of this land resulting from the expenditure of public funds. But the representatives of local agricultural interests who had been coopted into the policymaking bodies of the TVA succeeded in reversing this policy and adopting the procedure that only the minimum amount of land required for reservoirs and other facilities be acquired, thus enabling private investors to reap the benefits from the improved surrounding land.[16] Again, changes introduced to promote the adjustment of an organization to a hostile environment modified the organization's objectives.

The general principle illustrated by these changes is that in the course of adopting means to attain organizational goals the means may become ends-in-themselves that displace the original goals. In an innovating organization, whether political party, union, or government agency, this displacement tends to take the form, as we have just seen, of a retreat from the initial program to a more moderate and conservative program in the interest of maintaining the strength of the organization in an adverse environment. An example of this process in a voluntary association is furnished by Messinger, who describes how the fund-raising activities of the Townsend Organization were transformed from means into ends-in-themselves as new social conditions rendered its original objectives obsolete.[17] But in old and established bureaucracies the displacement of goals typically assumes a different form—the one to which Merton referred when he introduced the concept—namely, a rigid conformity with official procedures at the expense of the objectives they are designed to accomplish, which results from bureaucratic pressures and an overemphasis on discipline. In short, displacement of goals underlies the very tendencies associated with the stereotype "bureaucracy." In Merton's own words:

Adherence to the rules, originally conceived as a means, becomes transformed into an end-in-itself; there occurs the familiar process of *displacement of goals* whereby "an instrumental value becomes a terminal value." Discipline, readily interpreted as conformance with regulations, whatever the situation, is seen not as a measure designed for specific purposes but becomes an immediate value in the life-organization of the bureaucrat. This emphasis, re-

16 *Ibid.*, pp. 196–204.
17 Sheldon L. Messinger, "Organizational Transformation," *American Sociological Review*, 20 (1955), pp. 3–10.

sulting from the displacement of the original goals, develops into rigidities and an inability to adjust readily.[18]

The very opposite processes, however, have also been observed in bureaucracies. For example, the orientations of officials in a government agency established to enforce New Deal legislation revealed a decade later not an inclination to retreat from the original reform program but a tendency to use it as a steppingstone for further reforms.[19] The earlier goals were not displaced by means that became ends-in-themselves but rather were succeeded by more advanced objectives. Officials advocated legislation that would make the agency responsible for administering more advanced reforms. While officials were in part guided by an idealistic attachment to furthering the program of the New Deal, their career interests provided additional strong incentives for their support of new programs. For once the original mission of getting the new laws generally accepted was accomplished, the task of continuing enforcement involved narrower and more routine responsibilities. These tasks were not as interesting as instituting new reforms and, furthermore, could be accomplished with a smaller staff. Indeed, reductions of staff had already taken place and more threatened to follow. New reform programs would create new challenges that would make the work more interesting and necessitate staff expansions that would avert the threat of layoff and improve the promotion chances of the present personnel. The economic as well as the psychological interests of these officials motivated them to advocate new reform objectives.

This succession of goals, the opposite of the displacement of goals, has also been observed in labor unions. Hart's study of a local of the United Automobile Workers in Windsor shows that this union had expanded its activities far beyond the function of representing workers in relation to management by providing a variety of services to members, such as loans, counseling, consumer cooperatives, and health care.[20] This proliferation of goals apparently occurred when the accomplishment of the union's original objectives had become routine, because the industry was thoroughly organized and industry-wide collective bargaining was carried out by the international union. Local union leaders, consequently, had reason to fear that members might look upon them as dispensable, and this possibility threatened their position (just as the indispensability of union leaders strengthens

[18] Robert K. Merton, *Social Theory and Social Structure* (2d ed.), Glencoe, Ill.: Free Press, 1957, p. 199 (italics in original).

[19] See Peter M. Blau, *The Dynamics of Bureaucracy,* Chicago: University of Chicago Press, 1955, pp. 193–200.

[20] C. W. M. Hart, "Industrial Relations Research and Social Theory," *Canadian Journal of Economics and Political Science,* 15 (1949), pp. 53–73.

their position, as Michels pointed out). To avert this threat and fortify their position, union leaders instituted various services to members that would make them and the local again important to the membership.[21] A final example of the succession of goals is furnished by a voluntary association. On the basis of his study of a large service organization staffed by volunteers—the National Foundation for Infantile Paralysis—Sills correctly predicted that this organization would turn to new programs with the accomplishment of its original objectives.[22] This prediction was based on the facts that the organization had received wide public acceptance, had successfully attained its initial objectives, and was governed by a corporate-type structure that had the capacity and interest to establish new policies as well as the power to implement them.

What conditions govern whether the displacement of goals or the succession of goals is the prevailing trend in an organization? A crucial factor seems to be the organization's relation to its environment. As long as its very survival is threatened by a hostile environment, its officers will seek to strengthen the organization by building up its administrative machinery and searching for external sources of support. This process is often accompanied by a retreat from the original goal to more modest objectives, as exemplified by the history of the Tennessee Valley Authority and by the tendencies in socialist parties and unions in imperial Germany. But if the community permits an organization to succeed in achieving its initial objectives, the staff's interest in preserving the organization and expanding its jurisdiction will lead to the advocacy and adoption of more advanced goals, as illustrated by the federal agency, the Windsor local as well as other American unions, and the National Foundation. This explanation, however, does not account for the rigid conformity with procedures found in many old bureaucracies that are not at all threatened by the community. Perhaps the environment must supply stimulating challenges as well as support to organizations for flexibility and the succession of goals to develop, just as both these conditions seem to be needed for individual creativity (see the study by Pelz discussed in Chapter V).

Is it correct to speak of increased bureaucratization in those organizations where original goals are succeeded by more advanced ones? Yes, in the sense that the change involves increased scope and power for the bureaucracy; no, in the sense that it involves less preoccupation with administrative procedures as ends-in-themselves. The strain is toward innovation, not rigidity, and in this sense represents

---

21 Lipset *et al. (op. cit.,* p. 407) have noted that an important latent consequence of the proliferation of activities in unions is to encourage more active participation by members.

22 David L. Sills, *The Volunteers,* Glencoe, Ill.: Free Press, 1957, pp. 253–268.

a debureaucratizing tendency. We turn now to a discussion of some other forms of debureaucratization.

Debureaucratization. Less attention has been devoted to processes leading to reduced bureaucratization than to those leading to increased bureaucratization. A recent article by Katz and Eisenstadt analyzes some cases of debureaucratization reported in previous studies, most of which deal with tendencies to relax hierarchical authority.[23] It has been observed, for example, that army discipline, strict lines of authority, and social distance between officers and men were less pronounced in combat than in peacetime, particularly if the combat unit was isolated from other units. A study of an industrial concern found that miners were able successfully to resist attempts by management to increase bureaucratization while factory workers in the same company could not. Research also indicates that men on the night shift in industrial plants were less subject to hierarchical authority and discipline than men on the day shift. Katz and Eisenstadt suggest that the common elements in these situations are the presence of physical danger and the isolation of the unit from the larger organization. Both of these conditions make superiors in some respects dependent on their subordinates, and their dependence constrains them to refrain from using authoritarian or coercive measures in performing their duties and to rely, instead, on more personal, nonbureaucratic means of motivating cooperative effort. Katz and Eisenstadt infer from their secondary analysis that dependence of officials on their subordinates promotes debureaucratization, and that this principle applies to dependence on clients as well as on subordinates in an organization. They further extend this principle by following a lead of Parsons and including in the concept of dependence not only the fact that a client or subordinate has the power to influence the life-chances of an official but also the mere fact that the former is capable of disrupting the role performance of the latter.[24]

Data to illustrate this conclusion are gathered by Katz and Eisenstadt in their study of the contacts between immigrants and bureaucrats in Israel. Official-client relations depend on the abilities of both parties properly to perform their roles. Since immigrants who came to Israel from non-Western countries typically did not know what was expected of a bureaucratic client, their inability to act appropriately in this role disturbed the official-client relationship. For

[23] Elihu Katz and S. N. Eisenstadt, "Some Sociological Observations on the Response of Israeli Organizations to New Immigrants," *Administrative Science Quarterly*, 5 (1960), pp. 113–133.

[24] Parsons notes that although the parents have power over the life-chances of the child, they are also dependent on the child, because he or she is capable of disrupting the family system. See Talcott Parsons and Robert F. Bales, *Family, Socialization and Interaction Process*, Glencoe, Ill.: Free Press, 1955, pp. 46–47, footnote 18.

example, immigrants sometimes tried to bargain with the bus driver over the amount of the fare or to debate the route the bus was to travel. In such situations, an official was obliged to teach his clients how to play their role before he could properly perform his. Again, the public-health nurse had to teach her prospective clients which of their problems she could deal with and which ones were outside her sphere of competence. But the diffuse relations with clients that developed as officials assumed the role of teacher and counselor tended to impinge on their specific roles as representatives of a given bureaucracy. It led to debureaucratization and occasionally to entirely new role relationships independent of the initial bureaucratic ones. Some of the instructors sent by the government to immigrant villages, for instance, came to assume boundary roles mediating between the government and "their" village and, in the extreme case, turned into representatives of the immigrant group or even into leaders of movements furthering this group's interests.

The hypothesis that the dependence of officials on clients (or subordinates) lessens the degree of bureaucratization can be tested with data from County Agency previously presented in another connection. It will be recalled that in our comparison of the Public Assistance Division and the Child Welfare Division of County Agency it was noted that the clients of the latter were not only children but also foster parents, on whose cooperation operations in CWD were dependent, while there was much less dependence on the recipients of public assistance in PAD. The prediction is, therefore, that CWD should be less bureaucratized than PAD. The findings support this conclusion. Thus, caseloads were smaller in CWD, and there was more opportunity for casework in this division. Assignment of cases was less bureaucratic in CWD—not by geographic area, as in PAD, but by matching the severity of the problem with the experience of the worker. Since no case reassignments were necessary in CWD when the client changed residence, worker-client relations were more stable and workers were not considered to be interchangeable. Finally, the feelings of the client about the race of the worker were taken into account in CWD but not in PAD. (Note that lack of bureaucratization, even if in the interest of giving professional considerations wider scope, opens the door to racial discrimination.) These differences conform to the prediction. With only two cases, however, one cannot say with confidence whether these differences in bureaucratization actually were the result of the greater dependence of CWD on clients or were due to other conditions, such as the fact that CWD served children or that it had legal responsibility for their care.

Diamond presents an extreme case of debureaucratization in his discussion of an organization that became a society.[25] The Virginia Company was established in 1607 as a business concern to exploit the riches of a new continent and the labors of native peoples. Virginia, however, provided conditions different from those that had been faced by similar companies in India, Mexico, and Peru. Native labor refused to be mobilized, and mineral wealth was not to be found. Hence, it proved necessary to establish an agricultural community based on imported labor, and the company had to devote its efforts to recruiting the necessary voluntary labor from England. After these laborers had arrived, they were subjected to strict discipline enforced by a military regime and by religious sanctions. However, not enough men responded to the call, and the Company was forced to offer more and more concessions to serve as inducements for migrating. The terms under which the laborers could obtain land were eased, women were sent to Virginia to become the wives of the settlers, and martial law was gradually limited as representatives of the settlers were given some voice in government. As a consequence of these changes settlers became involved in a complex network of statuses, many of them outside the organization of the Virginia Company.

At one time in Virginia, the single relationship that existed between persons rested upon the positions they occupied in the Company's table of organization. As a result of the efforts made by the Company to get persons to accept that relationship, however, each person in Virginia had become the occupant of several statuses, for now there were rich and poor in Virginia, landowners and renters, masters and servants, old residents and newcomers, married and single, men and women; and the simultaneous possession of these statuses involved the holder in a network of relationships, some congruent and some incompatible, with his organizational relationship.[26]

Gradually, settlers felt that their statuses outside the Company were the more important, and they were no longer willing to accept organization position as the primary basis of legitimate authority. Thus, a society emerged where before there had been only a formal organization, a transformation that constitutes the polar case of debureaucratization.

EMERGENT PATTERNS

Informal Organization. The formal organization sets the stage for the emergence of informal social processes. Much emphasis has been placed on the influence exerted by the emergent informal relations and group

[25] Sigmund Diamond, "From Organization to Society," *The American Journal of Sociology*, 63 (1958), pp. 457–475.
[26] *Ibid.*, p. 471.

norms as they mold the patterns of conduct of the members of the organization. But formal institutions help to shape the characteristics of the informal organization, and this process has received far less attention than it merits. This latter process is exemplified by our analysis of the implications of the presence of a procedure manual for consultation networks in the two welfare agencies.

Oldtimers were more likely to be respected for their competence as caseworkers than newcomers in both agencies, and respected workers were more likely than others to be regularly consulted by colleagues in both. But in City Agency, where there was no procedure manual, seniority exerted an additional independent influence on a worker's participation in consultation, whereas it did not in County Agency, where all workers possessed a procedure manual. Only in City Agency did we find that oldtimers were disproportionately often consulted, and that newcomers consulted others disproportionately often. These relationships were not affected by holding constant the respect a worker's competence commanded. Worrying about the work, on the other hand, was associated with consulting colleagues frequently in County Agency but not in City Agency. The absence of a procedure manual apparently puts a premium on experience in the organization, with the result that seniority as such, regardless of whether it is accompanied by superior competence or not, has much impact on the patterns of informal communication among workers. In the presence of a procedure manual, which serves as a substitute for personal experience and reduces differences in the objective need for advice between workers, the subjectively felt need for approval and support, as indicated by worrying, exerts more influence on the tendency to seek advice. Here we see how an aspect of the formal institutions—the existence of a procedure manual—affects the informal relations that emerge among peers and, specifically, the significance that various characteristics of workers have for their informal status in the work group.

Another example of the influence of conditions in the formal organization on informal processes is provided by the finding from the study of City Agency that work pressures promoted the development of consulting relations that were perceived as reciprocal. Such reciprocity in a group's consultations conditioned the relationship between the pressures on individual workers and their consultation practices. Thus, if high reciprocity in the work group made consultants easily accessible, the greater the work pressure the more often did the individual consult with others. But in low-reciprocity groups, where consulting involved more effort, the greater the work pressure the less often did the worker consult his fellows.

If the formal structure influences the development of informal patterns, this emergent group structure, in turn, influences operations.

One important aspect of the informal structure is group cohesiveness. Earlier studies have shown that cohesion determines the degree of control that the group can exert over its members. Our research indicates that high cohesion made workers more independent of and more detached toward clients. Group values and norms, too, influence operations. We found that the work group's prevailing orientation to clients influenced a worker's approach to clients irrespective of what his own orientation was. Value orientations also affect the group norms that develop. For example, proclient values in groups seemed to give rise to the norm that clients should be given more independence, which helped protect clients against any individual worker who might not share these values. Group norms often regulate productivity. Whether they encourage a high or low level of productivity apparently depends on whether maximum productivity corresponds to or conflicts with the values and interests of the work group. If economic conditions are bad and workers fear layoffs, and if competition threatens group solidarity, then group pressures tend to restrict output. In the absence of such fears, however, and if a cooperative task makes workers dependent on one another and averts the danger of competition, group pressures tend to increase output. The former situation prevailed in Roethlisberger and Dickson's Bank Wiring Observation Room, the latter, in Walker's automated steel mill.[27]

Conformity to group pressure is associated with informal status. When the central values and norms of the group are involved, only outcasts are apt to deviate, and deviant tendencies are penalized by loss of informal status in the group. But in less salient areas, such as the prevailing climate of opinion in a group, the better integrated person seems to be more capable of resisting group pressures than the one who has still to win full acceptance. Informal status was also found to influence the orientations of workers to both their clients and their colleagues. Newcomers were more likely than oldtimers to be procedure-oriented rather than service-oriented in their approach to welfare clients, presumably because a lack of familiarity with procedures engenders anxiety and rigidity. Social support from peers seems to have mitigated such anxiety, as was indicated by the finding that newcomers who were socially integrated were just as apt to be service-oriented as oldtimers and much more so than unintegrated newcomers. With regard to colleagues, newcomers who were not yet accepted among their fellow workers were more concerned with being highly thought of by their peers than newcomers who had already achieved an integrated position among them. In contrast, oldtimers who were not highly inte-

[27] See F. J. Roethlisberger and William J. Dickson, *Management and the Worker*, Cambridge, Mass.: Harvard University Press, 1939, pp. 379–524; and Charles R. Walker, *Toward the Automatic Factory*, New Haven: Yale University Press, 1957, pp. 80–83.

grated among colleagues were less interested in their colleagues' opinions of them than oldtimers who had gained full acceptance. Apparently, the importance of peers as a reference group tended to increase over time for those workers who had achieved an integrated position but to decrease over time for those who had failed to attain a secure informal status. These are some illustrations of the internal dynamics characteristic of the emergence in work groups of informal organizations, which exert a pronounced effect on the operations in the formal organization.

Supervision. Emergent processes characterize authority relations as well as peer relations. Formal conditions and informal processes are even more closely intertwined in hierarchical relations than in peer-group patterns. Effective supervision requires extending the scope of authority beyond the narrow limits rooted in the formal contract. The successful supervisor must do more than maintain discipline and compliance with official orders—he must encourage his subordinates to exert effort, to assume responsibility, and to exercise initiative. His ability to obligate subordinates is of crucial importance for extending his influence over them and motivating them to follow his guidance and suggestions readily. The formal organization aids him in creating social obligations among subordinates. Thus, the promotion procedure is designed to assure that the supervisor has the competence to furnish subordinates with assistance in the form of advice and training. His position of greater power and centrality in the communication network enables him to extend a variety of services to subordinates—to shield them against demands of management, to obtain staff services for them, to back them in controversies with other departments, and many others. Formal rules and sanctions and his status prerogatives provide opportunities for obligating subordinates simply by refraining from enforcing or exercising them. While official institutions supply the superior with the tools for rendering services to subordinates, he may or may not be able to take advantage of these and actually succeed in obligating subordinates to him.

To establish authority over his subordinates, the supervisor must be able and willing to furnish services that command their respect and allegiance. For the collective loyalty of subordinates is what legitimates his exercise of control over them and transforms it into authority. When respect for the supervisor and feelings of obligation to him prevail in a group, they give rise to a consensus that, since it is in the common interest to maintain his good will, his directives and requests must be followed. Once these group norms enforce compliance with the supervisor's directives, his influence becomes independent of the use of coercive sanctions, or of persuasion, or even of the need to oblige particular subordinates in exchange for every request made of them. In short, group loyalty is the core of the value orientation that legitimates the supervisor's exercise of authority over subordinates, inasmuch as it leads to the development of group agreement that his requests are to be followed voluntarily and of group constraints that enforce this social agreement.

The formal organization cannot create feelings of loyalty to superiors among subordinates, but it can create conditions that promote them. Hence while the superior's informal practices determine the actual scope of his authority over subordinates, formal institutions can encourage or interfere with the development of effective authority relationships. We have already mentioned several examples of how official procedures increase the chances that supervisors can and will render services to subordinates. Let us add one illustration of how the formal structure can discourage superiors from acting in ways that would undermine the loyalty of their subordinates and their authority. A flat structure—an obtuse hierarchical pyramid—by increasing the number of their subordinates, prevents superiors from supervising too closely and thereby alienating their subordinates. At the same time, this flat structure prevents them from leaning too heavily on their own superiors and thus losing their independence and the respect of their subordinates. Further, it makes it less likely that superiors become overinvolved with their subordinates, simply because there are so many of them, and it consequently promotes detachment.

The supervisor has often been described as "the man in the middle," a description which suggests the significance of his relations to levels both above and below him. Data from a variety of organizations, including the two welfare agencies, indicate that some social distance from both subordinates and superiors is important for effective supervision. For example, detachment from subordinates was found to be associated with high productivity, and independence from superiors, with greater solidarity in the work group. And both kinds of social distance, although the two were hardly related to one another, were associated with commanding the loyalty of subordinates. In seeking to ascertain the source of the social support that permits a supervisor to remain independent from his superior and detached from his subordinates, we hypothesized that the supervisor's own peer group serves this function. Empirical findings negated this hypothesis, however, probably because the social relations among supervisors on the same level were not salient for them in the organizations studied. A possible alternative explanation is that the loyalty of subordinates might have provided the support needed for supervisors to maintain their independence and detachment.

Commanding the loyalty of subordinates and expressing loyalty to superiors were inversely related for City Agency supervisors. This difference suggests that superiors and subordinates function as alternative sources of social support for the supervisor. If he receives support from one source, he has less reason to seek it from the other. This finding (yet to be confirmed in research) raises an interesting paradox: if a manager commands the loyalty of his subordinates, who are supervisors, they will be under less pressure to seek to win the loyalty of their own subordinates, a condition which would be dysfunctional for their effectiveness. Conversely, a manager's inability to command the loyalty of his subordinates would have important latent functions for their effectiveness as supervisors, since it would constrain them to try to earn the respect and loyalty of their subordinates and thus foster independence from the manager and detachment toward subordinates. These speculations would imply that effective supervision can be expected only on alternate levels in the hierarchy, not on all levels, and (if they prove to be correct) they may explain in part why multilevel hierarchies have serious shortcomings.

Somewhat parallel conclusions can be drawn from two case studies of managerial succession. Gouldner reports on a new top manager who had recently been brought to a gypsum plant from outside and was under heavy pressure from the management of the company that owned the plant to improve production.[28] The new manager, in obvious contrast to his predecessor, was a stranger, unfamiliar with the network of informal relations in the plant, and he had as yet to earn the loyalty of the personnel of the organization. These typical characteristics of the role of successor constrained the manager to resort to bureaucratic mechanisms, such as elaborate rules and close supervision, in order to improve productivity. Such innovations alienated subordinates further. Since loyalty to him did not develop, the manager found it necessary to maintain control by further bureaucratization. Perhaps he felt too loyal to his superiors to permit him to win the loyalty of his subordinates. A recent case study by Guest deals with a very similar situation.[29] Again, a new manager was brought to a plant from the outside and put under pressure by the company who owned the plant to improve production. In this case, however, the new manager sought to achieve the same goal by opposite means. He tried, successfully, to raise productivity by relaxing the bureaucratic rules that had been set up under his predecessor and by refraining from using formal sanctions, thereby promoting loyalty.

Why did the two managerial successors use opposite strategies? A crucial difference between the two situations in which the new managers found themselves was that the predecessor in the gypsum plant

[28] Alvin W. Gouldner, *Patterns of Industrial Bureaucracy*, Glencoe, Ill.: Free Press, 1954, pp. 45–101.
[29] Robert H. Guest, "Managerial Succession," paper read at the meetings of the American Sociological Association, New York, 1960.

had commanded the high loyalty of his staff, whereas the predecessor in the second case had been generally disliked. The predecessor's practices appear to have served as reference standards for judging the new manager, which made it difficult for Gouldner's manager but easy for Guest's to win the approval of employees. Since the successor to an unpopular manager could rather easily earn the loyalty of subordinates, there was little need for him to resort to bureaucratic mechanisms to establish control over operations. From these and the foregoing conclusions, the following hypothesis may be inferred: a manager's ability to command the loyalty of his subordinates is inversely related to both his predecessor's and his superior's ability to command loyalty.

Conflict and Change. There seems to be a relation of mutual dependence between conflict and change in formal organizations: changes in the social structure often precipitate conflict, and conflicts tend to generate innovations.[30] Thus, conflicts between bureaucrats and clients frequently give rise to new practices which help to resolve or mitigate such disturbances, as exemplified by the custom of complaining and joking about clients to colleagues. This practice tended to reduce tensions and improve operations, albeit at the cost of less considerate treatment of clients. In those situations where clients are a part of the organization rather than simply isolated persons in occasional contact with it, conflicts between them and officials affect their social structure as well as that of the officials. An illustration is the elaborate network of relations that develops among prisoners as they attempt to gain some control over their environment in opposition to the formal system. This emergent organization among prisoners affects and is affected by the organization of the officials, particularly the guards. The connective tissues linking staff and client groups in mental hospitals appear to be extremely sensitive, inasmuch as even covert conflicts and disagreements among the staff have important repercussions among patients.

Bureaucratic formalization is one method for reducing uncertainty in formal organizations. Official procedures provide precise "performance programs,"[31] which prescribe the appropriate reactions to recurrent situations and furnish established guides for decision-making. But uncertainty cannot be completely eliminated. Change, whether due to new external developments impinging on the organization or to internal modifications, produces situations without established precedents. Besides, some exigencies that may arise cannot be anticipated,

---

[30] These statements apply to two distinct types of conflict: (1) conflict between principles that govern organizational conduct—a good example is the conflict between providing services to clients versus checking their eligibility for assistance; and (2) conflict between persons or groups, which, of course, is sometimes due to conflicts between the principles that govern their performance.

[31] On this concept, see James G. March and Herbert A. Simon, *Organizations*, New York: Wiley, 1958, pp. 141–142.

and the more complex the tasks, the more do attempts to prescribe behavior too rigidly interfere with the ability to make expert judgments in terms of abstract professional standards. Finally, procedures that lessen uncertainty for one group may increase it for another. For example, Gouldner points out that short-term employment contracts increase management's ability to deal with fluctuations in the market but at the same time reduce the certainty of employees concerning their job situations.[32] Informal patterns typically develop precisely in these areas of uncertainty and are attempts to cope with them. Where the uncertainty is one-sided, as when organizational policies increase the certainty of management at the expense of that of the workers, the informal organization of workers is likely to conflict with managerial objectives. If management policies deny employment security to workers, for instance, the workers' informal practices may take the form of restricting output to protect themselves against layoff and to reduce competition for scarce positions. But where the uncertainty is two-sided, not a handicap to one group and an advantage to another, informal patterns often arise that serve to organize operations in the interests of organization objectives.

Both Jaques and Dalton have noted that an individual's ability to stand uncertainty and ambiguity governs the scope of the responsibility he will seek.[33] Dalton suggests that strong managers, as opposed to weak ones, move into areas of uncertainty in the hope of extending their responsibility and influence. Power struggles develop as various managers seek to organize these pockets of uncertainty in the interest of their departments, and coalitions are formed to effect this organization. These power struggles, and the changes and uncertainties they bring, offer welcome opportunities to middle-level managers to extend their responsibility. The interests of strong managers in expanding their influence in such contests help the organization to adapt to change, since they cause these managers to welcome rather than to resist it. In the highly bureaucratized French tobacco monopoly, Crozier

---

[32] Alvin W. Gouldner, "Discussion" of Wilbert E. Moore's "Industrial Sociology," *American Sociological Review*, 13 (1948), pp. 396–400. Abegglen presents a description of the opposite situation in Japanese factories, where a permanent employment contract increases the certainty of workers but makes management more insecure by handicapping it in its attempts to adjust to changing market conditions or to introduce new technologies. James C. Abegglen, *The Japanese Factory*, Glencoe, Ill.: Free Press, 1958, pp. 11–25.

[33] Elliott Jaques, *The Measurement of Responsibility*, London: Tavistock Publications, 1956, pp. 85–106; and Melville Dalton, *Men Who Manage*, New York: Wiley, 1959, pp. 243–248, 252–255. Both Jaques and Dalton tend to view this characteristic—the individual's capacity to stand ambiguity—in psychological or sociopsychological terms whereas we would prefer to concentrate attention on the individual's position in the social structure as it influences his ability to cope with prolonged uncertainty.

found, power struggles developed in the one major remaining area of uncertainty—machine breakdown.[34] Conflicts occurred between maintenance and production personnel as the maintenance staff and, particularly, the managers in charge of it expanded their area of control and invaded that of line officials. Informal power accrued to the experts whose technical skills enabled them to cope with uncertainty. For knowledge of technical principles facilitates handling uncertainty in two ways: by making it possible to deal with emergencies, such as machine breakdowns, and by increasing the ability to stand uncertainty for prolonged periods.

Processes similar to those that govern conflicts within organizations characterize the conflicts between organizations. Thus, the coalitions and mergers of organizations to achieve dominance in a market can be looked on as a method of reducing uncertainty. Competition between firms increases the certainty of the public in the fairness of the prices charged but at the same time decreases the certainty of firms, which often react by trying to improve the security of their position by developing formal and informal ties with competitors. As uncertainties are reduced in one area (for example, between sellers in a common market) they arise in others (for example, between buyers and sellers), and the power struggle begins again in a new arena.

DILEMMAS OF FORMAL ORGANIZATION

We shall review three dilemmas of formal organization: (1) coordination and communication; (2) bureaucratic discipline and professional expertness; (3) managerial planning and initiative.

Coordination and Communication. The experiments and field studies on communication and performance we have reviewed lead to the conclusion that the free flow of communication contributes to problem-solving. There are three ways in which decisions are improved by the unrestricted exchange of ideas, criticisms, and advice. First, social support relieves the anxieties engendered by decision-making. In the discussion of problems with others, their social approval of the first step taken toward a solution mitigates the anxieties that might otherwise create a blocking of associations, and it thus facilitates reaching a solution. Once consultation patterns have become established, moreover, the very knowledge that advice is readily accessible makes it less disturbing to encounter a difficult problem, and the experience of being consulted by others strengthens self-confidence; both factors lessen anxieties that impede decision-making.

[34] Michel Crozier, *The French Bureaucratic System,* Stanford: Stanford University Press (forthcoming).

Second, communication processes provide an error-correction mechanism. Different persons are guided by different frameworks in their approach to a given problem, and the differences make it easier for them to detect the mistakes and blind spots in the suggestions of one another. Although social support and error correction are in some respects opposite processes, both of them are, nevertheless, important for problem-solving, as indicated by Pelz's finding that optimum research performance is associated with consulting some colleagues whose orientation differs from one's own (who challenge one's ideas) and some who share one's orientation (who support one's ideas).[35]

Third, the competition for respect that occurs in the course of discussing problems furnishes incentives for making good suggestions and for criticizing the apparently poor suggestions of others.

While the free flow of communication improves problem-solving, it impedes coordination. Unrestricted communication creates a battleground of ideas; the battle helps in selecting the only correct or best among several alternative suggestions, but makes it difficult to come to an agreement; and coordination always requires agreeing on *one* master-plan, even though different plans might do equally well. Processes of social communication, consequently, make the performance of groups superior to that of indviduals when the task is finding the best solution to a problem but inferior when the task is one of coordination.

Hierarchical differentiation is dysfunctional for decision-making because it interferes with the free flow of communication. Studies of experimental and work groups have shown that status differences restrict the participation of low-status members, channel a disproportionate amount of communication to high-status members, discourage criticism of the suggestions of the highs, encourage rejecting correct suggestions of the lows, and reduce the work satisfaction of the lows and their motivation to make contributions. All these factors are detrimental to effective problem-solving. If hierarchical differentiation does not block but frees the flow of communication, however, it improves decision-making; this observation indicates that the adverse effects that hierarchical differentiation typically has for problem-solving are specifically due to the obstacles to free communication it usually creates. But the very restriction of communication that makes hierarchical differentiation dysfunctional for problem-solving improves performance when the task is essentially one of coordination. Experiments with various communication networks show that differentiation, centralized direction, and restricted communication are necessary for efficient coordination. However, the achievement of such a differentiated organization—

[35] Donald C. Pelz, "Some Social Factors Related to Performance in a Research Organization," *Administrative Science Quarterly*, 1 (1956), pp. 310–325.

itself a problem-solving task—seems to have been easier for groups in which communication flowed freely than for those where it was experimentally restricted.

These conclusions point to a fundamental dilemma in formal organizations. Organizations require, of course, both effective coordination and effective problem-solving to discharge their functions. But the very mechanism through which hierarchical differentiation improves coordination—restricting and directing the flow of communications—is what impedes problem-solving. In peer groups, moreover, the free flow of communication that contributes to problem-solving also creates an informal differentiation of status as some members earn the respect and deference of others, and this differentiation, once established, creates obstacles to communication. This dilemma appears to be inherent in the conflicting requirements of coordination and problem-solving. To be sure, some types of centralized direction are more compatible with work on complex problems than others, but the fundamental dilemma posed by the need for unrestricted and for restricted communication cannot be resolved—it must be endured.

Bureaucratic Discipline and Professional Expertness. Weber's approach to the study of administration fails to distinguish the principles that govern bureaucratic organizations from professional principles, as both Parsons and Gouldner have emphasized.[36] To be sure, these two sets of principles have much in common. Both require that decisions be governed by universalistic standards independent of any personal considerations in the particular cases handled. The orientations of both professionals and bureaucrats are expected to be impersonal and detached, a principle designed to facilitate rational judgment. Both bureaucracy and professionalism are marked by specialized competence based on technical training and limit the officials's or professional's authority to a specialized area of jurisdiction. Both professionals and bureaucrats occupy an achieved rather than ascribed status, with the selection of personnel governed by such performance criteria as competence and training. These are important similarities, but they should not be allowed to obscure the equally important differences between the two.

The first difference between the organizing principles of a profession and those of a bureaucracy is that the professional is bound by a norm of service and a code of ethics to represent the welfare and interests of his clients, whereas the bureaucrat's foremost responsibility is to represent and promote the interests of his organization. Only in the case of service organizations do the ultimate objectives of serving clients

---

[36] Talcott Parsons, "Introduction" to Max Weber, *The Theory of Social and Economic Organization*, A. M. Henderson and Talcott Parsons (trans.) and Talcott Parsons (ed.), Glencoe, Ill.: Free Press and Falcon's Wing Press, 1947, pp. 58–60; and Gouldner, *Patterns of Industrial Bureaucracy, op. cit.*, pp. 22–24.

and serving the organization coincide, and even here the specific immediate objectives often conflict. For a service organization is oriented to serving the collective interests of its entire clientele, which demands that the interests of some clients may have to be sacrificed to further those of the majority or of future clients, while the distinctive feature of the professional orientation is that each client's interests reign supreme and must not be sacrificed for the sake of the welfare of other clients.

A second basic difference concerns the source of authority. The bureaucratic official's authority rests on a legal contract backed by formal sanctions, but the professional's authority is rooted in his acknowledged technical expertness. Although some technical competence may be required for performing the duties of a customs official, it is not this skill but his legal status that authorizes the customs inspector to decide whether goods can be imported duty-free or not. An individual is legally obligated to submit to the authority of the policeman, whatever he thinks of his decision, but the same person submits to the authority of his doctor because, and only if, he acknowledges that the doctor has the technical knowledge to determine whether he should have surgery, medicine, or neither.

A third difference, related to the foregoing, is that the bureaucrat's decisions are expected to be governed by disciplined compliance with directives from superiors, whereas the professional's are to be governed by internalized professional standards. To be sure, superiors may be more highly qualified in a field than their subordinates. The crucial problem, however, is that bureaucratic management must base its decisions in part on administrative considerations, which often conflict with purely professional considerations.

Finally, the differences between the two systems are reflected in the locus of the last court of appeal in case of disagreement. When a decision of a bureaucrat is questioned, the final judgment of whether he is right or not is a prerogative of management, but when a decision of a professional is questioned, the right of reviewing its correctness is reserved to his professional colleague group. The actions of the professional expert, therefore, are under the ultimate control of his peers who have the same specialized skills as he, whereas control over the bureaucrat's action is exercised by superiors in the organization whose technical skills tend to differ from his. One complains to the medical society or to the bar association about a physician's or a lawyer's actions, and there his professional colleagues will judge whether or not the complaint is justified; but one complains to a mechanic's boss about a mechanic's actions, and the boss who judges the mechanic is typically not an expert mechanic himself.

With increasing numbers of professionals being employed in

bureaucratic settings, much attention has been directed toward examining conflicts between the demands of the administrative organization and those of professional standards. These conflicts usually find expression in contrasting orientations of employees; some adopt management as their major reference group, and others, their professional colleagues. The significance of this difference is indicated by the fact that studies of professionals or semiprofessionals in formal organizations have consistently found that the conflict between bureaucratic and professional orientation is a fundamental issue. Hughes reports conflicts between itinerants and the homeguard in numerous work settings;[37] Francis and Stone emphasize the distinction between a service and a procedure orientation in their study of a public employment agency;[38] and Gouldner focuses on the contrast between cosmopolitan and local orientations in his study of a college faculty.[39] Our research, too, found that semiprofessional workers in a public assistance agency could be differentiated on the basis of whether their orientation was confined to the organization or extended to the profession of social work. Those oriented to their profession tended to be less attached to the welfare agency, more critical of its operations—particularly of service to clients—and less confined by administrative procedure. Although a professional orientation motivates a person to do better work in terms of professional standards, it also gives him a basis for ignoring administrative considerations and thus may lead to poorer performance in terms of the standards of the organization. Thus, professionally oriented caseworkers were more apt than others to fail to visit their clients on schedule.

Research on production organizations in widely different social contexts indicates that a rational organization for the collective pursuit of formally established goals may exist whether or not the specific mechanism employed for this purpose is a bureaucratic structure. Stinchcombe presents a comparative analysis of construction and mass-production industries in our highly complex and industrialized society.[40] Udy reports a quantitative investigation of rudimentary production organizations in a large number of simple, non-Western societies.[41] Despite the great difference in source materials, the two studies arrive at essentially the same conclusion. The findings of both indicate that a

[37] Everett C. Hughes, *Men and Their Work*, Glencoe, Ill.: Free Press, 1958, pp. 31, 129–130, 136.

[38] Roy G. Francis and Robert C. Stone, *Service and Procedure in Bureaucracy*, Minneapolis: University of Minnesota Press, 1956.

[39] Alvin W. Gouldner, "Cosmopolitans and Locals," *Administrative Science Quarterly*, 2 (1957), pp. 281–306.

[40] Arthur L. Stinchcombe, "Bureaucratic and Craft Administration of Production," *Administrative Science Quarterly*, 4 (1959), pp. 168–187.

[41] Stanley H. Udy, Jr., " 'Bureaucracy' and 'Rationality' in Weber's Theory," *American Sociological Review*, 24 (1959), pp. 791–795.

rational formal organization may be but is not necessarily bureaucratic. Specifically, the fact that an organization is governed by such rational principles as specialization, rewards for performance, and contractual agreements is independent of the existence of a bureaucratic structure, that is, a hierarchy of authority and an administrative apparatus. Stinchcombe concludes that the professionalized labor force in the construction industry serves as an alternative to bureaucratization for assuring rational production, because seasonal fluctuations in this industry make it impractical to maintain continuous bureaucratic organizations. Seasonal variation, however, is not the only condition that encourages employment of a professional labor force; another is the complexity of the services to be performed. When the over-all responsibility of the organization cannot be broken down into fairly routine specialized tasks—as exemplified by organizations responsible for research, the care of the ill, and casework service—expert judgments of professionals rather than disciplined compliance with the commands of superiors must govern operations in the interest of efficiency.

Professional expertness and bureaucratic discipline may be viewed as alternative methods of coping with areas of uncertainy. Discipline does so by reducing the scope of uncertainty; expertness, by providing the knowledge and social support that enable individuals to cope with uncertainty and thus to assume more responsibility. The dilemma, however, remains and, indeed, affects wider and wider circles as the number of people subject to both these conflicting control mechanisms grows, since the work of professionals is increasingly carried out in bureaucratic organizations, and since operations in bureaucracies seem to become increasingly professionalized, modern warfare being a conspicuous example.

Managerial Planning and Initiative. The need for centralized planning and individual initiative poses a third dilemma for formal organizations—or, perhaps more correctly, a third manifestation of the basic dilemma between order and freedom.[42] Notwithstanding the importance of free communication, freedom to follow one's best professional judgment, and conditions permitting the exercise of initiative, effective coordination in a large organization requires some centralized direction. But the assumption that managerial coordination necessitates control through a hierarchy of authority is questionable, since it can be and often is achieved by other methods, notably through various types of impersonal mechanisms of control designed by management.

The assembly line is such an impersonal mechanism through which managerial planning effects coordination of the production proc-

---

[42] See the discussion of the dilemma between bureaucracy and enterprise, as he calls it, by Marshall Dimock, *Administrative Vitality*, New York: Harper, 1959.

esses without the use of directives that are passed down the hierarchy. As a matter of fact, the impersonal constraints exerted on operators tend to reverse the flow of demand in the hierarchy. Since the moving line makes most of the demands on workers, the role of the foreman is changed from one who primarily makes demands on workers to one who responds to their demands for help and assistance, and similar changes occur on higher levels. There is centralized direction, but it is not attained through commands transmitted down the hierarchy.

Performance records are another impersonal mechanism of control, one suitable for controlling nonmanual as well as manual tasks. The regular evaluation of employee performance on the basis of quantitative records of accomplished results exerts constraints that obviate the need for routine supervisory checking. Performance records, like the assembly line, reverse the flow of demand in the organization and cast the supervisor in the role of adviser and helper to workers rather than in the role of a person who makes continual demands on them. This evaluation system also facilitates coordination, since it centralizes the direction of operations in the hands of the higher managers who design the records.

Both performance records and assembly lines minimize reliance on hierarchical authority and discipline to control operations and, therefore, improve relations between supervisors and subordinates. However, there is an important difference between these two mechanisms. Assembly-line production reduces the discretion workers can exercise and hence lowers their work satisfaction. In contrast, evaluation of performance on the basis of a quantitative record of results achieved increases the discretion employees are allowed to exercise and thus raises their work satisfaction.

We had expected that automation would be an impersonal control mechanism more similar in its consequences to performance records than to the assembly line. We further anticipated that most workers in automated plants, where routine tasks are performed by machines, would be technical experts engaged in maintenance and trouble-shooting, and that they, consequently, would enjoy more discretion and have higher work satisfaction. The surprising findings of studies conducted in automated organizations by Walker, Faunce, and Mann and Williams is that the average level of skill and responsibility of workers was not superior to the level that had existed prior to automation.[43] The discretion permitted workers had not been increased. Indeed, in the automated factory studied by Faunce, supervision was closer than on

[43] Walker, *op. cit.*; William A. Faunce, "Automation in the Automobile Industry," *American Sociological Review*, 23 (1958), pp. 401–407; and Floyd C. Mann and Lawrence K. Williams, "Observations of the Dynamics of a Change to Electronic Data-Processing Equipment," *Administrative Science Quarterly*, 5 (1960), pp. 217–256.

the assembly line, because foremen were concerned with preventing costly machine breakdowns. Since automation removed some of the higher positions in the organization as well as some lower ones, it reduced chances for advancement, a situation which was a source of considerable dissatisfaction. It appears that automated plants have not yet reorganized their work processes to take full advantage of the technological innovations. This reorganization would require, in our opinion, the training or recruitment of expert mechanics and the redesigning of the division of labor to include minor machine maintenance in the duties of operators. Under these conditions, machine breakdowns, or the impending danger of them, would not lead to closer supervision as it did in the plants studied, and the highly technical operations would permit the exercise of considerable discretion.

It is conceivable that union pressure to increase wage rates on automated jobs will force management to institute such a reorganization. Higher labor costs constrain management to attempt to improve productivity, and one means for accomplishing this improvement is through further automation that eliminates routine jobs. The remaining highly paid workers could be held responsible for acquiring the skills needed for the maintenance functions now discharged by foremen or specialists. Such changes would give them more discretion, lessen the need for close supervision, and thus probably raise work satisfaction. These predictions are in line with Melman's conclusion that union pressures and high wages have induced management to introduce technological innovations more rapidly than would otherwise have been the case.[44] Such a professionalization of the labor force might also require a reorganization of the reward system, since piece rates do not furnish incentives suited for professionalized tasks. Even in the semiautomated department studied by Walker, where tasks were far from professionalized, and where workers were quite satisfied with their rate of pay, there was much dissatisfaction with the piece-rate system for failing to take mental work and judgment into account. A reward system that emphasizes advancement chances rather than immediate earnings and evaluation of results rather than sheer productivity would seem to furnish more effective incentives for professionalized tasks.

Managerial planning of the production process and a professionalized labor force that can exercise initiative and is motivated to do so by opportunities for advancement would sharply reduce the need for hierarchical supervision and control through directives passed down the pyramid of authority. Indeed, coordination appears to be achieved frequently through centralized planning and by means of direct communication between responsible managers (as in Simpson's spinning depart-

[44] See Seymour Melman, *Decision-making and Productivity*, Oxford, England: Basil Blackwell, 1958, pp. 105–106, 141–143.

ment cited in Chapter VII) rather than through the cumbersome process of passing messages up and down the hierarchy. But our suggestion that managerial planning interferes less with the exercise of initiative than hierarchical authority is not meant to imply that the dilemma between managerial control and initiative is resolved. The best that can be hoped for, as Bendix has suggested, is that

. . . the employees of all ranks in industry and government strike a balance between compliance and initiative, that they temper their adherence to formal rules by a judicious exercise of independent judgement and that they fit their initiative into the framework of the formal regulation.[45]

But even this best is too much to expect. For this balance is continually disrupted by the need for more order on the one hand and the need for more freedom on the other.

DIALECTICAL PROCESSES OF CHANGE

The conception of dilemma directs attention to the inevitability of conflict and change in organizations. Mary Parker Follett, an astute observer of administrative practice, has noted: "When we think that we have *solved* a problem, well, by the very process of solving, new elements or forces come into the situation and you have a new problem on your hands to be solved."[46] The innovations instituted to solve one problem often create others because effectiveness in an organization depends on many different factors, some of which are incompatible with others; hence, the dilemma. The very improvements in some conditions that further the achievement of the organization's objectives often interfere with other conditions equally important for this purpose. A by now familiar example is that hierarchical differentiation promotes coordination but simultaneously restricts the communication processes that benefit decision-making.

New problems are internally generated in organizations in the process of solving old ones. However, the experience gained in solving earlier problems is not lost but contributes to the search for solutions to later problems. These facts suggest that the process of organzational development is dialectical—problems appear, and while the process of solving them tends to give rise to new problems, learning has occurred

45 Reinhard Bendix, "Bureaucracy," *American Sociological Review*, 12 (1947), p. 503.
46 Mary Parker Follett, "The Process of Control," Luther Gulick and L. Urwick (eds.), *Papers on the Science of Administration*, New York: Institute of Public Administration, 1937, p. 166 (italics in original).

which influences how the new challenges are met.[47] Consequently, effectiveness in an organization improves as a result of accumulated experience. These dialectical processes are illustrated by the introduction of assembly-line production. This new production method raised productivity and effected centralized control and coordination without the need for hierarchical directives. However, by routinizing tasks and lowering work satisfaction, the assembly line created problems of absenteeism and turnover—problems that were particularly serious given the interdependence of operations on the assembly line. Management had succeeded in solving one set of problems, but the mechanism by which they were solved produced new problems which were quite different from those that had existed in earlier stages of mechanization. Contrary to our expectations, the introduction of automation has not yet met the problems created by monotonous tasks and low work satisfaction. But should these problems be solved through a reorganization of the work force that requires operators to assume more responsibility, as we have suggested, management would no doubt again be faced with new difficulties. For example, increased responsibility and discretion in performing complex, interdependent tasks might engender anxieties over decision-making which would impede effective performance, and these new problems would require management to devote attention to developing mechanisms that reduce such anxieties.

Conflicts of interest between various groups or persons in the organization are another source of dialectical change. What constitutes satisfactory adjustment for one group may be the opposite for another, since different interests serve as the criteria of adjustment. Thus, when the efforts of managers are judged by the results they achieve and they are given freedom to exercise responsibility and initiative in achieving them, conflicts between them are likely to ensue. For each manager will seek to promote the interests and expand the jurisdiction of his department, and his endeavors will bring him into conflict with others who have staked out the same claims. Compromises will be reached and coalitions will be formed, but since the responsibilities and interests of the managers continue to differ, new conflicts are apt to arise as changing conditions produce new challenges. Moreover, as various occupational subgroups in the organization try to improve their economic position, their interests may come into conflict, particularly if the success of one group upsets the existing status hierarchy and motivates the others it has displaced to recoup their advantage. Conflicts of interest are most conspicuous in the relation between union and management. The union is interested in obtaining higher wages and better working

[47] If we classify problems into dichotomies or other very broad categories, it inevitably seems as if the same ones recur, simply because all new ones are put into one of the few existing categories.

conditions, while management is interested in lowering costs and improving productivity. Collective bargaining furnishes mechanisms for resolving issues, but the conflicting interests generate new ones. Thus, management introduces new machines in an attempt to improve efficiency, disturbing the existing adjustment and producing a variety of difficulties with which the union has to deal. Similarly, once workers have attained the right to collective bargaining, they use it to fight for pensions and other fringe benefits, thereby creating new problems for management.

Another source of disruption and change is turnover in personnel. Valuable experience is lost as older workers are replaced by new trainees, and social ties are disrupted by transfers and loss of personnel. As we have seen, the methods available to a new manager in discharging his responsibilities are dependent in part on those of his predecessor. If the latter commanded the loyalty of subordinates, the successor will find it difficult to do so and be constrained to resort to bureaucratic methods, whereas the successor to an authoritarian bureaucrat will find it advantageous to use more informal managerial practices. Again we see that organizational developments alternate in direction in a dialectical pattern. The succession of goals leads to such an alternating pattern of change in the relations between organizations. Once earlier objectives are achieved, management seeks new objectives and by doing so disturbs the existing equilibrium in the network of organizations. The dominance of one organization in a sector restores order as former competitors become exchange partners, but further power struggles are stimulated by a further succession of goals as groups of sellers start to compete with groups of buyers for dominant power over a set of related markets.

In mutual-benefit associations, there is still another source of dialectical change. These organizations are subject to conflicts that arise from the dilemma posed by their twofold formal purpose. One purpose, just as in the case of other organizations, is the effective accomplishment of the specific objectives of the organization—for example, improving employment conditions in the case of unions. But another distinctive purpose of these associations is to provide their members with a mechanism for arriving at agreements on their common objectives. For to serve the interests of its members a mutual-benefit association must furnish mechanisms for ascertaining what their collective objectives are as well as mechanisms for implementing them, and the ascertaining of objectives requires democratic self-government and freedom of dissent. Endeavors to attain one of these purposes frequently impede the attainment of the other. In the interests of effective accomplishment of union objectives, as Michels has pointed out, democratic processes are often set aside. Conversely, preoccupation with democratic self-government and freedom of dissent may interfere with efforts to implement the common objectives. But the study by Lipset and his colleagues shows that a strong union which has accomplished some of its specific objectives can and sometimes does turn its attention and energy to maintaining internal democracy.

Democratic societies are in this respect organized like mutual-benefit associations. They have the double purpose of remaining strong enough to survive and yet maintaining the freedoms that permit the democratic establishment of common objectives. Under current conditions in the world, the issue of promoting national security and strength versus preserving civil liberties and freedom of dissent poses the dilemma most sharply. No final solution is possible for this dilemma. Indeed, attempts finally to resolve it tend to sacrifice one purpose for the other and thus endanger the very nature of democratic societies. For we surely need to survive in order to preserve our democratic institutions, but we just as surely do not want to survive at the cost of losing our freedom.

Description and Comparison
of the Two Welfare Agencies

In 1957 Blau conducted a study of a city welfare agency in a large metropolis,[1] which we call "City Agency." In 1959 Scott carried out a study of a county welfare agency in a smaller urban center in a neighboring state,[2] which we refer to as "County Agency." In part the two studies were concerned with different problems; for example, the orientation of caseworkers was a main focus of Scott's investigation, while Blau's centered more on supervision. But in part the second study replicated the first, notably the material on relations among colleagues, providing opportunities for systematic comparison. We want to say a few words about data collection and then describe the two agencies to point out the similarities that make them comparable as well as the differences that furnish the basis for the comparative analysis.

Both investigations dealt primarily with the professional staffs of the agencies rather than the clerical or purely administrative employees. Data were collected in City Agency by systematic as well as unstructured observation, interviewing, and analysis of records and documents. Of a total of 70 caseworkers, 60 (86 per cent) in two field sections consented to be interviewed, as did 10 of the 12 supervisors directly in charge of them (all 12 supervisors as well as many workers and most of the higher supervisory staff had been informally interviewed). The systematic interviews were conducted after the period of observation either in a private room at the agency or at the worker's home, as he preferred. The study of County Agency employed unstructured and systematic observation, interviewing, a self-administered questionnaire, and the analysis of records and documents. Systematic data on workers were collected primarily by questionnaire subsequent to the period of observation. Of the 92 caseworkers, 90 (98 per cent) returned a lengthy questionnaire. Interviews were conducted with 11 of the 12 first-line supervisors during office hours.

Both organizations were public agencies charged with the respon-

[1] Philip M. Marcus served as research assistant for this study. Funds for it were made available by the Social Science Research Committee of the University of Chicago.
[2] A predoctoral training fellowship from the Social Science Research Council provided financial support for this study.

sibility of administering assistance to those in need. Functions, in addition to dispensing financial assistance, included the providing of minimal casework services to clients—particularly services aimed at rehabilitation—and the placement and supervision of children in foster homes and institutions. City Agency, located in a metropolis of several million persons, handled about 40,000 active cases and employed about 1,000 persons. There were six hierarchical levels, five above the operating employees. The first-line supervisors were in charge of units containing five or six workers. County Agency served a city of approximately 100,000 persons and its surrounding county. The caseload for this agency averaged about 6,000, and approximately 150 persons were employed, organized into four hierarchical levels, three above the caseworker or clerk. The average unit under the first-line supervisor contained seven workers.

The two agencies were engaged in different types of welfare programs. County Agency administered the categorical welfare programs, which include Aid to Dependent Children, Aid to the Blind, and Old Age Assistance (ADC, BA, OAA). These programs operate with federal, state, and local funds, and were established to provide aid to special types of needy persons on a relatively long-term basis. This agency also placed children in foster homes and institutions and supervised their care. City Agency was in charge of the general assistance program. This program, financed by state and local funds, was intended to supplement the categorical welfare programs by assisting persons in need who were unable to qualify for one of the categorical programs. The differences in these programs have important implications for worker-client relations in the two agencies. The workers in County Agency, being engaged in providing long-term categorical assistance, were able to establish more permanent relations with their clients than were City Agency workers. On the other hand, requirements for assistance were more rigid and the process of investigating client eligibility was more lengthy in County Agency. Another difference between the agencies was that the County program included no provisions for the granting of immediate or even emergency relief; clients requiring such aid had to be referred to other agencies. City Agency did grant such emergency relief; in fact, it served as "a court of last appeal" for the city's needy.

The duties of the public-assistance caseworkers in the two agencies were essentially similar. They were primarily engaged in determining the eligibility of clients for public assistance and, whenever possible, providing casework services to them. The workers interviewed in City Agency were all engaged in administering the general assistance program although other types of caseworkers were employed there. In County Agency, not only public-assistance workers but also those engaged in all other programs were included in the study. The bulk of these other workers were serving child-welfare or adult-service cases. Caseloads for public-assistance workers averaged over 100 cases per worker in both agencies. The caseloads for child-welfare and adult-service workers in County Agency were much smaller, averaging about 50 cases per worker.

City Agency was the more specialized in some respects, and County Agency in others. There were certainly more specialized departments in City Agency; medical, employment, and legal services, for example, were set up as separate departments. The worker whose case indicated a need for help in one of these areas referred the client there for service. In County Agency, each worker had to perform these services for his clients, if they were to be performed at all, since no specialists were available. On the other hand, County Agency had specialized workers engaged in "intensive" casework (that is, carrying a smaller number of cases in order that more time could be devoted to each case), whereas City Agency did not employ such workers.

The two agencies also differed in the manner in which procedures and regulations were transmitted to workers. In County Agency each worker possessed a personal copy of the "County Manual," a large loose-leaf volume containing all the rules and procedures governing the operations of the casework staff. This manual was regularly and painstakingly revised, and workers were admonished to consult it before approaching their supervisor for help in solving problems. In City Agency there was no such manual, and while changes in procedures were periodically distributed to the workers in the form of mimeographed bulletins, there were no requirements for filing them in a permanent binder.

Turning to the conditions of employment in the two agencies, the hiring of workers in City Agency was governed by its own regulations, whereas the County Agency workers were under state Civil Service and underwent an appropriate examination. The salaries were essentially similar in the two agencies: beginning at about $300 per month, each agency provided for regular increments for experience to a maximum about 50 per cent above the starting figure. Turnover in City Agency was much higher than in County, one important consequence of this turnover being that there were always several vacant positions whose caseloads had to be covered by other workers. Such a situation, which did not exist in County Agency, no doubt served to increase work pressures somewhat in City Agency. Finally, provisions were made for educational leave in both agencies, but several kinds of scholarship aid were available to workers in County Agency which were lacking in City Agency.

The director of City Agency did not have a professional degree in social work nor did he possess any experience in this field prior to his appointment. The director of County Agency, on the other hand, held advanced degrees both in social work and in social-work administration. His professional orientation was reflected in his extensive efforts to improve welfare legislation in the state as well as in certain agency programs he had set up, such as the educational inducements mentioned above. The educational differences marking the two staffs appear to reflect the differences between the directors' orientations. Although 28 per cent of the City staff had one year or more of graduate work as opposed to 9 per cent of the County staff, if we consider only graduate training in social work the differences are reversed: only 17 per cent of the City staff had any graduate training in social work in contrast to 42 per cent of the County staff. There is little difference between the first-line supervisors of the two agencies in amount of total education or in amount of social-work education. But in the upper levels of the organizations differences again appear: all of the heads of professional departments in County Agency held a graduate degree in social work, but not all of their counterparts in City Agency held such a degree.

Considering finally the background differences of the personnel in the two agencies, County Agency employed more women, more persons under 30, and more persons with children at home than did City Agency. In addition, County Agency contained a larger number of workers with more than three years' seniority; and its workers were more likely than City's to state that they expected still to be employed by the agency several years in the future. The latter differences are, of course, related to the higher turnover of staff in City Agency. Apparently, the position of caseworker was often a temporary job in City Agency.

These differences in personnel are no doubt partly due to differences in the management and the program of the two agencies. However, they probably also reflect another important factor: there was more opportunity for workers in the metropolitan area to step into the more desirable positions offered by private agencies. County Agency did not face this kind of competition for its personnel inasmuch as there were few private agencies in the county and they tended to be relatively small and weak. Other employment opportunities for college graduates were probably also better in the large metropolis than in the less diversified smaller community. Finally, more workers in City Agency came from working-class families (as indicated by father's occupation) than was the case in County Agency. Social work seems to have been more frequently an avenue of upward mobility for City Agency workers than for those in County Agency.

Bibliography

[Compiled by Patricia Denton in collaboration with the authors]

The period since 1945—especially since 1950—has seen a rapid increase of interest in the study of formal organization. Systematic compilation of the literature in this field becomes consequently a more pressing and difficult task. The more than 800 items in the bibliography which follows represent a third of a larger bibliography which we have compiled.[1] Several major sources have facilitated this work: *Sociological Abstracts* (published since 1953), the abstracts in *Administrative Science Quarterly* (since 1956), and several previous bibliographies, notably Merton *et al.* (1952), Eisenstadt (1958), March and Simon (1958), and Barton (1960).[2]

In making our selections, we placed emphasis on the following types of literature: (1) empirical studies of formal organizations and closely related discussions; (2) studies utilizing a sociological approach, that is, emphasizing structural rather than strictly psychological or purely administrative problems; and (3) publications in the English language which appeared during the past decade. The application of these criteria has necessarily led to the underrepresentation in our bibliography of large bodies of literature which might well have been included in a more comprehensive listing—such as work on public and business administration, small-group experiments, studies of decision-making, discussions of occupations and professions, and reflections based on practical experience with organizational problems. At the end of the bibliography, however, the reader will find a list of other bibliographies which will serve as a supplementary guide to some of these areas.

The references below are arranged alphabetically by author and chronologically under author. In addition, each item has been assigned a three-part code which roughly indicates the type of study, type of organization, and major subject matter reported in the book or article. The following is an explanation of the code:

I. TYPE OF STUDY

1. Empirical study of one organization, or of one or more segments of a single organization.
2. Empirical study of more than one organization or of their segments.
3. Research on related problems, typically studies that focus either on the

---

[1] This work has been financed by a Ford Foundation Business Problems Fellowship.

[2] Full references are cited below in the list of bibliographies.

characteristics of a population associated with organizations or on some problems that often occur in organizations, for example, research on the publics of organizations, participation in organizations, decision-making, conformity, professionalism.

4. Theoretical and methodological analyses.
5. General discussions and surveys of the literature, possibly drawing on some empirical studies but not reporting original research.
6. Readers, collected papers, and texts which cannot be classified in a single one of the above categories.

II. TYPE OF ORGANIZATION

M   *Mutual benefit associations,* in general.
Mu Labor unions.
Mv Voluntary associations (except unions), such as political parties, interest groups, religious organizations, philanthropic organizations, professional associations.
B . *Business concerns,* in general.
Bi Industrial concerns, for example, manufacturing firms.
Bc Commercial concerns, for example, stores.
S   *Service organizations,* mixed types (such as medical schools) and in general.
Sm Medical organizations, notably hospitals.
Ss Social work, educational, and other service organizations.
C   *Commonweal organizations,* including military services, (nonservice) government agencies, (noncommercial) research organizations.
V   *Various kinds* of organizations (several of the four basic types).
O   Not about organizations.

III. MAJOR TOPIC

1. *Approach and method:* the concept and study of formal organizations; critiques and reviews of various approaches to the study of formal organization; methods and research procedures.
2. *Theories and typologies* of organizations.
3. *Publics:* relations between organization and public (both public-in-contact and public-at-large), orientation of officials to public and of public to organization, organization of public, and the like.
4. *Peer groups:* informal relations and norms; performance, morale, and attitudes (especially of the rank and file).
5. *Communication patterns* among peers and in hierarchical structures.
6. *Supervision,* authority relationship, and leadership.
7. *Management* of the organization: policy formation, planning; impersonal mechanisms of control (such as automation), hierarchical structure in general.
8. *Social context:* interorganization relations, cross-cultural comparisons, relations between the community and the organization, influence of cultural values and ideologies on the organization.
9. *Dynamics:* change, dialectical processes, bureaucratization and the problem of democratic control, the individual personality and the organization.

O. *Occupations and professions:* orientations and characteristics of occupational groups (especially, professional vs. bureaucratic), relations within and between occupational groups, occupational origins, careers, and job mobility of organization members.

X. *General discussions,* covering a variety of topics, such as texts.

According to this scheme, an empirical investigation of the effects of automation in one industrial organization (such as Walker, 1957) would be coded as 1/Bi/7. But the code should be taken only as a rough—although we hope nevertheless useful—guide to content.

The code also serves to integrate the bibliography with the text of this book. Part II (type of organization) is derived from the typology proposed in Chapter II. Categories 1–9 of Part III (subject matter) correspond in general to the key topics dealt with in chapters with a corresponding number. Most of the items footnoted in the text may also be found in the bibliography, although the topic code of a reference does not necessarily correspond to the chapter where it is cited, since a study primarily concerned with one topic may be cited for a specific reason under quite another.

Abegglen, James C. *The Japanese Factory.* Glencoe, Ill.: Free Press, 1958. **2/Bi/8**

Ackoff, Russell L. "Automatic Management: A Forecast and Its Educational Implications," *Management Science,* 2 (1955), 55–60. **5/B/7**

Adams, Richard N., and Jack J. Preiss (eds.). *Human Organization Research.* Homewood, Ill.: Dorsey, 1960. **6/V/1**

Adams, Stuart. "Social Climate and Productivity in Small Military Groups," *American Sociological Review,* 19 (1954), 421–425. **1/C/4**

Adler, H. G. "Ideas Toward a Sociology of the Concentration Camp," *American Journal of Sociology,* 63 (1958), 513–522. **5/C/1**

Administrative Science Quarterly, 5, entire issue No. 1 (1960), 1–179. **6/C/8**

Adorno, Theodor W., and Walter Dirks (eds.). "Betriebsklima: Eine Industriesoziologische Untersuchung aus dem Ruhrgebiet (Industrial Climate: A Sociology of Industry Study from the Ruhr District)," *Frankfurter Beitrage zur Soziologie,* 3 (1955). **1/Bi/6**

Alexander, K. J. W. "Membership Participation in a Printing Trade Union," *Sociological Review,* 2 (1954), 161–168. **1/Mu/9**

Allport, Floyd H. "The Influence of the Group Upon Association and Thought," *Journal of Experimental Psychology,* 3 (1920), 159–182. **3/O/5**

Almond, Gabriel, and Harold D. Lasswell, "Aggressive Behavior by Clients toward Public Relief Administrators," *American Political Science Review,* 28 (1934), 643–655. **1/Ss/3**

Anderson, Theodore R., and Seymour Warkov. "Organizational Size and Functional Complexity: A Study of Administration in Hospitals," *American Sociological Review,* 26 (1961), 23–28. **2/Sm/8, 9**

Anonymous. "Informal Social Organization in the Army," *American Journal of Sociology,* 51 (1946), 365–370. **2/C/4**

Anonymous. "The Making of the Infantryman," *American Journal of Sociology*, 51 (1946), 376–379. 5/C/O

Apple, Dorrian (ed.). *Sociological Studies of Health and Sickness*. New York: McGraw-Hill, 1960. 6/Sm/X

Archibald, Katherine. *Wartime Shipyard*. Berkeley: University of California Press, 1947. 1/Bi/4

Arensberg, Conrad M. "Industry and the Community," *American Journal of Sociology*, 48 (1942), 1–12. 5/B/1, 8

—— "Behavior and Organization: Industrial Studies," in John H. Rohrer and Muzafer Sherif (eds.), *Social Psychology at the Crossroads*, New York: Harper, 1951, 324–352. 5/Bi/1

—— *et al.* (eds.). *Research in Industrial Human Relations*. New York: Harper, 1957. 6/B, Mu/X

—— and Douglas MacGregor. "Determination of Morale in an Industrial Company," *Applied Anthropology*, 1 (1942), 12–34. 1/Bi/7

—— and Geoffrey Tootell. "Plant Sociology," in Mirra Komarovsky (ed.), *Common Frontiers of the Social Sciences*, Glencoe, Ill.: Free Press, 1957, 310–337. 5/Bi/1

Argyle, Michael, Godfrey Gardner, and Frank Cioffi. "Supervisory Methods Related to Productivity, Absenteeism, and Labour Turnover," *Human Relations* 11 (1958), 23–40. 2/Bi/6

Argyris, Chris. *Executive Leadership*. New York: Harper, 1953. 1/Bi/7

—— "The Fusion of an Individual with the Organization," *American Sociological Review*, 19 (1954), 267–272. 1/Bc/4, O

—— *Organization of a Bank*. New Haven: Labor and Management Center, Yale University, 1954. 1/Bc/4, 6

—— *Diagnosing Human Relations in Organizations: A Case Study of a Hospital*. New Haven: Labor and Management Center, Yale University, 1956. 1/Sm/4, O

—— *Personality and Organization*. New York: Harper, 1957. 5/B/9, O

Armytage, W. H. G. "The Superseding of the Private Patron: Recent Developments in the English Civic Universities, 1930–52," *American Journal of Economics and Sociology*, 13 (1954), 305–322. 3/Ss/8, 9

Aubert, Vilhelm, and Oddvar Arner. "On the Social Structure of the Ship," *Acta Sociologica*, 3 (1958), 200–219. 2/Bi/8

Aurbach, Herbert A. "Social Stratification in the Collective Agricultural Settlements in Israel," *Rural Sociology*, 18 (1953), 25–34. 5/Mv/6, 9

Babchuk, Nicholas, and William J. Goode. "Work Incentives in a Self-Determined Group," *American Sociological Review*, 16 (1951), 679–687. 1/Bc/4

—— Ruth Marsey, and C. Wayne Gordon. "Men and Women in Community Agencies: A Note on Power and Prestige," *American Sociological Review*, 25 (1960), 399–403. 2/Mv/8

Baehr, Melany E., and Richard Renck. "The Definition and Measurement of Employee Morale," *Administrative Science Quarterly*, 3 (1958), 157–184. 3/B/4

Baker, Alton W., and Ralph C. Davis. *Ratios of Staff to Line Employees and Stages of Differentiation of Staff Functions*. Columbus: Bureau of Business Research, College of Commerce and Administration, Ohio State University, 1954. 2/Bi/9

Baker, Helen, and Robert R. France. *Centralization and Decentralization in Industrial Relations.* Princeton, N.J.: Industrial Relations Section, Princeton University, 1954. 2/Bi/7

Bakke, E. Wight. *Bonds of Organization.* New York: Harper, 1950. 2/Bc, Mu/4, 7, O

Bales, Robert F. *Interaction Process Analysis.* Cambridge, Mass.: Addison-Wesley, 1950. 4/O/1

————— A. Paul Hare, and Edgar F. Borgotta. "Structure and Dynamics of Small Groups: A Review of Four Variables," in Joseph B. Gittler (ed.), *Review of Sociology,* New York: Wiley, 1957, 391–422. 5/O/1

Banks, E. P. "Methodological Problems in the Study of Psychiatric Wards," *Social Forces,* 34 (1956), 277–280. 1/Sm/1, 3

Banks, Olive. *The Attitudes of Steelworkers to Technical Change.* Liverpool: Liverpool University Press, 1960. 1/Bi/4,9

Barber, Bernard. "Participation and Mass Apathy in Associations," in Alvin W. Gouldner (ed.), *Studies in Leadership,* New York: Harper, 1950, 477–504. 3/M/8

Barnard, Chester I. *The Functions of the Executive.* Cambridge, Mass.: Harvard University Press, 1938. 4/B/7

————— *Organization and Management.* Cambridge, Mass.: Harvard University Press, 1948. 5/V/X

Barton, Allen H., and Bo Anderson. "Change in an Organizational System: Formalization of a Qualitative Study," in Amitai Etzioni (ed.), *Complex Organizations,* New York: Holt, Rinehart, and Winston, 1961, 400–418. 2/C/1, 3, 5

Bass, Bernard M. *Leadership, Psychology, and Organizational Behavior.* New York: Harper, 1960. 6/V/5, 6

Bauder, Ward W. *Objectives and Activities of Special-Interest Organizations in Kentucky.* Lexington, Ky.: Agricultural Extension Service, Bulletin No. 639, 1956. 2/Mv/9

Baumgartel, Howard. "Leadership, Motivations, and Attitudes in Research Laboratories," *Journal of Social Issues,* 12 (1956), 24–31. 1/C/6, O

————— "Leadership Style as a Variable in Research Administration," *Administrative Science Quarterly,* 2 (1957), 344–360. 1/C/6

Bavelas, Alex. "Communication Patterns in Task-Oriented Groups," in Daniel Lerner and Harold D. Lasswell (eds.), *The Policy Sciences,* Stanford: Stanford University Press, 1951, 193–202. 3/O/5

Beal, George M. "Additional Hypotheses in Participation Research," *Rural Sociology,* 21 (1956), 249–256. 5/M/9

Becker, Howard S. "The Professional Dance Musician and His Audience," *American Journal of Sociology,* 57 (1951), 136–144. 3/Bc/3

————— "The Career of the Chicago Public Schoolteacher," *American Journal of Sociology,* 57 (1952), 470–477. 1/Ss/3, O

————— "The Teacher in the Authority System of the Public School," *Journal of Educational Sociology,* 27 (1953), 128–141. 2/Ss/3

————— and James W. Carper. "The Development of Identification with an Occupation," *American Journal of Sociology,* 61 (1956), 289–298. 1/Ss/O

————— and James W. Carper, "The Elements of Identification with an Occupation," *American Sociological Review,* 21 (1956), 341–348. 1/Ss/O

——— and Blanche Geer. "The Fate of Idealism in Medical School," *American Sociological Review*, 23 (1958), 50–56. 1/S/3,O

——— and Blanche Geer. "Latent Culture: A Note on the Theory of Latent Social Roles," *Administrative Science Quarterly*, 5 (1960), 304–313. 5/S/8,O

Behrend, Hilde. "Absence and Labour Turnover in a Changing Economic Climate," *Occupational Psychology*, 27 (1953), 69–79. 2/Bi/8

——— "Financial Incentives as the Expression of a System of Beliefs," *British Journal of Sociology*, 10 (1959), 137–147. 2/Bi/7

Belknap, Ivan. *The Human Problems of a State Mental Hospital*. New York: McGraw-Hill, 1956. 1/Sm/3

Bell, Daniel. *Work and Its Discontents*. Boston: Beacon, 1956. 5/B/7,O

Bell, Wendell, and Maryanne T. Force. "Urban Neighborhood Types and Participation in Formal Associations," *American Sociological Review*, 21 (1956), 25–34. 3/M/8

——— and Maryanne T. Force. "Social Structure and Participation in Different Types of Formal Associations," *Social Forces*, 34 (1956), 345–350. 3/M/8

Ben-David, Joseph. "The Professional Role of the Physician in Bureaucratized Medicine: A Study in Role Conflict," *Human Relations*, 11 (1958), 255–274. 2/Sm/3,O

——— "Roles and Innovations in Medicine," *American Journal of Sociology*, 65 (1960), 557–568. 3/C/8,9,O

——— "Scientific Productivity and Academic Organization in Nineteenth Century Medicine," *American Sociological Review*, 25 (1960), 828–843. 3/C/8

Bendix, Reinhard. "Bureaucracy and the Problem of Power," *Public Administration Review*, 5 (1945), 194–209. 5/V/8,9

——— "Bureaucracy: The Problem and Its Setting," *American Sociological Review*, 12 (1947), 493–507. 5/V/1,9

——— *Higher Civil Servants in American Society*. Boulder: University of Colorado Press, 1949. 3/C/O

——— "Bureaucratization in Industry," in Arthur Kornhauser *et al.* (eds.), *Industrial Conflict*, New York: McGraw-Hill, 1954, 164–175. 5/B/8,9

———*Work and Authority in Industry*. New York: Wiley, 1956. 3,4/B/8,9

——— *Max Weber: An Intellectual Portrait*. Garden City, N.Y.: Doubleday, 1960. 4/O/2

Bennett, Edith B. "Discussion, Decision, Commitment and Consensus in 'Group Decision,' " *Human Relations*, 8 (1955), 251–273. 3/O/5

Bennis, Warren G. "The Effect on Academic Goods of Their Market," *American Journal of Sociology*, 62 (1956), 28–33. 1/C/3

——— "Values and Organization in a University Social Research Group," *American Sociological Review*, 21 (1956), 555–563. 1/C/O

——— "Leadership Theory and Administrative Behavior: The Problem of Authority," *Administrative Science Quarterly*, 4 (1959), 260–301. 5/V/6

——— N. Berkowitz, M. Affinito, and M. Malone. "Reference Groups and Loyalties in the Out-Patient Department," *Administrative Science Quarterly*, 2 (1958), 481–500. 3/Sm/O

——— N. Berkowitz, M. Affinito, and M. Malone. "Authority, Power, and the

Ability to Influence," *Human Relations,* 11 (1958), 143–155. 2/Sm/6,0

Berelson, Bernard R., Paul F. Lazarsfeld, and William N. McPhee. *Voting.* Chicago: University of Chicago Press, 1954. 3/O/8

Berger, Morroe. "Law and Custom in the Army," *Social Forces,* 25 (1946), 82–87. 5/C/6

——— "Bureaucracy East and West," *Administrative Science Quarterly,* 1 (1957), 518–529. 3/C/8,O

——— *Bureaucracy and Society in Modern Egypt: A Study of the Higher Civil Service.* Princeton, N.J.: Princeton University Press, 1957. 3/C/8,O

Berkman, Paul L. "Life Aboard an Armed Guard Ship," *American Journal of Sociology,* 51 (1946), 380–387. 2/C/4

Berkowitz, Leonard. "Group Standards, Cohesiveness, and Productivity," *Human Relations,* 7 (1954), 509–519. 3/O/4

——— "Group Norms among Bomber Crews: Patterns of Perceived Crew Attitudes, 'Actual' Crew Attitudes, and Crew Liking Related to Air-Crew Effectiveness in Far Eastern Combat," *Sociometry,* 19 (1956), 141–153. 2/C/4

Berkowitz, Norman H., and Warren G. Bennis. "Interaction Patterns in Formal Service-Oriented Organizations," *Administrative Science Quarterly,* 6 (1961), 25–50. 1/Sm/6

Berle, Adolf A., Jr., and Gardiner C. Means. *The Modern Corporation and Private Property.* New York: Macmillan, 1932. 2/B/8,9

Berliner, Joseph S. *Factory and Manager in the USSR.* Cambridge, Mass.: Harvard University Press, 1957. 3/Bi/7,8

Bernstein, Marver H. *Regulating Business by Independent Commission.* Princeton, N.J.: Princeton University Press, 1955. 5/C/3,9

Bidwell, Charles E. "Some Effects of Administrative Behavior: A Study in Role Theory," *Administrative Science Quarterly,* 2 (1957), 163–181. 2/Ss/6

——— "The Young Professional in the Army: A Study of Occupational Identity," *American Sociological Review,* 26 (1961), 360–372. 1/C/O

Bierstedt, Robert. "The Problem of Authority," in Morroe Berger *et al.* (eds.), *Freedom and Control in Modern Society,* New York: Van Nostrand, 1954, 67–81. 4/O/2,6

Bigman, Stanley. "Rivals in Conformity," *Journalism Quarterly,* 25 (1948), 127–131. 2/Bc/7

Blau, Peter M. *The Dynamics of Bureaucracy.* Chicago: University of Chicago Press, 1955. 2/Ss,C/4,9

——— *Bureaucracy in Modern Society.* New York: Random House, 1956. 5/V/2,4,6

——— "Formal Organization: Dimensions of Analysis," *American Journal of Sociology,* 63 (1957), 58–69. 5/V/1,4,9

——— "Social Integration, Social Rank, and Processes of Interaction," *Human Organization,* 18 (1959–60), 152–157. 2/S,C/4

——— "Structural Effects," *American Sociological Review,* 25 (1960), 178–193. 1/Ss/1,4

——— "A Theory of Social Integration," *American Journal of Sociology,* 65 (1960), 545–556. 4/O/2,5

—— "Patterns of Deviation in Work Groups," *Sociometry*, 23 (1960), 245–261. 1/Ss/4

—— "Orientation toward Clients in a Public Welfare Agency," *Administrative Science Quarterly*, 5 (1960), 341–361. 1/Ss/3,4

Bonser, Howard J., and Herbert W. Butt. *Selective Participation of Farmers and Their Wives in Rural Organizations*. Knoxville: Tennessee Agricultural Experimental Station Bulletin, No. 257, 1957. 3/Mv/8

Bottomore, Thomas. "La Mobilité Sociale dans la Haute Administration Française (Social Mobility in the High French Government Administration)," *Cahiers Internationaux de Sociologie*, 13 (1952), 167–178. 3/C/O

—— "Social Stratification in Voluntary Organizations," in D. V. Glass (ed.), *Social Mobility in Britain*, Glencoe, Ill.: Free Press, 1954, 349–382. 2/Mv/8

Boulding, Kenneth E. "Toward a General Theory of Growth," *Canadian Journal of Economic and Political Science*, 19 (1953), 326–340. 4/V/2,9

Brady, Robert A. *Business as a System of Power*. New York: Columbia University Press, 1943. 5/B/8

Breed, Warren. "Social Control in the Newsroom: A Functional Analysis," *Social Forces*, 33 (1955), 326–335. 2/Bc/4,6

Brookover, W. B. "Research on Teacher and Administrator Roles," *Journal of Educational Sociology*, 29 (1955), 2–13. 5/Ss/3,O

Brown, Julia S. "Union Size as a Function of Intra-Union Conflict," *Human Relations*, 9 (1956), 75–89. 1/Mu/9

Brown, Paula. "Bureaucracy in a Government Laboratory," *Social Forces*, 32 (1954), 259–268. 1/C/O

—— and Clovis Shepherd. "Factionalism and Organizational Change in a Research Laboratory," *Social Problems*, 3 (1956), 235–243. 1/C/9

Bryson, Lyman. "Notes on a Theory of Advice," *Political Science Quarterly*, 66 (1951), 321–339. 4/V/5

Burchard, Waldo W. "Role Conflicts of Military Chaplains," *American Sociological Review*, 19 (1954), 528–535. 3/C/O

Burin, Frederic S. "Bureaucracy and National Socialism: A Reconsideration of Weberian Theory," in Robert K. Merton *et al.* (eds.), *Reader in Bureaucracy*, Glencoe, Ill.: Free Press, 1952, 33–48. 4/C/8,9

Burling, Temple, Edith M. Lentz, and Robert N. Wilson. *The Give and Take in Hospitals*. New York: Putnam, 1956. 2/Sm/4

Burnham, James. *The Managerial Revolution*. New York: John Day, 1941. 5/V/7,9

Burns, Tom. "The Directions of Activity and Communicating in a Departmental Executive Group," *Human Relations*, 7 (1954), 73–97. 1/Bi/6

—— "The Reference of Conduct in Small Groups: Cliques and Cabals in Occupational Milieux," *Human Relations*, 8 (1955), 467–486. 4/V/4

Cadwallader, Mervyn L. "The Cybernetic Analysis of Change in Complex Social Organizations," *American Journal of Sociology*, 65 (1959), 154–157. 4/V/1,5,9

Caldwell, Morris G. "Group Dynamics in the Prison Community," *Journal of Criminal Law and Criminology*, 46 (1956), 648–657. 2/C/3

Campbell, Donald T., and Thelma H. McCormack. "Military Experience and

Attitudes toward Authority," *American Journal of Sociology*, 62 (1957), 482–490. 1/C/6

Campbell, H. "Some Effects of Joint Consultation on the Status and Role of the Supervisor," *Occupational Psychology*, 27 (1953), 200–206. 2/Bi/6

Caplow, Theodore, "The Criteria of Organizational Success," *Social Forces*, 32 (1953), 1–9. 4/V/1,2,9

―――― *The Sociology of Work*. Minneapolis: University of Minnesota Press, 1954. 6/V/X

―――― "Organizational Size," *Administrative Science Quarterly*, 1 (1957), 484–505. 4/V/9

―――― and Reece J. McGee. *The Academic Marketplace*. New York: Basic Books, 1958. 2/Ss/O

Carlson, Sune. *Executive Behavior*. Stockholm: Strömberg Aktiebolag, 1951. 1/Bi/5,7

Carr-Saunders, Alexander M., and P. A. Wilson. *The Professions*. Oxford: Clarendon, 1933. 5/O/O

Carter, Launor, William Haythorn, Beatrice Meirowitz, and John Lanzetta. "The Relation of Categorizations and Ratings in the Observation of Group Behavior," *Human Relations*, 4 (1951), 239–254. 3/O/1

Cartwright, Dorwin (ed.). *Studies in Social Power*. Ann Arbor: Institute for Social Research, University of Michigan, 1959. 6/V/X

―――― and Alvin Zander (eds.). *Group Dynamics*. Evanston, Ill.: Row, Peterson, 1953. 6/O/5,6

Cassinelli, C. W. "The Law of Oligarchy," *American Political Science Review*, 47 (1953), 773–784. 4/V/9

Cattell, R. B., David R. Saunders, and Glen I. Stice. "The Dimensions of Syntality in Small Groups," *Human Relations*, 6 (1953), 351–356. 4/O/1

Caudill, William. *The Psychiatric Hospital as a Small Society*. Cambridge, Mass.: Harvard University Press, 1958. 1/Sm/3,5

―――― "Around the Clock Patient Care in Japanese Psychiatric Hospitals: The Role of the *Tsukisoi*," *American Sociological Review*, 26 (1961), 204–214. 3/Sm/3,0

―――― Fred C. Redlich, Helen R. Gilmore, and Eugene B. Brody. "Social Structure and Interaction Processes on a Psychiatric Ward," *American Journal of Orthopsychiatry*, 22 (1952), 314–334. 1/Sm/3

Chambers, Rosalind C. "A Study of Three Voluntary Organizations," in D. V. Glass (ed.), *Social Mobility in Britain*, Glencoe, Ill.: Free Press, 1954, 383–406. 2/Mv/8

Chandler, Margaret K., and Leonard R. Sayles. *Contracting Out: A Study of Management Decision Making*. New York: Graduate School of Business, Columbia University, 1959. 2/Bi/7,8

Chapin, F. Stuart. "The Optimum Size of Institutions—A Theory of the Large Group," *American Journal of Sociology*, 62 (1957), 449–460. 2/Mv/9

―――― and John E. Tsouderos. "Formalization Observed in Ten Voluntary Associations: Concepts, Morphology, Process," *Social Forces*, 33 (1955), 306–309. 2/Mv/9

―――― and John E. Tsouderos. "The Formalization Process in Voluntary Organizations," *Social Forces*, 34 (1956), 342–344. 2/Mv/9

Chapple, Eliot D. "Measuring Human Relations: An Introduction to the Study of the Interaction of Individuals," *Genetic Psychology Monographs,* 22 (1940), 3–147. 4/O/1

Chinoy, Ely. *Automobile Workers and the American Dream.* Garden City, N.Y.: Doubleday, 1955. 3/Bi/O

Christner, Charlotte A., and John K. Hemphill. "Leader Behavior of B-29 Commanders and Changes in Crew Members' Attitudes toward the Crew," *Sociometry,* 18 (1955), 82–87. 1/C/6

Cicourel, Aaron V. "Front and Back of Organizational Leadership: A Case Study," *Pacific Sociological Review,* 1 (1958), 54–58. 1/Mv/9

Cillié, François S. *Centralization or Decentralization?* New York: Teachers College, Columbia University, 1940. 2/Ss/7

Clark, Burton R. *Adult Education in Transition.* Berkeley: University of California Press, 1956. 1/Ss/3

——— *The Open Door College.* New York: McGraw-Hill, 1960. 1/Ss/3,8

Clark, Donald F., and Russell L. Ackoff. "A Report on Some Organizational Experiments," *Operations Research,* 7 (1959), 279–293. 3/V/1,5,7

Cleland, Sherill. *The Influence of Plant Size on Industrial Relations.* Princeton, N.J.: Princeton University Press, 1955. 2/Bi/7

Clemmer, Donald. *The Prison Community.* Boston: Christopher, 1940. 1/C/3

Cloward, Richard A. *et al. Theoretical Studies in Social Organization of the Prison.* New York: Social Science Research Council, 1960. 6/C/3,9

Coates, Charles H., and Roland J. Pellegrin. "Executives and Supervisors: Contrasting Self-Conceptions and Conceptions of Each Other," *American Sciological Review,* 22 (1957), 217–220. 2/V/O

——— and Roland J. Pellegrin. "Executives and Supervisors: Informal Factors in Differential Bureaucratic Promotion," *Administrative Science Quarterly,* 2 (1957), 200–215. 3/V/8

Coch, Lester, and John R. P. French, Jr. "Overcoming Resistance to Change," *Human Relations,* 1 (1948), 512–532. 1/Bi/5,9

Cohen, Arthur R. "Situational Structure, Self-Esteem and Threat-Oriented Reactions to Power," in Dorwin Cartwright (ed.), *Studies in Social Power,* Ann Arbor: Institute for Social Research, University of Michigan, 1959, 35–52. 1/Bc/6

Coleman, James S. *Community Conflict.* Glencoe, Ill.: Free Press, 1957. 5/O/8

——— "The Adolescent Subculture and Academic Achievement," *American Journal of Sociology,* 65 (1960), 337–347. 3/Ss/3

——— Elihu Katz, and Herbert Menzel. "The Diffusion of an Innovation among Physicians," *Sociometry,* 20 (1957), 253–270. 3/Sm/1,3,4

Coleman, John R. "The Compulsive Pressures of Democracy in Unionism," *American Journal of Sociology,* 61 (1956), 519–526. 5/Mu/9

Collins, Orvis. "Ethnic Behavior in Industry: Sponsorship and Rejection in a New England Factory," *American Journal of Sociology,* 51 (1946), 293–298. 1/Bi/4,8

——— Melville Dalton, and Donald Roy. "Restriction of Output and Social Cleavage in Industry," *Applied Anthropology,* 5 (1946), 1–14. 2/Bi/4

Commons, John R. *Legal Foundations of Capitalism.* New York: Macmillan, 1924. 4/B/2

Comrey, A. L., J. M. Pfiffner, and W. S. High. *Factors Influencing Organiza-*

tional Effectiveness, Los Angeles: University of Southern California, Final Technical Report, The Office of Naval Research, 1954. 2/V/4,6

Constas, Helen. "Max Weber's Two Conceptions of Bureaucracy," *American Journal of Sociology,* 63 (1958), 400–409. 4/C/8,9

Cooper, Homer Chassell. "Perception of Subgroup Power and Intensity of Affiliation with a Large Organization," *American Sociological Review,* 26 (1961), 272–274. 2/Mv/4

Corey, Lewis. "Problems of the Peace: IV. The Middle Class," *Antioch Review,* 5 (1945), 69–87. 3/O/O

Corwin, Ronald G. "The Professional Employee: A Study of Conflict in Nursing Roles," *American Journal of Sociology,* 66 (1961), 604–615. 3/S/O

Coser, Lewis. *The Functions of Social Conflict.* Glencoe, Ill.: Free Press, 1956. 4/O/2

Coser, Rose Laub. "Authority and Decision-making in a Hospital," *American Sociological Review,* 23 (1958), 56–63. 1/Sm/6

——— "Insulation From Observability and Types of Social Conformity," *American Sociological Review,* 26 (1961), 28–39. 5/V/6

Cressey, Donald R. "Achievement of an Unstated Organizational Goal: An Observation on Prisons," *Pacific Sociological Review,* 1 (1958), 43–49. 2/C/3

——— "Contradictory Directives in Complex Organizations: The Case of the Prison," *Administrative Science Quarterly,* 4 (1959), 1–19. 1/C/3,7

——— (ed.), *The Prison: Studies in Institutional Organization and Change.* New York: Holt, Rinehart and Winston, 1961. 6/C/X

——— and Witold Krassowski. "Inmate Organization and Anomie in American Prisons and Soviet Labor Camps," *Social Problems,* 5 (1957–58), 217–230. 2/C/3,8

Crozier, Michael. "Human Relations at the Management Level in a Bureaucratic System of Organization," *Human Organization,* 20 (1961), 51–64. 2/C/7

——— *The French Bureaucratic System.* Stanford: Stanford University Press (forthcoming). 2/C/7,9

Cutright, Phillips, and Peter H. Rossi. "Party Organization in Primary Elections," *American Journal of Sociology,* 64 (1958), 262–269. 3/Mv/3

Cyert, Richard M., and James G. March. "Organizational Factors in the Theory of Oligopoly," *Quarterly Journal of Economics,* 70 (1956), 44–64. 4/B/7

——— Herbert A. Simon, and Donald B. Trow. "Observation of a Business Decision," *Journal of Business,* 29 (1956), 237–248. 1/B/7

Daheim, Hansjürgen. "Desorganisationsprozesse in Einem Bürobetrieb (Processes of Disorganization in an Office)," *Kölner Zeitschrift für Soziologie und Sozialpsychologie,* 10 (1958), 256–271. 1/Bc/6,9

Dahl, Robert A., and Charles E. Lindblom. *Politics, Economics, and Welfare.* New York: Harper, 1953. 4/V/2,8

Dale, John D. *Wage Incentives and Productivity.* New York: George Elliott, 1958. 2/Bi/7

Dalton, Melville. "Conflicts between Staff and Line Managerial Officers,"

American Sociological Review, 15 (1950), 342–351. 2/Bi/7

———"Unofficial Union-Management Relations," *American Sociological Review*, 15 (1950), 611–619. 2/Bi/4,8,O

——— *Men Who Manage*. New York: Wiley, 1959. 2/B/4,7,9

Daniels, Morris J. "Affect and Its Control in the Medical Intern," *American Journal of Sociology*, 66 (1960), 259–267. 3/Sm/3

Darley, John G., Neal Gross, and William C. Martin. "Studies of Group Behavior: Factors Associated with the Productivity of Groups," *Journal of Applied Psychology*, 36 (1952), 396–403. 1/Mv/4,6

Davies, Arthur K. "Bureaucratic Patterns in the Navy Officer Corps," *Social Forces*, 27 (1948), 143–153. 1/C/2,9,O

Davis, F. James. "Conceptions of Official Leader Roles in the Air Force," *Social Forces*, 32 (1954), 253–258. 2/C/6

Davis, James A., Joe L. Spaeth, and Carolyn Huson. "A Technique for Analyzing the Effects of Group Composition," *American Sociological Review*, 26 (1961), 215–225. 1/Mv/1,4

Dean, Lois R. "Social Integration, Attitudes, and Union Activity," *Industrial and Labor Relations Review*, 8 (1954), 48–58. 2/Mu/8

Dearborn, DeWitt C., and Herbert A. Simon. "Selective Perception: A Note on the Departmental Identifications of Executives," *Sociometry*, 21 (1958), 140–144. 1/Bi/7

de Grazia, Alfred. "The Science and Values of Administration—I, II," *Administrative Science Quarterly*, 5 (1960–61), 362–397 and 556–582. 5/V/1,2

Delany, William. "Some Field Notes on the Problem of Access in Organizational Research," *Administrative Science Quarterly*, 5 (1960), 448–457. 4/Ss,C/1

Demerath, Nicholas J., and John W. Thibaut. "Small Groups and Administrative Organizations," *Administrative Science Quarterly*, 1 (1956), 139–154. 4/V/1

Dennis, Wayne (ed.). *Current Trends in Industrial Psychology*. Pittsburgh: University of Pittsburgh Press, 1949. 6/Bi/X

Deutsch, Morton. "A Theory of Cooperation and Competition," *Human Relations*, 2 (1949), 129–152. 4/O/5

———"An Experimental Study of the Effects of Cooperation and Competition upon Group Process," *Human Relations*, 2 (1949), 199–232. 3/O/5

Diamond, Sigmund. "From Organization to Society: Viriginia in the 17th Century," *American Journal of Sociology*, 63 (1958), 457–475. 1/B/8,9

Dill, William R. "Environment as an Influence on Managerial Autonomy," *Administrative Science Quarterly*, 2 (1958), 409–443. 2/B/7,8

Dimock, Marshall E. *The Executive in Action*. New York: Harper, 1945. 5/C/7

——— *Administrative Vitality*. New York: Harper, 1959. 5/V/X

Dittes, James E., and Harold H. Kelley. "Effects of Different Conditions of Acceptance upon Conformity to Group Norms," *Journal of Abnormal and Social Psychology*, 53 (1956), 100–107. 3/O/5

Dornbusch, Sanford M. "The Military Academy as an Assimilating Institution," *Social Forces*, 33 (1955), 316–321. 1/C/O

Dorsey, John T., Jr. "A Communication Model for Administration," *Administrative Science Quarterly*, 2 (1957), 307–324. 4/V/5,7

Dotson, Floyd. "Patterns of Voluntary Association among Urban Working-

Class Families," *American Sociological Review,* 16 (1951), 687–693. 3/Mv/8

Drucker, Peter F. *Concept of the Corporation.* New York: John Day, 1946. 1/Bi/7,8

—— "The Employee Society," *American Journal of Sociology,* 58 (1953), 358–363. 5/B/8

Dubin, Robert. *Human Relations in Administration.* New York: Prentice-Hall, 1951. 6/V/X

—— "Power and Union-Management Relations," *Administrative Science Quarterly,* 2 (1957), 60–81. 4/Mu/8,9

—— *Working Union-Management Relations.* Englewood Cliffs, N.J.: Prentice-Hall, 1958. 6/Mu/8

—— *The World of Work.* Englewood Cliffs, N.J.: Prentice-Hall, 1958. 6/B/O

—— "Human Relations in Formal Organizations," *Review of Educational Research,* 29 (1959), 357–366. 5/V/1,6

Duncan, Otis Dudley. "Urbanization and Retail Specialization," *Social Forces,* 30 (1952), 267–271. 2/Bc/8

—— and Leo F. Schnore. "Cultural, Behavioral, and Ecological Perspectives in the Study of Social Organization," *American Journal of Sociology,* 65 (1959), 132–146. 4/O/1,8

Durkheim, Emile. *The Division of Labor in Society.* Tr. George Simpson. Glencoe, Ill.: Free Press, 1947. 4/O/8,9

Duverger, Maurice. *Political Parties.* New York: Wiley, 1954. 4/Mv/2

Dynes, Russell R. "Church-Sect Typology and Socio-Economic Status," *American Sociological Review,* 20 (1955), 555–560. 2,3/Mv/8

—— "The Relation of Community Characteristics to Religious Organization and Behavior," in Marvin B. Sussman (ed.), *Community Structure and Analysis,* New York: Crowell, 1959, 253–268. 3/Mv/8

Eaton, Joseph W. "Social Processes of Professional Teamwork," *American Sociological Review,* 16 (1951), 707–713. 5/C/5,O

Ehrmann, Henry W. "French Bureaucracy and Organized Interests," *Administrative Science Quarterly,* 5 (1961), 534–555. 2/C/3,8,O

Eisenstadt, S. N. "Political Struggle in Bureaucratic Societies," *World Politics,* 9 (1956), 15–36. 4/C/2

—— *The Comparative Analysis of Historical Political Systems.* New York: Committee on Comparative Politics, Social Science Research Council, 1958. 4/C/8

—— "Bureaucracy, Bureaucratization, and Debureaucratization," *Administrative Science Quarterly,* 4 (1959), 302–320. 4/V/9

Elder, R. E. "The Public Studies Division of the Department of State: Public Opinion Analysts in the Formulation and Conduct of American Foreign Policy," *Western Political Quarterly,* 10 (1957), 783–792. 1/C/3

Entwisle, Doris R., and John Walton. "Observations on the Span of Control," *Administrative Science Quarterly,* 5 (1961), 522–533. 2/B,Ss/7

Etzioni, Amitai. "Solidaric Work Groups in Collective Settlements," *Human Organization,* 16 (1957), 2–6. 2/Mv/3,4

—— "Human Relations and the Foreman," *Pacific Sociological Review,* 1 (1958), 33–38. 5/Bi/6,8

—— "Administration and the Consumer," *Administrative Science Quarterly*, 3 (1958), 251–264. 5/V/3

—— "The Functional Differentiation of Elites in the *Kibbutz*," *American Journal of Sociology*, 64 (1959), 476–487. 3/Mv/8,9

—— "Authority Structure and Organizational Effectiveness," *Administrative Science Quarterly*, 4 (1959), 43–67. 5/V/2,7,O

—— "Two Approaches to Organizational Analysis: A Critique and a Suggestion," *Administrative Science Quarterly*, 5 (1960), 257–278. 5/V/9

—— (ed.). *Complex Organizations: A Sociological Reader.* New York: Holt, Rinehart and Winston, 1961. 6/V/**X**

Fallers, Lloyd A. *Bantu Bureaucracy.* Cambridge, England: W. Heffer, 1956. 3/C/8,9

Fanshel, David. "A Study of Case Workers' Perceptions of their Clients," *Social Casework*, 39 (1958), 543–551. 1/Ss/3

Faunce, William A. "Automation in the Automobile Industry: Some Consequences for In-plant Social Structure," *Amercian Sociological Review*, 23 (1958), 401–407. 1/Bi/7

Feld, M. D. "Information and Authority: The Structure of Military Organization," *American Sociological Review*, 24 (1959), 15–22. 5/C/7

Festinger, Leon, and Daniel Katz (eds.). *Research Methods in the Behavioral Sciences.* New York: Dryden, 1953. 4/O/1

—— Stanley Schachter, and Kurt Back. *Social Pressures in Informal Groups.* New York: Harper, 1950. 3/O,Mv/4

Fichter, Joseph H. *Southern Parish. Vol. I: Dynamics of a City Church.* Chicago: University of Chicago Press, 1951. 1/Mv/8

—— *Social Relations in the Urban Parish.* Chicago: University of Chicago Press, 1954. 3/Mv/8

—— *Parochial School: A Sociological Study.* Notre Dame, Ind.: University of Notre Dame Press, 1958. 1/Ss/3,8

Fiedler, Fred E. "A Note on Leadership Theory: The Effect of Social Barriers between Leaders and Followers," *Sociometry*, 20 (1957), 87–94. 3/V/6

—— *Leader Attitudes and Group Effectiveness.* Urbana: University of Illinois Press, 1958. 3/V/6

Field, Mark G. "Structured Strain in the Role of the Soviet Physician," *American Journal of Sociology*, 58 (1953), 493–502. 3/Sm/3,8

Finer, Herman. "Officials and the Public," *Public Administration*, 9 (1931), 23–36. 5/C/3,8

—— "Critics of Bureaucracy," *Political Science Quarterly*, 60 (1945), 100–112. 5/C/1

Fisher, Burton R., and Stephen B. Withey. *Big Business as the People See It.* Ann Arbor: Institute for Social Research, University of Michigan, 1951. 3/B/3

Fiske, Marjorie. *Book Selection and Censorship.* Berkeley and Los Angeles: University of California Press, 1959. 2/Ss/8

Fleishman, Edwin A. "Leadership Climate, Human Relations Training, and Supervisory Behavior," *Personnel Psychology*, 6 (1953), 205–222. 1/Bi/6

Foa, Uriel G. "The Foreman-Worker Interaction: A Research Design," *Sociometry*, 18 (1955), 226–244. 4/Bi/6

────── "A Test of the Foreman-Worker Relationship," *Personnel Psychology,* 9 (1956), 469–486. 4/Bi/1,6

Folkman, William S. "Board Members as Decision Makers in Farmers' Cooperatives," *Rural Sociology,* 23 (1958), 239–252. 2/Mv./8

Follett, Mary Parker. "The Process of Control," in Luther Gulick and L. Urwick (eds.), *Papers on the Science of Administration,* New York: Institute of Public Administration, 1937, 159–169. 5/V/7,9

Foote, Nelson N. "The Professionalization of Labor in Detroit," *American Journal of Sociology,* 58 (1953), 371–380. 5/Bi/7,O

Foreman, Paul B. "Guide Theory for the Study of Informal Inmate Relations," *South Western Social Science Quarterly,* 34 (1953), 34–46. 5/C/3,4

────── "Buchenwald and Modern Prisoner-of-War Detention Policy," *Social Forces,* 37 (1959), 289–298. 3/C/3

Foskett, John M. "Social Structure and Social Participation," *American Sociological Review,* 20 (1955), 431–438. 3/Mv/8

Fox, John B., and Jerome F. Scott. *Absenteeism: Management's Problem.* Boston: Graduate School of Business Administration, Business Research Studies No. 29, Harvard University, 1943. 2/Bi/4

Francis, Roy G., and Robert C. Stone. *Service and Procedure in Bureaucracy.* Minneapolis: University of Minnesota Press, 1956. 1/Ss/3,4,6

Frank, Andrew Gunder. "Goal Ambiguity and Conflicting Standards: An Approach to the Study of Organization," *Human Organization,* 17 (1958–59), 8–13. 5/Bi/7,9

Freeman, Felton D. "The Army as a Social Structure," *Social Forces,* 27 (1948), 78–83. 5/C/2

Freeman, Howard E., Edwin Novak, and Leo G. Reeder. "Correlates of Membership in Voluntary Associations," *American Sociological Review,* 22 (1957), 528–533. 3/Mv/8

Freidson, Eliot (ed.). *Student Government, Student Leaders and the American College.* Philadelphia: U.S. National Student Association, 1955. 2/Ss/3

────── "Client Control and Medical Practice," *American Journal of Sociology,* 65 (1960), 374–382. 3,5/Sm/3,8

French, Cecil L. "Correlates of Success in Retail Selling," *American Journal of Sociology,* 66 (1960), 128–134. 1/Bc/4

French, John R. P., Jr., and Richard Snyder. "Leadership and Interpersonal Power," in Dorwin Cartwright (ed.), *Studies in Social Power,* Ann Arbor: Institute for Social Research, University of Michigan, 1959, 118–149. 3/O/6

Friedmann, Georges. "Outline for a Psycho-Sociology of Assembly Line Work," *Human Organization,* 12 (1954), 15–20. 4/Bi/7

────── *Industrial Society.* Glencoe, Ill.: Free Press, 1955. 5/Bi/4,7

Friedsam, H. J. "Bureaucrats as Heroes," *Social Forces,* 32 (1954), 269–274. 3/O/O

Galbraith, John Kenneth. *American Capitalism: The Concept of Countervailing Power.* Boston: Houghton Mifflin, 1952. 4/B/2,8,9

────── *The Affluent Society.* Boston: Houghton Mifflin, 1958. 5/O/9

Garceau, Oliver. *The Political Life of the American Medical Association.* Cambridge, Mass.: Harvard University Press, 1941. 1/Mv/8

——— *The Public Library in the Political Process.* New York: Columbia University Press, 1949. 2/Ss/8

——— and Corinne Silverman. "A Pressure Group and the Pressured: A Case Report," *American Political Science Review,* 48 (1954), 672–691. 1/Mv,C/8

Gardner, Burleigh B. *Human Relations in Industry.* Chicago: Irwin, 1945. 6/Bi/X

——— and William F. Whyte. "The Man in the Middle: Position and Problems of the Foreman," *Applied Anthropology,* 4 (1945), 1–28. 2/Bi/6

Georgopoulos, Basil S., and Arnold S. Tannenbaum. "A Study of Organizational Effectiveness," *American Sociological Review,* 22 (1957), 534–540. 1/Bc/1,2

Gerard, R. W. "Problems in the Institutionalization of Higher Education: An Analysis Based on Historical Materials," *Behavioral Science,* 2 (1957), 134–146. 3/Ss,C/9

Gerth, Hans H., and C. Wright Mills. "A Marx for the Managers," *Ethics,* 52 (1942), 200–215. 5/B/1

——— and C. Wright Mills (tr. and eds.), *From Max Weber: Essays in Sociology.* New York: Oxford University Press, 1946. 4/V/2

Getzels, J. W., and E. G. Guba. "Role, Role Conflict and Effectiveness: An Empirical Study," *American Sociological Review,* 19 (1954), 164–175. 2/C/O

Goffman, Erving. "The Nature of Deference and Demeanor," *American Anthropologist,* 58 (1956), 473–502. 4/Sm/3,5

——— *The Presentation of Self in Everyday Life.* Edinburgh: University of Edinburgh Press, 1956. 4/O/4

——— "The Characteristics of Total Institutions," in Walter Reed Institute of Research, *Symposium on Preventive and Social Psychiatry,* Washington, D.C.: U.S. Government Printing Office, 1957, 43–84. 4/V/2

Gold, Martin, and Carol Slater. "Office, Factory, Store—and Family: A Study of Integration Setting," *American Sociological Review,* 23 (1958), 64–74. 3/O/8

Goldner, Fred H. "Organizations and Their Environment: Roles at Their Boundary." Unpublished paper read at the meetings of the American Sociological Association, New York, 1960. 1/Bi/8

Goldstein, Bernard. "Some Aspects of the Nature of Unionism among Salaried Professionals in Industry," *American Sociological Review,* 20 (1955), 199–205. 5/Mu/3,O

Goldthrope, John H. "Technical Organization as a Factor in Supervisor-Worker Conflict: Some Preliminary Observations on a Study Made in the Mining Industry," *British Journal of Sociology,* 10 (1959), 213–230. 5/Bi/6,7

Gomberg, William. "The Use of Psychology in Industry: A Trade Union Point of View," *Management Science,* 3 (1957), 348–370. 5/B/1

Goodacre, Daniel M., III. "The Use of a Sociometric Test as a Predictor of Combat Unit Effectiveness," *Sociometry,* 14 (1951), 148–152. 1/C/4

Goode, William J. "Community within a Community: The Professions," *American Sociological Review*, 22 (1957), 194–200. 4/O/3,O

————— and Irving Fowler. "Incentive Factors in a Low-Morale Plant," *American Sociological Review*, 14 (1949), 618–624. 1/Bi/4

Gordon, C. Wayne. *The Social System of the High School*. Glencoe, Ill.: Free Press, 1957. 1/Ss/3

————— and Nicholas Babchuk. "A Typology of Voluntary Associations," *American Sociological Review*, 24 (1959), 22–29. 4/Mv/2

Gordon, Robert A. *Business Leadership in the Large Corporation*. Washington, D.C.: Brookings Institution, 1945. 2/B/7,8

Gore, William J. "Administrative Decision-Making in Federal Field Offices," *Public Administration Review*, 16 (1956), 281–291. 2/C/7

Gosnell, Harold F. *Machine Politics: Chicago Model*. Chicago: University of Chicago Press, 1937. 3/Mv/3,O

Goss, Mary E. W. "Influence and Authority among Physicians in an Outpatient Clinic," *American Sociological Review*, 26 (1961), 39–50. 1/Sm/6,O

Gouldner, Alvin W. "Attitudes of 'Progressive' Trade Union Leaders," *American Journal of Sociology*, 52 (1947), 389–392. 3/Mu/O

————— (ed). *Studies in Leadership*. New York: Harper, 1950. 6/V/X

————— *Patterns of Industrial Bureaucracy*. Glencoe, Ill.: Free Press, 1954. 1/Bi/7,9

————— *Wildcat Strike*. Yellow Springs, Ohio: Antioch Press, 1954. 1/Bi/4,7,9

————— "Metaphysical Pathos and the Theory of Bureaucracy," *American Political Science Review*, 49 (1955), 496–507. 4/V/9

————— "Cosmopolitans and Locals: Toward an Analysis of Latent Social Roles—I, II," *Administrative Science Quarterly*, 2 (1957–58), 281–306 and 444–480. 1/Ss/2,O

————— "Organizational Analysis," in Robert K. Merton *et al.* (eds.), *Sociology Today*, New York: Basic Books, 1959, 400–428. 5/V/1,2

Gouldner, Helen P. "Dimensions of Organizational Commitment," *Administrative Science Quarterly*, 4 (1960), 468–490. 1/Mv/8

Granick, David. *The Red Executive: A Study of the Organization Man in Russian Industry*. Garden City, N.Y.: Doubleday, 1960. 3/Bi/7,8,O

Greenblatt, Milton, Daniel J. Levinson, and Richard Williams (eds.), *The Patient and the Mental Hospital*. Glencoe, Ill.: Free Press, 1957. 6/Sm/X

————— Richard H. York, and Esther Lucile Brown. *From Custodial to Therapeutic Patient Care in Mental Hospitals*. New York: Russell Sage Foundation, 1955. 2/Sm/3,5

Greenwood, Ernest. "Attributes of a Profession," *Social Work*, 2 (1957), 45–55. 5/O/3,O

Greer, Scott. "Situational Pressures and Functional Role of the Labor Leader," *Social Forces*, 32 (1953), 41–45. 2/Mu/9

Gross, Edward. "Some Functional Consequences of Primary Controls in Formal Work Organizations," *American Sociological Review*, 18 (1953), 368–373. 2/Bi, C/4

————— *Work and Society*. New York: Crowell, 1958. 6/B/X

Gross, Neal. "The Sociology of Education," in Robert K. Merton *et al.* (eds.), *Sociology Today*, New York: Basic Books, 1959, 128–152. 5/Ss/3,8,O

————— William C. Martin, and John G. Darley. "Studies of Group Behavior:

Leadership Structures in Small Organized Groups," *Journal of Abnormal and Social Psychology*, 48 (1953), 429–432. 1/Mv/6

——— Ward S. Mason, and Alexander W. McEachern. *Explorations in Role Analysis: Studies of the School Superintendency Role.* New York: Wiley, 1958. 2/Ss/7,8

Grusky, Oscar. "Role Conflict in Organization: A Study of Prison Camp Officials," *Administrative Science Quarterly*, 3 (1959), 452–472. 1/C/3,7,9

——— "Organizational Goals and the Behavior of Informal Leaders," *American Journal of Sociology*, 65 (1959), 59–67. 1/C/3

Guest, Robert H. "Managerial Succession: Two Studies Compared." Unpublished paper read at the meetings of the American Sociological Association, New York, 1960. 2/Bi/7,9

Guetzkow, Harold (ed.). *Groups, Leadership and Men.* Pittsburgh: Carnegie, 1951. 6/V/5,6

——— and Anne E. Bowes. "The Development of Organizations in a Laboratory," *Management Science*, 3 (1957), 380–402. 3/B/1

——— and William R. Dill. "Factors in the Organizational Development of Task-Oriented Groups," *Sociometry*, 20 (1957), 175–204. 3/O/5

——— and John Gyr. "An Analysis of Conflict in Decision-Making Groups," *Human Relations*, 7 (1954), 367–381. 2/B,C/4

——— and Herbert A. Simon. "The Impact of Certain Communication Nets upon Organization and Performance in Task-Oriented Groups," *Management Science*, 1 (1955), 233–250. 3/O/5

Gulick, Luther, and L. Urwick (eds.), *Papers on the Science of Administration.* New York: Institute of Public Administration, 1937. 6/V/2,6,7,9

Gusfield, Joseph R. "Social Structure and Moral Reform: A Study of the Women's Christian Temperance Union," *American Journal of Sociology*, 61 (1955), 221–232. 1/Mv/9

——— "The Problem of Generations in an Organizational Structure," *Social Forces*, 35 (1957), 323–330. 1/Mv/9

——— "Equalitarianism and Bureaucratic Recruitment," *Administrative Science Quarterly*, 2 (1958), 521–541. 5/V/9,O

Habenstein, Robert A., and Edwin A. Christ. *Professionalizer, Traditionalizer, and Utilizer.* Columbia: University of Missouri Press, 1955. 3/Sm/O

Haire, Mason. "Size, Shape, and Function in Industrial Organizations," *Human Organization*, 14 (1955), 17–22. 4/Bi/9

——— (ed.). *Modern Organization Theory.* New York: Wiley, 1959. 6/V/X

Hall, Oswald. "The Informal Organization of the Medical Profession," *Canadian Journal of Economics and Political Science*, 12 (1946), 30–44. 3/Sm/4,O

Hall, Robert L. "Social Influence on the Aircraft Commander's Role," *American Sociological Review*, 20 (1955), 292–299. 1/C/6

Halpin, Andrew W. "The Leadership Behavior and Combat Performances of Airplane Commanders," *Journal of Abnormal and Social Psychology*, 49 (1954), 19–22. 2/C/6

———"The Leader Behavior and Leadership Ideology of Educational Administrators and Aircraft Commanders," *Harvard Educational Reveiw*, 25 (1955), 18–32. 2/Ss, C/6

——— *The Leadership Behavior of School Superintendents.* Columbus: Ohio State University Press, 1956. 2/Ss/6

Hamilton, David. "The Ceremonial Aspect of Corporate Organization," *American Journal of Economics and Sociology,* 16 (1956), 11–23. 5/B/2

Harbison, Frederick H., and Eugene W. Burgess. "Modern Management in Western Europe," *American Journal of Sociology,* 60 (1954), 15–23: 5/B/7,8

——— E. Köchling, F. H. Cassell, and H. C. Ruebman. "Steel Management on Two Continents," *Management Science,* 2 (1955), 31–39. 2/Bi/8

Hardin, Einar. "Computer Automation, Work Environment, and Employee Satisfaction: A Case Study," *Industrial and Labor Relations Review,* 13 (1960), 559–567. 1/Bc/7

Hare, A. Paul, Edgar F. Borgotta, and Robert F. Bales (eds.). *Small Groups.* New York: Knopf, 1955. 6/O/5,6

Harrison, Paul M. *Authority and Power in the Free Church Tradition.* Princeton, N.J.: Princeton University Press, 1959. 1/Mv/2,3,9

——— "Weber's Categories of Authority and Voluntary Associations," *American Sociological Review,* 25 (1960), 232–237. 1/Mv/2,9

Hart, C. W. M. "Industrial Relations Research and Social Theory," *Canadian Journal of Economics and Political Science,* 15 (1949), 53–73. 1/Mu/1,8,9

Hart, P. E., and E. H. Phelps-Brown. "The Sizes of Trade Unions: A Study in the Laws of Aggregation," *Economic Journal,* 67 (1957), 1–15. 2/Mu/9

Hartmann, Heinz. *Authority and Organization in German Management.* Princeton, N.J.: Princeton University Press, 1959. 2/B/7,8

Hartson, Louis D. "A Study of Voluntary Associations, Educational and Social, in Europe During the Period from 1100 to 1700," *Pedagogical Seminary,* 18 (1911), 10–30. 2/M/9

Haynes, F. E. "The Sociological Study of the Prison Community," *Journal of Criminal Law and Criminology,* 39 (1948), 432–440. 5/C/1,3

Haythorn, William, Arthur Couch, Don Haefner, Peter Langham, and Launor Carter. "The Effects of Varying Combinations of Authoritarian and Equalitarian Leaders and Followers," *Journal of Abnormal and Social Psychology,* 53 (1956), 210–219. 3/O/6

Heady, Ferrel. "Bureaucratic Theory and Comparative Administration," *Administrative Science Quarterly,* 3 (1959), 509–525. 5/V/2,8

——— "Recent Literature on Comparative Public Administration," *Administrative Science Quarterly,* 5 (1960), 134–154. 5/C/1

Heinicke, Christoph, and Robert F. Bales. "Developmental Trends in the Structure of Small Groups," *Sociometry,* 16 (1953), 7–38. 3/O/5

Henry, Jules. "The Formal Social Structure of a Psychiatric Hospital," *Psychiatry,* 17 (1954), 139–151. 1/Sm/6

Henry, William E. "The Business Executive: The Psychodynamics of a Social Role," *American Journal of Sociology,* 54 (1949), 286–291. 3/B/O

Herring, E. Pendleton. *Public Administration and the Public Interest.* New York: McGraw-Hill, 1936. 5/C/3

Hetzler, Stanley A. "Variations in Role-playing Patterns among Different Echelons of Bureaucratic Leaders," *American Sociological Review,* 20 (1955), 700–706. 3/C/4,6

Hill, J. M. M. "The Time-Span of Discretion in Job Analysis," *Human Relations*, 9 (1956), 295–323. 4/Bi/6,7

Hodges, Wayne. *Company and Community*. New York: Harper, 1958. 5/B/8

Hogewind, F. J. E. "Invloed van de Chef op Struktuur en Arbeidsklimaat van de Werkgroep (The Impact of the Supervisor on Structure and Climate of the Work Group)," *Mens en Onderneming*, 10 (1956), 431–445. 5/Bi/6

Hollander, E. P. "Authoritarianism and Leadership Choice in a Military Setting," *Journal of Abnormal and Social Psychology*, 49 (1954), 365–370. 1/C/4

Hollingshead, August B., and Frederick C. Redlich. *Social Class and Mental Illness*. New York: Wiley, 1958. 3/Sm/3,8

Homans, George C. "The Small Warship," *American Sociological Review*, 11 (1946), 294–300. 2/C/4,5,6

—— *The Human Group*. New York: Harcourt, Brace, 1950. 4/V/2

—— "The Cash Posters: A Study of a Group of Working Girls," *American Sociological Review*, 19 (1954), 724–733. 1/Bc/4

—— "Social Behavior as Exchange," *American Journal of Sociology*, 63 (1958), 597–606. 4/O/2

—— *Social Behavior: Its Elementary Forms*. New York: Harcourt, Brace, and World, 1961. 4/O/2

Hoppock, Robert. *Job Satisfaction*. New York: Harper, 1935. 3/V/4,O

Horsfall, Alexander B., and Conrad M. Arensberg. "Teamwork and Productivity in a Shoe Factory," *Human Organization*, 8 (1949), 13–25. 1,4/Bi/1,4

Hughes, Everett C. "The Ecological Aspect of Institutions," *American Sociological Review*, 1 (1936), 180–189. 1/V/2

—— "The Knitting of Racial Groups in Industry," *American Sociological Review*, 11 (1946), 512–519. 2/Bi/4,8

—— "Memorandum on Going Concerns." Unpublished paper read before the Society for Applied Anthropology, 1952. 5/V/2

—— *Men and Their Work*. Glencoe, Ill.: Free Press, 1958. 4/V/2

Hurwitz, Jacob I., Alvin F. Zander, and Bernard Hymovitch. "Some Effects of Power on the Relations among Group Members," in Dorwin Cartwright and Alvin Zander (eds.), *Group Dynamics*, Evanston, Ill.: Row, Peterson, 1953, 483–492. 3/O/5

Hyneman, Charles S. *Bureaucracy in a Democracy*. New York: Harper, 1950. 5/C/8,9

Ingham, Herbert, and Leslie Taylor Harrington. "Pyramid Structure—A Pattern for Comparative Measurements," *The Manager*, 24 (1956), 657–660. 4/B/1,8

Jackman, Norman R. "Collective Protest in Relocation Centers," *American Journal of Sociology*, 63 (1957), 264–272. 2/C/3

Jackson, Jay M. "Reference Group Processes in a Formal Organization," *Sociometry*, 22 (1959), 307–327. 1/Ss/4,O

Jaco, E. Gartley (ed.), *Patients, Physicians and Illness*. Glencoe, Ill.: Free Press, 1958. 6/Sm/X

Jacobs, Paul. "Union Democracy and the Public Good," *Commentary*, 25 (1958), 68–74. 5/Mu/9

Jacobson, Eugene. "The Growth of Groups in a Voluntary Organization," *Journal of Social Issues*, 12 (1956), 18–23. 1/Mv/9

—— Robert L. Kahn, Floyd C. Mann, and Nancy C. Morse (eds.). "Human Relations Research in Large Organizations," *Journal of Social Issues,* 7, entire issue No. 3 (1951), 1–74. 6/**B,C**/1,4,5,6

Janowitz, Morris. *The Community Press in an Urban Setting.* Glencoe, Ill.: Free Press, 1952. 3/**Bc**/8

—— "Changing Patterns of Organizational Authority: The Military Establishment," *Administrative Science Quarterly,* 3 (1959), 473–493. 1/**C**/6

—— *Sociology and the Military Establishment.* New York: Russell Sage Foundation, 1959. 5/**C**/7,9

—— *The Professional Soldier.* Glencoe, Ill.: Free Press, 1960. 1/**C**/7,9,**O**

—— and William Delany. "The Bureaucrat and the Public: A Study of Informational Perspectives," *Administrative Science Quarterly,* 2 (1957), 141–162. 2/**C**/3

—— Deil Wright, and William Delany. *Public Administration and the Public: Perspectives toward Government in a Metropolitan Community.* Ann Arbor: Institute of Public Administration, University of Michigan, 1958. 3/**S, C**/3

Jaques, Elliott. *The Changing Culture of the Factory.* New York: Dryden, 1952. 1/**Bi**/7,9

——*The Measurement of Responsibility.* Cambridge, Mass.: Harvard University Press, 1956. 4/**V**/1,7

Jones, Maxwell *et al. The Therapeutic Community.* New York: Basic Books, 1953. 3/**Sm**/3

Josephson, Eric. "Irrational Leadership in Formal Organizations," *Social Forces,* 31 (1952), 109–117. 5/**V**/6,9

Kadushin, Charles. "Individual Decisions to Undertake Psychotherapy," *Administrative Science Quarterly,* 3 (1958), 379–411. 3/**Sm**/3

Kahn, Robert L., and Daniel Katz. "Leadership Practices in Relation to Productivity and Morale," in Dorwin Cartwright and Alvin Zander (eds.), *Group Dynamics,* Evanston, Ill.: Row, Peterson, 1953, 612–628. 2/**B**/6

—— Floyd C. Mann, and Stanley Seashore (eds.). "Human Relations Research in Large Organizations: II." *Journal of Social Issues,* 12, entire issue No. 2 (1956). 6/**V**/**X**

Kaplan, Max. "Telopractice: A Symphony Orchestra as It Prepares for a Concert," *Social Forces,* 33 (1955), 352–355. 1/**Mv**/8,9

Kaplan, Norman. "The Role of the Research Administrator," *Administrative Science Quarterly,* 4 (1959), 20–42. 2/**C**/**O**

—— "Research Administration and the Administrator: U.S.S.R. and U.S.," *Administrative Science Quarterly,* 6 (1961), 51–72. 2/**C**/8,**O**

Kaplan, Sidney J. "Up from the Ranks on a Fast Escalator," *American Sociological Review,* 24 (1959), 79–81. 3/**B**/8,**O**

Karsh, Bernard, Joel Seidman, and Daisy M. Lilienthal. "The Union Organizer and His Tactics: A Case Study," *American Journal of Sociology,* 59 (1953), 113–122. 1/**Bi, Mu**/8

Katona, George. *Psychological Analysis of Economic Behavior.* New York: McGraw-Hill, 1951. 3/**B**/2

Katz, Daniel, and Robert L. Kahn. "Some Recent Findings in Human Relations Research in Industry," in Guy E. Swanson *et al.* (eds.), *Readings in Social Psychology,* Rev. ed., New York: Holt, 1952, 650–665. 2/**B**/4,6

—— Nathan Maccoby, Gerald Gurin, and Lucretia G. Floor. *Productivity, Supervision, and Morale among Railroad Workers.* Ann Arbor: Institute for Social Research, University of Michigan, 1951. 1/Bi/4,6

—— Nathan Maccoby, and Nancy C. Morse. *Productivity, Supervision, and Morale in an Office Situation.* Ann Arbor: Institute for Social Research, University of Michigan, 1950. 1/Bc/4,6

Katz, Elihu. "The Two-Step Flow of Communication: An Up-to-Date Report on an Hypothesis," *Public Opinion Quarterly,* 21 (1957), 61–78. 5/O/5

—— and S. N. Eisenstadt. "Some Sociological Observations on the Response of Israeli Organizations to New Immigrants," *Administrative Science Quarterly,* 5 (1960), 113–133. 3,5/V/3,9

—— and Paul F. Lazarsfeld. *Personal Influence.* Glencoe, Ill.: Free Press, 1955. 3/O/5

Kaufman, Herbert. "Emerging Conflicts in the Doctrines of Public Administration," *American Political Science Review,* 50 (1956), 1057–1074. 5/C/1

—— *The Forest Ranger: A Study in Administrative Behavior.* Baltimore: Johns Hopkins Press, 1960. 1/C/7,O

Kelley, Harold H. "Communications in Experimentally Created Hierarchies," *Human Relations,* 4 (1951), 39–56. 3/O/5

—— and Martin M. Shapiro. "An Experiment on Conformity to Group Norms Where Conformity is Detrimental to Group Achievement," *American Sociological Review,* 19 (1954), 667–677. 3/O/5

Kelsall, R. K. *Higher Civil Servants in Britain: From 1870 to the Present Day.* London: Routledge and Kegan Paul, 1955. 3/C/O

Kerr, Clark, and Lloyd H. S. Fisher. "Plant Sociology: The Elite and the Aborigines," in Mirra Komarovsky (ed.), *Common Frontiers of the Social Sciences,* Glencoe, Ill.: Free Press, 1957, 281–309. 5/Bi/1,8

—— and Abraham Siegel. "The Interindustry Propensity to Strike—An International Comparison," in Arthur Kornhauser *et al.* (eds.), *Industrial Conflict,* New York: McGraw-Hill, 1954, 189–212. 2/B, Mu/8

Kerr, Willard A. "Labor Turnover and Its Correlates," *Journal of Applied Psychology,* 31 (1947), 366–371. 2/Bi/4

Kincaid, Harry V., and Margaret Bright. "Interviewing the Business Elite," *American Journal of Sociology,* 63 (1957), 304–311. 4/B/1

Kohrer, Wayne C. "On Clienteles of the Agricultural Extension Service," *Rural Sociology,* 20 (1955), 299–303. 3/C/3

Komarovsky, Mirra. "Voluntary Associations of Urban Dwellers," *American Sociological Review,* 11 (1946), 686–698. 3/Mv/8

König, René. "Einige Grundsätzliche Bemerkungen über die Mikroanalyse in der Betriebssoziologie (Some Fundamental Remarks on Micro-Analysis in Industrial Sociology), *Kölner Zeitschrift für Soziologie und Soziopsychologie,* 8 (1956), 46–64. 4/Bi/4

Kornhauser, Arthur, Robert Dubin, and Arthur M. Ross (eds.), *Industrial Conflict,* New York: McGraw-Hill, 1954. 6/Bi, Mu/7,8

Kornhauser, William R. "The Negro Union Official: A Study of Sponsorship and Control," *American Journal of Sociology,* 57 (1952), 443–452. 2/Mu/3,O

Kounin, Jacob, Norman Polansky, Bruce Biddle, Herbert Coburn, and Augustus Fenn. "Experimental Studies of Clients' Reactions to Initial Interviews," *Human Relations,* 9 (1956), 265–293. 3/S/3

Kriesberg, Louis. "Occupational Controls among Steel Distributors," *American Journal of Sociology,* 61 (1955), 203–212. 2/Bi/8

—— "Industrial Sociology 1945–55," in Hans L. Zetterberg (ed.), *Sociology in the United States of America,* Paris: UNESCO, 1956, 71–77. 5/Bi/1

Krugman, Herbert E. "Salesman in Conflict: A Challenge to Marketing," *Journal of Marketing,* 23 (1958), 59–61. 1/Bc/3

Lahne, Herbert J., and Joseph Kovner. "Local Union Structure: Formality and Reality," *Industrial and Labor Relations Review,* 9 (1955), 24–31. 2/Mu/8,9

Lamson, Robert W. "The Present Strains between Science and Government," *Social Forces,* 33 (1955), 360–367. 5/C/O

Landsberger, Henry A. "Interaction Process Analysis of the Mediation of Labor-Management Disputes," *Journal of Abnormal and Social Psychology,* 51 (1955), 552–558. 3/Mu, B/4

—— *Hawthorne Revisited.* Ithaca, N.Y.: Cornell University Press, 1958. 5/Bi/1

Lane, Robert E. *The Regulation of Businessmen.* New Haven: Yale University Press, 1954. 3/B/8

Lanzetta, John T., and Thornton B. Roby. "Group Performance as a Function of Work-Distribution Patterns and Task Load," *Sociometry,* 19 (1956), 95–104. 3/O/7

—— and Thornton B. Roby, "Effects of Work-Group Structure and Certain Task Variables on Group Performance," *Journal of Abnormal and Social Psychology,* 53 (1956), 307–314. 3/O/5

Laski, Harold J. "Bureaucracy," in *Encyclopedia of the Social Sciences,* Vol. 3, New York: Macmillan, 1930, 70–73. 5/C/9

Lawrence, Paul R. *The Changing of Organizational Behavior Patterns: A Case Study of Decentralization.* Boston: Graduate School of Business Administration, Harvard University, 1958. 1/Bc/7,9

Lazarsfeld, Paul F. "Reflections on Business," *American Journal of Sociology,* 65 (1959), 1–31. 5/B/1,3,7

—— and Robert K. Merton. "Friendship as Social Process," in Morroe Berger *et al.* (eds.), *Freedom and Control in Modern Society,* New York: Van Nostrand, 1954, 18–66. 3/O/4

—— and Morris Rosenberg (eds.), *The Language of Social Research,* Glencoe, Ill.: Free Press, 1955. 6/O/1

—— and Wagner Thielens, Jr. *The Academic Mind.* Glencoe, Ill.: Free Press, 1958. 2/Ss/O

Leavitt, Harold J. "Some Effects of Certain Communication Patterns on Group Performance," *Journal of Abnormal and Social Psychology,* 46 (1951), 38–50. 3/O/5

—— *Managerial Psychology.* Chicago: University of Chicago Press, 1958. 5/B/5,7,O

Lefton, Mark, Simon Dinitz, and Benjamin Pasamanick. "Decision-Making in a Mental Hospital: Real, Perceived, and Ideal," *American Sociological Review,* 24 (1959), 822–829. 1/Sm/7

Leighton, Alexander H. *The Governing of Men.* Princeton, N.J.: Princeton University Press, 1945. 1/C/3,8

Leiserson, Avery. *Administrative Regulation: A Study in the Representation of Interests.* Chicago: University of Chicago Press, 1942. 3/M, C/8

Lenski, Gerhard E. "Status Crystallization: A Non-Vertical Dimension of Social Status," *American Sociological Review,* 19 (1954), 405–413. 3/O/1

——— "Social Participation and Status Crystallization," *American Sociological Review,* 21 (1956), 458–464. 3/Mv/8

Lentz, Edith M. "Hospital Administration—One of a Species," *Administrative Science Quarterly,* 1 (1957), 444–463. 5/Sm/2,8,9

Levine, Sol, and Paul E. White. "Exchange as a Conceptual Framework for the Study of Interorganizational Relationships," *Administrative Science Quarterly,* 5 (1961), 583–601. 2/Mv, S/8

Lewis, Ralph. "Officer-Enlisted Men's Relationships," *American Journal of Sociology,* 52 (1947), 410–419. 3/C/6

Lieberson, Stanley. "Ethnic Groups and the Practice of Medicine," *American Sociological Review,* 23 (1958), 542–549. 3/Sm/8

——— "The Division of Labor in Banking," *American Journal of Sociology,* 66 (1961), 491–496. 2/Bc/8

Likert, Rensis. "Measuring Organizational Performance," *Harvard Business Review,* 36 (1958), 41–50. 5/B/7

——— "A Motivational Approach to a Modified Theory of Organization and Management," in Mason Haire (ed.), *Modern Organization Theory,* New York: Wiley, 1959, 184–217. 4/B/2,4,7

——— and Samuel P. Hayes, Jr. (eds.). *Some Applications of Behavioural Research,* New York: UNESCO Publications Center, 1957. 6/V/X

Lindzey, Gardner (ed.). *Handbook of Social Psychology.* 2 vols. Cambridge, Mass.: Addison-Wesley, 1954. 6/O/1,2

Lippitt, Ronald, Norman Polansky, and Sidney Rosen. "The Dynamics of Power," *Human Relations,* 5 (1952), 37–64. 2/Ss/3,5

——— Jeanne Watson, and Bruce Westley. *The Dynamics of Planned Change.* New York: Harcourt, Brace, 1958. 3/V/3,8,9

Lipset, Seymour M. *Agrarian Socialism.* Berkeley and Los Angeles: University of California Press, 1950. 1/Mv/8,9

——— "The Political Process in Trade Unions: A Theoretical Statement," in Morroe Berger *et al.* (eds.), *Freedom and Control in Modern Society,* New York: Van Nostrand, 1954, 82–124. 4/Mu/9

——— *Political Man: The Social Bases of Politics.* Garden City, N.Y.: Doubleday, 1960. 3/M,C/8,9

——— Martin A. Trow, and James S. Coleman. *Union Democracy.* Glencoe, Ill.: Free Press, 1956. 2/Mu/9

Litchfield, Edward H. "Notes on a General Theory of Administration," *Administrative Science Quarterly,* 1 (1956), 3–29. 4/V/2

Little, Roger W. "The 'Sick' Soldier and the Medical Ward Officer," *Human Organization,* 15 (1956), 22–24. 1/C/3,O

Litwak, Eugene. "Voluntary Associations and Neighborhood Cohesion," *American Sociological Review,* 26 (1961), 258–271. 3/Mv,B/8

Lockwood, David. *The Blackcoated Worker: A Study in Class Consciousness.* London: George Allen and Unwin, 1958. 3/V/O

Loeb, Martin B. "Some Dominant Cultural Themes in a Psychiatric Hospital," *Social Problems,* 4 (1956), 17–21. 1/Sm/X

Lombard, George F. *Behavior in a Selling Group.* Cambridge, Mass.: Graduate School of Business Administration, Harvard University, 1955. 1/Bc/3,4

Long, Norton E. "The Local Community as an Ecology of Games," *American Journal of Sociology,* 64 (1958), 251–261. 5/V/8

Lorge, Irving, David Fox, Joel Davitz, and Marlin Brenner. "A Survey of Studies Contrasting the Quality of Group Performance and Individual Performance, 1920–1957," *Psychological Bulletin,* 55 (1958), 337–372. 5/O/5

―――― and Herbert Solomon. "Two Models of Group Behavior in the Solution of Eureka-type Problems," *Psychometrika,* 20 (1955), 139–148. 3/O/5

Maccoby, Eleanor E., Theodore M. Newcomb, and Eugene L. Hartley (eds.). *Readings in Social Psychology,* 3d ed. New York: Holt, 1958. 6/O/X

Maccoby, Herbert. "Controversy, Neutrality, and Higher Education," *American Sociological Review,* 25 (1960), 884–893. 2/Ss/8,O

Mack, Raymond W. "The Prestige System of an Air Base: Squadron Ranking and Morale," *American Sociological Review,* 19 (1954), 281–287. 2/C/4

―――― "Occupational Ideology and the Determinate Role," *Social Forces,* 36 (1957), 37–44. 3/O/O

Mackenzie, W. J. M. "Pressure Groups in British Government," *British Journal of Sociology,* 6 (1955), 133–148. 4/Mv/2

MacRae, Duncan, Jr. "The Relation between Roll Call Votes and Constituencies in the Massachusetts House of Representatives," *American Political Science Review,* 46 (1952), 1046–1055. 1/C/8

―――― "The Role of the State Legislator in Massachusetts," *American Sociological Review,* 19 (1954), 185–194. 1/C/3,O

Magistretti, Franca. "Sociological Factors in the Structuring of Industrial Workers' Teams," *American Journal of Sociology,* 65 (1960), 536–540. 2/Bi/4,8

Maier, Norman R. F., and Allen R. Solem. "The Contribution of a Discussion Leader to the Quality of Group Thinking," *Human Relations,* 5 (1952), 277–288. 3/O/5

Man and Automation. Proceedings of the Society for Applied Anthropology. New Haven: Technology Project, Yale University, 1956. 6/B/7

Mann, Floyd C., and Richard L. Hoffman. *Automation and the Worker: A Study of Social Change in Power Plants.* New York: Holt, 1960. 2/Bi/7

―――― and Lawrence K. Williams. "Observations on the Dynamics of a Change to Electronic Data-Processing Equipment," *Administrative Science Quarterly,* 5 (1960), 217–256. 1/Bc/7

Mann, Peter H. "The Marine Radioman—A British Contribution," *American Journal of Sociology,* 63 (1957), 39–41. 1/B/4

Mannheim, Karl. *Freedom, Power, and Democratic Planning.* New York: Oxford University Press, 1950. 4/O/9

March, James G., and Herbert A. Simon. *Organizations.* New York: Wiley, 1958. 4/V/2

Marcus, Philip M. "Expressive and Instrumental Groups: Toward a Theory of Group Structure," *American Journal of Sociology*, 66 (1960), 54–59. 1/Ss/4

Marriott, R. "Size of Working Group and Output," *Occupational Psychology*, 23 (1949), 47–57. 2/Bi/4

Marschak, Jacob. "Elements for a Theory of Teams," *Management Science*, 1 (1955), 127–137. 4/V/5,7

Martin, John M. "Social-Cultural Differences: Barriers in Case Work with Delinquents," *Social Work*, 2 (1957), 22–25. 5/Ss/3,8

Martin, Norman H. "Differential Decisions in the Management of an Industrial Plant," *Journal of Business*, 29 (1956), 249–260. 1/Bi/7

—— and Anselm L. Strauss. "Patterns of Mobility within Industrial Organizations," *Journal of Business*, 29 (1956), 101–110. 5/B/O

Marvick, Dwaine. *Career Perspectives in a Bureaucratic Setting*. Ann Arbor: University of Michigan Press, 1954. 1/C/O

—— "Expectations Concerning Power in a Bureaucratic Arena," *Administrative Science Quarterly*, 2 (1958), 542–549. 1/C/4,6

Marx, Fritz Morstein. *The Administrative State*. Chicago: University of Chicago Press, 1957. 5/C/9,O

Matthews, Donald R. *The Social Background of Political Decision-Makers*. Garden City, N.Y.: Doubleday, 1954. 1/C/8,O

—— *U.S. Senators and their World*. Chapel Hill: University of North Carolina Press, 1960. 3/C/3,4,O

Matthewson, Stanley B. *Restriction of Output among Unorganized Workers*. New York: Viking, 1931. 3/Bi/4

Mayer, Kurt. "Business Enterprise: Traditional Symbol of Opportunity," *British Journal of Sociology*, 4 (1953), 160–180. 3/B/O

Mayo, Elton. "Revery and Industrial Fatigue," *Journal of Personnel Research*, 3 (1924), 273–281. 1/Bi/4

—— *The Human Problems of an Industrial Civilization*. New York: Macmillan, 1933. 1/Bi/4,8

—— *The Social Problems of an Industrial Civilization*. Boston: Graduate School of Business Administration, Harvard University, 1945. 5/Bi/4,7,8

—— and George Lombard. *Teamwork and Labor Turnover in the Aircraft Industry of Southern California*. Boston: Graduate School of Business Administration, Harvard University, 1944. 1/Bi/4

McCleery, Richard H. *Policy Change in Prison Management*. East Lansing: Governmental Research Bureau, Michigan State University, 1957. 1/C/3,9

McCorkle, Lloyd, and Richard Korn. "Resocialization within Walls," *Annals of the American Academy of Political and Social Science*, 239 (1954), 88–98. 5/C/3

McCormack, Thelma H. "The Druggists' Dilemma: Problems of a Marginal Occupation," *American Journal of Sociology*, 61 (1956), 308–315. 3/O/O

McCurdy, Harold G., and Wallace E. Lambert. "The Efficiency of Small Human Groups in the Solution of Problems Requiring Genuine Co-operation," *Journal of Personality*, 20 (1952), 478–494. 3/O/5

McEwen, William J. "Position Conflict and Professional Orientation in a Research Organization," *Administrative Science Quarterly*, 1 (1956), 208–224. 1/C/O

McKenzie, R. T. "Pressure Groups in British Government," *British Journal of Sociology*, 6 (1955), 123–132. 2/Mv/8,9

McMurry, Robert N. "Recruitment, Dependency, and Morale in the Banking Industry," *Administrative Science Quarterly*, 3 (1958), 87–117. 2/Bc/O

Medalia, Nahum Z., and Delbert C. Miller. "Human Relations Leadership and the Association of Morale and Efficiency in Work Groups: A Controlled Study with Small Military Units," *Social Forces*, 33 (1955), 348–352. 2/C/6

Melbin, Murray. "Organization Practice and Individual Behavior: Absenteeism among Psychiatric Aides," *American Sociological Review*, 26 (1961), 14–23. 2/Sm/4,O

Melman, Seymour. "The Rise of Administrative Overhead in the Manufacturing Industries of the United States, 1899–1947," *Oxford Economic Papers*, 3 (1951), 62–112. 2/Bi/9

—— *Dynamic Factors in Industrial Productivity*. Oxford: Basil Blackwell, 1956. 3/Bi/8,9

—— *Decision Making and Productivity*. New York: Wiley, 1958. 1/Bi/4,7

Meltzer, Leo. "Scientific Productivity in Organizational Settings," *Journal of Social Issues*, 12 (1956), 32–40. 3/C/O

Merton, Robert K. "Bureaucratic Structure and Personality," *Social Forces*, 18 (1940), 560–568. 4/V/O

—— "Role of the Intellectual in Public Bureaucracy," *Social Forces*, 23 (1945), 405–415. 5/C/O

—— "Patterns of Influence: A Study of Interpersonal Influence of Communications Behavior in a Local Community," in Paul F. Lazarsfeld and Frank N. Stanton (eds.), *Communications Research, 1948–1949*, New York: Harper, 1949, 180–219. 3/O/O

—— "The Role Set: Problems in Sociological Theory," *British Journal of Sociology*, 8 (1957), 106–120. 4/V/3,8

—— *Social Theory and Social Structure*. Rev. ed. Glencoe, Ill.: Free Press, 1957. 4/V/2

—— Leonard Broom, and Leonard S. Cottrell, Jr. (eds.). *Sociology Today*. New York: Basic Books, 1959. 6/O/X

—— Alisa Gray, Barbara Hockey, and Hanan C. Selvin (eds.). *Reader in Bureaucracy*. Glencoe, Ill.: Free Press, 1952. 6/V/X

—— and Paul F. Lazarsfeld (eds.). *Continuities in Social Research: Studies in the Scope and Method of "The American Soldier."* Glencoe, Ill.: Free Press, 1950. 6/C/1,2,4

—— George C. Reader, and Patricia L. Kendall (eds.). *The Student Physician: Introductory Studies in the Sociology of Medical Education.* Cambridge, Mass.: Harvard University Press, 1957. 6/S/3,O

Messinger, Sheldon L. "Organizational Transformation: A Case Study of a Declining Social Movement," *American Sociological Review*, 20 (1955), 3–10. 1/Mv/9

Meyerson, Martin, and Edward C. Banfield. *Politics, Planning and the Public Interest*. Glencoe, Ill.: Free Press, 1955. 1/C/8

Michels, Robert. *Political Parties*. Tr. Eden Paul and Cedar Paul. Glencoe, Ill.: Free Press, 1949 (first published 1915). 4/Mu/2,9

Miller, Daniel R., and Guy E. Swanson. *The Changing American Parent.* New York: Wiley, 1958. 3/O/O

Miller, Delbert C. "Industry and Community Power Structure: A Comparative Study of an American and an English City," *American Sociological Review,* 23 (1958), 9–15. 3/B/8

—— and William H. Form. *Industrial Sociology: An Introduction to the Sociology of Work Relations.* New York: Harper, 1951. 6/Bi/X

Miller, Walter B. "Implications of Lower-Class Culture for Social Work," *Social Service Review,* 33 (1959), 219–236. 5/Ss/3

Millet, J. H. "British Interest-Group Tactics: A Case Study," *Political Science Quarterly,* 72 (1957), 71–82. 1/Mv/8

Mills, C. Wright. *The New Men of Power.* New York: Harcourt, Brace, 1948. 3/Mu/7,9

—— *White Collar: The American Middle Classes.* New York: Oxford University Press, 1951. 3/O/O

Mills, Theodore. *Group Structure and the Newcomer: An Experimental Study of Group Expansion.* Oslo: Oslo University Press, Studies in Society No. 1, 1957. 3/V/4

Minnis, Mhyra S. "Cleavage in Women's Organizations: A Reflection of the Social Structures of a City," *American Sociological Review,* 18 (1953), 47–53. 2/Mv/8

Mises, Ludwig von. *Bureaucracy.* New Haven: Yale University Press, 1944. 4/C/2

Mishler, Elliot G., and Asher Tropp. "Status and Interaction in a Psychiatric Hospital," *Human Relations,* 9 (1956), 187–205. 1/Sm/4,8

Mitchell, William C. "Occupational Role Strains: The American Elective Public Official," *Administrative Science Quarterly,* 3 (1958), 210–228. 5/C/3,O

Mooney, James D., and Alan C. Reiley. *The Principles of Organization.* New York: Harper, 1939. 5/V/7

Moore, David G., and Richard Renck. "The Professional Employee in Industry," *Journal of Business,* 28 (1955), 58–66. 3/Bi/4,O

Moore, Joan W. "Patterns of Women's Participation in Voluntary Associations," *American Journal of Sociology,* 66 (1961), 592–603. 2/Mv/8

Moore, Wilbert E. *Industrial Relations and the Social Order.* New York: Macmillan, 1946. 6/V/X

—— "Industrial Sociology: Status and Prospects," *American Sociological Review,* 13 (1948), 382–391; discussions, 391–400. 5/B/1

Moreno, Jacob L. *Who Shall Survive? Foundations of Sociometry, Group Psychotherapy, and Sociodrama.* Washington, D.C.: Nervous and Mental Disease Publishing Company, 1934. 4/O/1

Morgenthau, Hans J. "The Impact of the Loyalty-Security Measures on the State Department," *Bulletin of Atomic Scientists,* 11 (1955), 134–140. 5/C/6,9

Morse, Nancy C. *Satisfactions in the White-Collar Job.* Ann Arbor: Institute for Social Research, University of Michigan, 1953. 1/Bc/4,6,O

—— and Everett Reimer. "The Experimental Change of a Major Organizational Variable," *Journal of Abnormal and Social Psychology,* 52 (1956), 120–129. 1/B/6

——— and Robert S. Weiss. "The Function and Meaning of Work and the Job," *American Sociological Review*, 20 (1955), 191–198. 3/O/4,O

Mort, Paul R., and Francis G. Cornell. *American Schools in Transition*. New York: Teachers College, Columbia University, 1941. 2/Ss/8,9

Mulder, Maul. "Communication Structure, Decision Structure and Group Performance," *Sociometry*, 23 (1960), 1–14. 3/O/5

Mumford, Enid M. "Social Behavior in Small Work Groups," *Sociological Review*, 7 (1959), 137–157. 2/Bi/4

Murphy, Robert F. "Credit vs. Cash: A Case Study," *Human Organization*, 14 (1955), 26–28. 1/Bi/8

Myers, Charles A., and George P. Shultz. *The Dynamics of a Labor Market*. New York: Prentice-Hall, 1951. 3/B/8,O

——— and John G. Turnbull. "Line and Staff in Industrial Relations," *Harvard Business Review*, 34 (1956), 113–124. 2/B/7

Myers, Jerome K., and Leslie Schaffer. "Social Stratification and Psychiatric Practice: A Study of an Out-Patient Clinic," *American Sociological Review*, 19 (1954), 307–310. 1/Sm/3,8

Naegle, Kaspar D. "Clergymen, Teachers and Psychiatrists: A Study in Roles and Socialization," *Canadian Journal of Economics and Political Science*, 22 (1956), 46–62. 3/S/3,O

Newcomb, Theodore M. *Personality and Social Change*. New York: Dryden, 1957. 1/Ss/3

Newman, Donald J. "Public Attitudes toward a Form of White Collar Crime," *Social Problems*, 4 (1957), 228–232. 3/C/3

Niles, Mary Cushing H. *Middle Management: The Job of the Junior Administrator*. Rev. ed. New York: Harper, 1949. 5/B/6

Nixon, Raymond B. "Concentration and Absenteeism in Daily Newspaper Ownership," *Journalism Quarterly*, 22 (1945), 97–114. 3/Bc/8

——— "Trends in Daily Newspaper Ownership Since 1945," *Journalism Quarterly*, 31 (1954), 3–14. 3/Bc/8

Nyman, Richmond C. *Union-Management Cooperation in the 'Stretch-Out'*. New Haven: Yale University Press, 1934. 1/Bi/7,8

Ohlin, Lloyd E., and William C. Lawrence. "Social Interaction among Clients as a Treatment Problem," *Social Work*, 4 (1959), 3–13. 4/Ss/3

Olmstead, Donald W. "Organizational Leadership and Social Structure in a Small City," *American Sociological Review*, 19 (1954), 273–281. 3/M/8

Page, Charles H. "Bureaucracy's Other Face," *Social Forces*, 25 (1946), 88–94. 1/C/4

——— "Bureaucracy and Higher Education," *The Journal of General Education*, 5 (1951), 91–100. 5/Ss/9

Parkinson, C. Northcote. *Parkinson's Law and Other Studies in Administration*. Boston: Houghton, Mifflin, 1957. 5/V/9

Parsons, Talcott. *The Social System*. Glencoe, Ill.: Free Press, 1951. 4/O/2

——— *Essays in Sociological Theory*. Rev. ed. Glencoe, Ill.: Free Press, 1954. 4/O/2

——— "Suggestions for a Sociological Approach to the Theory of Organizations, I, II," *Administrative Science Quarterly*, 1 (1956), 63–85 and 225–239. 4/V/2

———— *Structure and Process in Modern Societies.* Glencoe, Ill.: Free Press, 1960. 4/V/2

———— and Robert F. Bales. *Family, Socialization and Interaction Process.* Glencoe, Ill.: Free Press, 1955. 4/O/2

———— Robert F. Bales, and Edward A. Shils. *Working Papers in the Theory of Action.* Glencoe, Ill.: Free Press, 1953. 4/O/2

———— and Neil J. Smelser. *Economy and Society.* Glencoe, Ill.: Free Press, 1956. 4/V/2

Paterson, Thomas T. *Morale in War and Work.* London: Max Parrish, 1955. 1/C/4

Payne, Raymond. "An Approach to the Study of Relative Prestige of Formal Organizations," *Social Forces*, 32 (1954), 244–247. 3/V/8

———— "Citizen Conception of the School's Ideal Role among Youth Service Agencies: An Aspect of School-Community Relations Research," *Journal of Educational Sociology*, 29 (1955), 82–88. 3/Ss/8

Pearson, Judson B., Gordon H. Barker, and Rodney D. Elliott. "Sales Success and Job Satisfaction," *American Sociological Review*, 22 (1957), 424–427. 1/Bc/4

Pellegrin, Ronald J., and Charles H. Coates. "Absentee-Owned Corporations and Community Power Structure," *American Journal of Sociology*, 61 (1956), 413–419. 3/B/8

Pelz, Donald C. "Influence: A Key to Effective Leadership in the First-Line Supervisor," *Personnel*, 29 (1952), 209–217. 1/Bc/6

———— "Some Social Factors Related to Performance in a Research Organization," *Administrative Science Quarterly*, 1 (1956), 310–325. 1/C/5

———— "Interaction and Attitudes between Scientists and the Auxiliary Staff: I. Viewpoints of Staff," and "II. Viewpoints of Scientists," *Administrative Science Quarterly*, 4 (1959–60), 321–326 and 410–425. 1/C/5

Pemberton, H. Earl. "The Effect of a Social Crisis on the Curve of Diffusion," *American Sociological Review*, 2 (1937), 55–61. 2/Mv/8,9

Perlmutter, Howard V., and Germaine de Montmollin. "Group Learning of Nonsense Syllables," *Journal of Abnormal and Social Psychology*, 47 (1952), 762–769. 3/O/5

Perrow, Charles. "Organizational Prestige: Some Functions and Dysfunctions," *American Journal of Sociology*, 66 (1961), 335–341. 1,5/Sm,V/3,8

Pfautz, Harold W. "The Sociology of Secularization: Religious Groups," *American Journal of Sociology*, 61 (1955), 121–128. 4/Mv/2,9

Pierce, Truman M. *Controllable Community Characteristics Related to the Quality of Education.* New York: Teachers College, Columbia University, 1947. 2/Ss/8

Polansky, Norman, William Bowen, Lucille Gordon, and Conrad Nathan. "Social Workers in Society: Results of a Sampling Study," *Social Work Journal*, 34 (1953), 74–80. 3/Ss/3,O

———— and Jacob Kounin. "Client's Reaction to Initial Interviews," *Human Relations*, 9 (1956), 237–264. 3/S/1,3

Popiel, Gerald. "Bureaucracy in the Mass Industrial Union," *American Journal of Economics and Sociology*, 15 (1955), 49–58. 4/Mu/9

Powell, F. DeSales. "Origins and Perspectives of the International Representative," *American Catholic Sociological Review*, 19 (1958), 210–223. 2/Mu/3,9

Presthus, Robert V. "Social Bases of Bureaucratic Organization," *Social Forces*, 38 (1959), 103–109. 5/V/8

—— "Authority in Organizations," *Public Administration Review*, 20 (1960), 86–91. 5/V/6

Price, James. "Continuity in Social Research: TVA and the Grass Roots," *Pacific Sociological Review*, 1 (1958), 63–68. 4/V/8,9

Purcell, Theodore V. *The Worker Speaks His Mind on Company and Union*. Cambridge, Mass.: Harvard University Press, 1953. 1/Bi,Mu/4,8,O

—— *Blue Collar Man: Patterns of Dual Allegiance in Industry*. Cambridge, Mass.: Harvard University Press, 1960. 1/Mv,Bi/4,O

Rapoport, Robert N., and Rhona Sofer Rapoport. " 'Democratization' and Authority in a Therapeutic Community," *Behavioral Science*, 2 (1957), 128–133. 5/Sm/3

—— and Eileen Skellern. "Some Therapeutic Functions of Administrative Disturbance," *Administrative Science Quarterly*, 2 (1957), 82–96. 5/Sm/5

Rauh, Morton A. *College and University Trusteeship*. Yellow Springs, Ohio: Antioch Press, 1959. 2/Ss/7

Raven, Bertram H., and John R. P. French, Jr. "Legitimate Power, Coercive Power, and Observability in Social Influence," *Sociometry*, 21 (1958), 83–97. 3/V/6

Record, Jane C. "The Marine Radioman's Struggle for Status," *American Journal of Sociology*, 62 (1957), 353–359. 3/B,Mu/4,8

Reissman, Leonard. "A Study of Role Conceptions in Bureaucracy," *Social Forces*, 27 (1949), 305–310. 3/C/3,O

—— "Class, Leisure, and Social Participation," *American Sociological Review*, 19 (1954), 76–84. 3/Mu/8

—— and John H. Rohrer (eds.). *Change and Dilemma in the Nursing Profession, Studies of Nursing Services in a Large General Hospital*. New York: Putnam, 1957. 1/Sm/X

Reitzes, Dietrich. "The Role of Organizational Structures," *Journal of Social Issues*, 9 (1953), 37–44. 3/M/8

Rettig, Solomon, Frank N. Jacobson, and Benjamin Pasamanick. "Status Overestimation, Objective Status, and Job Satisfaction among Professions," *American Sociological Review*, 23 (1958), 75–81. 3/S/8,O

Rice, A. K. *Productivity and Social Organization: The Ahmedabad Experiment*. London: Tavistock Publications, 1958. 1/Bi/7,9

Richardson, Frederick L., and Charles R. Walker. *Human Relations in an Expanding Company*. New Haven: Labor and Management Center, Yale University, 1948. 1/Bi/4,7,9

Richardson, Stephen A. "Organizational Contrasts on British and American Ships," *Administrative Science Quarterly*, 1 (1956), 189–207. 2/C/8

Riesman, David. *The Lonely Crowd*. New Haven: Yale University Press, 1950. 4/O/2

Roberts, David R. "A General Theory of Executive Compensation, Based on Statistically Tested Propositions," *Quarterly Journal of Economics*, 70 (1956), 270–294. 4/B/7

—— *Executive Compensation*. Glencoe, Ill.: Free Press, 1959. 2/B/7

Robinson, James A. "Decision Making in the House Rules Committee," *Administrative Science Quarterly*, 3 (1958), 73–86. 3/C/3,5

Roethlisberger, Fritz J. "The Foreman: Master and Victim of Double Talk," *Harvard Business Review*, 23 (1945), 283–298. 5/Bi/6

—— and William J. Dickson. *Management and the Worker*. Cambridge, Mass.: Harvard University Press, 1939. 1/Bi/4

Rose, Arnold. "The Social Structure of the Army," *American Journal of Sociology*, 51 (1946), 361–364. 5/C/6,8

—— *Union Solidarity*. Minneapolis: University of Minnesota Press, 1952. 1/Mu/4,O

—— "Voluntary Association under Conditions of Competition and Conflict," *Social Forces*, 34 (1955), 159–163. 2/Mv/8

Rosen, Hjalmar, and R. A. Hudson Rosen. *The Union Member Speaks*. New York: Prentice-Hall, 1955. 1/Mu/4,5

Rosenfeld, Eva. "Social Stratification in a 'Classless Society,'" *American Sociological Review*, 16 (1951), 766–774. 2/Mv/6,9

Ross, Aileen D. "The Social Control of Philanthropy," *American Journal of Sociology*, 58 (1953), 451–460. 3/B,Mv/8

Roy, Donald. "Quota Restriction and Goldbricking in a Machine Shop," *American Journal of Sociology*, 57 (1952), 427–442. 1/Bi/4

—— "Work Satisfaction and Social Reward in Quota Achievement: An Analysis of Piecework Incentives," *American Sociological Review*, 18 (1953), 507–514. 1/Bi/4

—— "Efficiency and 'the Fix': Informal Intergroup Relations in a Piecework Machine Shop," *American Journal of Sociology*, 60 (1954), 255–266. 1/Bi/4

Saunders, J. V. D. "Characteristics of Hospitals and of Hospital Administrators Associated with Hospital-Community Relations in Mississipi," *Rural Sociology*, 25 (1960), 229–232. 2/Sm/8

Sayles, Leonard R. *Behavior of Industrial Work Groups*. New York: Wiley, 1958. 2/Bi/4,O

—— and George Strauss. *The Local Union*. New York: Harper, 1953. 2/Mu/5,9,O

Sayre, Wallace S. "The Recruitment and Training of Bureaucrats in the United States," *Annals of the American Academy of Political and Social Science*, 292 (1954), 39–44. 5/C/O

Schachter, Stanley, Norris Ellertson, Dorothy McBride, and Doris Gregory. "An Experimental Study of Cohesiveness and Productivity," *Human Relations*, 4 (1951), 229–238. 3/O/5

Schein, E. H. "Some Observations on Chinese Methods of Handling Prisoners of War," *Public Opinion Quarterly*, 20 (1956), 321–337. 3/C/3

Schrag, Clarence. "Leadership among Prison Inmates," *American Sociological Review*, 19 (1954), 37–42. 1/C/3

Schulze, Robert O. "The Role of Economic Dominants in Community Power Structure," *American Sociological Review*, 23 (1958), 3–9. 3/V/8,9

Schumpeter, Joseph A. *Capitalism, Socialism, and Democracy*. 2d ed., New York: Harper, 1947. 4/O/2

Schwartz, Richard D. "Functional Alternatives to Inequality," *American Sociological Review*, 20 (1955), 424–430. 2/Mv/6,8

Scott, Frances Gillespie. "Action Theory and Research in Social Organization," *American Journal of Sociology*, 64 (1959), 386–395. 5/Sm,C/2,3

Scott, John C., Jr. "Membership and Participation in Voluntary Associations," *American Sociological Review*, 22 (1957), 315–326. 3/Mv/8

Scott, W. H., A. H. Halsey, J. A. Banks, and T. Lupton. *Technical Change and Industrial Relations: A Study of the Relations Between Technical Change and Social Structure in a Large Steel Works*. Liverpool: Liverpool University Press, 1956. 1/Bi/4,9

Scott, W. Richard. "A Case Study of Professional Workers in a Bureaucratic Setting." Unpublished Ph.D. dissertation, Department of Sociology, University of Chicago, 1961. 1/Ss/3,4,O

Seashore, Stanley E. *Group Cohesiveness in the Industrial Work Group*. Ann Arbor: Institute for Social Research, University of Michigan, 1954. 1/Bi/4

Seeley, John R. *et al. Community Chest: A Case Study in Philanthropies*. Toronto: University of Toronto Press, 1957. 1/Mv/8

Seeman, Melvin. "Social Mobility and Administrative Behavior," *American Sociological Review*, 23 (1958), 633–642. 2/Ss/7,O

—— *Social Status and Leadership: The Case of the School Executive*. Columbus: College of Education, Ohio State University, 1960. 2/Ss/6,8

—— and John W. Evans. "Stratification and Hospital Care: I. The Performance of the Medical Intern," and "II. The Objective Criteria of Performance," *American Sociological Review*, 26 (1961), 67–80 and 193–204. 1/S/6

Seidman, Joel. "Democracy in Labor Unions," *Journal of Political Economy*, 61 (1953), 221–231. 5/Mu/9

—— Jack London, Bernard Karsh, and Daisy L. Tagliacozzo. *The Worker Views His Union*. Chicago: University of Chicago Press, 1958. 2/Mu/4,O

Seligman, Lester G. "Developments in the Presidency and the Conception of Political Leadership," *American Sociological Review*, 20 (1955), 706–712. 5/C/6

Selltiz, Claire, Marie Jahoda, Morton Deutsch, and Stuart W. Cook. *Research Methods in Social Relations*. Rev. ed. New York: Holt, 1959. 4/O/1

Selvin, Hanan C. *The Effects of Leadership*. Glencoe, Ill.: Free Press, 1960. 1/C/1,6

Selznick, Philip. "An Approach to a Theory of Bureaucracy," *American Sociological Review*, 8 (1943), 47–54. 4/V/2

—— "Foundations of the Theory of Organization," *American Sociological Review*, 13 (1948), 25–35. 4/V/2

—— *TVA and the Grass Roots*. Berkeley and Los Angeles: University of California Press, 1949. 1/C/8,9

—— *The Organizational Weapon: A Study of Bolshevik Strategy and Tactics*. New York: McGraw-Hill, 1952. 1/Mv/8,9

—— *Leadership in Administration*. Evanston, Ill.: Row, Peterson, 1957. 4/V/2,7

Shartle, Carroll. *Executive Performance and Leadership*. Englewood Cliffs, N.J.: Prentice-Hall, 1956. 5/V/7,O

Shaw, Marjorie E. "A Comparison of Individuals and Small Groups in the Rational Solution of Complex Problems," *American Journal of Psychology*, 44 (1932), 491–504. 3/O/5

Shaw, Marvin E. "A Comparison of Two Types of Leadership in Various Communication Nets," *Journal of Abnormal and Social Psychology,* 50 (1955), 127–134. 3/O/5,6

————— Gerard H. Rothschild, and John F. Strickland. "Decision Processes in Communication Nets," *Journal of Abnormal and Social Psychology,* 54 (1957), 323–330. 3/O/5

Shepard, Herbert A. "The Value System of a University Research Group," *American Sociological Review,* 19 (1954), 456–462. 1/C/5,O

Shepherd, Clovis, and Paula Brown. "Status, Prestige, and Esteem in a Research Organization," *Administrative Science Quarterly,* 1 (1956), 340–360. 1/C/4,O

Sheppard, Harold L. "The Treatment of Unionism in 'Managerial Sociology," *American Sociological Review,* 14 (1949), 310–313. 5/Mu/1

————— "Approaches to Conflict in American Industrial Sociology," *British Journal of Sociology,* 5 (1954), 324–341. 5/Mu/1,8

Sherif, Muzafer. "A Preliminary Experimental Study of Inter-Group Relations," in John H. Rohrer and Muzafer Sherif (eds.), *Social Psychology at the Crossroads,* New York: Harper, 1951, 388–424. 3/Ss/3

————— "Superordinate Goals in the Reduction of Intergroup Conflict," *American Journal of Sociology,* 63 (1958), 349–356. 3/Ss/3,9

Shils, Edward A. "Primary Groups in the American Army," in Robert K. Merton and Paul F. Lazarsfeld (eds.), *Continuities in Social Research: Studies in the Scope and Method of "The American Soldier."* Glencoe, Ill.: Free Press, 1950, 16–39. 2/C/4

————— and Morris Janowitz. "Cohesion and Disintegration in the *Wehrmacht* in World War II," *Public Opinion Quarterly,* 12 (1948), 280–315. 1/C/4

Shubik, Martin. "Games, Decisions and Industrial Organization," *Management Science,* 6 (1960), 455–474. 5/Bi/1

Sills, David L. *The Volunteers.* Glencoe, Ill.: Free Press, 1957. 1/Mv/8,9

Simmel, Georg. *Conflict.* Tr. Kurt H. Wolff. *The Web of Group Affiliations.* Tr. Reinhard Bendix. Glencoe, Ill.: Free Press, 1955. 4/O/2

Simmons, Ozzie G. *Social Status and Public Health.* New York: Social Science Research Council, 1958. 5/Sm/3

————— James Davis, and Katherine Spencer. "Inter-Personal Strains in Release from a Mental Hospital," *Social Problems,* 4 (1956), 21–28. 1/Sm/3

Simon, Abraham J. "Social Structure of Clinics and Patient Improvement," *Administrative Science Quarterly,* 4 (1959), 197–206. 1/Sm/3

Simon, Herbert A. "Birth of an Organization: The Economic Cooperation Administration," *Public Administration Review,* 13 (1953), 227–236. 1/C/9

————— "Staff and Management Controls," *Annals of the American Academy of Political and Social Science,* 292 (1954), 95–103 5/B,C/7,O

————— *Administrative Behavior.* 2d ed. New York: Macmillan, 1957. 5/V/X

————— "The Compensation of Executives," *Sociometry,* 20 (1957), 32–35. 4/B/1,7

————— *Models of Man.* New York: Wiley, 1957. 6/V/1,2

————— *The New Science of Management Decision.* New York: Harper, 1960. 5/B/7

————— Harold Guetzkow, George Kozmetsky, and Gordon Tyndall. *Central-*

ization vs. Decentralization in Organizing the Controller's Department.
New York: Controllership Foundation, 1954. 2/B/7

—— Donald W. Smithburg, and Victor A. Thompson. *Public Administration.* New York: Knopf, 1950. 6/C/X

Simpson, Richard L. "Vertical and Horizontal Communication in Formal Organizations," *Administrative Science Quarterly,* 4 (1959), 188–196. 1/Bi/6

Sirota, David. "Some Effects of Promotional Frustration on Employee's Understanding of, and Attitudes toward Management," *Sociometry,* 22 (1959), 273–278. 1/Bi/4,O

Slater, Philip E. "Role Differentiation in Small Groups," *American Sociological Review,* 20 (1955), 300–310. 3/O/4

Slesinger, Jonathan A. *A Model for the Comparative Study of Public Bureaucracies.* Ann Arbor: Institute of Public Administration, University of Michigan, 1957. 5/V/2

Slichter, Sumner H. *Trade Unions in a Free Society.* Cambridge, Mass.: Harvard University Press, 1947. 5/Mu/8,9

Smigel, Erwin O. "Public Attitudes toward 'Chiseling' with Reference to Unemployment Compensation," *American Sociological Review,* 18 (1953), 59–67. 3/Ss/3

—— "Public Attitudes toward Stealing as Related to the Size of the Victim Organization," *American Sociological Review,* 21 (1956), 320–337. 3/B,C/3

—— "Interviewing a Legal Elite: The Wall Street Lawyer," *American Journal of Sociology,* 64 (1958), 159–164. 4/Bc/1

—— "The Impact of Recruitment on the Organization of the Large Law Firm," *American Sociological Review,* 25 (1960), 56–66. 2/Bc/8,9

Smith, Edmund Arthur. "Bureaucratic Organization: Selective or Saturative," *Administrative Science Quarterly,* 2 (1957), 361–375. 4/C/2,8

Smith, Ewart E. "The Effects of Clear and Unclear Role Expectations on a Group Productivity and Defensiveness," *Journal of Abnormal and Social Psychology,* 55 (1957), 213–217. 3/O/4

Snyder, Eloise C. "The Supreme Court as a Small Group," *Social Forces,* 36 (1958), 232–238. 1/C/4

Soemardjan, Selo. "Bureaucratic Organization in a Time of Revolution," *Administrative Science Quarterly,* 2 (1957), 182–199. 2/C,Bi/8

Sofer, Cyril. "Reactions to Administrative Change: A Study of Staff Relations in Three British Hospitals," *Human Relations,* 8 (1955), 291–316. 2/Sm/9

Solomon, David N. "Sociological Research in a Military Organization," *Canadian Journal of Economics and Political Science,* 20 (1954), 531–541. 5/C/2,9

—— "Professional Persons in Bureaucratic Organizations," in Walter Reed Army Institute of Research, *Symposium on Preventive and Social Psychiatry,* Washington, D.C.: U.S. Government Printing Office, 1957, 253–266. 5/V/O

Soni, B. D. "Sociological Analysis of Legal Profession: A Study of Mechanisms in Lawyer-Client Relationship," *Journal of Social Sciences* (India), 1 (1958), 63–70. 3/Bc/3

Spindler, G. Dearborn. "The Military—A Systematic Analysis," *Social Forces,* 27 (1948), 83–88. 5/C/2

Spinrad, William. "Correlates of Trade Union Participation: A Summary of the Literature," *American Sociological Review,* 25 (1960), 237–244. 5/Mu/8

Spiro, Melford E. *Kibbutz: Venture in Utopia.* Cambridge, Mass.: Harvard University Press, 1956. 1/Mv/X

Stanton, Alfred H., and Morris S. Schwartz. *The Mental Hopital.* New York: Basic Books, 1954. 1/Sm/3,5

Stewart, Donald D. "The Place of Volunteer Participation in a Bureaucratic Organization," *Social Forces,* 29 (1951), 311–317. 1/C/7,9

Stewart, Rosemary. "Management Succession," *The Manager,* 23 (1955), 579–582 and 676–679. 2/Bi/O

Stinchcombe, Arthur L. "Bureaucratic and Craft Administration of Production: A Comparative Study," *Administrative Science Quarterly,* 4 (1959), 168–187. 2/Bi/2,7,O

———— "The Sociology of Organization and the Theory of the Firm," *Pacific Sociological Review,* 3 (1960), 75–82. 4/V/1

Stogdill, Ralph M. "The Sociometry of Working Relationships in Formal Organizations," *Sociometry,* 12 (1949), 276–286. 2/C/1,4,6

———— "Interaction among Superiors and Subordinates," in J. L. Moreno (ed.), *Sociometry and the Science of Man,* New York: Beacon, 1956, 296–301. 1/C/4,6

———— *Leadership and Structures of Personal Interaction.* Columbus: Bureau of Business Research, College of Commerce and Administration, Ohio State University, 1957. 2/C/7,9

———— Ellis L. Scott, and William E. Jaynes. *Leadership and Role Expectations.* Columbus: Bureau of Business Research, College of Commerce and Administration, Ohio State University, 1956. 1/C/6,O

———— Carroll L. Shartle, Robert L. Wherry, and William E. Jaynes. "A Factorial Study of Administrative Behavior," *Personnel Psychology,* 8 (1955), 165–180. 2/C/6,O

———— Carroll L. Shartle, and associates. *Patterns of Administrative Performance.* Columbus: Bureau of Business Research, College of Commerce and Administration, Ohio State University, 1956. 2/C, Bi/6,O

Stone, Gregory P. "City Shoppers and Urban Identification: Observations on the Social Psychology of City Life," *American Journal of Sociology,* 60 (1954), 36–45. 3/Bc/3

Stone, Robert C. "Mobility Factors as They Affect Workers' Attitudes and Conduct toward Incentive Systems," *American Sociological Review,* 17 (1952), 58–64. 2/B/4,O

———— "Conflicting Approaches to the Study of Worker-Manager Relations," *Social Forces,* 31 (1952), 117–124. 5/B/1

———— "Factory Organization and Vertical Mobility," *American Sociological Review,* 18 (1953), 28–35. 2/Bi/O

Stouffer, Samuel A. *et al. The American Soldier.* Vols. I and II of *Studies in Social Psychology during World War II.* Princeton, N.J.: Princeton University Press, 1949. 2/C/4,6

Strauss, George. "Factors in the Unionization of a Utilities Company: A Case Study," *Human Organization,* 12 (1953), 17–25. 1/Mu/8

—— "The Set-Up Man: A Case Study of Organizational Change," *Human Organization,* 13 (1954), 17–25. 1/Bi/9

—— "Control by the Membership in Building Trades Unions," *American Journal of Sociology,* 61 (1956), 527–535. 2/Mu/9

—— "The Changing Role of the Working Supervisor," *Journal of Business,* 30 (1957), 202–211. 2/Bi, Sm/6

Strodtbeck, Fred L., Rita M. James, and Charles Hawkins. "Social Status in Jury Deliberations," *American Sociological Review,* 22 (1957), 713–719. 3/C/5,8

—— and Richard D. Mann. "Sex Role Differentiation in Jury Deliberations," *Sociometry,* 19 (1956), 3–11. 3/C/8

—— and Marvin B. Sussman. "Of Time, the City, and the 'One Year Guaranty': The Relations between Watch Owners and Repairers," *American Journal of Sociology,* 61 (1956), 602–609. 3/Bc/3

Stuart-Bunning G. H. "The Personal Relations of Officials with the Public," *Public Administration,* 9 (1931), 36–40. 5/C/3

Sullivan, Richard C. "Administrative-Faculty Relationships in Colleges and Universities," *Journal of Higher Education,* 27 (1956), 308–326. 5/Ss/7,O

Sumner, William Graham. *Folkways.* Boston: Ginn, 1907. 4/O/2

Suojanen, Waino W. "Leadership, Authority, and the Span of Control," *Advanced Management,* 22 (1957), 17–22. 5/B, C/2,7

Swanson, Charles E. "Midcity Daily," *Journalism Quarterly,* 26 (1949), 20–28, 172–180, and 304–310. 1/Bc/3,7

Sykes, Gresham M. "The Corruption of Authority and Rehabilitation," *Social Forces,* 34 (1956), 257–262. 1/C/3

—— *The Society of Captives: A Study of a Maximum Security Prison.* Princeton, N.J.: Princeton University Press, 1958. 1/C/3,8

Taft, Philip. *The Structure and Government of Labor Unions.* Cambridge, Mass.: Harvard University Press, 1954. 2/Mu/9,O

Talacchi, Sergio. "Organization Size, Individual Attitudes and Behavior: An Empirical Study," *Administrative Science Quarterly,* 5 (1960), 398–420. 2/B/4,9

Talmon-Garber, Y. "Social Differentiation in Cooperative Communities," *British Journal of Sociology,* 3 (1952), 339–357. 2/Mv/9

Tannenbaum, Arnold S. "Control and Effectiveness in a Voluntary Organization," *American Journal of Sociology,* 67 (1961), 33–46. 1/Mv/6,9

—— and Basil S. Georgopoulos. "The Distribution of Control in Formal Organizations," *Social Forces,* 36 (1957), 44–50. 4/V/6

—— and Robert L. Kahn. *Participation in Union Locals.* White Plains, N.Y.: Row, Peterson, 1958. 2/Mu/8,9

Tawney, R. H. *Religion and the Rise of Capitalism.* New York: Harcourt, Brace, 1937. 4/O/2

Taylor, Donald W., Paul C. Berry, and Clifford H. Block. "Does Group Participation when Using Brainstorming Facilitate or Inhibit Creative Thinking?" *Administrative Science Quarterly,* 3 (1958), 23–47. 3/O/5

—— and William L. Faust. "Twenty Questions: Efficiency in Problem Solving as a Function of Size of Group," *Journal of Experimental Psychology,* 44 (1952), 360–368. 3/O/5

Taylor, Robert K. "The Social Control Function in Casework," *Social Casework,* 39 (1958), 17–21. 5/Ss/3,8

Tead, Ordway. *The Art of Administration.* New York: McGraw-Hill, 1951. 5/V/X

Terrien, Frederic W., and Donald L. Mills. "The Effect of Changing Size upon the Internal Structure of Organizations," *American Sociological Review,* 20 (1955), 11–13. 2/Ss/9

Thibaut, John W., and Harold H. Kelley. *The Social Psychology of Groups.* New York: Wiley, 1959. 4/O/5

Thomas, Edwin J. "Role Conceptions and Organizational Size," *American Sociological Review,* 24 (1959), 30–37. 1/Ss/8

Thompson, James D. "On Building an Administrative Science," *Administrative Science Quarterly,* 1 (1956), 102–111. 4/V/1

—— "Authority and Power in 'Identical' Organizations," *American Journal of Sociology,* 62 (1956), 290–301. 2/B, C/6

—— "Organizational Management of Conflict," *Administrative Science Quarterly,* 4 (1960), 389–409. 5/V/2,8

—— and Frederick L. Bates. "Technology, Organization, and Administration," *Administrative Science Quarterly,* 2 (1957), 325–343. 4/Bi, S/8,9

—— et al. (eds.). *Comparative Studies in Administration.* Pittsburgh: University of Pittsburgh Press, 1959. 6/V/X

—— and William J. McEwen. "Organizational Goals and Environment: Goal-Setting as an Interaction Process," *American Sociological Review,* 23 (1958), 23–31. 4/V/3,8

—— and Arthur Tuden. "Strategies, Structures, and Processes of Organizational Decision," in James D. Thompson *et al.* (eds.), *Comparative Studies in Administration,* Pittsburgh: University of Pittsburgh Press, 1959, 195–216. 4/V/2

Thompson, Victor A. "Hierarchy, Specialization, and Organizational Conflict," *Administrative Science Quarterly,* 5 (1961), 485–521. 5/V/5,6

Thorndike R. L. "On What Type of Task Will a Group Do Well?" *Journal of Abnormal and Social Psychology,* 33 (1938), 409–413. 3/O/5

Thorner, Isidor. "Nursing: The Functional Significance of An Institutional Pattern," *American Sociological Review,* 20 (1955), 531–538. 4/Sm/3

Thrall, Robert M., and Robert C. Angell. "The Mapping of Community Organizations," *Sociometry,* 17 (1954), 244–271. 4/V/1,8

Torrance, E. Paul. "Some Consequences of Power Differences on Decision-Making in Permanent and Temporary Three-Man Groups," in A. Paul Hare *et al.* (eds.), *Small Groups,* New York: Knopf, 1955, 482–492. 1/C/5

Treinen, Heiner. "Eine Arbeitsgruppe am Fliessband: Sozialstruktur und Formen der Beaufsichtigung (A Conveyor-Belt Work Group: The Social Structure and Types of Supervision)," *Kölner Zeitschrift für Soziologie und Sozialpsychologie,* 8 (1956), 73–83. 1/Bi/7

Trice, Harrison M. "A Study of the Process of Affiliation with Alcoholics Anonymous," *Quarterly Journal of Studies on Alcohol,* 18 (1957), 39–54. 1/Mv/3

Trist, E. L., and E. K. Bamforth. "Some Social and Psychological Consequences of the Longwall Method of Coal-Getting," *Human Relations,* 4 (1951), 3–38. 2/Bi/4,7

Truman, David B. *The Governmental Process.* New York: Knopf, 1951. 5/M,C/2,8,9

Tsouderos, John E. "Organizational Change in Terms of a Series of Selected Variables," *American Sociological Review,* 20 (1955), 206–210. 2/Mv/9

Tumin, Melvin M. "Some Disfunctions of Institutional Imbalances," *Behavioral Science,* 1 (1956), 218–223. 4/V/8

Turner, Ralph H. "The Navy Disbursing Officer as a Bureaucrat," *American Sociological Review,* 12 (1947), 342–348. 1/C/4,6

—— and Lewis M. Killian. *Collective Behavior.* Englewood Cliffs, N.J.: Prentice-Hall, 1957. 6/Mv/3,9

Udy, Stanley H., Jr. " 'Bureaucratic' Elements in Organizations: Some Research Findings," *American Sociological Review,* 23 (1958), 415–418. 2/Bi/8,9

—— "The Structure of Authority in Non-Industrial Production Organizations," *American Journal of Sociology,* 64 (1959), 582–584. 2/Bi/8

—— " 'Bureaucracy' and 'Rationality' in Weber's Theory," *American Sociological Review,* 24 (1959), 791–795. 2/Bi/2,8,9

—— *Organization of Work: A Comparative Analysis of Production among Non-Industrial Peoples.* New Haven: Human Relations Area Files Press, 1959. 2/Bi/8

—— "Technology, Society, and Production Organization." Unpublished paper read at the meetings of the American Sociological Association, New York, 1960. 2/Bi/8

Ulmer, S. Sidney. "Judicial Review as Political Behavior: A Temporary Check on Congress," *Administrative Science Quarterly,* 4 (1960), 426–445. 1/C/5

University of Liverpool, Social Science Department. *The Dock Worker.* Liverpool: University Press of Liverpool, 1954. 1/Bi/4,6,O

Urwick, Lyndall F. *The Elements of Administration.* New York: Harper, 1943. 5/V/X

—— "The Manager's Span of Control," *Harvard Business Review,* 34 (1956), 39–47. 5/V/6

Van Zelst, Raymond H. "Validation of A Sociometric Regrouping Procedure," *Journal of Abnormal and Social Psychology,* 48 (1952), 299–301. 1/Bi/4

Vinter, Robert D. and Morris Janowitz. "Effective Institutions for Juvenile Delinquents: A Research Statement," *Social Service Review,* 33 (1959), 118–130. 4/Ss/3,8

Viteles, Morris S. *Motivation and Morale in Industry.* New York: Norton, 1953. 5/B/4,6

Vollmer, Howard M. "Member Commitment and Organizational Competence in Religious Orders," *Berkeley Publications in Society and Institutions,* 3 (1957), 13–26. 2/Mv/2

—— *Employee Rights and the Employment Relationship.* Berkeley and Los Angeles: University of California Press, 1960. 2/B, C/1,6,7

Vroom, Victor H. "The Effects of Attitudes on Perception of Organizational Goals," *Human Relations,* 13 (1960), 229–240. 1/Bi/4

Waldo, Dwight. *The Administrative State.* New York: Ronald,'1948. 4/C/2

—— *The Study of Public Administration.* Garden City, N.Y.: Doubleday, 1956. 5/V/X

Walker, Charles R. *Toward the Automatic Factory*. New Haven: Yale University Press, 1957. 1/Bi/7

———— and Robert H. Guest. *The Man on the Assembly Line*. Cambridge, Mass.: Harvard University Press, 1952. 1/Bi/4,7

———— Robert H. Guest, and Arthur N. Turner. *The Foreman on the Assembly Line*. Cambridge, Mass.: Harvard University Press, 1956. 1/Bi/6,7

Wallace, Anthony F. C., and Harold A. Rashkis. "The Relation of Staff Consensus to Patient Disturbance on Mental Hospital Wards," *American Sociological Review*, 24 (1959), 829–835. 1/Sm/3

Ward, Conor K. "Some Aspects of the Social Structure of a Roman Catholic Parish," *Sociological Review*, 6 (1956), 75–93. 3/Mv/3,8

Wardwell, Walter I. "Social Integration, Bureaucratization and the Professions," *Social Forces*, 33 (1955), 356–359. 4/V/9,O

Warner, W. Lloyd, and James C. Abegglen. *Big Business Leaders in America*. New York: Harper, 1955. 3/B/O

———— and James C. Abegglen. *Occupational Mobility in American Business and Industry, 1928–1952*. Minneapolis: University of Minnesota Press, 1955. 3/B/O

———— and J. O. Low. *The Social System of the Modern Factory*. New Haven: Yale University Press, 1947. 1/Bi/7,8

———— and Norman H. Martin (eds.). *Industrial Man*. New York: Harper, 1959. 6/B/7,8,O

Warren, Roland L. "The Naval Reserve Officer: A Study in Assimilation," *American Sociological Review*, 11 (1946), 202–211. 5/C/O

———— "Toward a Typology of Extra-Community Controls Limiting Local Community Autonomy," *Social Forces*, 34 (1956), 338–341. 3/V/8

Watson, Goodwin (ed.). "The Psychological Problems of Bureaucracy," *Journal of Social Issues*, 1, entire issue No. 4 (1945). 6/V/3,9,O

Weber, Max. *The Protestant Ethic and the Spirit of Capitalism*. Tr. Talcott Parsons. New York: Scribner, 1930. 4/O/2

———— *The Theory of Social and Economic Organization*. Tr. A. M. Henderson and Talcott Parsons and ed. Talcott Parsons. Glencoe, Ill.: Free Press, and Falcon's Wing Press, 1947. 4/O/2

Weisman, Irving. "Impact of Setting upon Social Workers and Patients," *Social Work*, 2 (1957), 70–76. 5/S/3

Weiss, Edward C. "Relation of Personnel Statistics to Organizational Structure," *Personnel Psychology*, 10 (1957), 27–42. 2/B/7

Weiss, Robert S. *Processes of Organization*. Ann Arbor: Institute for Social Research, University of Michigan, 1956. 1/C/2,4,7

———— and Eugene Jacobson. "A Method for the Analysis of the Structure of Complex Organizations," *American Sociological Review*, 20 (1955), 661–668. 1/C/1

Wessen, Albert F. "Beobachtungen zur Sozialen Struktur des Krankenhauses (Observations on the Social Structure of the Hospital)," *Kölner Zeitschrift für Soziologie und Sozialpsychologie*, Supplement 3 (1958), 156–184. 1/Sm/6,O

Westerlund, Gunnar. *Group Leadership*. Stockholm: Nordisk Rotogravyr, 1952. 1/Bc/6

Westley, William A. "Violence and the Police," *American Journal of Sociology*, 59 (1953), 34–41. 1/C/3

——— "Secrecy and the Police," *Social Forces*, 34 (1956), 254–257. 1/C/3,4

White, Leonard D. *The Prestige Value of Public Employment.* Chicago: University of Chicago Press, 1929. 3/C/O

——— *Introduction to the Study of Public Administration.* 4th ed. New York: Macmillan, 1955. 5/V/X

White, R. Clyde. "Prestige of Social Work and the Social Worker," *Social Work Journal*, 36 (1955), 21–23, 33, 3/Ss/O

White, Ralph, and Ronald Lippitt. "Leader Behavior and Member Reaction in Three 'Social Climates'," in Dorwin Cartwright and Alvin Zander (eds.), *Group Dynamics*, Evanston, Ill.: Row, Peterson, 1953, 585–611. 3/V/6

——— and Ronald Lippitt. *Autocracy and Democracy.* New York: Harper, 1960. 3/O/6

Whitehead, T. N. *Leadership in a Free Society.* Cambridge, Mass.: Harvard University Press, 1936. 5/Bi/4,7,8

Whyte, William F. (ed.). *Industry and Society.* New York: McGraw-Hill 1946. 6/B/X

——— *Human Relations in the Restaurant Industry.* New York: McGraw-Hill, 1948. 2/Bc/4

——— "Small Groups and Large Organizations," in John H. Rohrer and Muzafer Sherif (eds.), *Social Psychology at the Crossroads*, New York: Harper, 1951, 297–312. 5/B/1

——— *Man and Organization: Three Problems in Human Relations in Industry.* Homewood, Ill.: Irwin, 1959. 5/B/1,7

——— *et al. Money and Motivation: An Analysis of Incentives in Industry.* New York: Harper, 1955. 5/Bi/4,7

Whyte, William H., Jr. *The Organization Man.* New York: Simon and Schuster, 1956. 5/V/O

Wilensky, Harold L. *Intellectuals in Labor Unions.* Glencoe, Ill.: Free Press, 1956. 2/Mu/7,O

——— and Charles N. Lebeaux. *Industrial Society and Social Welfare.* New York: Russell Sage Foundation, 1958. 5/Ss/8,O

Wilkening, Eugene A. "Consensus in Role Definition of County Extension Agents between the Agents and the Local Sponsoring Committee Members," *Rural Sociology*, 23 (1958), 184–197. 2/C/3

Willerman, Ben, and Leonard Swanson. "Group Prestige in Voluntary Organizations: A Study of College Sororities," *Human Relations*, 6 (1953), 57–77. 2/Mv/8

Williams, Warren S. "Class Differences in the Attitudes of Psychiatric Patients," *Social Problems*, 4 (1957), 240–244. 5/Sm/3,8

Wilson, Bryan R. "An Analysis of Sect Development," *American Sociological Review*, 24 (1959), 3–15. 4/Mv/2,9

Wilson, Logan. *The Academic Man: A Study in the Sociology of a Profession.* New York: Oxford University Press, 1942. 3/Ss/O

Wirdenius, Hans. *Supervisors at Work.* Stockholm: The Swedish Council for Personnel Administration, 1958. 2/Bi/1,6

Wispé, Lauren G. "A Sociometric Analysis of Conflicting Role-Expectancies," *American Journal of Sociology*, 61 (1955), 134–137. 1/Bc/8

—— and Kenneth E. Lloyd. "Some Situational and Psychological Determinants of the Desire for Structured Interpersonal Relations," *Journal of Abnormal and Social Psychology*, 51 (1955), 57–60. 1/Bc/9

Wolfensberger, Wolf P. "Attitudes of Alcoholics toward Mental Hospitals," *Quarterly Journal of Studies on Alcohol*, 19 (1958), 447–451. 1/Sm/3

Worcester, Dean A., Jr. "Standards of Faculty Tenure and Promotion: A Pure Theory," *Administrative Science Quarterly*, 2 (1957), 216–234. 4/Ss,C/6,O

Worthy, James C. "Organizational Structure and Employee Morale," *American Sociological Review*, 15 (1950), 169–179. 2/Bc/7

Wray, Donald E. "Marginal Men of Industry: The Foremen," *American Journal of Sociology*, 54 (1949), 298–301. 2/Bi/6

Wright, Charles R., and Herbert H. Hyman. "Voluntary Association Memberships of American Adults: Evidence from National Sample Surveys," *American Sociological Review*, 23 (1958), 284–294. 3/Mv/8

Zald, Mayer N. "The Correctional Institution for Juvenile Offenders: An Analysis of Organizational 'Character'," *Social Problems*, 8 (1960), 57–67. 5/C/2

Zaleznik, Abraham. *Worker Satisfaction and Development*. Boston: Graduate School of Business Administration, Harvard University, 1956. 1/Bi/4

—— C. R. Christensen, and F. J. Roethlisberger. *The Motivation, Productivity and Satisfaction of Workers: A Prediction Study*. Boston: Graduate School of Business Administration, Harvard University, 1958. 1/Bi/4

Zander, Alvin, Arthur R. Cohen, and Ezra Stotland. *Role Relations in the Mental Health Professions*. Ann Arbor: Institute for Social Research, University of Michigan, 1957. 3/S/4,O

Zeisel, Hans, Harry Kalven, Jr., and Bernard Buchholz. *Delay in the Court*. Boston: Little, Brown, 1959. 3/C/7

Zetterberg, Hans L. (ed.). *Sociology in the United States of America: A Trend Report*. Paris: UNESCO, 1956. 6/V/X

Ziller, Robert C. "Group Size: A Determinant of the Quality and Stability of Group Decisions," *Sociometry*, 20 (1957), 165–173. 3/O/5

—— "Four Techniques of Group Decision Making under Uncertainty," *Journal of Applied Psychology*, 41 (1957), 384–388. 2/C/6

BIBLIOGRAPHIES

(The following items contain sizeable bibliographies. Those denoted by asterisks have not been cited in the general bibliography above. The others have been.)

Adams, Richard N., and Jack J. Preiss (eds.). *Human Organization Research*. Homewood, Ill.: Dorsey, 1960.

* Barber, Bernard. "Sociology of Science—A Trend Report and Bibliography," *Current Sociology*, 5 (1956), 89–153.

* Barnes, Ralph M., and Norma A. Englert. *Bibliography of Industrial Engineering and Management Literature, to January 1, 1946.* 5th ed. Dubuque, Ia.: Wm. C. Brown, 1946.
* Barton, Allen. "Bibliography of Empirical Studies of Organizations." Project for Documentation of Advanced Training in Social Research, Columbia University, 1960. (Mimeographed.)
  Bass, Bernard M. *Leadership, Psychology, and Organizational Behavior.* New York: Harper, 1960.
* Beardsley, Seymour W., and Alvin G. Edgell. *Human Relations in International Affairs: A Guide to Significant Interpretation and Research.* Washington, D.C.: Public Affairs Press, 1956.
* Bendix, Reinhard, and Seymour M. Lipset. "Political Sociology—An Essay and Bibliography with Special Reference to the Development of Research in the United States of America and Western Europe," *Current Sociology,* 6 (1957), 77–170.
* Bowen, Howard R. *The Business Enterprise as a Subject for Research.* New York: Social Science Research Council, 1955.

  Caplow, Theodore. *The Sociology of Work.* Minneapolis: University of Minnesota Press, 1954.
  Caudill, William. *The Psychiatric Hospital as a Small Society.* Cambridge, Mass.: Harvard University Press, 1958.
* Chapin, F. Stuart. "Social Institutions and Voluntary Associations," in Joseph B. Gittler (ed.), *Review of Sociology,* New York: Wiley, 1957, 259–288.
* Child, Irvin L. "Morale: A Bibliographic Review," *Psychological Bulletin,* 38 (1941), 393–420.

* de Grazia, Alfred. *Human Relations in Public Administration: An Annotated Bibliography from the Fields of Anthropology, Industrial Management, Political Science, Psychology, Public Administration, and Sociology.* Chicago: Public Administration Service, 1949.
  Dubin, Robert. *The World of Work.* Englewood Cliffs, N.J.: Prentice-Hall, 1958.

* Eisenstadt, S. N. "Bureaucracy and Bureaucratization—A Trend Report and Bibliography," *Current Sociology,* 7 (1958), 99–164.

* Fox, Harland G., Walter D. Scott, Wayne K. Kirchner, and Thomas A. Mahoney. *Selected Annotated Bibliography on Leadership and Executive Development.* Minneapolis: University of Minnesota Press, 1954.
* Freeman, Howard E., and Leo G. Reeder. "Medical Sociology: A Review of the Literature," *American Sociological Review,* 22 (1957), 73–81.

* Gordon, C. Wayne. "The Sociology of Education," in Joseph B. Gittler (ed.), *Review of Sociology,* New York: Wiley, 1957, 500–519.
* Gore, William J., and Fred B. Silander. "A Bibliographical Essay on Decision Making," *Administrative Science Quarterly,* 4 (1959), 97–121.
  Greenblatt, Milton, Richard H. York, and Esther Lucile Brown. *From Custodial to Therapeutic Patient Care in Mental Hospitals.* New York: Russell Sage Foundation, 1955.
* Gusfield, Joseph R. "The Sociology of Politics," in Joseph B. Gittler (ed.), *Review of Sociology,* New York: Wiley, 1957, 520–530.

Hare, A. Paul, Edgar F. Borgotta, and Robert F. Bales (eds.). *Small Groups*. Knopf, 1955.

Hartmann, Heinz. *Authority and Organization in German Management*. Princeton, N.J.: Princeton University Press, 1959.

* Heady, Ferrel, and Sybil L. Stokes. *Comparative Public Administration: A Selective Annotated Bibliography*. 2d ed. Ann Arbor: Institute of Public Administration, University of Michigan, 1960.

* Lasswell, Harold D., Daniel Lerner, and C. Easton Rothwell. *The Comparative Study of Elites: An Introduction and Bibliography*. Stanford: Stanford University Press (Hoover Institute Studies. Series B: Elites, No. 1), 1952.

Lazarsfeld, Paul F. "Reflections on Business," *American Journal of Sociology*, 65 (1959), 1–31.

Lorge, Irving, David Fox, Joel Davitz, and Marlin Brenner. "A Survey of Studies Contrasting the Quality of Group Performance and Individual Performance, 1920–1957," *Psychological Bulletin*, 55 (1958), 337–372.

March, James G., and Herbert A. Simon. *Organizations*. New York: Wiley, 1958.

Merton, Robert K., Alisa P. Gray, Barbara Hockey, and Hanan C. Selvin. (eds.), *Reader in Bureaucracy*. Glencoe, Ill.: Free Press, 1952.

* Pittman, David J. "The Sociology of Religion," in Joseph B. Gittler (ed.), *Review of Sociology*, New York: Wiley, 1957, 546–558.

* Prestridge, V., and Donald E. Wray. *Industrial Sociology: An Annotated Bibliography*. Urbana: Institute of Labor and Industrial Relations, University of Illinois, 1953.

Spinrad, William. "Correlates of Trade Union Participation: A Summary of the Literature," *American Sociological Review*, 25 (1960), 237–244.

* Stogdill, Ralph M. *Individual Behavior and Group Achievement*. New York: Oxford University Press, 1959.

* Tagliacozzo, Daisy L. "Trade-Union Government, Its Nature and Its Problems: A Bibliographical Review, 1945–55," *American Journal of Sociology*, 61 (1956), 554–581.

Warner, W. Lloyd, and Norman H. Martin (eds.). *Industrial Man*. New York: Harper, 1959.

* Wasserman, Paul. *Measurement and Evaluation of Organizational Performance: An Annotated Bibliography*. Ithaca, N.Y.: Graduate School of Business and Public Administration, Cornell University, 1959.

* ———— and Fred S. Silander. *Decision-Making: An Annotated Bibliography*. Ithaca, N.Y.: Graduate School of Business and Public Administration, Cornell University, 1958.

* Whyte, William F., and Frank B. Miller. "Industrial Sociology," in Joseph B. Gittler (ed.), *Review of Sociology*, New York: Wiley, 1957, 289–345.

Zetterberg, Hans L. (ed.). *Sociology in the United States of America: A Trend Report*. Paris: UNESCO, 1956.

Index of Names

Abegglen, James C., 17n, 18n, 202n, 203n, 212, 241n
Ackoff, Russell L., 186n
Allport, Floyd H., 116–117, 118, 120
Almond, Gabriel, 81–82
Anderson, Theodore R., 227
Arensberg, Conrad, 83n
Argyle, Michael, 124n, 151
Argyris, Chris, 50, 131

Babchuk, Nicholas, 94
Bain, Robert K., 62n
Baker, Alton W., 226
Bales, Robert F., 16, 121n, 125, 145, 146n, 197n, 232n,
Barber, Bernard, 46n
Barnard, Chester I., 49, 141n, 145, 165
Barton, Allen H., 258
Bates, Frederick L., 214n
Bavelas, Alex, 126
Behrend, Hilde, 166
Belknap, Ivan C., ix
Bell, Wendell, 46n
Bendix, Reinhard, 30n, 77n, 87n, 88n, 141, 226, 250
Benét, Stephen Vincent, 5–6
Bennis, W. G., 69–71
Berelson, Bernard, 199n
Berger, Morroe, 17n, 137n, 202
Berle, Adolf A., 44n
Beyer, William C., 206n
Blau, Peter M., ix, 18, 19, 48n, 73n, 74n, 83, 95n, 97n, 98n, 101n, 105n, 120n, 129n, 130n, 131, 133n, 168n, 170n, 178n, 230n, 254
Blau, Zena Smith, x
Bogue, Donald J., 215n
Borash, Saul, 76
Boulding, Kenneth E., 216n, 217, 225
Braibanti, Ralph, 206n
Broom, Leonard, ix, 96n

Caplow, Theodore, 7n, 65, 71
Carter, Launor, 146
Cartwright, Dorwin, 122n, 124, 144n, 145n, 146n, 157n
Caudill, William A., 53, 80, 98–99, 146n, 163, 203
Chamberlin, Edward, 216
Chapple, Eliot D., 16, 146
Clark, Burton R., 53, 168n, 171, 201
Cloward, Richard A., 57
Coch, Lester, 20, 187n

Cohen, Arthur R., 157
Coleman, James S., 80, 198
Collins, Orvis, 200n
Commons, John R., 140
Comrey, A. L., 147n, 151, 154n, 157
Constas, Helen, 207n
Corey, Lewis, 64n
Crozier, Michael, 175–176, 241, 242n

Dale, John D., 166
Dalton, Melville, 169, 173–175, 198, 241
Davis, Ralph C., 226
Dean, Lois R., 200
Denton, Patricia, ix, 258
Deutsch, Morton, 19, 120n
Diamond, Sigmund, 233, 234n
Dickson, William J., 12n, 16n, 89–93, 191, 236
Dill, William R., 127n
Dimock, Marshall E., 130n, 166, 174n, 247n
Dittes, J. E., 104n
Dostoyevsky, Fyodor, 31n
Duncan, Otis Dudley, ix, 199n
Durkheim, Emile, 209–210, 211

Eisenstadt, S. N., 45n, 52n, 232–233, 258
Etzioni, Amitai W., 19n, 173

Fallers, Lloyd A., 204–205
Faunce, William A., 180, 181, 204, 247
Faust, William L., 117
Festinger, Leon, 18n, 20n, 96n
Fiedler, Fred E., 154
Fisher, Burton R., 75n
Foa, Uriel, 147
Follett, Mary Parker, 250
Form, William H., 199
Francis, Roy G., 18n, 207n, 246
French, John R. P., 20, 144, 145n, 187n

Galbraith, John Kenneth, 219, 221
Gerth, H. H., 32n, 33n
Goffman, Erving, 22n, 40n, 79n, 194
Goldman, Irving, 218n
Goldner, Fred H., 197
Goode, William J., 63, 94
Gouldner, Alvin W., 35, 46n, 48n, 65–66, 70, 71, 138, 153, 165, 188n, 196n, 207n, 239, 240, 241, 244, 246
Graicunas, V. A., 167
Grusky, Oscar, 57
Guest, Robert H., 89n, 176n, 239, 240
Guetzkow, Harold, 126, 127n

Gulick, Luther, 167n, 250n
Guttman, Louis, 65, 205

Haire, Mason, 19n, 154n, 166n, 175n, 225, 226n
Harbison, Frederick H., 204
Hare, A. Paul, 123n, 124n
Hart, C. W. M., 230
Hawley, Amos H., 214n
Heinicke, Christoph, 125
Henderson, A. M., 27n, 28n, 244n
Heron, Jayne Salzman, x
Heyns, Roger W., 16n
Hoffman, L. Richard, 182n
Homans, George C., 95, 104, 106, 143n
Hoover, Edgar M., 215n
Hopkins, Terrence K., 19n
Hughes, Everett C., 40n, 63n, 64n, 65, 171, 217n, 246
Hurwitz, Jacob I., 122

Jaco, E. Gartley, 122n
Janowitz, Morris, 52n, 55–56, 75–76, 174, 185
Jaques, Elliott, 161, 170, 241

Kahn, Robert L., 96n, 124n, 146n, 150n
Katz, Daniel, 14n, 18, 20n, 50, 96n, 124n, 146n, 150n
Katz, Elihu, 52n, 232–233
Kaufman, Herbert, 171
Kelley, Harold H., 104n, 122
Kerr, Clark, 47, 200, 201
Komarovsky, Mirra, 46
Kornhauser, Arthur, 47n, 87n, 200n
Kroeber, A. L., 4n

Lambert, W. E., 119n
Landsberger, Henry A., 93
Lasswell, Harold D., 81–82, 145
Lawrence, Paul, 145, 146n
Lazarsfeld, Paul F., 3n, 17n, 137n
Leavitt, Harold J., 126
Lebeaux, Charles N., 26n, 72n
Lefton, Mark, 190
Lenski, Gerhard E., 96n
Lewin, Kurt, 124
Likert, Rensis, 154n, 159n, 166, 175n
Lindzey, Gardner, 16n, 201n
Lippett, Ronald, 16n, 124, 125n, 144
Lipset, Seymour M., 15n, 16n, 46n, 47n, 48, 77n, 200, 201n, 228, 231n, 253
Litwak, Eugene, 207n
Lombard, George F., 95n
Lorge, Irving, 118n
Low, J. O., 180n, 201n

Maier, Norman R. F., 124
Mann, Floyd C., 182n, 247
March, James G., 14n, 37n, 87n, 240n, 258

Marcus, Philip M., 157n, 254n
Marshall, Alfred, 216
Marx, Karl, 15n
Matthewson, S. B., 93
Mayo, Elton, 12, 91, 95n, 109
McCurdy, H. G., 119n
McEwen, William J., 196–198
McGee, Reece J., 65, 71
Mead, Margaret, 218n
Means, Gardner C., 44n
Melman, Seymour, 191n, 211–214, 226, 249
Merton, Robert K., 22, 34n, 64n, 96n, 137n, 142, 143n, 145n, 195, 196n, 229, 230n, 258
Messinger, Sheldon L., 80, 229
Michels, Robert, 15n, 48, 227–228, 231, 252
Miller, Delbert C., 199
Mills, C. Wright, 32n, 33n
Mills, Donald L., 227
Montmollin, Germaine de, 117
Moore, Wilbert E., 172n, 241n
Moreno, Jacob L., 147
Mulder, Maul, 126n

Nagel, Ernest, 3n

Page, Charles H., 35n
Park, Robert E., 214n
Parkinson, C. Northcote, 225, 226
Parsons, Talcott, 4n, 27n, 28n, 35, 38–40, 41, 51n, 58, 63n, 121n, 165, 190n, 197n, 207n, 232, 244
Paul, Cedar, 48n, 227n
Paul, Eden, 48n, 227n
Pelz, Donald C., 138–139, 155, 231, 243
Perlmutter, Howard V., 117
Polansky, Norman, 77n
Presthus, Robert V., 206n

Rapoport, Anatol, 19n
Rashkis, Harold A., 54
Reissman, Leonard, 65
Richardson, Frederick L., 167, 212
Roberts, David R., 166
Robinson, Joan, 216
Roethlisberger, F. J., 12n, 16n, 89–93, 191, 236
Rohrer, John H., 83n, 111n, 122n
Rosenberg, Morris, 3n
Roy, Donald, 94

Sawyer, Jack, 101n
Sayles, Leonard R., 47, 100n, 109–111, 200
Schachter, Stanley, 96n
Schwartz, Morris S., 53, 189n
Scott, Joy Whitney, x
Scott, Nancy Levinson, x
Scott, W. Richard, x, 66n, 189n, 254

Seashore, Stanley E., 12n, 96, 109, 110
Seidman, Joel, 48n, 201n
Selltiz, Claire, 15n
Selznick, Philip, 18n, 35, 141n, 165, 228, 229n
Shapiro, M. M., 104n
Shaw, Marjorie E., 118
Shepard, Herbert A., 131–133
Sherif, Muzafer, 83n, 111n, 122n
Siegel, Abraham, 47, 200, 201
Sills, David L., 231
Simmel, Georg, 197
Simon, Herbert A., 14n, 28n, 36–38, 42, 58, 87n, 126, 166n, 168n, 240n, 258
Simpson, George, 210n
Simpson, Richard L., 181, 184, 249
Smith, Adam, 219
Snyder, Richard, 144, 145n
Soemardjan, Selo, 206n
Solem, Allen R., 124
Solomon, Herbert, 118n
Spinrad, William, 47–48, 201n
Stanton, Alfred H., 53, 189n
Stelling, Joan, x
Stinchcombe, Arthur L., 207–208, 209, 246, 247
Stone, Robert C., 18n, 207n, 246
Strauss, George, 47, 200
Sumner, William Graham, 4, 5n
Swanson, Guy E., 96n
Sykes, Gresham M., 80

Tagliacozzo, Daisy L., 201n
Taylor, Donald W., 117
Taylor, Frederick W., 87
Temporary National Economic Committee, 219
Terrien, Frederic W., 227
Thielens, Wagner, Jr., 17n
Thomas, Edwin J., 200n
Thompson, James D., 41, 42, 196–198, 214n
Thorndike, E. L., 199n
Thorndike, R. L., 118, 119n

Tocqueville, Alexis de, 15n
Torrance, E. Paul, 123, 124n
Tuden, Arthur, 41, 42
Turner, Ralph H., 35n

Udy, Stanley H., 26, 205–206, 208–210, 224, 246
Urwick, L., 167n, 250n

Veblen, Thorstein, 219
Vernon, Raymond, 215n

Walker, Charles R., 89n, 167, 176–178, 181, 182n, 191, 192n, 212, 236, 248, 249
Wallace, Anthony F. C., 54
Warkov, Seymour, 227
Warner, W. Lloyd, 18n, 180n, 201n
Weber, Max, 9, 15n, 27, 28, 30–36, 42, 56, 58, 65, 165, 206–207, 208, 224, 244
Weiss, Robert S., 131n
Wessen, Albert F. 122
Westerlund, Gunnar, 150
White, Leonard D., 80
White, R. Clyde, 77n
White, Ralph, 124, 125n
Whyte, William F., 82–83, 100, 111n, 145, 166
Whyte, William H., Jr., 175
Wilensky, Harold L., 26n, 65, 71, 72n, 172
Williams, Lawrence K., 182n, 247
Williams, Robin M., Jr., 40n, 216n
Wirdenius, Hans, 146
Withey, Stephen B., 75n
Wolff, Kurt H., 197n
Worthy, James C., 166, 168

Yule, G. Udney, 209

Zaleznik, Abraham, 89n, 95n, 110, 131
Zander, Alvin, 122n, 124n, 146n
Zelditch, Morris, Jr., 19n

Index of Topics

Acceptance: see Integration
Administrative
  apparatus, 7–8, 15, 207–209, 212–214, 224, 225–228, 231, 247
  decision-making; see Decision-making, and administrative structure
  efficiency, 33, 34, 43, 45, 49–50, 227–228
  leadership, 141, 165, 167
  staff among Soga, 204–205
Advice: see Consultation
Allegiance: see Loyalty
Ambiguity, 110, 157, 194, 198, 204, 241; see also Uncertainty
Apathy, 45–48
Approach
  comparative: see Comparative approach
  human-relations: see Human-relations approach
  sociopsychological: see Sociopsychological approach
  structural: see Structural approach
Approval, social, 84–85, 102, 119–120, 123, 125, 162, 235, 242
Assembly line, 88–89, 167, 176–178, 179–181, 184, 186, 212, 247–248, 251
Authority; see also Expertness, and discipline; Hierarchy; Supervision
  concept of, 27–30, 61, 140–145, 165, 169, 237–238, 245
  and coordination; see Coordination, and hierarchy
  and leadership, 141–145, 150
  line, 172–173
  strict; see Supervision, authoritarian
  Weber's types, 30–32
Automation, 20, 180–183, 184, 186, 191–192, 204, 248–249, 251
Autonomy, 155, 156, 171, 182, 197, 235; see also Responsibility, scope of

Bank Wiring Observation Room, 16, 91–93, 95, 191–192, 236
Beneficiary: see Concept of, prime beneficiary
Boundary
  of organization, 194
  role, 197–198, 233
  status, 122
Bravery, 56
Bureaucracy; see also Hierarchy; Administrative, apparatus

careers in, 33, 61, 88, 175, 207–209, 224
characteristics of, 7–8, 32–33, 194–195, 205–209, 224, 246–247
and democracy, ix, 15; see also Democracy, pseudo
in nonindustrial societies, 202–206, 208–209, 210
Weber's theory of, 9, 32–36, 206–208; see also Expertness, and discipline
Bureaucratization, 8, 10, 31, 45, 63n, 113, 175–176, 204–205, 207–209, 225–231, 232, 239
Business concerns, 5, 43–45, 49–51, 58–59, 62, 81, 195, 224, 234; see also Types of organizations

Caseload, 74, 78, 135–136, 233, 256
Casework service: see Orientation, service and procedure
Centralization, 126, 171–172, 182, 185, 204, 227–228, 247–248
Change
  dialectical, 250–253
  in industry, 211–214
  in market structure, 215–221
  in organization, 10, 44, 100, 174–175, 193, 206, 212, 216–217, 222–232, 234, 239–242
Charismatic authority, 31–32, 176
Clients, 42, 43, 44, 54, 61–62, 95, 188–190; see also Orientation, to clients; Public
  aggressive, 81–82
  checking on: see Orientation, service and procedure
  conflicts with, 81–85, 240
  delegating responsibility to, 102–104, 156
  diffuse relations with, 233
  dissatisfaction of, 77
  power of, 78–79, 232, 233
  service to, 51, 78, 190, 255
  subservience to, 52–53
Close supervision, 158n, 168, 177, 179–182, 186, 238–239, 248–249; see Supervision, authoritarian
Coalitions, 174, 191, 197, 220, 241–242
Code for bibliography, 258–260
Cohesion, 80, 84, 95–96, 107–108, 109–111, 112, 130, 156, 169, 192, 236
Collaboration and performance, 119, 125–128, 139, 242–249

Commensalism, 214; see also Competition

Commercial organizations, 49–51, 82–83, 182

Common value orientation: see Orientation, shared; Values, social

Commonweal organizations, 41, 43–45, 50, 54–59, 62, 79, 81, 224; see also Types of organizations

Communication; see also Consultation; Interaction, social
   concept of, 116
   free flow of, 119–120, 124–128, 131–134, 139, 242–244, 247
   vertical and horizontal, 49, 130–134, 172, 181, 184

Community
   conflict, 198–199
   and organizations, 199–202

Comparative approach, 14, 25–26, 111, 114–115, 223

Comparisons
   cross-cultural, 87n, 202–206, 208–209, 224–225, 246–247
   of professional and bureaucratic principles, 60–63
   of styles of supervision, 148–159
   of two divisions, 77–79
   of two hierarchical levels, 160–163
   of two industries, 207–208
   of two organizations, 132
   of work groups, 95–96, 100–104, 107–111

Competition, 93, 94, 116–117, 122–123, 192, 236, 243
   and cooperation, 120–121, 196–197
   and exchange, 214, 217–221, 252
   between organizations, 197, 214–216, 242
   for personnel, 257

Complexity, 7, 19, 88, 205–206, 223–227; see also Technological, complexity

Concept of
   authority, 27–30, 140–145
   communication, 116
   culture, 4–5
   dilemma, 222, 250–251
   formal organization, 1, 2, 5–8, 32–40, 223–224
   informal organization, 6–7, 35
   persuasion, 28
   power, 27–28
   prime beneficiary, 42–44
   profession, 60–63
   social interaction, 116
   social organization, 1–5
   social relations, 3–4
   social structure, 3–4
   solidarity, 109
   status, 96–97

Conceptual scheme, 8–9, 33–34, 38–40

Conflict; see also Expertness, and discipline
   and change, 10, 240–242
   with clients: see Clients, conflict with
   community, 198–199
   in demands, 72n, 195–196
   between departments, 60, 156–157
   of interest, 62, 190, 251–252
   lineage–state, 204–205
   in loyalty, 64–71, 162–164, 202, 246
   among managers, 174–176
   among staff, 24–25, 53–54
   between staff and line, 173–174, 177, 192–193
   between superior and subordinate, 178, 179

Conformity; see also Norms, social
   to group norms, 92, 96, 104–107, 236
   to legal standards, 129, 183
   to official procedures, 73–74, 129, 130, 166, 229, 231
   to role expectations, 5, 22n
   to superior's directives, 188, 237

Consultation, 121
   homophily in, 137–139, 243
   interdepartmental, 184–185
   in law-enforcement agency, 129–134, 217
   in machine shop, 131
   reciprocity in, 133–137, 156, 158, 235
   in research organization, 131–132, 138–139, 243
   and status differentiation, 133–135, 217–218
   among supervisors, 160–161
   in welfare agency, 112–114, 235

Continuity of employment: see Bureaucracy, career in

Contract, 140–141, 205–206, 210, 225, 245, 257

Control mechanisms, impersonal, 37, 39, 167, 171–172, 176–183, 185–186, 191, 193, 238, 247–248

Cooperation: see Collaboration and performance; Competition and cooperation

Cooptation, 196, 228–229

Coordination, 7, 32, 34–35, 88, 167–180, 192, 209, 210, 224, 242–244, 247–250, 251
   and hierarchy, 33, 139, 167, 177, 183–185, 193
   and task performance, 119, 125–128, 139, 242–244

Cosmopolitans and locals, 64–71, 138, 246

Craftsmanship: see Professional, labor force

Creativity, 56, 132, 231

Cross pressure, 82–83, 155, 199

Cui bono, 42–44

Custodial organizations, 56–57, 79–80

Debureaucratization, 231–234

Decentralization: see Centralization

Decision-making
  and administrative structure, 33, 36–38, 41–42, 165, 167, 240, 243, 250
  anxieties over, 119, 130–131, 134, 170, 242, 251
  centralization of, 126–127, 182
  and consultation, 113, 130–131, 242, 244
  impersonal, 202
  pseudo-democratic, 187–188, 190, 191, 193
  and unofficial norms, 6
Deference, 133, 134–135, 217, 244
Democracy
  belief in, 4
  external, 15, 43, 55–56
  internal, 16, 43, 45–49, 55, 186, 227–228
  pseudo, 186–191, 193
  versus strength, 227–228, 252–253
Dependence
  on subordinates, 232–233
  on superior, 131–132, 204, 205–206, 208, 210
Depression, 93, 181, 191–192
Detachment, 22–23, 33, 34, 103–104, 107–108, 149, 154–155, 159–163, 168, 176, 188, 203, 224, 236, 238–239, 244
Deviation: see Conformity
Dilemma
  of caseworkers, 74
  concept of, 222, 250–251
  coordination and communication, 139, 172–173, 242–244, 250
  discipline and expertness, 172–173, 244–247
  of group problem-solving, 121n
  methodological, 10–13, 222–223
  of mutual-benefit association, 48, 228, 252–253
  planning and initiative, 247–250
  of prison officials, 57
Discipline: see Expertness, and discipline; Authority
Discretion, 129–130, 175, 179–183, 186, 248–249; see also Responsibility
Displacement of goals, 178n, 228–231
Disturbance
  of observer, 21–25
  collective, 53–54
Division of labor: see Specialization
Dominance, 215, 242, 252
Domination, 52, 141–142, 185, 216
Dysfunctions, 34–35, 85, 121–124, 133, 139, 151–152, 153, 178n, 180, 183, 192, 240, 243

Ecology
  office, 111–112
  organizational, 214–217

of supervision, 170–172
  urban, 199, 214–215
Educational organizations, 53, 80–81, 201–202, 227
Efficiency: see Administrative, efficiency; Industrial productivity
Eligibility: see Orientation, service and procedure
Employment agency, 83–85, 178–180
Environment, 9, 199–205, 214
Error correction, 118–123, 138–139, 243
Ethnic minorities, 4, 46–47, 75, 79, 109–110, 199–200
Evaluation of results, 129–130, 166, 179, 185, 192, 249
Evolution, 205–206, 210–211
Exchange, 29, 35, 132, 133–134, 214, 217–221, 237
Executive leadership: see Administrative, leadership
Expandability, 215–217
Experience: see Seniority
Expertness, 23–24, 32, 33, 34, 61, 63, 176, 182–183; see also Professional
  and discipline, 35–36, 63, 165, 172–173, 185, 192, 207–209, 242, 244–247

Fear of layoff, 93, 181, 191–192
Feedback, 195
Field experiment, 19–20
Flow of demand, 82–83, 177–179, 180n, 248
Foreman: see Supervision
Fragmented time: see Time perspective
Free association, 116–117
Functions, 34–35, 40, 44, 50, 51, 80, 85, 92–94, 112, 113, 124–128, 130, 132–133, 139, 142, 168, 174–175, 178–180, 184, 185, 193, 199, 202, 212, 238, 239, 240; see also Responsibility

Group
  climate, 100–106, 124, 236
  composition, 108–110
  and individual performance, 116–119, 243
  norms: see Norms, work group
  pressure, 29, 74n, 101–104, 124, 191, 193, 236; see also Resistance against group pressure
  status, 3–4, 100, 110
  structure 3, 4, 6, 9–10, 13, 80, 83–86, 87, 89, 100–115, 235
Growth: see Size; Expandability

Heterogeneity: see Homogeneity
Heterophily: see Homogeneity
Hierarchy
  of authority and coordination, 183–185, 193, 247–250

levels in, 39, 60, 162–164, 169, 234
and performance, 123–128
structure of, 6, 19, 32, 34, 37–39, 165,
167–172, 185, 187–188, 205–210,
224, 225, 228, 232, 234, 238, 247,
255
Homogeneity, 109–110, 137–139
Homophily, see Homogeneity
Hospitals: see Medical organizations
Human-relations approach, 87–89, 153
Hypotheses
explanatory, 11, 115, 121, 128, 200–
201, 216, 240
implicit in ideal type, 33–34
testing of, 11, 15–16, 19–20, 40, 90,
105–106, 159–161, 206–207, 223, 233,
238

Ideal type, 33–34, 206
Illumination experiments, 89–90
Impersonal orientation: see Detachment
Incentive system: see Reward system
Industrial organizations, 89–93, 96, 109–
111, 174–178, 180–182, 191–192,
196, 202–204, 211, 226–227, 232,
239
Industrial productivity, 211–214
Industrial research, 12, 87–88
Informal organization; see also Group,
structure
concept of, 6–7, 35
of the public, 79–81
of work group, 12, 89–100, 224, 234–
237, 241
Initiative: see Responsibility, discretion
Integration
among colleagues, 97–98, 104–107,
235–237
among supervisors, 159–161, 238
Interaction, social, 1, 3–4, 5, 16, 17, 20,
47, 51, 57, 82, 91, 92, 102, 112, 116–
124, 129, 145–146, 156, 160, 177,
179, 180–181, 223
between organizations, 197
of supervisor, 149, 156, 160–161, 177,
179–181, 185
Interdependent tasks: see Specialization
Interlocking memberships, 198–199

Joking, 84–85, 240

Labor cost, 211–212, 249
Labor unions: see Unions
Law-enforcement agency, 129–134, 187–
188, 230
Legal authority, 31–32, 140–141, 245
Loyalty
familial, 202
to organization, 39, 49, 64–71, 246
to supervisor, 105–106, 143–145, 150,

153, 155, 158–159, 162–164, 168,
237–240, 252

Machine breakdown, 175, 180–182, 249
Managerial ideology, 87–88, 141
Managerial planning, 166–167, 185, 191,
209, 247–250; see also Control mechanisms, impersonal
Managerial succession, 239–240, 252
Marginal utility, 133
Mechanization, 180–181, 184–186, 193,
211–212, 213, 251; see also Assembly line; Automation; Technological
Medical organizations, 53–54, 80, 98–99,
173, 190–191, 196, 203, 227
Methods of research; see also Hypotheses,
testing of
case study, 12
experimental, 13, 14, 19–20, 128
field study, 20–25, 128, 253
interviewing, 17, 145, 146–147
observation, 16–17, 21–25, 80, 94, 145–
146
sociometric, 107, 147
in study of supervision, 145–148
survey, 11, 18
use of documents, 17–18
Military elite, 55–56
Military organizations, 1, 54–56, 185, 223,
225, 232
Models of management, 165–167
Mule-spinning department, 90–91
Mutual-benefit associations, 43–49, 52, 58,
59, 62, 186, 196, 220, 227–228, 229,
252–253; see also Types of organizations

Natural experiment, 20
Network
of communication, 126–127
of social relations, 3–4, 89, 91, 107
Norms; see also Conformity
and authority, 29, 142–143
community, 199–200
development of, 4, 6, 84–85, 103–104
functions of, 80, 85, 92–93
professional, 61, 66, 244
work group, 85, 89, 91–94, 97, 100–107,
121, 236, 237

Obligations
contractual: see Contract
social, 24, 30, 46, 57, 134, 142–143,
237
Observability: see Visibility
Oligarchy, 45, 48, 227–228
Opportunities for advancement, 70–71, 88,
131, 181, 192, 249, 257
Organization man, 175

Orientation
 to change, 73n, 156
 to clients, 9, 33, 58, 60, 73–74, 84, 101–
  108, 111–113, 151–152, 188, 190,
  236, 244–245
 of consultants, 137–139
 professional and bureaucratic, 60–74,
  111–112, 138, 174, 188, 202, 246
 of public, 9, 58, 60, 74–77
 service and procedure, 97–98, 101–102,
  150, 151–152, 156, 163, 174, 200,
  236, 240n, 246
 shared, 2, 4, 13, 28–30, 39, 41–42,
  137–138, 209; see also Values, social
 of supervisor, 147
 therapeutic, 57, 188–191
Outcast, 56–57, 80, 106
Outline of book, 8–10

Participation
 in conferences, 4, 20, 98–99, 122–123
 in decision-making, 187, 190–191, 193
 in organizations, 46–47, 198–199, 205–
  206
 in unions, 47–48, 109–111, 200
Performance
 and cohesion, 95–96
 and consultation, 130–134, 137–139,
  242–244
 and group norms, 92–94, 236
 and group pressure, 101–102
 and incentive plan, 191–192, 193
 and informal relations, 90–91
 and informal status, 94–95, 243
 and orientation, 73–74
 and social interaction, 116–121, 138–
  139
 and status differentiation, 123–128
 and supervision, 14, 50, 125n, 150–
  159, 163
Performance records, 18, 129, 171, 178–
  180, 193, 248
Planning: see Managerial planning
Popularity, 99–100, 104, 107–108, 113–
  114, 160, 217
Power, 22, 30, 38, 103
 bureaucratic, 52, 141, 142, 157, 227–
  228, 231, 237
 community, 199
 concealed, 190
 concept of, 25–28
 countervailing, 219–221, 252
 and expertness, 175–176
 and exploitation, 210–211, 218
 military, 55–56
 of public, 60, 78–79, 232–238
 in relational network, 123, 195, 196,
  217, 232
 struggles, 174–175, 193, 220, 241–242,
  252

 of work group, 110, 191
Pressure
 cross: see Cross pressure
 group: see Group pressure
 work: see Work pressure
Prestige; see also Status; Respect
 among students, 80–81
 of agency division, 78–79
 of caseworkers, 77
 of public officials, 76, 202
Problem-solving: see Performance; Decision-making
Procedure manual, 111, 113–114, 171,
  235, 256
Productivity; see Industrial productivity;
  Supervision, and productivity
Professional; see also Expertness; Responsibility
 and bureaucratic principles, 36, 60–64,
  72, 78, 190, 208–209, 244–247
 and business principles, 61–62
 commitment, 65–74, 114, 207
 control, 62–63
 court of appeal, 245
 judgment, 35–36, 42, 51, 63 165, 173,
  185, 189, 190, 204, 241, 247
 labor force, 207–208, 247, 249
 management, 111–112, 209, 257
 opportunities, 70–71
 service, 43, 45, 51, 61–62
Psychiatric approach: see Supervision,
  therapy-oriented
Public
 attitudes to government of, 75–76
 impact on organization of, 77–79, 83–
  85, 201–202, 232–233, 240
 -in-contact, 42, 51, 59–60, 79–81, 194;
  see also Clients
 knowledge of government of, 75
 organization of, 79–81, 196, 219–220
Pyramid, shape of: see Hierarchical, structure

Rationality
 in administration, 33, 36–38, 207–209,
  246–247
 of output restriction, 92–93
Reciprocity: see Consultation, reciprocity in
Reference group, 65–74, 99–100, 161, 237
Relations between organizations, 7, 9,
  194–199, 214–215, 221
Relay Assembly Test Room, 90
Research
 industrial: see Industrial research
 procedures: see Methods of research
 small group: see Small group research
 and theory: see Theory, and research
Research organizations, 131–132, 138–139
Resistance against group pressure, 104–
  107

Respect, 108, 114, 125, 235, 237; see also
   Status
   competition for, 121–123
   earning colleagues', 132–134, 168, 244
   for supervisor, 108, 143, 144, 162–163,
      239
Responsibility; see also Functions
   on automated jobs, 180–182, 248–249
   and conflict, 173–175, 190, 241–242
   interdependent, 183–186, 192
   legal, 129, 233
   managerial, 140–141, 165, 167–170,
      174, 177, 252
   scope of, 37, 39, 170–171, 172, 191,
      230, 241, 247, 251
   of welfare agency, 190, 253–254
   willingness to assume, 129–130, 149,
      152, 153, 163, 167, 247
Rest periods, 90–91
Reward system, 129–130, 166, 167, 186,
   187–188, 191–192, 205–206, 208,
   225, 249
   informal, 94–95, 132–134
Role set, 195
Routinization, 31, 46, 230

Sanctions, 4, 62, 63, 84, 92, 102, 141,
   142–144, 237, 239; see also Approval, social; Reward system
Satisfaction, 48, 49, 50–51, 104, 124,
   130, 150–151, 153, 155, 163, 175,
   178n, 179–183, 186, 191, 243, 248–
   249, 251
Scientific management, 87
Seasonal fluctuations, 207, 209, 247
Self-confidence, 114, 130, 133, 136–137,
   139, 158–159, 242
Seniority, 33, 35, 66n, 97, 100, 109–110,
   111, 113–114, 131, 160, 175, 235–
   237, 252, 257
Service organizations, 41, 43–45, 50, 51–
   54, 57, 58, 60, 62, 79, 81, 153, 224,
   244–245; see also Types of organizations
Shared values: see Orientation, shared;
   Values, social
Shortage
   material, 212
   staff, 112, 256
Size, 7, 40, 87, 88, 200, 216n, 223–227
Small-group research, 13
Social constraints: see also Control mechanisms, impersonal
   and authority, 29, 143–144
   on communication, 121–128
   of group structure, 100–108
   on group structure, 24, 83–86, 108–
      115, 235
   on organization, 77–79
   two types of 2–5

Social contact: see Interaction, social
Social cost: see Dysfunctions
Social density, 198–199, 209, 211
Social distance, 33, 149, 153–154, 159,
   232, 238
Sociopsychological approach, 38, 81–83,
   86
Solidarity, 51, 93, 109–111, 120–121,
   128, 150, 156–157, 158, 160–161,
   163, 200–201, 209, 236, 238
Span of control, 168–169, 171, 238
Specialization, 32, 34, 60–61, 110–111,
   167, 180, 199, 208, 216, 224, 225,
   244, 247, 256
   parallel and interdependent, 183–185,
      192, 193
   in simple organization, 205–206, 209–
      211
Staff
   administrative: see Administrative, ap-
      paratus
   and line, 172–174, 177
   professional, 44, 253
   shortage, 112
   and type of authority, 32
Statistical records: see Performance records
Status; see also Authority; Popularity;
   Power; Prestige; Respect
   achieved and ascribed, 61, 204, 225,
      244
   background, 110
   and communication, 14, 83, 116, 122–
      126, 131–134, 243–244
   community, 201, 203, 210, 225, 234
   and conformity, 80, 92, 104–107, 236
   differentiation, 3–4, 6, 19, 122–128,
      132, 133–135, 139, 217–218, 234
   dimensions of, 96–97
   family, 203
   and performance, 94–95, 97
   prerogatives, 142
   in relation to public, 57, 60, 76
   and relations with colleagues, 5, 51,
      98–100, 217, 235
   and service orientation, 52, 97–98, 236
   socio-economic, 46–47, 49, 75, 79, 82,
      251
Strategies, 41–42, 110, 141–142, 147,
   187, 195–198, 239
Strike propensity, 200–201
Structural approach, 81–86, 88–89
Structural effects, 100–108
Structure: see Concept of, social structure;
   Group, structure; Hierarchy, structure
Succession of goals, 230–231
Supervision; see also Span of control
   authoritarian, 124, 142, 148–149, 150–
      153, 155–156, 163, 232, 252
   close: see Close supervision

consistent, 157–159, 163
detached, 149, 153, 155, 159, 159–163,
168, 176, 203, 238–239
and impersonal control mechanisms,
176–182
independence in, 148–150, 155–157,
160–163, 168, 238–239.
and loyalty: see Loyalty, to supervisor
and productivity, 14, 50, 90, 144–145,
150–155, 157, 163
therapy–oriented, 188–191
Support, social, 64, 80, 84–85, 95, 107–
108, 113, 119–122, 125, 130, 138–
139, 156, 169, 235, 236, 238–239,
242–243, 247
Symbiosis, 214–215, 217–220; see also
Exchange
System problems, 38–39

Tactics: see Strategies
Technological
complexity, 185, 194–195, 209–212,
221; see also Assembly line; Automation; Mechanization
innovation, 203, 212, 249, 252
Theoretical
framework: see Conceptual scheme
generalization, 10–14, 25
Theory
of authority, 27–32
economic, 133, 215–217, 219
of formal organization, 27, 32–40
and research, 8–9
Time perspective, 169–170
Traditional authority, 30, 204
Turnover, 91, 111–112, 114, 176, 251,
252, 256, 257
Types of organizations
analytical, 40–57, 224
commercial, 49–51, 82–83, 182
custodial, 56–57, 79–80
educational, 53, 80–81, 201–202, 227
employment, 83–85, 178–180
industrial, 89–93, 96, 109–111, 174–

178, 180–182, 191–192, 196, 202–
204, 211, 226–227, 232, 239
law enforcement, 129–134, 187–188,
230
medical, 53–54, 80, 98–99, 173, 190–
191, 196, 203, 227
military, 1, 54–56, 185, 223, 225, 232
production and service, 40–41
research, 131–132, 138–139
unions, 1, 2, 5, 15–16, 44, 45, 47–49,
59, 60, 65, 93, 100, 109–111, 172,
191, 196–198, 200–201, 212, 227–
228, 230–231, 249, 251–252
welfare, 26, 66–74, 76–79, 97–107,
111–115, 146, 149, 151–163, 169,
188–189, 223, 233, 235, 238, 254–
257
Typologies, 40–45

Uncertainty, 119, 170, 175–176, 240–242,
247; see also Ambiguity
Union activity: see Participation, of membership; Solidarity
Unions, 1, 2, 5, 15–16, 44, 45, 47–49,
59, 60, 65, 93, 100, 109–111, 172,
191, 196–198, 200–201, 212, 227–
228, 230–231, 249, 251–252
Universalistic standards, 60–61, 244

Values, social, 4, 6, 39, 66, 80, 89, 97,
100–104, 106, 202, 203, 209, 236
legitimating authority, 28–30, 141,
143–144, 237–238
Visibility, 22, 69–70, 143, 149, 178, 195–
196
Voluntary compliance, 28, 29, 143–144

Web of organizations: see Relations between organizations
Welfare agencies, 26, 66–74, 76–79, 97–
107, 111–115, 146, 149, 151–163,
169, 188–189, 223, 233, 238, 254–257
Work pressure, 135–136, 235, 256
Worrying, 103–104, 105, 112–113, **235**